RENEWALS 458-4574
DATE DUE

**WITHDRAWN
UTSA LIBRARIES**

The Other Global City

Routledge Advances in Geography

1. The Other Global City
Edited by Shail Mayaram

The Other Global City

Edited by Shail Mayaram

Routledge
Taylor & Francis Group
New York   London

First published 2009
by Routledge
270 Madison Ave, New York, NY 10016

Simultaneously published in the UK
by Routledge
2 Park Square, Milton Park, Abingdon, Oxon OX14 4RN

Routledge is an imprint of the Taylor & Francis Group, an informa business

© 2009 Taylor & Francis

Typeset in Sabon by IBT Global.
Printed and bound in the United States of America on acid-free paper by IBT Global.

All rights reserved. No part of this book may be reprinted or reproduced or utilised in any form or by any electronic, mechanical, or other means, now known or hereafter invented, including photocopying and recording, or in any information storage or retrieval system, without permission in writing from the publishers.

Trademark Notice: Product or corporate names may be trademarks or registered trademarks, and are used only for identification and explanation without intent to infringe.

Library of Congress Cataloging in Publication Data

The other global city / edited by Shail Mayaram.
  p. cm.—(Routledge advances in geography ; 1)
Includes bibliographical references and index.
 1. Cities and towns—Asia. 2. Cosmopolitanism—Asia. I. Mayaram, Shail.
HT147.A2O84 2009
307.76095—dc22
                          2008025823

ISBN10: 0-415-99194-3 (hbk)
ISBN10: 0-203-88765-4 (ebk)

ISBN13: 978-0-415-99194-0 (hbk)
ISBN13: 978-0-203-88765-3 (ebk)

For Anirudh (1982–2005) whose light has made this possible.

Toward partial payment of my lifelong debt—pitr/guru rin—to the philosophers, Daya Krishna (1924–2007) and Ramachandra Gandhi (1937–2007).

All three embodied immensely joyful, creative, and caring ways of relating self and other.

Contents

List of Maps ... ix
List of Photographs ... xi
Prologue and Acknowledgments ... xiii

1 Introduction: Rereading Global Cities: Topographies of an Alternative Cosmopolitanism in Asia ... 1
   SHAIL MAYARAM

SECTION I
Cosmopolitanism and the State

2 Beneficence and Difference: Ottoman *Awqaf* and "Other" Subjects ... 35
   ENGIN F. ISIN

3 Living Together in Lhasa: Ethnic Relations, Coercive Amity, and Subaltern Cosmopolitanism ... 54
   EMILY T. YEH

4 Intelligent City: From Ethnic Governmentality to Ethnic Evolutionism ... 86
   AIHWA ONG

SECTION II
Cosmopolitanism Compromised/Denied

5 Impossible Cosmopolises: Dislocations and Relocations in Beirut and Delhi ... 101
   YASMEEN ARIF

6 Limiting Cosmopolitanism:
   Streetlife "Little India," Kuala Lumpur   131
   YEOH SENG GUAN

7 Invisibility and Cohabitation in Multiethnic Tokyo   161
   JOHN LIE

SECTION III
Cosmopolitan Microprocesses

8 Cairo Cosmopolitan:
   Living Together through Communal Divide, Almost   179
   ASEF BAYAT

9 Cosmopolitanism and the City:
   Interaction and Coexistence in Bukhara   202
   CAROLINE HUMPHREY, MAGNUS MARSDEN, AND VERA SKVIRSKAJA

Contributors   233
Index   237

Maps

P.1	Asia and its cities.	xiv
1.1	The "Silk Route."	12

Photographs

1.1	Sarai at Leh, Ladakh, India.	13
1.2	Hindu and Muslim workers' families living under a single roof.	25
1.3	Hindu and Muslim workers on a day's outing in Old Delhi.	25
3.1	Barkhor, vegetable market, Lhasa.	58
3.2	"Han Tibetans one family," near Lhasa, People's Republic of China.	66
3.3	"National culture belongs to the world," Lhasa, People's Republic of China.	80
6.1	Deepraya festival sales, Kuala Lumpur.	149
6.2	View of Jalan Masjid India during Deepa-raya festival.	150
8.1	Church, Khalafawi, Shubra, Cairo.	192
9.1	Vegetable market, Bukhara.	212

Prologue and Acknowledgments

This volume lies at the intersection of the debate on cosmopolitanism and the city. It is the outcome of a project I coordinated called Communities in Interaction that focused on relations between communities in Asian cities. The project proposal that I wrote initially arose from a discontent with the dominating knowledge on ethnic groups that has focused largely on alterity, conflict, and violence. This is the prevailing perspective that has oriented academic research, the publishing market, and the media, all of which thrive on narratives of conflict. It has fed into clones of the clash-of-civilizations argument that has also produced the idea of a homogenous Islam, ignoring what the Iranian theorist, Ramin Jahanbegloo, calls the intercultural imperative, the widespread evidence of dialogue between cultures. The project was concerned with understanding the complex totality of interethnic relations in urban contexts including aspects of violence, but also aspects of coexistence and conviviality.

The volume is not a conference volume or mere edited book, but consists of specially commissioned studies of the cities of Beirut, Cairo, Istanbul, Bukhara, Lhasa, Delhi, Kuala Lumpur, Singapore, and Tokyo.

A plurality of theoretical and methodological approaches characterizes the work ranging from the historical-ethnographic to the discursive-post-Foucauldian. The effort, as far as possible, was to involve Asian scholars who are either located in Asia or have spent formative years in the non-West and continue to be keenly concerned with its socioeconomic processes. To my regret, we were not able to obtain any scholar from China. Regrettably the focus of interest within the Chinese academy has been on economics—only now are signs of change visible.

The proposal derived from a concern that the pervasiveness and intensification of violence make it imperative that we begin to understand the complex project of "living together" between ethnic groups—somewhat crudely rendered in English as "coexistence." The exercise is particularly important as the "primordialist" framework of ethnicity has overwhelmed our understanding of interethnic relations in the previous decades, oriented our lens to the extent that we see only violence or the potential for violence the minute we think of collective identities. It is often presumed that the more serious divisions are likely to gel into fault lines.

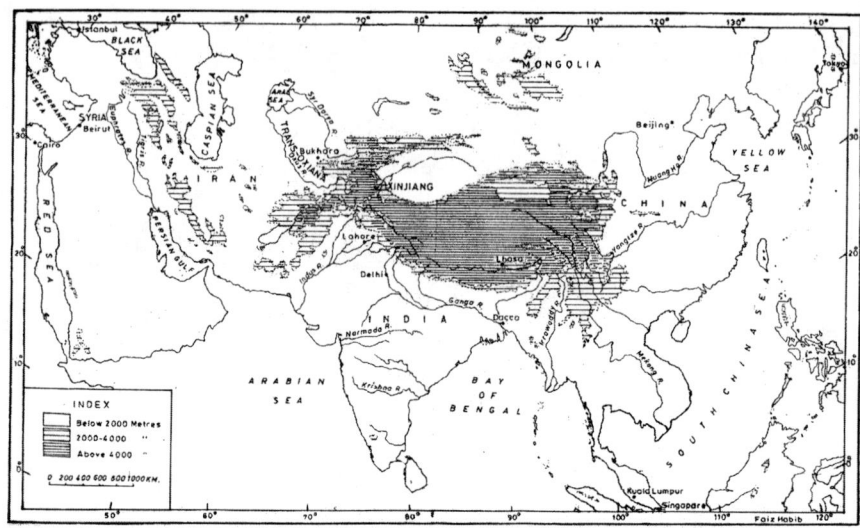

Map P.1 Asia and its cities. Map by Faiz Habib.

What is ignored by this "alterity industry" is that what is needed for a semblance of peace in this millennium is a greater understanding of processes whereby groups have fought and been indifferent to each other, but, nonetheless, have still managed to live together. Asian cities were chosen as the site of inquiry since the considerable evidence of networks and intersubjectivity that cuts across and through presumed boundaries and so-called fault lines has been theorized only in a preliminary way.

The project gave us an opportunity to investigate the following and other questions. What are other conceptualizations or translations of the term? What are the range of practices that we might identify as "cosmopolitan"? Cities are increasingly being cleaved into two with gated and even fortressed neighborhoods and ghettos that house the working-class poor, refugees, and migrants. Are there possibilities here of a subaltern cosmopolitanism? Another set of questions relates to political and social institutions. Does democracy foster pluralism or is it inimical to it? The concern, broadly speaking, was to identify aspects of sharedness in multicultural contexts that are defined by difference, by the politics of separate and bounded ethnicities. Another line of interest was in the city of the mind, in the lost and forgotten city, and in different imaginaries of the city, including the literary and the aesthetic.

There has been a growing interest in the question of cultural encounter. The dominant account is of Europe's representation of the otherness of non-Europe as manifest in cartography and colonialism, missionary evangelization, and orientalized knowledge. The question is also of the nature of encounter between Muslim, Hindu, Christian, and Buddhist religious communities and cultures that might be indigenous or agnostic. Alterity, boundary, and ethnicity tell us one part of the story. But can one go beyond the self/other polarity and indicate this other story of cultural encounter characterized by exchange, reciprocity, sharing, and sociality. What would be an archive of Living Together?

The exploration of Asian cities sought to identify what de Certeau calls the intertwined pedestrian pathways that are obscured by the panoptic (statist) and planned view of the city and by the disciplinary grids of history, anthropology, political science, and religious studies that work with boundaries entailed in the notion of civilization, culture, religion, ethnicity, and community. Ironically, my reading of this work took place on the very day of the collapse of the twin towers of the World Trade Center, which he uses to metaphor the imperial-panoptic view!

The project was dreamt up in a moment of madness. Living through it has meant experiencing the indescribable magic and horror of the city, a sense of both the miraculous and the miserable that megacities today convey and the exhilaration of learning as I took a giant stride out of the usual area of my research. Occasionally, there was despair and despondency as I struggled with the challenge but these feelings were compensated by significant moments of excitement—as when Caroline Humphrey and her postdocs proposed a study of Bukhara and proposed using the project to put together a larger volume on Bukhara; Asef Bayat wrote back enthusiastically, planning a larger project on West Asian cities; and the Institute for the Study of Islam in the Modern World (ISIM) went on to host a conference on the subject. Many more cities could have been included—Damascus, Dubai, Beijing, Shanghai, Kathmandu, Colombo, Dacca, Bangkok. . . . Our constraints were of funding and manageability. We hope, nonetheless, to have provided illustrations of the enterprise of rereading a city in terms of cosmopolitanism or its lack that can be used by others elsewhere.

I have been privileged to work with a particularly special group of scholars and have learned immensely from their research and writing. Unfortunately the structure of single-authored and segregated chapters obscures the dialogical process of being interlocutors to each other.

Susanne and Lloyd Rudolph helped me fine-tune the project proposal. It was navigated through bureaucratic processes within the Ford Foundation by Mark Robinson and Gowher Rizvi—who surprised me by requesting a meeting in my then "field" city of Ajmer, Rajasthan, India. The city studies were supported by a generous grant from the Ford Foundation. The contributors were put together with the lively assistance of Gautam Bhan and Sana Aiyar, who went through lists of names, cvs, and published work. The subsequent contributions of Himanshu Verma, Shireen Mirza, Subhashim Goswami, Dwaipayan Sen, Prajakti Kalra, and Mahendra Singh is gratefully acknowledged. Sifting through proposals for research collaborators, we drew frequently on advice from Ashis Nandy, who has an almost intuitive feel for the urban. Collectively I think we have been able to carve out a subfield of research and hope we will be able to challenge academic pedagogies.

Abhinav and Arvind are my anchors. I cannot think of having lived through this period without them and Daddy and Amma, Jijji, Sujata, Dilip, Ratna, Shaival, Phuong, Alaka, Sumi, Rajat, and Tin Tin. I owe a lot to the wonderful community of my colleagues at CSDS. A special thanks to my friends, Renu Addlakha, Kalpana, Surabhi, Daniel Raveh, Punam, Vidya, Beatrix, Arpana Caur, Jasjeet, Shankar Ramaswami. . . . All of you make life worth living.

Different incarnations of the book project have been presented at several fora: American University of Beirut, 18 October 2004; Columbia University, 3 April 2007; the University of Pittsburgh, 20 April 2007; SOAS, 16 May 2007, and the University of Sussex, 18 May 2007; the Delhi School of Economics, 9 March and 7 December 2007, and the India International Centre, 17 December 2007 and 28 January 2008. Numerous interlocutors will, perhaps, recognize their voices in the current version of the Introduction and I am especially grateful to Samir Khalaf, Gayatri Spivak, Sheldon Pollock, T. N. Madan, J. P. S. Uberoi, Rashmi Dube Bhatnagar, Sumi Madhok, Maya Unnithan-Kumar, Shankar Ramaswami, Aamir Mufti, Tarun Saint, Hilal Ahmed, and Deepak Mehta for orchestrating (and sometimes even coercing) these presentations and/or for perceptive comments. The work outside India was made possible by the hospitality of the Varmas, Panchals, Sehgals, Chardavoynes, Madhoks, Malaiyas, and Gulatis in the United States, the UK, Lebanon, and the UAE. Avinash, Dada, and Ramesh have patiently sustained my demanding library requests. Himanshu and Hilal have been frequently called upon for infrastructural assistance; Renu Bhasin contributed the index; and Kanhai, Bhagwati, Chatarpal, Hareram, Chaddha saab, Jagdish, Diwan Singh, Riyal saab, Jayshree, Ghanshyam, Rajkaran . . . have provided invaluable support at home and work.

The "city group" met collectively for the first time at CSDS, Delhi, in October 2005 at a workshop. The workshop was a rare one with detailed presentations, two discussants for each paper, and in-depth discussion on each city. Marriages are said to be made in heaven—in some cases workshops also play a role! Prajakti and Siddhartha Saxena (of the Bukhara team from Cambridge) met at the workshop and got married a year later.

Needless to say, the research questions are framed by my location in India, the megacity of Delhi and a nodal Third World research institute—which we notoriously call "the Centre." At the Centre for the Study of Developing Societies (CSDS) there has been a long-term interest in dissent, violence, the politics of culture, dialogue between civilizations, and a more recent interest in the city and the shahar, primarily in the Centre's Sarai Programme, which has put together impressive publications such as The Cities of Everyday Life and Shaharnama (Hindi), volumes 1 and 2, and City One, a conference on the South Asian city.

1 Introduction
Rereading Global Cities: Topographies of an Alternative Cosmopolitanism in Asia

Shail Mayaram

In addressing the problematic of Living Together, this book asks the question: What is it that holds cities together? What are the circumstances that lead to myriad partitions within cities, as well as to their annihilation as multiethnic cities. This work is about the (im)possibilities of cosmopolitan being in cities, in the past and the present. The Im (hyphen) possibilities folding into itself both the potentialities of the urban condition as well as its negation.

I argue that thinking about the city in the longue duree and as part of a topography of interconnected regions contests several dominant cartographies. First, imperial and nation-statist ways of reading cities that have occasioned the many and particularly violent territorial partitions of Asia including those of India and Palestine and have led to the utter devastation of cities.

Images of bombed cities permeate our consciousness. The universalism of cartography is mirrored in the singularity of coerced democracy. The strategic maps of military targets that these images are grounded on are countered by cultural and historical understandings of the city, its "scopic regimes" suggesting at alternative ways of seeing (Jay).[1]

Countercartographies of these devastated cities intimate different stories. Kabul, which has been what Uberoi calls a revolving door of Hindu, Buddhist, and Islamic civilizations.[2] Baghdad, located in a region that was the first to contribute language, law, and literature and known for its highly developed civil society institutions in the late nineteenth and the twentieth centuries, but that became grist to a hunger for oil and antiques. Najaf and Karbala, cities sacred for both Shi'i Islam and for Sunni Sufism. Basra, an important commercial city as also that of the great woman Sufi, Rabi'a al'Adawiyya (AD 717–801), who, as Schimmel reminds us, was the person who first introduced the element of absolute love in Islamic mysticism (*My soul is a woman* 34). Beirut, which represents the highly urban culture of Lebanon with Byblos located on the Mediterranean coast being one of the oldest inhabited cities in the world and an ancient crossroads of cultures for Phoenicians, Greeks, and Romans along with Sidon, Tyre, and Tripoli.[3] In Lebanon in 2006 a million people, a fourth of the population, were displaced by "precision bombing," a euphemism for an extended geopolitical war, aimed at destroying one of the most dynamic economies of the Middle East that had just been rebuilt after the civil war.

To understand the city then in terms of layers of geo-historic-cultural stratification, the fluid interpenetration of cultures is to reframe Lefebvre's famous question of who has the right to the city. It is also to ask whether cities have rights.

Second, thinking of the city in this way also questions discourses of knowledge including (post)Enlightenment cartographies that have divided the world into continents and clubbed them into regions to enable the management of territories by empires, states, and markets: the "Middle" East of European imperialism that has now become the MENA (the Middle East and North America) for transnational capital and "Asia Pacific," which comes from the Monroe Doctrine and the Cold War imagination.

The inclusion of Cairo and Istanbul in this project did not come from an Asian imperialism but was done in order to suggest their historical role as "bridge" cities constitutive of civilizations fostering the borderlands between Europe, Asia, and Africa.

Methodologically then our book is an effort to see cities and their histories in terms of interconnectedness, an approach that Andre Gunder Frank emphasized in *Re-Orient*—Spivak's comment of this being a "revision of a European world history" notwithstanding! The effort is to understand the city not in terms of its uniqueness but through its relations with other cities and regions. We highlight linkages between South, Central, West, and Southeast Asia that have been divided by the operations of West-oriented IR, area studies, and foreign policy establishments.[4]

This has important implications for thinking about spaces and identities. The Mediterranean, for instance, is tremendously important for the area that we call Lebanon today. Unfortunately even a theorist such as Balibar uses the term Euro-Mediterranean. Far more than a European lake, it was a borderlands in the making of which northern Africa contributed as did the Middle Eastern land bridge that connected with the Indian Ocean.[5] This is mirrored in the contemporary articulation of identities, as when Mai Ghoussoub, writer, artist, and publisher of Saqi Books, asserts that being a Beiruti means being able to read from left to right and right to left.[6] This is a different way of looking at identities than the horizontality of multiple identities that Amartya Sen refers to or the double self of psychologists.

Cities are palimpsest formations, horizontally and vertically. Lefebvre's *The Production of Space* signaled the spatial turn in urban studies.[7] My own predilection has been to understand how time sediments in spatial organization and in subjectivities. Lefebvre seems more concerned with the structure and form of cities, their materiality, than with the messy, lived life of its inhabitants. His datum is distinctively European.

In contrast to the proliferation of published work on Western cities, there has been a yawning gap in the relatively limited research on non-Western cities. Nonetheless, there have been important recent contributions—Huyssen's exploration of urban imaginaries, drawing upon Charles Taylor's conception of social imaginary, highlights how cities both reflect and contest cultural globalization; Drieskens et al. explore how urban structures deny citizenship;

Introduction   3

and Sassen's project on global networks highlights connections between the global and midrange cities of the global south (*Global Networks*).

My work on the Hindu-Muslim sacred city was a part of this project with all of its cosmological cartographical cityscapes. For considerations of space I have kept both this and a theoretical chapter on cosmopolitanism aside. Both will be published independently.

This book engages with three arenas and the literature each of these has generated, the idea of Asia, the debate on global cities, and cosmopolitanism.

THE IDEA OF ASIA

Why a book on Asian cities? Asia originated as a European imaginary and it is neither a continent nor a territorial unity, I have been asked. The category Asian cities is also new. Asia might well be a European construction but the construction has assumed a hyperreality for over two of the previous centuries that has fed into the making of identities. Tagore saw himself as a citizen of Asia (Bharucha, *Another Asia*). At the Bandung Conference representatives of some twenty-nine states from Asia, Africa, and the Caribbean collected, visualizing the birth of a new, decolonized Asia.[8]

Further, Asia is a complex unity defined by the trade routes of the Indian Ocean and the Silk Route; the overlapping religions which have come to be called Hinduism, Buddhism, Islam, Judaism, Christianity and other cosmologies; the spread of kingly polities from India and of sultanates from Iran and their overlay on kin- and clan-based polities; the traumatic experience of colonialism and modernity, its counterresponse in nationalism and the transition to the nation-state; and more recently, the rise of transnationalisms, political, economic, and religious ideological; and the influence of the newly industrialized economies (NIEs) of Korea and Singapore models that have exercised an overwhelming influence over China and India.[9]

More recently it has been argued that the first "global economy" developed in Asia with the emergence of a maritime economy in the Indian Ocean. Monsoon Asia connected Mesopotamia, India, China, and Indonesia. Chaudhuri and Wink point out that this was the area, stretching from East Africa to Indonesia, that was overlaid by Islam for a thousand years (Chaudhuri, *Asia Before Europe*; Chaudhuri, *Trade and Civilisation*; Wink). Europe established its supremacy over this region from the mid-eighteenth century, although Wink argues that Western superiority was established only in the nineteenth century and that the tide has already begun turning against Western dominance.

Asia is characterized by a very high degree of plurality (Vatsyayana). It is simultaneous with notions of difference and civilizational or cultural unity such as Arabiya or Farsiyat or Jambudvipa for India as well as the experience of Japan and China, which were never directly colonized. Debates continue to rage as to whether Turkey, Japan, and Israel are a part of Asia.

As an aspect of this plurality we need to rethink Asia demographically as a continent having been on the move, historically and in the present. This relates to the travel and livelihood of peoples, pastoral and merchant, flows of literati, and religious specialists including of brahmans and bhikkus, sufis, Ismaili and Christian missionaries, artists and craftspersons, musicians and medical practitioners, and the new transhumance of elites, workers, and refugees. Constituted by migration, in the case of Asia what needs to be problematized is the fact of settlement, why eventually people settled in one place, what the sedentarizing pressures were, and the continuum and tension between the pastoral and sedentary.

The idea of the pastoral must gird readings of the city, which is normally understood in terms sedentarization. The pastoral itself must be seen not in terms of livelihood alone, but as involving the circulation of ideas, languages, texts, aesthetic forms, genres, and goods that travel with their purveyors across borders and boundaries.

The interface between the pastoral and the urban was important for cities of the Mediterranean such as Damascus and Beirut. One aspect of the debate on urban design in the project of rebuilding Beirut after the Civil War highlighted the importance of the *maidan*. This had to do with how reconstructed Beirut could provide a setting for cosmopolitan being. Harvard-based architect, Hashim Sarkis, argued that the traditional public space of the *maidan*, which had been obliterated in the making of modern Beirut, be reinstated as a site where people from the hinterland had once camped in a space of exchange between peasant, pastoralist, and city dweller.

The importance of the pastoral is exemplified by Bukhara, although here it had terrible outcomes as when the Mongol armies of horse archers who came from the steppes of Inner Asia unleashed their destruction on the cities of Baghdad, Bukhara, and Samarqand. The Mongols under Cinggiz Khan (d. 1277), as yet un-Islamicized and un-Persianized, were infamous for their slaughter of urban populations.

Population movements can also have uncosmopolitan structures and outcomes as in the case of indentured labor to the Caribbean, an interstitial space between Africa, Asia, and Europe.[10]

We witness in our times an extraordinary flow of persons, ideas, images, wealth, and new communication technologies that yield a dramatic sense of the global interconnectedness of the world. The city has a new globality that is quite different from the old. Apart from the transnational spaces produced by capitalism, whether in the corporate sector or immigrant workers, there is also the life of transnational civil society including of religious and avowedly secular organizations. The flows of migrant labor include domestic and sex workers: Sri Lankan maids in Beirut, Central Asian sex workers in Dubai, and Bangladeshi bar girls in Bombay. These, as the Bukhara study suggests, have exploitative dimensions but also entrepreneurial possibilities.[11]

Should we train our imagination to allow "Asia" to emerge as a continent, Spivak asks (212). She reminds us of the attempt to think of it as one continent in its plurality, rather than reduce it only to a regional identity. Spivak's book is an exercise in imagining pluralized Asia, which is distinct from the pan-Asianism of Shinpei Goto, Sun Yat Sen, and Rabindranath Tagore.[12]

This plurality is brought forth in Bharucha's exploration of the friendship (between two cultural icons of Asia, India's foremost poet-artist-educator, Rabindranath Tagore [1861–1941], and the Japanese art historian and curator, Okakura Tenshin [1862–1913]) (*Another Asia*). Tagore enables Okakura Tenshin to travel deep into Another Asia that in spite of its fuzzy ideals has greater emotional depth and humanitarian insight, but it is Okakura Tenshin who catalyzes the very idea of Asia for Tagore. Both have very divergent constructions of Asia. Tagore was critical of the violent face of nationalism that was potentially destructive of civilization while Okakura's vision of Asian unity was hierarchical, and even racist.

Bharucha raises the question of the relationship between the New and Old Asia, with its "living traditions" of epic, ritual, and cultural performance. Is it possible to have a different idea of Asia, contrary to the statist valorization of Asian Values as repackaged neoliberalism? We hope through this book to raise these questions and possibly provide some answers.

OF "GLOBAL" CITIES

The second arena of our engagement is with the "global cities" literature. If New York's Manhattan Island is the model for Hong Kong, Shanghai has become one for Mumbai.

The urban phenomenon is one of the major transformations of our times. This is reflected in the large body of research of the past two decades and the profusion of city "readers." The UN report titled *State of the World's Cities, 2006-7* indicates the dimensions of demographic transition, as for the first time in history the population of cities outnumbers that of rural areas. This signals the proportional decline of the peasant-based, agricultural economy. By 2030 five billion persons are expected to inhabit cities. Further, with the number of slum dwellers expected to cross the one billion mark, the expectation is for all cities to be cleaved into a citadel/ghetto binary. A third of the population of cities will stand deprived of adequate housing and have few basic services.

Our title is a play on the question, What is a global city? It derives from an engagement with Sassen's provocative work on the global city (Sassen, *Cities in a World Economy*; Sassen, *The Global City*).[13] While her work was path-breaking in suggesting the transformation of the world economy since the mid-1970s leading to the new social formation of global cities and finance as a constitutive function of globality, it almost negates the prior and present existence of *other* global cities that have been and are based not merely on financial, but on other transactions; on labor, but on numerous other population flows; and not on transnational homogenous economic space alone but a cross-regional heterogeneous politico-cultural space.

It relates to contemporary globalization but also to a far more decentered world system and to multiple pasts and plural visions for Asian global cities that have been hierarchized surely but have not been as polarized as in the present. While Sassen's work is compelling, indicating the far-reaching transformations in the global economy in the 1980s, its focus on global financial and labor flows ignores political, religious, moral, and aesthetic perspectives.[14]

Underlying this is the much-debated question of what precisely the global/local is? Who/what authorizes the world/global city? Sassen's first list identified three global cities in New York, London, and Tokyo and was revised to include Miami, Toronto, Sao Paulo, Hong Kong, Frankfurt, Zurich, Amsterdam, Paris, Mexico City, and Sydney (*Cities in a World Economy*). On another ranking of "world cities" Manila qualifies, but not Shanghai and Mumbai. Abrahamson's is one of the most recent attempts to designate global cities on a continuum through composite economic and cultural ranking. The enterprise of the hierarchization of cities continues with London, New York, Paris, and Tokyo being "central hubs" of the global network; a second tier including Hong Kong, Osaka, Toronto, and Zurich; and a third tier consisting of Miami, Milan, San Francisco, Sao Paulo, and Singapore. These are ranked on a Global Cities Composite Economic Index (based on the presence and quantum of stock exchanges, banks and financial institutions, multinational corporations, and services firms) and a Cultural Industries Composite Index (including those of recorded music, movies, television). New York, needless to say, leads on all counts and London, Paris, and Tokyo follow. Osaka and Singapore achieve a score of 20 and 10 respectively (on a hierarchical continuum of 0–70) (Abrahamson chs. 7–8).

In Abrahamson's account culture is reduced to entertainment and its industries. There is no space for the globality of religious centers that might spawn transnational religious movements or for centers of knowledge and learning that are not mere nodes in the "information" economy/network society. In the case of the former, Delhi is the headquarters of the Islami Markaz, the font of the worldwide operations of the Tablighi Jama'at (see Mayaram, "Do Hindu and Islamic").

There has been much criticism of this paradigmatic approach to global cities. King asserts that all cities are global cities. Robinson points out that all contemporary cities are ordinary, diverse, creative, modern, and distinctive and calls for more cosmopolitan urban theory. With the West becoming the site of production of unlocated urban theory, Third World cities have fallen "off the map," as it were. To aim to be a global city might well be a clarion call to ruin, Robinson asserts (*Ordinary Cities*). Huyssen adds that terms like globalization and global city implicitly hierarchize cities.[15]

The global city has, nonetheless, been set up as an imagined destination for city planners and middle classes. Hence the slogan of radical civil society articulated at the Asian Social Forum—No more world-class cities!

My own emphasis is on multiple indices of globality including that of state and empire, sect and science, knowledge and culture. Byzantium/Constantinople/Istanbul was a global city for over fifteen centuries. Istanbul was a base for the operations of the Naqshbandiyya Sufi order that connected the three regions of Central Asia, Ottoman Turkey, and India. The names of several *tekkes* in Istanbul like Ozbekler, Buhara, and Kasgar and the names of its shaykhs such as Bukhari, Kabuli, or Kashmiri intimate their global world. The Bukharan Khwaja Nasir ad-Din Ubaydullah Ahrar had established the Naqshbandiyya as the dominant Sufi order in all regions of Inner Asia and sent disciples to Iran, Hijaz, and Anatolia. His murid, Molla Abdullah Ilahi, moved to Istanbul and established the first Naqshbandi *tekke* and gave sermons there (including at Ayasofya) that were attended by scholars and even by Sultan Mehmed Fatih. Ilahi's own murid, Shaykh Ahmad Bukhari, was from Bukhara and he built a series of *tekkes* patronized by Sultan Bayezid II. This historic role of the Naqshbandis was shared by the Qadiriyya and the Shadiliyya Sufi orders (Algar).[16]

In Asia city and country were often connected in a ritual economy centered on the monastery, temple, shrine, or pilgrimage center. In the Sunni Islamic world, the khanaqah was a place where some found spiritual succor and others just refuge for the night. The Naqshbandi and the Qadiri were the two great universal Sufi orders that emerged from Central Asia and spread through the Islamic world. The travel and connections of its members bound these lands culturally and spiritually.

Abbasid Baghdad was a global city for science. Scholars from different backgrounds, regions, and religions from Spain to India worked on Greek, Syrian, Persian, and Sanskrit texts. Al Mansur ordered the building of the Dar al Hikma, the House of Wisdom, in which a hundred thousand works were collected. Muslims, Christians, and Jews jointly explored an intellectual heritage of medicine and metaphysics (Peters ch. 4). Arab astronomy used the knowledge of the Bedouin; Babylonian and Indian works helped build an Arab algebra. Connections were established between Baghdad and Byzantium as envoys were sent by the caliph to bring back the work of Greek, Nestorian, and Christian scholars. Under the rule of Harun al Rashid, Hunayn Ibn Ishaq (808–873) headed a team of translators and copyists who translated Plato, Aristotle, and Hippocrates from the Greek. Arabic was the language of al Qur'an, of a conquest polity, but it was also that of science and medicine (exhibit, Department of Islamic Arts, Louvre, Paris). It was here that the hospital was invented. This would be the knowledge that would later make possible European expansion and the geographical "discoveries" of the Enlightenment, acclaimed as Western knowledge.

There was an eclecticism in the early Islamic city and polity—the Prophet Mohammad's Covenant with Jews and Christians made Medina a city acclaimed for its tolerance—but it was also circumscribed. The mystic, Al-Hallaj (858–922), was tortured and publicly crucified, said to have been beheaded and even dismembered, by the Abbasid rulers for what they pronounced were theological errors. They authored fierce Sunni repression—their secret agents poisoned four of the ten Fatimid imams in Cairo (Hitti).[17]

In addition, one can think of the globality of cities from the point of view of cinema or the arts. Bombay would rank on multiple indices even though it is rated a regional center in this literature.[18] Kapur describes Bombay as the privileged metropolis, the colonial port city and center of finance capitalism that up to the 1980s nurtured one of world's biggest urban industrial working-class movements. It has now emerged as *the* city of film and *modernist* imaging in art with Bombay and Baroda becoming centers of an expressly urban art and its related discourse (Kapur; Kapur and Rajadhyaksha). Singapore has been projecting itself as "the global city of the arts" (Bharucha, "Consumed in Singapore").

It is important to recover these complex pasts of the Other Global City, for they intimate histories of cosmopolitan being, its aspirations, contestations, and limitations. Models of the globe are important for the awareness of the world, particularly since several societies currently seem to have developed an amnesia with respect to their cosmopolitan cultural pasts and cosmopolitan possibilities in the futures present. The contemporary claim is to the world being flattened (Friedman). It is not only that in earlier periods plural conceptions of time have prevailed but that we also fail to comprehend those in the present.[19] The argument about the end of history and sovereignty ignores the current re-enchantment of the globe, the return of the idea of the sacred with all its complex temporalities that constantly disrupt secularized-linear time. Mythic and other temporalities permeate and disrupt global time (re)constituting subjective time. Is this nemesis for having ignored the time of tribal and forest, peasant and pastoral communities?

This reductionist view of time is echoed in Castells, who postulates the new global order on the capacity to store and process information and generate knowledge. Information underlies the production of goods, the growth of services and decision making. Visvanathan points out how his celebration of space-time compression ignores the politics of knowledge including of alternative knowledges. He cites Jackson's comment both in his *Altars of Unhewn Stone* and in personal conversations, regarding his puzzlement of why America is called a high-information society, Africa and India being rendered "low-information societies," despite the former having reduced its varieties of apples from 160 to 5! The informational explosion is contrasted with species extinction at the rate of one thousand species a year or so, especially in the tropics, coupled with the genetic truncation of major crops, which is a major loss of biological information. "By being insensitive to the fate of different knowledges and their link to livelihood, lifestyles and forms of life, Castells becomes a mere cheerleader of the latest form of R&D management as a model for a wider politics." He ignores the right of many forms of knowledge to exist as all knowledges are seen as partial and complementary. Corporate time is the domain of instant time; ecological time is the time of the movements and of large parts of civil/political society. Castells's information society enacts by default one of the oldest myths of the Western scientific regime—the myth of the perpetual machine. Vishvanathan concludes, "Net time . . . has no sense of the cosmic. There is about the network society a sense of necrophilic time, amnestic time, the time of nuclearism, the genocidal time of obsolescence and instant wars. . . . What one needs to probe are the notions of pathology, health, normalcy of the network society." What Castells fails to understand is that ethnicity is not merely about identity but about the right to different forms of lived time required by a universe of diversities.

OF COSMOPOLITANISM

Cities are and have been permeated by hierarchies of power, caste, race, class, and gender. But cities have also manifested the ethical idea of living together with strangers. How is the stranger apprehended and related to? Are there shared imaginaries and grammars that are rooted in everyday perceptions of being in the world? What are the practices that we might see as making possible Living Together, enabling us to capture at least some of the fluidity and diversity of social formations we encounter in urban spaces? Aihwa Ong has repeatedly asserted that the stranger is embedded in the global marketplace. The old philosophico-sociological question, however, is whether the self can rise above its social determination.

Given the burgeoning literature and a celebratory, popular notion of the cosmopolitan signified by the eclecticism of dress and food, taste and travel, I have found it useful to begin with a negative analytic, what cosmopolitanism is not. It is not corporate globalization or statist multiculturalism of postcolonial Asian states metaphored in the image-slogan, "Malaysia as truly Asia" or "Han-Tibetans one people." It is also not the liberal project of a cosmopolitan world order that identifies it in global governance (Held; Held and Archibuigi; Held et al.).

Global governance has hardly lived up to the Kantian vision of perpetual peace. Held's anticipation of cosmopolitan democracy and Archibuigi's reform project for the United Nations are undercut by the actual working of the Security Council. The very idea of global society is a fiction, deeply fractured and divided into nation-states as the world is today and rendered an impossibility by the armaments industry—the nexus between industry and state and nonstate structures of power.

Virtually all the studies in this book bring out the dark side of modern Asian polities. There has been Japan's hypernationalist past, the developmentalist state and the denial of difference of its others that John Lie brings out. Malaysia's majoritarian-authoritarian present, as Seng Guan puts it, attempts to exorcise the ghosts of polytheism that undervalue the Hindu-Buddhist civilizations that predated the Malacca sultanate in the peninsula.[20] In Tibet, Emily Yeh demonstrates how China authorizes a coercive cosmopolitanism achieved by the policy of *minzu tuanjie,* which is really the idea of cultural homogeneity achieved through assimilation into the mainstream. This has led to the crushing of dissent in Tibet and a demographic and developmental colonization.

Each of the contributors has their own take on theories and empirics of cosmopolitanism. Yet there is substantial agreement that it is not about diversity, world travel, and global flows and that it has non-Western and non-elite connotations and multiple vernacularizations. *Nyingjé* grounded cosmopolitanism in pre-1950s Lhasa and continues to still play a role today. Translated as compassion, it is also the notion of seeing familiar selves in others deriving from the idea of reincarnation—that lowly human being might actually be my mother from a previous life. Yeh argues that this gives us clues to subaltern cosmopolitanism. The Japanese idea of *kyosei* (*kyo* meaning together and *sei* meaning living) translates as living together, coexistence, coliving, symbiosis, and conviviality. Mayeda points out that it is captured, albeit inadequately, in the coexistence of man-woman, of human beings, and of humanity with nature. Elsewhere I have suggested that mapping translations of cosmopolitanism in Chinese, Sanskrit or Persian might lead to an enlargement of our social lexicon (Mayaram, "Debating Cosmoplitanism"). Isin refers to cosmopolitanism as an ethic; Arif to mundane cosmopolitanism; and Ong to cosmopolitanism in the lower case.

There is a rich literature on new cosmopolitanism that has been useful in thinking beyond the Enlightenment notions of cosmopolitanism and civilization—the idea of multiple cosmopolitanisms or the notion of critical cosmopolitanism first used by Mignolo (Pollock et al.; Mignolo) and Werbner's conceptualization of new including vernacular and feminist cosmopolitanisms.[21]

It is useful to make a distinction between cosmopolitanism as a descriptive category, which refers to, as Zubaida puts it, cosmopolitan individuals and lifeworlds, ideologies, milieus, and movements and to cosmopolitanism as a normative category. Isn't terror cosmopolitan, I have been asked? Whether one vests terror in state or in civil society, any ideological discourse that involves the denial of life and livelihood is, in my view, intrinsically anticosmopolitan.

My personal position is that a theoretical revamping of cosmopolitanism is required on the lines of citizenship and democracy studies, which no longer merely vests citizenship with the discourse of rights. Hence my preference for a notion of cosmopolitan being, a conception of being as becoming, a processual understanding of personhood as also of relating self/other, suggesting that it might involve (un)learning. This is distinct from cosmopolitanism that is rendered just another *ism*. This means also the possibility of the demonic self and the antithesis of cosmopolitan being in annihilatory projects.

Divergent from the approach that suggests that the cosmopolitan is about universal belonging and rootedness, we maintain that it codifies not only limited gesture of tolerance, but affirms the other's right to social and cultural being. It is demonstrative then of the capacity of the self to relate to non self not in denial, negation, otherness, and annihilatory politics but in feelings ranging from prejudice, ethnocentrism, and indifference, to civility, accommodation, dialogue, mutual respect, learning, and sharing to compassion, friendship, and even love. It is the human capacity to craft the self suggesting work and care and the capacity to learn from the other. Ironically, the cosmopolitan is rarely found in civilizations that have claimed monopolies of it!

Cosmopolitan being is not about belonging—for this will always entail a membership and exclusion—but about a relation and the capacity of the self to relate to non self affirmatively, as also to the natural and animal word and to earth. It can involve the imaginative seeing of oneself in another or perceiving the other as necessary for the self but not in an instrumental, functional way.[22]

LIVING TOGETHER

In this section I theorize a notion of alternative cosmopolitanisms building on practices that we might identify as "cosmopolitan." A recent argument developed by Varshney in the Indian, and now Southeast Asian context, makes interethnic peace contingent upon civic life. This derives from a long-standing theoretical framework that views associational life as indexical of "development." Strong associational forms of civic engagement, such as integrated business organizations, trade unions, political parties, and professional associations, are able to control outbreaks of ethnic violence, Varshney maintains.

Ashis Nandy's study of Cochin postulates an alternative cosmoplitanism on an epic imagination where no person is completely (im)perfect, neither human beings nor gods *(Time Warps)*. Each of the cultures of the cosmoplitan city thinks of itself as the most superior but simultaneously recognises the others right to exist. The postulation of such a universal, however, makes it difficult to explain violence without a resort to a binary view of good tradition/bad modernity. Indeed, the contradiction is apparent in his own writing on the simultaneity of heroism and violence.

Asia's cosmopolitan milieus, however, arose from a complex array of structures and practices and no single variable can give us a key to interethnic peace. These fostered exchanges, fluidities, and transactions. I attempt to map some of the sources below, drawing upon the contributions in this volume and other research.

1. Religion- and Trade-Based Cosmopolitanism

Trade and religion have been closely connected in Asia. In the context of Buddhism, for instance, monasteries provided credit to traders and reciprocal lay patronage was extended to the monasteries, which were often set up along trade routes leading to an extensive network of Buddhist cities.

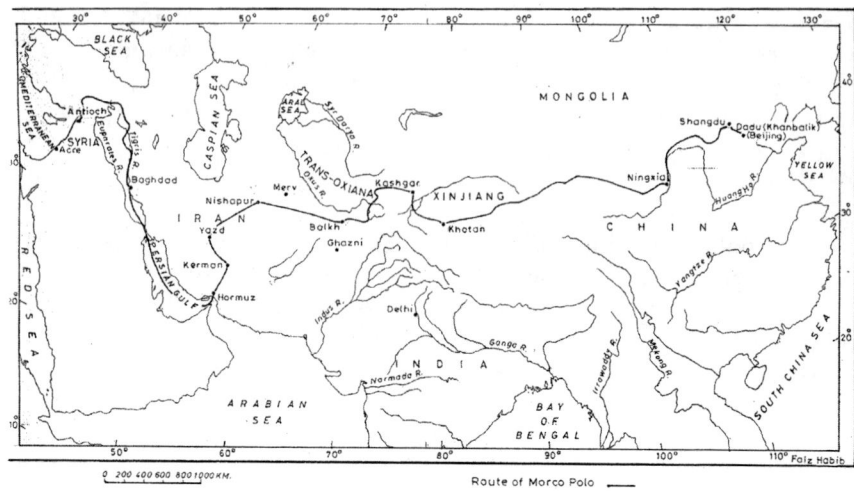

Map 1.1 The "Silk Route." Map by Faiz Habib.

The Silk Route exemplifies the connection between trade and religion. Samarqand's famous mural of the Ambassadors' Painting, "Afrasiab," shows a delegation from the Chinese Court bringing gifts of silk to the King of Samarqand and Turkic delegates with their long plaits. Dunhuang—the site of the loot of Aurel Stein who took from there hundreds of crates of manuscripts, paintings, and artifacts—in the present Gansu Province of western China has a history of two thousand years. I was surprised to learn when I visited Leh, in the Indian state of Jammu and Kashmir in the summer of 2005, that the city, which was on an ancillary node of the Silk Route, actually continued to harbor an active caravan trade till the partition of the subcontinent. The cities of Kanchi and Kampuchea suggest the flow between the Chola and Cambodian Empires as Narayanan has pointed out.

I have been working for some time now on the Indo-Islamic sacred city of Ajmer/Pushkar, which is the city of the great Hindu god, Brahma, and of a Sufi saint of the Chishti order who is actually referred to as Nabi-i Hind (the Prophet of India that some would undoubtedly regard as a heresy). The Chishti order received considerable Mughal patronage and grew into the most important site of pilgrimage in the subcontinent for Muslims but has always attracted numerous non-Muslims as well. The pilgrimage bazaar is a particularly important site of exchanges between Hindus and Muslims and continues even in post-partition India. A poster collected by Yousuf Saeed shows Burrraq, the Prophet's horse for his *me'raj* (Ascension to Heaven), with the face of a Hindu goddess and against the background of the Taj Mahal.

The bazaar is quite different from the neoliberal market, whether it is the Khan al-Khalili market representing the moment of Cairo's great prosperity at the juncture of the East-West spice trade, the Grand Bazaar

Photo 1.1 Sarai at Leh, Ladakh, India. Photo by Shail Mayaram.

of Istanbul, the Mughal mina bazaar, a *souk* for everyday supplies in Tripoli, or a weekly *hat* in Delhi. Descriptions range from Ibn Battuta's wonderful fourteenth-century account that describes an interregional network of cities with Cairo as the largest and intellectually liveliest metropolis of his time to that of Levi-Strauss in whose composite account of a newly partitioned South Asia one can recognize the sights, sounds, and smells of many bazaars.

Trade fostered close relations between Turks and Venetians, sometimes in open defiance of the Catholic Church (Exhibition, Metropolitan Museum, 2007). Delacroix's paintings capture the well-to-do families of Jewish merchants in Algeria and Morocco.

Elsewhere I have argued that suffering and ritual healing continue to provide contexts for social interaction across religious boundaries—even if occasionally one comes across a killer such as Suketu Mehta did, who seeks redress for his daughter from a Muslim holy man yet seeks to kill Muslims (see also Mayaram, "Living Together"). A good deal of evidence for this came from the studies of the project. In Bukhara the *mazar* that is usually seen as "Muslim" space still attracts Russians, Koreans, and even Jews, being attributed with specific healing properties such as curing hearing or speech defects. In Singapore the rationalization of land use consequent to urban planning in the 1960s and the attendant land scarcity led to the merger and co-location of several sacred sites associated with Sikh, Taoist, Buddhist, and Hindu traditions and occasioned new encounters and interaction between religious communities (Sinha).

In Kuala Lumpur in the building of the world's largest mall at Brickfields, lower-level functionaries exempted some nine Ganesh and other temples from demolition, suggesting a negotiation between the lower bureaucracy and minorities despite the Islamization of the state under Mahathir (Baxstrom). Baxstrom describes the Seng Hong Tokong temple whose iconography includes altars for Kali, Buddha, and Chinese folk gods and is seen as being able to rid the earth of spirits. The temple is patronized by Tamils and Chinese devotees whose self-ascription is Hindu-Buddhist and Buddhist-Hindu-Christian. He refers to this as an unstated but shared grammar of the everyday that holds the community together.

There is in China a new interest in Confucianism, Buddhism, and Tibetan medicine. It says something about cultural politics in China that Sun Shuyun's retracing of Xuanzang's (Hsuan Tsang) 16,000-mile journey should become a bestseller. Shuyun grew up in a period where the Maoist state heavily censored the domestic so that her grandmother's stories of monks are silenced but deeply affect her cultural subconscious. The novel is about memory, personal, familial, and civilizational.

The castigation of the modern/neoliberal market is evident in many of the studies. In Lhasa, Yeh points out that the surface veneer of interaction between Tibetans and Han Chinese in the property market barely hides tensions. In Kuala Lumpur, Seng Guan brings home the ethnicization of the market. In Singapore, the state marks expatriate Indians as preferred citizens in its effort to build the Intelligent City.

State Forms and Institutions

The role of the institutional-legal fabric in Asia intimates different visions of power. Abu-Lughod stresses the role of the Pax Mongolica under Kublai Khan (1260–1294) and Timur (1294–1307) who sustained the overland trade.

After the conquest of Constantinople by the Turks in 1453 the city was pillaged for three days, but soon thereafter Sultan Mehmet undertook the rebuilding of the city, which was repopulated by bringing in Turks, Greeks, and Armenians from Asia Minor and Thrace who inhabited Stamboul and Galata. With a population of 500,000, Istanbul was the largest city in Europe in the sixteenth century (contemporary London and Paris were below 200,000), presiding over the oldest of the three Muslim empires and the longest-lived.

Engin Isin's study explores Ottoman rule from an institutional-state perspective exploring law and governance as an institution of citizenship. He highlights the institution of *awqaf* or the inalienable endowment through the gifting of property that was used by the millet or autonomous national religious communities to provide public services such as schools, libraries, markets, hospitals, baths, sarais, and aqueducts. Since this entitlement was available to all people of the book including Jews and Christians, it enabled the negotiation of difference.

Isin cautions us of the limits of Ottoman cosmopolitanism, a term we use cautiously: non-Muslim endowments could not be used to print non-Islamic religious texts; regulations restricted settlement and movement of non-Muslim subjects in the city; and only monotheist religious groups or *dhimmis* were accommodated. He demonstrates, nonetheless, how Ottoman legal practice creatively worked through Islamic law, for instance, by declaring the monastic *waqf* of Mount Athos, a premier Orthodox monastery in Greece to be family *waqf* and, hence, exempt from confiscation. While difference was cognized in law and norms, non-Muslim subjects were, nonetheless, able to exercise rights such as freedom of conscience and religion and to provide services within their own millet.

Engin's work invites one to think of *waqf*-endowed spaces as not only contributing to the growth of Ottoman cities (as well as medieval cities like Cairo and Delhi) by building its infrastructure of mosques, libraries, bazaars, and hamans but also as providing contexts for exchange, say, of gossip or information. Karavanserai were usually a complex of a kitchen, bakery, olive press, and stables where travelers could find free food and shelter after they arrived in the city. Not surprisingly, the Ottoman Turkic term for the cosmopolitan, which relates to the stranger/traveler, is *musafir parbalik* (musafir = Arabic, parba = Persian, and lik = Turkic). The architectural and other activity generated by endowments enabled exchanges between architects, tradesmen, artisans, and craftspersons. Armenian architects and painters were influenced by the Genovese. Court patronage of Venetian painters brought in seductive styles of realism deeply affecting Ottoman miniaturists' styles and subjects, a world of light and murderous shadows that Orhan Pamuk explores—mark also the role of the Jewish matchmaking woman in the novel *My name is red*.

State cosmopolitanism is suggested by the Mughal capitals of Fatehpur Sikri/Akbarabad/Agra and Delhi/Shahjahanabad. Sikri houses Akbar's 'Ibadatkhana where religious debates were held with Muslim theologians, Hindus, Parsis, Jains, and Christians; suggests the ritual and architectural incorporation of the Chishtiyya Sufis and of the shrine of Salim Chishti; and also has a yogic quarter where Akbar himself undertook worship of sun (Schimmel, *The Empire of the Great Mughals*). The Emperor was the author of the Mughal-Rajput alliance and his court historian, Abul Fazl, wrote *A'in-i Akbari*, an India-centric history. Akbar also made a gift of red sandstone to the Govinda deva temple. Under the influence of a larger sufic belief in the unity in multiplicity, known as *wahdat-ul-wujud* (doctrine of Unity of Being inspired by Ibn Arabi), he launched a massive project of the translation of Sanskrit texts in Persian. Akbar's vision of the idea of *sulh-i kul* (peace with all), Alam maintains, saw all religions as leading to salvation and he inaugurated a new period of tolerance. Like Kublai Khan, Akbar wanted to understand Christianity and undertook a dialogue with the Jesuits whose interest instead was in converting him!

Akbar, we need to recognize, was no Asoka who renounced violence after the Battle of Kalinga! It was he who authorized the attack on the Pathan Raushaniyya for their "heresies." It was his grandson, Dara Shikoh, who epitomized the philosopher-prince and foregrounded a different notion of power. According to the Iranian philosopher, Daryush Shayegan, Dara represents a dialogue in meta-history and is the founder of comparative philosophy. Like Akbar he was interested in other religions and studied the Old Testament, the Gospels, and Hindu religious texts, particularly the Upanishads. It was in the sacred books of the Hindus that he claimed to have discovered the hermeneutical key enabling him to unveil the sealed meanings of Qur'anic verses. While Akbar wanted a universal religion, Din-i Ilahi, whereby Hindus and Muslims could rise above confessional prejudice, Dara's dream was loftier in trying to revisualize power.

A miniature of Dara's meeting with Khwaja Khizr metaphors Islam's encounter with the pagan, for Khwaja Khizr is a saint/deity of water revered by sailors and fishermen. Another popular theme of miniatures is Dara learning from faqirs and sufis, a tradition that comes from the mirror of princes literature dating back to Firdausi's *Shahnama*.

The making of the modern state is a transformational moment for multireligious, multiethnic societies. But combined with the technologies of the modern state, it produces anticosmopolitan consequences. One version of the separation of state and religion produced socialist societies. Humphrey, Marsden, and Skvirskaya point out how Soviet social engineering involved liquidation and exile of entire ethnic groups as "enemies of people"; coerced diversification through resettlement of population of Russians, Crimean and Volga Tatars, Germans, and others under Khrushchev and Brezhnev; forced housing arrangements; the destruction of mosques, madrasas, and public baths; the disappearance of trade and religion as occupations and hence, of older forms of coexistence based on trading and religious cosmopolitanism. The coercive cosmopolitanism of universal communist citizenship emphasized interethnic marriage but suppressed modes of religious piety and ethnicity. There are continuities in the post-Soviet city framed by the Uzbek State's authorizing of a new nationalist ideology and authoritarian political regime. The mahallas have been reorganized to represent monopolistic administration and contrast with the layered diversity of people's pasts.

In Japan, John Lie's earlier work has identified the dominance of the ideology of monoethnicity after the 1960s, when it became a principal predicate of Japaneseness, a discourse that collapses state, nation, and ethnicity (as well as class and culture) (*Multiethnic Japan*). Lie maintains that given the dominant ideology of monoethnicity, interethnic encounters are not recognized even when they do occur. A normative blanket prevails over metropolitan Tokyo—disputes, brawls and altercations occur, but are not recognized and are swiftly contained. Nationalism in Japan manifests as an anti-imperialist and antistatist ideology envisaging a monoethnic and peaceful Japan. Ironically, it was Japan's imperial project that articulated the notion of a multiethnic Japan!

Both Delhi and Istanbul face a troubled encounter with modernity, which means the nation and the secular state. In contrast to nineteenth-century Istanbul, which had a 50% population of Christians, Istanbul is rendered a monoethnic megapolis by Kemalist Turkey, which is 98% Turkish. Pamuk's city-biography highlights the attacks on Greek businesses, churches, and women in the 1950s, often sponsored by the state (*Istanbul*). Delhi witnesses massacres in 1857 before the Raj is established and Muslims are excluded from the city for several weeks (Dalrymple, *The Last Mughal*). A century later, in 1947, imperialism and nationalism wreak havoc on the Indian capital. But a constitution is arrived at in which the principles of mutual respect for all religions and an alternative secularism, not of the wall of separation but based on the principle of let all religions flourish, is encoded (Bhargava, "The Distinctiveness"; Bhargava, "Secularism"). In 1984, again there is horrific violence against the Sikhs with the complicity of the state and the ruling party. Yasmeen Arif's contribution highlights the continued marginality of Sikh widows, their perceptions of the failure of justice as none of the guilty involved in 1984 were arrested or prosecuted.

Are there processes of healing after genocidal violence? Not recovery—for the pain is always there for those who have lost dear ones and suffered the disruption of lives and livelihoods. But on occasion political processes contribute, even as they are also a part of the making of violence—a Sikh became prime minister of India and the Congress has even come to power in the Punjab. One hopes that the presence of Islamists in the Turkish public sphere will deepen ethical stances toward Christians, Kurds and others more than was possible under secularist governance.

The Neighborhood

Ashis Nandy uses his study of Cochin to identify the city as the site of prejudice and ethnocentrism and sees the neighborhood as exemplifying this. Chatterji and Mehta suggest how intimacy and violence go together in the neighborhood and national boundaries are reproduced in everyday speech acts, performative of violence. In both Bombay and Delhi, the sources of violence came from *within* the neighborhood and did not involve outsiders.

There are other stories and other worlds in the neighborhood. Humphrey et al. describe the neighborhood as a spatio-cultural formation arising around interlinked streets, but also an institutional complex identified with a set of practices. The rhythms of ritual life bring people together—the carpet denotes a material artifact of coexistence, akin to the *dastarkhan,* which is literally a tablecloth but also signifies hospitality, a particular manner of receiving and serving guests and eating food communally in a fairly widespread area including Indo-Islamic India, Afghanistan, and Kazakhastan. In Uzbek *andisha* is similar to Persianate *adab,* which refers to courtesy, respect, and appropriateness (Metcalf). Life cycle rites are occasions for feasts served to persons seated on carpets, along with wine and song and an exchange of gifts. The participants usually belong to different ethnic/religious backgrounds and might be Christian or Muslim, Uzbek or Turk. The authors emphasize how the city is in dialogue with the diversity of its past as they map the sites of sociality: the *chaikhana* (tea house), the places were men play their games, the cafés, the hamams, and the markets, which include the more impersonal large covered markets, the smaller early morning open-air vegetable and fruit markets where gossip and neighborhood news is exchanged, and the tourist markets that give opportunities to youthful subjectivities, to meet strangers, explore budding sexualities, and learn languages. . . .

Asef Bayat, an Iranian who has lived and taught in Cairo, explores the middle-class neighborhood of Shubra in Cairo comprising diverse ethnicities. The Christian Copts, who belong to the oldest churches in the world and whose presence goes back to the fourth century when Egypt was Christian, were a *dhimmi* or non-Muslim group subject to the payment of the *jizya* tax; their upwardly mobile status in premodern Cairo had been akin to that of Jews in Istanbul and Christian Maronites in Beirut. As the literati of oceanic commerce, they were concentrated in the port town but also lived *within* the walled city, in contrast to their ghettoization in Europe.

Ethnic violence has intensified in the south of Egypt and more recently in Alexandria, and in the previous century one of the most powerful Islamist movements developed in the form of the Society of Muslim Brotherhood. Nonetheless, Bayat demonstrates how Copts simultaneously have a shared homeland, history, and culture with Muslims. He explores practices of neighborliness: Muslims who attend Christian schools and Copts who go to Muslim *awqaf* schools; the mutuality of cleaning sidewalks and quotidian conversation; watching over each other's business and borrowing food and money; an overlapping ritual life manifest in attending each other's festivities. Some households even keep both Qur'an and Bible at home and there is also a world of furtive sexuality exemplified by Muslim-Copt romances. Public spaces and electoral politics bring people together as in the campaign of 2002 when a Muslim campaigned on sectarian lines but other Muslims went ahead and elected a Christian candidate in Shubra. The study of Cairo suggests the paradox of the urban, how the city is the site of deep-seated contradictions in terms of shared time and space. Among Muslims and Copts, then, there is knowledge and awareness of the other, but there are is also fear among Copts for their future. After considerable migration and through media and information flows, they have been reconstituted into a distanciated, virtual community.

Yasmeen Arif's discussion of Beirut leads one to reflect on the specificity of "downtown" as a social formation in the non-West. This was particularly important in a city in which the primary settlement pattern was segmentary due to migration histories and occasionally the communal tension in the countryside. Thus, Shi'is and Palestinians, that is, the poor, lived to the south, Sunni Muslims in west Beirut, and Maronite Christians in the prosperous neighborhoods of East Beirut, all of which were interspersed with pockets of Druze, Greek Orthodox, and Armenian settlements. The character of the old downtown derived from its souks, multiconfessional neighborhoods, and city center framed by the memory of an older cosmopolitanism. Downtown, as Arif suggests, was simultaneously a materiality and memory and a future that Lebanon aspired to. What a former Druze resident calls the *ruh-al-wataniye* was tragically destroyed by the civil war, the iconic cosmopolitan city bombed out, as it were. The violence led to myriad partitions and the obliteration of shared public spaces. Residents have memories of friendships that they see as having been overwritten by the insularity in the confessionally homogenous neighborhoods. A Kurdish woman and Jewish woman speak of their friendship with Shi'i neighbors. Even at the height of the Israeli aggression and civil war, households extended each other mutual support. In the postconflict geography many want to return to these mixed areas of residence even after having lived for several years in the more ethnically homogenous neighborhoods.

ASIAN URBAN FUTURES: POSSIBILITIES OF A SUBALTERN COSMOPOLITANISM?

Asia has become the main theater of the War on Terror.[23] Modern imperialisms of various kinds have brought ruin to multiethnic state forms and been midwives to coerced nation-state and "democratic transitions."

Any effort to theorize cosmopolitanism must be undertaken back-to-back with a theory of violence, which sunders fabrics of sociality. The so-called security concerns of foreign policy rarely consider that cities are repositories of civilizational conversations carried out over centuries or that its inhabitants might be bearers of memories that draw upon a culture's geological stratum. State and intelligence departments are oriented to power games of dominoes that rarely recognize the complex identities that are represented by cities, countries, and civilizations. Armies, paramilitaries, and precision bombs are sent in to pulverize peoples.

Across Asia postcolonial societies have experienced a range of authoritarian states ranging from benevolent monarchies and presidencies to military dictatorships extending from Egypt and the UAE, through Afghanistan and Pakistan right up to China, Singapore, and Malaysia. Most cities and countries today witness the play of democracy and its antithesis and of cosmopolitan being and the decosmopolitanizing of cities and regions. Modernity and the rise of the nation-state have been the two major forces disruptive of older transnationalisms. The quest for security and upward mobility has altered ethnoscapes of civilizations and cities. Dalrymple points out that after centuries of largely peaceful coexistence with their Muslim neighbors Christians are now leaving the Middle East—at present a small minority of 14 million struggle to live amid 180 million non-Christians. In the last twenty years there has been an outflux of two million who have left for America, Australia, and Europe. In Istanbul the last descendants of the Byzantines are leaving what was once the capital of Christendom; in the east of Turkey the Syrian Orthodox Church is virtually extinct; in Lebanon the Christian Maronites have lost the long civil war and their stranglehold on political power; several Palestinian Christians have left Palestine and Israel; and the Copts in Egypt fear an Islamic revolution (Dalrymple, *From the Holy Mountain* 19–20).

In the last three decades Asian elites, in the process of packaging and marketing a new glitzy Asia, are authorizing new discourses of violence involving nuclearization, greater income disparities, and exclusivist policies toward refugees and immigrants. Asiacentricity, Bharucha reminds us, can be as ethnocentric as Eurocentricity.

Circulation, commerce, communication, it is believed, are central to cities, which are the great financial and executive centers of the world-all other places and their economies erased from view, as it were. No other time is cognized but the time of capital, of instantaneous bank transfers. Cities, in turn, become depoliticized phantasms, rendering obsolete times of those who are not part of global networks.

There is obviously something dramatically new happening in Asian societies, with respect to state and sovereignty, city and cosmopolitanism. A new state form is emerging from the death throes of the postdevelopmentalist, postbureaucratic, and postwelfarist state midwived by neoliberal economic reforms. Sovereignty seeks to enter a new phase of entrepreneurial governmentality, enabling it to transcend the circumscribed territorialities identified with the Westphalian nation-state system and to reformat the Asian city. A new visualization of state power is entailed and new roles for its elites as the calculative state marshals capital, experts, knowledge, and skills oriented to reformatting the Asian city/state. Ong directs attention to the re-embedment of the nation-state in the territoriality of global capitalism and transnational civil society.[24] There is also the converse process of the embedment of global capital in the territoriality of nation-state. Overlapping sovereignties with corporations and civil society make the metropolis a hub of resources, actors, and institutions with a distinctive ecosystem. Postcolonial ruling groups continue to seek power and profit, deftly combining capitalism with nationalism and a cosmopolitanism imitative of the West but that is also extraordinarily nubile and flexible. This is the larger field this book captures—of the city caught in the travails of nationalism, statism, capitalism, and imperialism and yet the author of its destiny, of the future of the nation-state, and of Asia.

Across Asia the entrepreneurial state is matched by the growth of a class of transnational cultural entrepreneurs. Ong points out that in the case of China they are educated in the West but owe loyalty to the Chinese nation. They work as cross-cultural mediators fashioning a modern subjectivity and a different modernity for China, making it the most industrializing nation in the world. Among them are the yompies (young, outwardly mobile professionals), in their late twenties and thirties with a self-image as global citizens, who are often loosely connected with other Asian, mainly Chinese yompies from Singapore, China, Malaysia, and India (Ong, *Neoliberalism as Exception* chs. 6, 10). This New Asian technocratic elite that includes managers and middle men, capitalists and professionals is to be found in Beirut, Delhi, Kuala Lumpur, and Shanghai. These are the new patrons of global cuisines frequenting restaurants and bars.

As we confront the politics of violence and religious transnationalisms in our times, we also need to ask questions about the "politics of piety" that might be authorized by Hindu, Muslim, Buddhist, or Sikh discourses. Mahmood questions hegemonic notions of secular-liberal sociability and governance but does not address the implications of pietist and Islamist notions of sociality for different communities. Her ethnography does not investigate the attitude of women in the mosque movement toward minorities; how their transformative power as ethical subjects might be deployed vis-à-vis the non Muslim other; and how they use ethico-politics or moral principles to relate to intersubjective lives. This is particularly surprising given her restoration of Aristotle over Kant. Kant's assertion that morality was a matter of reason independent of the context of social virtues or habit displaced the tradition of Aristotelian ethics that emphasized habituated virtue over the "good" or the "right." The intertwining of the ethical and political suggests a view of agency that emerges from "within semantic and institutional networks that define and make possible particular ways of relating to people, things, and oneself," asserts Mahmood (citing Asad 78). But what is the way in which Egyptian women relate to their immediate neighbors, the ethnic other so-called, we are not told. A crucial lapse in an account of piety in contemporary Cairo.

Modes of cosmopolitan being have to do with memory that is equally about forgetting and silencing, an amnesia that characterizes Asian elites as also (non)Western intellectuals. Sassen's own implicit thesis is of the global city as a site of radical cultural erasure. This work on the Asian city is as much about this dynamic as about the need to remember and restore to memory these suppressed and silenced other urban imaginaries:

That even as Beirut is bombed we need to remember that this is an area that was part of the Holy Land.

That the Bamiyan Buddhas had survived in the Kabul Valley for some one thousand years and that it was the monks of the Kabul valley who took Buddhism to China.

That Kublai Khan had yogis and tantrikas at his court.

That the Tang dynasty emphasized "learn from the West," which meant to get a sutra and not as the Chinese interpret it now as looking toward Europe and the United States.

That Bombay, the city of fisherfolk and the port city, has been hugely hospitable to migrants including "untouchables," who felt emancipated in the city, and is not just the nativist city of Marathi speakers. For Rushdie Bombay is "the city of lost histories." But the "torn corpse of the old city" is buried by the skyscrapers that are the "tombstones" marking the burial of India's most diverse city.

That Delhi's cosmopolitanism came from its Indo-Islamic, particularly Perso-Turkic character.

The civilizational costs of the loss of memory are enormous. More infrequently one can identify flashes of remembrance. An older dialogue between Buddhism and Islam is represented in the published dialogue between Chingiz Aitmatov (a cultural icon of the former Soviet Union who wrote in both Kyrgyz and Russian) and Daisaku Ikeda, the Japanese Buddhist thinker. In another exchange of Aitmatov with the Kazakh writer, Mukhtar Shakhanov, published as *The Hunter's Lament over the Precipice: A Confession at the End of the Century,* he refers to an Asian Renaissance that preceded the European, which they locate between the tenth and twelfth centuries. Shakhanov writes of the word "mankurt" among Turkic peoples as suggesting the minority nationalities in the Soviet Union who were forced to forget their pasts—"the full forgetting of one's past can lead to spiritual mankurtism," he points out.

Sometimes the flashes may not even be recognized whether by subjects or observers. The Jewish philosopher, Erich Auerbach, is an important figure of German exile, but it is important to speculate on why he seeks refuge in Istanbul. Mufti maintains that "it was precisely his distance from home—in all senses of the word—that made possible the superb undertaking of Mimesis." But in a deeper sense Auerbach is at home-in-exile, given its importance for fleeing European Jews seeking refuge.

It is possibly also modes of memory that make the new Asian megacities sites of struggle, where, as Thornton and Songok put it, East meets West "in a maelstrom of urban chaos." "Like a body rejecting an organ transplant, Asian societies tend to be highly resistant to the cultural habiliments of neoliberal restructuration. Its intransigent commercialism has to be force-fed, and its social immune system violently suppressed, to make the transplant work. The scene of these climactic struggles is the new Asian megacity." Thornton and Songok see themselves as authors of a chaos school and clash-oriented approach. They, nonetheless, acknowledge that the resilient otherness that our book documents is what makes a sustained clash possible. As Thornton pointed out to me, "Were these cultural others not so deeply ingrained and so difficult to expunge, the clash phase of Asian globalization would be over in a flash (personal communication, 1 March 2007; see also *Development without Freedom*)."

Nonetheless, what is emerging in contemporary Asia is the splitting of cities, ruling and proletarian, of SEZs and shantytowns. Davis's apocalyptic account maintains that slums are likely to be the permanent battlefields of the twenty-first century. His work foregrounds the slum as a paradigm of the city, the camp à la Agamben, although the latter's argument is that it is the camp rather than the city that is the fundamental biopolitical paradigm of the West (*Homo Sacer* 32; *State of Exception* 64). Davis sees the rise of this informal urban proletariat as a wholly original development unforeseen by either classical Marxism or neoliberal theory. He envisages an impending world war between the American empire and the slum's poor: a "war on terrorism" arising at the conjuncture of corrupt leadership, institutional failure, and IMF-imposed Structural Adjustment Programs, leading to a massive transfer of wealth from poor to rich.

Are the great slums, as a terrified Victorian middle class once imagined, volcanoes waiting to erupt? Are the souls of the new urban poor waiting to feed the vultures of fundamentalist ideologies such as Hindu fundamentalism in Mumbai, Islamism in Casablanca and Cairo, Pentecostalism in Kinshasa and Rio de Janeiro that have produced the street gangs in Cape Town and San Salvador or suicide bombers elsewhere? While the quest is for imperial order they have the gods of chaos on their side, Davis concludes.

Cities, however, need to recognize that while the slum is the site of biopolitical modernity and extreme vulnerability, poised as it is on homelessness and violence it is often also the site of productivity, creativity, and sociality. The dark side of the city, as Ashis Nandy puts it, is also the redemptive village in the city that comes with all its parochialisms, its localisms, as it were.[25] This urban underclass is disconnected from industrialization, but not from the services sector or even economic growth. Indeed, the double-digit growth of the Asian Tigers and Giants so-called depend on them. *The slum is the vital city.*

Davis, to my mind, reduces the informal urban proletariat to mere victims of history. He expresses an old European fear of the crowd, the mob. One needs to see the city in terms of both dystopias and utopias. Davis ignores that migrants and workers might be bearers of vibrant counter-imaginaries of the city, of citizenship, democracy, and justice. The challenge, of course, is whether urban elites/planners will be able to cognize these in their imaginaries as they make and remake cities. Neuwirth's discussion of squatters is far more nuanced as he invests it with productivity and entrepreneurship. But he, likewise, does not tell us much of the textures of interethnic relations in the shantytowns, the resource conservation, the sociality, and the aesthetics of their lives.[26]

The slum is the site of prejudice, conflict, and exclusion but also one of cohabitation and conflictual coexistence, where difference is encountered and confronted, hate speech articulated but also negotiated. A slum contains in itself many possibilities. Its population can be disciplined to provide an amenable working class as in China's SEZs or it can be converted into a camp as in the case of the Palestinian camp of Burj al-Barajneh in Beirut—where older exchanges between Beiruti Shi'is and Palestinians turned horrifically violent.[27] It can provide fertile ground for recruitment to (hyper)nationalisms or to antistatist ideologies such as radical Islamism.

One of my questions for our project was of the possibilities of a subaltern cosmopolitanism drawing upon new subjectivities, coalitions, and alliances relating to interethnic relations in the multiethnic city-slum, in political society and as an outcome of the deepening of democracy.

In India subaltern groups were involved in partition violence, one of the greatest events of mass violence ever, in the 1960s and again since the 1980s. The violence in Delhi in 1984 and in Gujarat in 2002 involved dalits and tribals. Nonetheless, in the crevices of society one sometimes witnesses glimpses of cosmopolitan being. In the slum demolitions of some 100,000 tenements in Mumbai in 2006, Chander and Goswami demonstrate that Hindu and Muslim "Bhaiyas" (primarily from Uttar Pradesh) protested their homelessness and displacement, suggesting that slums are not merely cleaved along the communal lines identified by Appadurai, Chatterji and

Mehta, and Mehta.[28] Lapierre describes a Calcutta slum in which a Christian woman affected by leprosy is looked after by her neighbors.

Ramaswami's research on migrant workers in Delhi indicates their sense of exclusion from the ruling city as they do not have a sense of belonging as a *nagarik* or *vasi* of Delhi.[29] Hindu and Muslim workers are given to both stereotypes and prejudices mirrored in their sexualized banter. But there are flashes of a subaltern cosmopolitanism in the multiple languages that a migrant worker is exposed to and begins to speak; in the possibilities of new intimacies between men and women; in a Muslim worker prevailing upon a Hindu couple to cook simai, the ritual food for Eid and their invitation to other workers to feast on it; in their joint resistance to the exploitation of the nonresident capitalist ("Marginal Civilizens"; "Togethering Contra Othering")[30]

Subaltern visions for democracy, citizenship, and justice come alive in their discourse. This is a political imaginary in which there will be *asli prajatantra* as opposed to the *rakshasi prajatantra,* real versus demonic democracy. This will be a domain of dignity for them (*asli samman* and *asli svagata* contrasted with the *nakli samman* and the *svagata dande ka*).[31] It will, above all, be a world in which they get proper remuneration for their work; where there is *talmel* rather than individuating competition and the pursuit of self-interest. Such visions are also in circulation among people of what is called the "informal sector," in hawkers' and vendors' organizations.[32]

This is a perspective that entails a different idea of the subject. Negri gestures in this direction. He elucidates the idea of the productive *bios* as Agamben is "unable to account for the productive dimension of the *bios* and ends up blocking the *bios* on a naturalistic plain (life as *zoe*) or on a generically anthropological negativity (sacredness, bareness, exclusion, or camp). . . ." His negativity leaves the subject a mystery without any positive construction of being (235–6). We need to construct a new political subject from the margin of the biopolitical fabric, Negri points out. This is a need to understand power in biopolitical terms as "we are immersed in Power; we are within Power and harbor no illusion of being outside of it or being on the margins" (235–6, 237). Poverty, Negri argues, is both a being *inside* and a being *against*. The resistance of the poor is productive of new spaces of creation and circulation. The poor are excluded from the world they produce but that power becomes resistance and resistance nourishes new power. There is obviously a different conception of power at work here in Negri's elucidation of Spinoza, which is not the case of poverty as "bare life" but rather of a power to create the world.[33]

As I sift through Shankar's photographs for inclusion in this book, I see that there are many vignettes from workers' lives—more sharedness than I thought. Hindu and Muslim workers' families live together in the same flat and Hindu and Muslim workers go for an outing to Old Delhi. Another worker lies in a hospital bed and is visited by several of his Hindu co-workers. In yet another in the aftermath of the demolition of a

Introduction 25

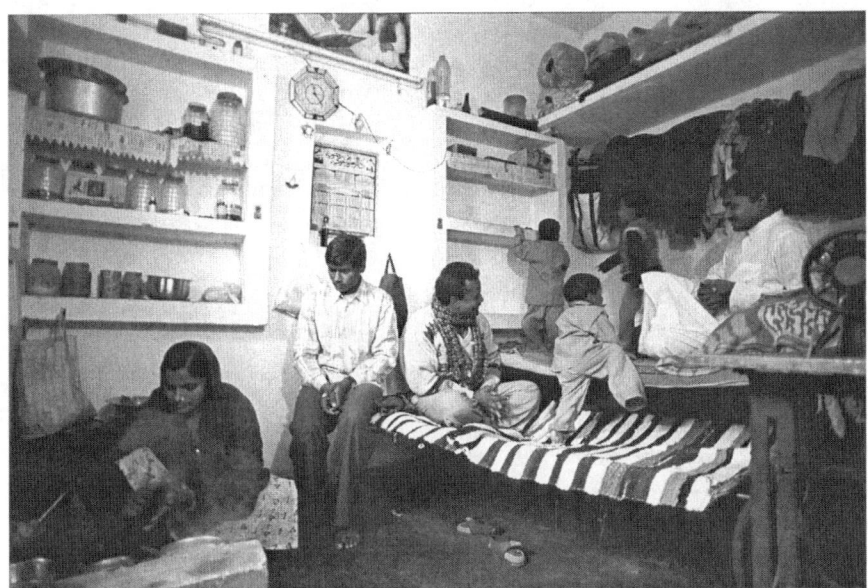

Photograph 1.2 Hindu and Muslim workers' families living under a single roof. Photo by Shankar Ramaswami.

Photograph 1.3 Hindu and Muslim workers on a day's outing in Old Delhi. Photo by Shankar Ramaswami.

hutment of a Muslim worker, Hindu workers are taking him and his family to their homes.

Subaltern cosmopolitanism is not a fully satisfactory term, but these images give it body. It can also have civilizational dimensions. Gayatri Spivak mentioned to me the one occasion when she used the term subaltern cosmopolitanism. Where a journalist is trying to probe from Armenian women their response to the genocide by the Turks and they make a gesture that she reads as one of forgiveness, let the past be done with. . . .

NOTES

1. Weber uses the *Washington Post* term "targets of opportunity."
2. For an elaboration of the idea of the Hindu Kush frontier between the Oxus and the Indus and between Central and South Asia, see Uberoi. He describes the frontier not as a boundary but a zone, physical, ecological, geopolitical, ethnolinguistic, or cultural. The central Hindu Kush are "one of the crossroads of Asia, a true frontier . . . which divides, interrelates and interchanges, for the mountain barrier was crossed and re-crossed by people, things and ideas in either direction in history and pre-history" (185). The mountains not only divided central and southern Asia, but also interconnected the two parts of Asia into a system of interrelations. "For the history of the frontier is the history of mutuality and the logic of interrelations or it is nothing," Uberoi writes. In the colonial period alone was the life of the frontier almost stilled. See Uberoi ("Between the Oxus and the Indus").
3. For a detailed account see Mayaram ("Beirut").
4. The issue of earlier modes and moments of modernity (the early modern) and of globalization has recently been raised. Fletcher affirms the need for a horizontally integrative macrohistory, pointing out that while "historians are alert to vertical continuities (the persistence of tradition, etc), they are blind to horizontal ones." He identifies a period of early modernity characterized by population growth, growth of regional cities and towns, the rise of urban commercial classes, religious revival and missionary movements, rural unrest, and decline of nomadism (Fletcher). See also Subrahmanyam on this period between the mid-fourteenth and mid-eighteenth centuries.
5. On the relation between Europe and Africa, see Bernal and the debate his work generated.
6. Presentation to Conference on Public Spheres, American University of Beirut, Beirut, 22–24 October 2004.
7. Harvey's reformulation suggests a threefold view of space-time: as absolute, a "thing in itself" (the space of Newton and Descartes); relative space (Euclid and non-Euclidean geometries and Einstein's shift from space *and* time to space-time); and relational space (signaled by Leibniz's objection to Newton that God is inside absolute space and time (ch. 3).
8. On the continuity between colonization and decolonization represented by the Bandung Conference, particularly of the pedagogical model of politics implicit in the Nehruvian development vision that continued up to the 1960s, see Chakrabarty. The moment represented what Heidegger called the Europeanization of the earth.
9. Uberoi points out that the Asian frontier provides a connective tissue between two parts of Asia ("The structural concept of the Asian frontier"). This is a vast chain of mountains, plateaus, deserts, and steppes that divides central or

inner Asia, whose waters have no oceanic outlets, and outer Asia. He characterizes a true frontier as an autonomous region that represents the conjunction, the unity, and the opposition of two or more regions so that they together form a patterned whole. The essential nature and diachronic rhythm of the frontier is to change in time from a firm dividing line into its opposite, a meeting point, and back again, thus renewing itself as well as those on either side.

10. Jean Rhys's marvelous prequel to *Jane Eyre* is an account of the double displacement of slaves and of white creoles displaced following the Emancipation Act by a new wave of colonizers. Antoinette is the Gothic secret of *Jane Eyre*. She and her mother become ghosts, women relegated to "madness" by Victorian society. Here is the dialogue of the colonial margin with the metropolitan center when Rochester says, "Slavery was not a matter of liking or disliking. It was a question of justice" and Antoinette responds, "Justice, I've heard that word. It's a cold word. I tried it our [. . .] I wrote it down. I wrote it down several times and always it looked like a damn cold lie to me. There is no justice" (94).

11. See Ong's chapter titled "A Biocartography: Maids, Neoslavery, and NGOs," which demonstrates how neoliberal Asian lifestyle reduces domestic maids to slavelike labor. Foreign domestic workers in Singapore, Hong Kong, and Kuala Lumpur prop up the high standards of living of the middle class, who control wages, work permits, work and living conditions, and passports. These migrant women are exposed to violence and have no access to health services. There are 140,000 domestic workers in Singapore, 200,000 in Malaysia (Indonesian maids looked down upon despite their shared religion), and 240,000 in Hong Kong who are underpaid, starved, and battered (196).

12. In an interview Spivak indicates that "Asia can be for me a position without an identity" (Spivak).

13. Sassen argues that the transformation of the world economy since the mid-1970s has seen the emergence of a new social formation, that of global cities. Their growth has been fueled by the transnational mobility of capital as well as by the flows of information and labor. Up to the 1800s the world economy was trade based, located in multiple sites such as harbors, plantations, factories, and mines not necessarily identified with cities. Today the global city is the site of economic activity given the new centrality of banking, finance, and services, displacing the importance of manufacturing and production. Its emergence signals a spatial transformation of cities with export processing zones, offshore banking centers, financial markets, transnational corporations, banks, the transformation of neighborhoods into business districts, the growth of wage labor, and increased inequalities between rich and poor. International trade has been overshadowed by international financial flows. Foreign direct investment grew three times faster than export trade in the 1980s, and international financial flows were directed more at investment in services than at manufacturing.

14. William Thornton comments that Sassen's stress on the "'new temporality' of economic globalization is sociology written from the victor's perspectives." While she "defines her vaunted global city as a zone embedded in 'older temporalities and spatialities' her focus is almost entirely on the city as a shimmering 'global network.' The cultural embeddedness that she rhetorically alludes to is nowhere in evidence" (personal communication, 1 March 2007).

15. See Brenner and Kiel for a review of aspects of the debate.

16. This is not to deny that the Naqshbandi Sufis are a particularly orthodox school of sufis since they are seen as favoring the shar'iah and in view of their distance and hostility to Shi'ism, unlike other sufi orders. Two famous Indian Naqshbandis, Shaykh Ahmad Sirhindi and Shah Waliullah of the eighteenth century, continue to inspire all forms of Islamic movements in the subcontinent.

17. Cordoba, the capital of Umayyad-ruled Moorish Spain, acclaimed for its *convivencia* between Islamic, Christian, and Judaic faiths, saw the exile and burning of the books of Ibn Rushd or Averroes (1126–1198) for the "heresy" of combining Greek philosophy and Islam and proclaiming the autonomy of reason.
18. Mumbai along with Hong Kong, London, Manilla, Mumbai, and Toronto are described as tertiary centers of the global film industry and Cairo as a movie and television center of the Arab world (Abrahamson 165).
19. Raju points out that the Fifth Ecumenical Council held in AD 553 pronounced a curse on "cyclic" time, a curse that affected Western thought about time for centuries to come. The idea of rebirth of souls that had prevailed in the context of early Christianity came to be rejected. Augustine formulated a notion of sin that for the first time made heaven and hell eternal and quasi-cyclic time was substituted by apocalyptic time. Raju maintains that the categories "linear" and "cyclic" are defective, since each category incorporates many different pictures of time. Among Ricoeur's masterly insights was pointing out that the calendar bridges lived and universal time and also invents a third form of time that is mythic time.
20. Ong has pointed out how Islamic governmentality in Malaysia and the pact of what is projected as multicultural and moderate Islam with Islamic feminism both position themselves against Islamist civil society (ch. 1).
21. See also Dharwadker; Appiah; and Mayaram, "Debating Cosmopolitanism" for a detailed discussion.
22. In a presentation at the East West Philosophy Conference, Spivak spoke of education as imagination, as meaning the capacity to visualize, seeing that which is not before one's eyes and acting against one's self-interest. Even the latter is sufficient—if one acts against self-interest, one must be seeing something beyond the "obvious." I am grateful to Daniel Raveh for having brought this to my attention.
23. Ninan Koshy cited in Spivak (1).
24. Neoliberalism, Ong points out, is a new relationship between power and knowledge, sovereignty and territoriality. Governing becomes a transformative-technical rather than politico-ideological intervention. Drawing on Carl Schmitt's formulation that the sovereign derives not from monopoly to coerce or rule but decides on the exception to the juridical order, Ong formulates the exception very differently from Agamben. For Agamben civilization represents normativity and the death camp is the zone of exception of absolutized exclusion and suspension of rights and life itself. But in contemporary Asian societies, Ong argues, authoritarian sovereigns create exceptions in zones endowed with new economic freedoms, autonomies, opportunities, and resources for its elites to forge transnational connections, but where workers rights are subject to suspension (ch. 1). Ong sees the state not as a singularity but as an ever shifting assemblage of planning, operations, and tactics informed by neoliberal reason.
25. Keynote address to City One, Conference, CSDS.
26. Kaneez Hasna's doctoral work at the University of Oxford indicates how migrant Bangladeshi women bring to the city beliefs that the plants that they nurture will attract clouds and bring rain.
27. Personal interview, Olfat Khalil Mahmoud, Beirut, 23 Oct. 2004.
28. Chander and Goswami contend that within slums, language and region are more salient lines of division than religion. Thus the politics of Marathi-speaking natives might lead to confrontations with UP bhaiyyas (which include both Hindus and Muslims)
29. Ramaswami points to the fact that *vasi* is an expansive notion that relates to existential senses of centeredness, relatedness, and mutual belonging to

places, persons, ways of life, and the nonhuman world, which is constricted in the idea of the *nagarika,* the normative ideal of equal citizenship.
30. The workers launched an agitation when the factory was closed by Michael Ayun, who markets designer silverware in upmarket American department stores at the cost of considerable personal injury and ill-health to workers. As I personally witnessed their struggle carried out over months in front of the offices of a nonresponsive print media and the apartment building of the nonresident capitalist, I thought of how difficult trade unionism and a nonviolent satyagraha have been rendered in our neoliberal times. But networks led to a web site creating counterpressure on buyers for supporting unethical practices, leading to a recognition of workers' demands.
31. Mark the same usage of the word—*danda* (rod) of the policeman and *danda,* the coercive power of the state.
32. My colleague, Madhu Kishwar, has fought at the cost of physical violence to herself for the rights of hawkers and vendors to the city. See her articles in *Manushi;* also Mayaram, "Living Together."
33. "Bare life" is the opposite of Spinozian power and joy of the body. "Spinoza systematically overturns all the ontological positions that characterize *Dasein* as unproductive," writes Negri (236). Elsewhere in a review Negri maintains that there are two Agambens—a Heideggerian Agamben concerned with existentiality, death, bare life and a Spinozist Agamben with a more positive metaphysics. See Colin McQuillan, "The Political Life of Giorgio Agamben" <http://garnet.acns.fsu.edu/~nr03/mcquillan.htm>.

WORKS CITED

Abrahamson, Mark. *Global Cities.* Oxford: Oxford UP, 2004.
Abu-Lughod, Janet L. *Before European Hegemony: The World System AD 1250–1350.* New York: Oxford UP, 1989.
Agamben, Giorgio. *Homo Sacer: Sovereign Power and Bare Life.* Stanford, Standford UP, 1995.
———. *State of Exception.* Chicago: Chicago UP, 2005.
Alam, Muzaffar. *The Languages of Political Islam in India c. 1200–1800.* New Delhi: Permanent Black, 2004.
Algar, Hamid. "A Brief History of the Naqshbandi Order." *Naqshbandis: Historical Developments and Present Situation of a Muslim Mystical Order.* Ed. M. Gaborieau, Alexandre Popovic, and Thierry Zarcone. Istanbul: İnstitut Francais d'Etudes Anatoliennes d'Istanbul, 1985. 3–44.
Appadurai, Arjun. "Spectral Housing and Urban Cleansing: Notes on Millennial Mumbai." *Public Culture* 12.3 (2000): 627–51.
Appiah, Kwame Anthony. *Cosmopolitanism: Ethics in a World of Strangers.* New York: Norton, 2006.
Batuta, Ibn. *The Travels of Ibn Batuta.* 1829. London: Darf, 1984.
Baxstrom, Richard. "Wrecking Balls, Religion, and the (Re)production of the Local in Brickfields, Kuala Lumpur." Unpublished paper.
Bernal, Martin. *Black Athena: The Afroasiatic Roots of Classical Civilization.* New Brunswick: Rutgers UP, 1987.
Bhargava, Rajeev. "The Distinctiveness of Indian Secularism." *The Future of Secularism.* Ed. T. N. Srinivasan. Delhi: Oxford UP, 2007. 20–53.
———. "What is Secularism for?" *Secularism and its Critics.* Ed. Rajeev Bhargava. Delhi: Oxford UP, 1988. 486–542.

Bharucha, R. *Another Asia: Rabindranath Tagore and Okakura Tenshin*. Delhi: Oxford UP, 2006.
———. "Consumed in Singapore: The Intercultural Spectacle of Lear." *Theatre* 31.1 (2001): 107–27.
Brenner, Neil, and Roger Keil, eds. *The Global Cities Reader*. Abingdon, Eng.: Routledge, 2006.
Castells, Manuel. *The Rise of the Network Society*. Oxford: Blackwell, 1996.
Chakrabarty, Dipesh. "Legacies of Bandung: Decolonisation and the Politics of Culture." *Economic and Political Weekly* (12 Nov. 2005): 4812–18.
Chander, Naveen, and Naresh Goswami. "Dastan-i Mumbai, Qissa-i Shanghai," Research study. Delhi: Sarai, 2006.
Chatterji, Roma, and Deepak Mehta. *Living with Violence: An Anthropology of Events and Everyday Life*. Delhi: Routledge, 2007.
Chaudhuri, K. N. *Asia Before Europe: Economy and Civilisation of the Indian Ocean from the Rise of Islam to 1750*. Cambridge: Cambridge UP, 1992.
———. *Trade and Civilisation in the Indian Ocean: An Economic History from the Rise of Islam to 1750*. Cambridge: Cambridge UP, 1992.
Dalrymple, William. *The Last Mughal: The Fall of a Dynasty, Delhi 1857*. Delhi: Penguin/Viking, 2006.
———. *From the Holy Mountain: A Journey in the Shadow of Byzantium*. Delhi: Penguin, 1977.
Davis, Mike. *Planet of the Slums*. London: Verso, 2006.
de Certeau, Michel. (1984). "Walking in the City." *The Practice of Everyday Life*. Trans. Steven Rendall. Berkeley: U of California P. 91–111
Dharwadker, Vinay. "Cosmopolitanism in Its Time and Place." *Cosmopolitan Geographies*. Ed. Vinay Dharwadker. Abingdon, Eng.: Routledge, 2001. 1–13.
Drieskens, Barbara, Franck Mermier, and Heiko Wommen, eds. *Cities of the South: Citizenship and Exclusion in the 21st Century*. London: Saqi, 2007.
Fletcher, Joseph. "Integrative History: Parallels and Interconnections in the Early Modern Period, 1500–1800." *Journal of Turkish Studies* 9 (1985): 37–57.
Frank, Andre Gunder. *ReOrient: Global Economy in the Asian Age*. Berkeley: U of California P, 1998.
Friedman, Thomas L. *The World Is Flat: The Globalized World in the Twenty-First Century*. London: Penguin, 2006.
Harvey, David. *Spaces of Global Capitalism: Towards a Theory of Uneven Geographical Development*. London: Verso, 2006.
Held, David. *Democracy and the Global Order*. Stanford: Stanford UP, 1995.
Held, David, and Daniele Archibiugi, eds. *Cosmopolitan Democracy*. Stanford: Stanford UP, 1995.
Held, David, Anthony McGrew, David Goldblatt, and Jonathan Perratone. *Global Transformations: Politics, Economics, and Culture*. Stanford: Stanford UP, 1999.
Hitti, Phillip Khurri. *Capital Cities of Arab Islam*. Minneapolis: University of Minnesota Press, 1973.
Huyssen, Andreas. "Introduction: World Cultures, World Cities." *Other Cities, Other Worlds: Urban Imaginaries in a Globalizing World*. Ed. Andreas Huyssen. Durham: Duke UP, 2008. 1–26.
Jay, Martin. "Scopic Regimes of Modernity." *Vision and Visuality*. Ed. H. Foster. Seattle: Dia Art Foundation, 1988. 3–28.
Kapur, Geeta. "subTerrain: Artists Dig the Contemporary." *body.city: Siting Contemporary Culture in India*. Ed. Indira Chandrasekhar and Peter C. Seel. New Delhi: Tulika, 2003. 46–83.
Kapur, Geeta, and Ashish Rajadhyaksha. "Bombay/Mumbai 1992–2001." *Century City: Art and Culture in the Modern Metropolis*. Ed. Iwona Blazwick. London: Tate, 2001.

King, Anthony D. *Spaces of Global Cultures: Architecture Urbanism Identity.* London: Routledge, 2004.
Lapierre, Dominique. *City of Joy.* New York: Grand Central, 1988.
Lefebvre, Henri. *The Production of Space.* Oxford: Blackwell, 1991.
Levi-Strauss, Claude. *Tristes Tropiques.* Harmondsworth: Penguin, 1976.
Lie, John. *Multiethnic Japan.* Harvard: Cambridge University Press, 2001.
Ludden, David. "History Outside Civilization and the Mobility of South Asia." *South Asia* 17.1 (1994): 1–23.
Mahmood, Saba. *Politics of Piety: The Islamic Revival and the Feminist Subject.* Princeton: Princeton UP, 2005.
Mayaram, Shail. "Beirut: Time for Another Requiem?" *The Hindu* 11 Aug. 2006 <http://www.thehindu.com/2006/08/11/stories/2006081104541200.htm>.
———. "Debating Cosmopolitanism: Towards a Framework for Understanding Inter-Ethnic Relations in Asian Cities." Draft, n.d.
———. "Do Hindu and Islamic Transnational Religious Movements Represent Cosmopolitanism and Difference?" *Assertive Religious Identities: India and Europe.* Ed. Satish Saberwal and Mushirul Hasan. Delhi: Manohar, 2006. 323–55.
———. "Living Together: Ajmer as a Paradigm for the (South) Asian City." *Living Together Separately: Cultural India in History and Politics.* Ed. Mushirul Hasan and Asim Roy. New Delhi: Oxford UP, 2005. 145–71.
Mayeda, Sengaku. Asoka's dharma and Shiio's kyosei-Buddhism and social order in Ancient India and contemporary Japan. Unpublished paper, Interim World Philosophy Congress, Delhi, 2006.
Mehta, Suketu. *Maximum City.* Delhi: Viking, 2004.
Metcalf, Barbara D., ed. *Moral Conduct and Authority: The Place of Adab in South Asian Islam.* Berkeley: U of California P, 1984.
Mignolo, Walter D. "The Many Faces of Cosmopolis." *Public Culture* 12.3 (2000): 129–53.
Mufti, Aamir R. "Auerbach in Istanbul: Edward Said, Secular Criticism, and the Question of Minority Culture." *Critical Inquiry* 25 (1998): 95–125.
Nandy, Ashis. *Time Warps: The Insistent Politics of Silent and Evasive Pasts.* Delhi: Permanent Black, 2002.
Narayanan, Vasudha. From Kanchi to Kampuchea. Keynote address, First International Conference on Religions in the Indic Civilsation, Delhi, 28–21 December 2003.
Neuwirth, Robert. *Shadow Cities: A Billion Squatters, a New Urban World.* New York: Routledge, 2005.
Ong, Aihwa. *Neoliberalism as Exception: Mutations in Citizenship and Sovereignty.* Durham: Duke UP, 2006.
Pamuk, Orhan. *Istanbul: Memories of a City.* London: Faber, 2005.
———. *My Name Is Red.* New York: Vintage, 2002.
Peters, F. E. "The Early Muslim Empires: Umayyads, Abbasids, Fatimids." *Islam: The Religious and Political Life of a World Community.* Ed. M. Kelly. New York: Praeger, 1984. 73–93.
Pollock, Sheldon, Homi K. Bhabha, Carol A. Breckenridge, and Dipesh Chakrabarty. "Cosmopolitanisms." *Public Culture* 12.3 (2000): 577–89.
Raju, C. K. *The Eleven Pictures of Time: The Physics, Philosophy, and Politics of Time Beliefs.* New Delhi: Sage, 2003.
Ramaswami, Shankar. "Marginal Civilizens: Migrant Workers' Lives and Thought Worlds in Contemporary Delhi." Seminar on Democracy's Marginal Citizens. Lokniti, CSDS, Delhi. 19–20 November 2004.
———. "Togethering Contra Othering: Hindu-Muslim Inter-Relations in Proletarian Delhi." Seminar on Situating NGOs and Civil Society in Conflict Prevention and Peacebuilding Work: Constructing a Framework. India International Centre, New Delhi. 4 October 2006.

Rhys, Jean. *Wide Sargossa Sea.* London: Penguin, 1966.
Ricoeur, Paul. *Time and Narrative.* Chicago and London: U of Chicago P, 1988.
Robinson, Jennifer. "Global and World Cities: A View from Off the Map." *International Journal of Urban and Regional Research* 26.3 (2002): 531–54.
Robinson, Jennifer. *Ordinary Cities: Between Modernity and Development.* London: Routledge, 2006.
Saeed, Yousuf. Mecca versus the local shrine: the dilemma of orientation in the popular religious art of Indian Muslims. *India's popular culture: Iconic spaces and fluid images.* Ed. Jyotindra Jain. Mumbai, *Marg.* 59 (2007): 76–89.
Sassen, Saskia. *The Global City: New York, London, Tokyo.* Princeton: Princeton UP, 1991.
———. *Cities in a World Economy.* Thousand Oaks: Pine Forge, 1994.
———, ed. *Global Networks, Linked Cities.* New York: Routledge, 2002.
Schimmel, Annemarie. *The Empire of the Great Mughals: History, Art and Culture.* Delhi: Oxford UP, 2005.
———. *My Soul Is a Woman: The Feminine in Islam.* Cairo: American U in Cairo P, 1998.
Sen, Amartya. *Identity and Violence: The Illusion of Destiny.* New York: Norton.
Shayegan, Daryush. (2007). "Dara Shikuh." Dialogue on India and Iran. India International Centre, Delhi, 10–12 March. Unpublished paper.
Shuyun, Sun. *Ten Thousand Miles Without a Cloud.* London: HarperCollins, 2003.
Sinha, Vineeta. "Merging 'Different' Spaces: Enabling Religious Encounters Through Pragmatic Utilization of Space?" *Contributions to Indian Sociology* 37 (2003): 459–94.
Spivak, Gayatri Chakravorty. *Other Asias.* Oxford: Blackwell, 2008.
Subrahmanyam, Sanjay. "Connected Histories: Notes Towards a Reconfiguration of Early Modern Eurasia." *Modern Asian Studies* 31.3 (1997): 735–62.
Thornton, William H. and Songok Han Thornton. *Development without Freedom: The Politics of Asian Globalization.* Ashgate, 2008.
Uberoi, Jit Pal Singh. "Between the Oxus and the Indus: A Local History of the Frontier 500 BC–1925 AD." *Central Asia: Movement of Peoples and Ideas from Times Prehistoric to Modern.* Ed. Amalendu Guha. Delhi: Indian Council for Cultural Relations/Vikas. 182–9.
———. "The structural concept of the Asian frontier." History and society: Essays in honour of Niharranjan Ray. Ed. Debiprasad Chattopadhyaya. Calcutta: KP Bagchi, 1978. 67–77.
Varshney, Ashutosh. *Ethnic Conflict and Civic Life: Hindus and Muslims in India.* London: Yale University Press, 2002.
Vatsyayana, Kapila. "Preface." *Sacred Landscapes in Asia: Shared Traditions, Multiple Histories.* Ed. Himanshu Prabha Ray. New Delhi: Manohar, 2007. vii–ix.
Visvanathan, Shiv. "Knowledge and Information in the Network Society." *Seminar* 503. 2001. vii-ix.
Weber, Samuel. *Targets of Opportunity: On Militarization of Thinking.* New York: Fordham UP, 2005.
Werbner, Pnina. *Anthropology and the New Cosmoplitanism: Rooted, Feminist and Vernacular Perspectives.* UK: Berg, 2008.
———. "On Working Class Cosmopolitans and the Creation of Transnational Ethnic Worlds." *Social Anthropology* 7.1 (1999): 17–35.
Wink, André. *Al-Hind: The Making of the Indo-Islamic World.* Leiden: Brill, 1996.
Zubaida, Sami. "Cosmopolitanism and the Middle East." Cosmopolitanism, Identity and Authenticity in the Middle East. Ed. Roel Meijr. London: Routledge, 1999. 15–33.

Section I
Cosmopolitanism and the State

2 Beneficence and Difference
Ottoman *Awqaf* and "Other" Subjects
Engin F. Isin

INTRODUCTION

As the Ottoman Empire expanded into three continents throughout the fifteenth century, the encounter with the "other" became a generalized condition of governing the empire. From the moment of its conquest by the Ottomans and their realization that governing Constantinople would involve dealing with already constituted social groups, Istanbul has always had to deal with negotiating differences among groups. When Constantinople was conquered in 1453, it was almost deserted. As is well known, Ottomans began repopulating Istanbul by transferring people from other conquered territories such as the Peloponnesian Salonika (modern Thessalonica) and the Greek islands. By about 1480 the population rose to between sixty thousand and seventy thousand (Inalcik). While Hagia Sophia and other Byzantine churches were transformed into mosques, the Greek patriarchate was retained and was moved to the Church of the Pammakaristos Virgin (Mosque of Fethiye), later to find a permanent home in the Fener quarter. The capital of the Ottoman Empire was transferred to Constantinople from Adrianople (Edirne) in 1457. Within a century, *Konstantiniye* (as Ottomans called the city for a long time) was transformed into a "cosmopolitan" imperial city with inhabitants drawn from all corners of the empire and negotiating their differences, inventing along the way various legal, political, social, and cultural institutions with which such negotiations took place. I place the term cosmopolitan in quotation marks to indicate that I will increasingly turn critical toward the concept understood simply as presence of multiplicity, diversity, and plurality in a given space (Zubaida, "Cosmopolitanism and the Middle East"). By contrast, I will work toward a conception of cosmopolitanism as an ethic enabling and instituting practices of negotiation of differences without either reducing them or effacing such differences.

Modern historians of the empire called the variegated Ottoman institutions for negotiating difference collectively as the "millet system" (Braude, "Millet Sistemi'nin İlginç Tarihi"; Reppeto; Stefanov). Millet is a generic term used to describe Muslim or non-Muslim religious groups and their affiliations. Millet is often translated into English as "nation" though it would be anachronistic to define these groups as modern nations or even modern incipient nations. What complicates this history is that these millets did indeed develop *and* fulfill national aspirations in the modern sense later in the nineteenth century. Thus, I prefer to discuss these with the sociological concept "social group" or simply "group" to avoid anachronism or historicism.

These groups had various governing rights and privileges within the framework of Ottoman imperial administration (Braude and Lewis). The two major non-Muslim groups were Jews and Christians. The latter included Greeks and Armenians. These groups practiced various collective rights and privileges. A religious authority governed each, which was also responsible for its obedience to imperial administration. The head of the Orthodox Greek millet, for example, was the ecumenical patriarch of Constantinople. The patriarch's position as leader of that millet gave him also substantial secular powers. Whether to call these rights and privileges as "autonomous" or even "autocephalous" is open to debate. But not unlike guilds and corporations of medieval European cities these groups were able to negotiate considerable scope for rights and privileges that obviously prompted many historians to use such terms as "autonomy" with relative ease.

Much has been written about Ottoman millets and the way their subjects governed themselves and how the relations between these millets and Ottoman imperial administration were regulated (Braude, "Foundation Myths," "Millet Sistemi'nin İlginç Tarihi"; Karpat; Stefanov). While I will have occasion later to make some observations on these various "autonomous" or even "autocephalous" rights, I shall be chiefly concerned with them within the context of the *waqf* as an institution of beneficence. Like the millet system, Ottoman *awqaf* have also been investigated quite extensively (Çizakça; Singer; Van Leeuwen). *I am concerned here with the way in which awqaf were utilized by millets to govern relationships of authority within these groups, between them and other millets and between imperial authorities.* I shall focus on the issue of whether non-Muslim subjects of the empire were able to either establish *awqaf* as benefactors or use their services as beneficiaries. Thus, I will expand this issue not only to the right and privilege of founding non-Muslim *awqaf* as *benefactors* but also to use of *awqaf*-provided services as *beneficiaries*. Thus, neither the Ottoman millet system nor the Ottoman *waqf* is of concern by itself but the way in which the presence of the *waqf* institution enabled the constitutive Ottoman social groups to negotiate differences without either reducing or effacing such differences.

We do know that through thousands of *awqaf* established throughout the empire, neighborhoods and cities were built and governed. Especially in Istanbul the *waqf* became a beneficence institution that provided considerable amount of what moderns would call social services, ranging from libraries, soup kitchens, baths, fountains, hospitals, and religious buildings. We also know that while its principle was Islamic, *awqaf* were also founded by non-Muslim groups to provide various properties and services and were recognized by Ottoman authorities as legitimate and indispensable ways in which these groups were governed. The Islamic institution of beneficence that existed for centuries before the Ottoman Empire, which was then taken up by it, institutionalized, codified, and systematized to the extent that almost all social, cultural, religious, and economic services were provided by this institution by the eighteenth century. Under the Ottoman Empire the *waqf* became a systematic method of building cities by providing various services in well-thought-out nuclei (*külliye* or *imaret*) through which a definitive shape was given to cities (Ergin, *Türkiye'de Şehirciliğin Tarih-i İnkişafı*; Ergin, *Türk İmar Tarihinde Vakıflar*). Well-known *külliyes* that have given shape to Istanbul, for example, include Süleymaniye, Fatih, Şehzade, Eyüp Sultan, and Lâleli *külliyes* (Eyice; Kuban; Tanman). Throughout the empire thousands of madrasas, schools, libraries, mosques, caravanserais, business centers (*hans*), bazaars, fountains, bridges, hospitals, soup kitchens or almshouses, lodges, tombs, baths, and aqueducts were founded either as part of such *külliyes* or *imarets* or standing alone (Demirel). *Awqaf* could also include other immovable property such as rural land that yielded income for urban property as well as movable property such as cash, books, and other valuables. The *waqf* therefore involves a very complex economy and its urban properties cannot be isolated from rural properties. A *waqf* scholar, Nazif Öztürk (*Türk Yenileşme Tarihi Çerçevesinde Vakıf Müessesesi*), estimates that throughout the Ottoman Empire more than thirty-five thousand *awqaf* were founded, the majority of which were urban properties. That means a vast majority of Ottoman architecture and cities were built by the *waqf* system. According to Öztürk, these *awqaf*, by employing vast numbers of people and providing income, constituted about 16% of the Ottoman economy in the seventeenth century, about 27% in the eighteenth, and about 16% in the nineteenth century. Similarly, another *waqf* scholar, Murat Çizakça, estimates that by the end of the nineteenth century *awqaf* was providing more than 8% of total employment in the Ottoman Empire.

These are significant figures that illustrate the economic role and size of the *waqf*, but its cultural and social significance cannot be overemphasized (Yediyıldız, "Vakıf Müessesesinin 18," "Müessese-Toplum Münasebetleri Çerçevesinde 18," "Türk Vakıf Kurucularının Sosyal Tabakalaşmadaki Yeri, 1700–1800," "Türk Kültür Sistemi İçinde Vakfın Yeri"). It is important to note that this entire system of beneficence was not a centralized or state-driven practice. It was a gift-giving practice that combined Islamic philosophy with civic engagement: thus it can be appropriately called a civic gift-giving practice that should be distinguished from philanthropy and charity (Isin and Lefebvre). It is this aspect of civic gift-giving that would prove crucial for non-Muslim millets to negotiate their differences within the Ottoman imperial legal and political culture. Founding a *waqf* meant endowing privately held property for civic use in perpetuity for functions that are set out in its founding deed or charter (*vakfiye*) and according to the conditions specified therein. The *waqf* deed also set out the way in which the *waqf* property would be administered and maintained. The charter was registered and authenticated by a local judge (*kadı*) and did not require further approval. The principles underlying the *waqf* were then civism, perpetuity, autonomy, and beneficence. Among *awqaf* founders were prominent sultans, sultanas, and pashas, as well as much less prominent members of the Ottoman governing, religious, and merchant groups. More significantly, there were notable numbers of women and non-Muslim *waqf* founders, which needs to be investigated in terms of rights and duties.

This chapter outlines some thoughts on the role *awqaf* played as beneficence institutions enabling millet subjects to govern themselves, their relations between themselves and Ottoman imperial authorities, and other Muslim and non-Muslim subjects. The subject is vast but this chapter aims to provide not only a glimpse of how various groups negotiated otherness and difference but also insights into the rise of modern reformism and nationalism that displaced governing through millets and *awqaf*. Thus, the chapter is part of a broader investigation on "oriental citizenship," which interprets various social and political practices as citizenship (understood as a generalized otherness that enables negotiations of recognition, difference, and identity). I am investigating if, and to what extent, founding *awqaf* as gift-giving acts can be considered as "acts of citizenship" in Ottoman Empire in its classical age with a focus on Istanbul (Isin, *Being Political*; Isin, "Citizenship After Orientalism"; Isin and Lefebvre). I argue that Ottoman and Istanbul *awqaf* as institutions of negotiating differences and providing social institutions in the context of *awqaf* in Delhi, Cairo, Tehran, and Beirut can provide significant comparative insights on how groups both share and contest spaces to negotiate their difference in "cosmopolitan" contexts.

THE CLASSICAL AGE AND THE NON-MUSLIM *AWQAF*

There is a limited but slowly growing literature on how the non-Muslim *awqaf* instituted relations of obligations between non-Muslim subjects and imperial authorities (Güneri; Öztürk, *Türk Yenileşme Tarihi Çerçevesinde Vakıf Müessesesi*; Öztürk, *Azınlık Vakıfları*; Soykan 123–7; Stefanov). This literature has increasingly challenged views that often depicted non-Muslim *awqaf* as relatively stagnant and insignificant aspects of the Ottoman Empire. I will first discuss this literature briefly and then discuss more recent works by Eugenia Kermeli, Colin Imber, and Ron Shaham, which have further deepened and complicated our picture of the relationship between *awqaf* and millets. They begin to provide us useful insights as to how non-Muslim *awqaf* were implicated in the negotiation of otherness.

Millets and *Awqaf*

It is now widely accepted that, like the Muslim subjects of the Empire, non-Muslims were indeed allowed to stipulate the income of trust to their descendents in perpetuity (*waqf ehli*). More important, they were also eligible to found endowments with a distinct religious and public or civic nature (*waqf hayri*). However, there were also certain regulations and restrictions on the establishment of non-Muslim *awqaf*. For example, non-Muslims were not permitted to establish an endowment and trust for the renovation or establishment of synagogues and churches. Nor can non-Muslim *awqaf* be founded for the print or distribution of Bible or the Old Testament. Non-Muslims were allowed to found *awqaf* for churches and synagogues but they were not permitted to register their donations in the name of these religious institutions. In addition, they were not allowed to directly donate endowments and found *awqaf* for the church or synagogue personnel (e.g., monks or rabbis). But the endowments were permissible as long as beneficiaries were "poor and needy" and these establishments were used to serve "beneficial functions." Just how and for whom a *waqf* function would be deemed beneficial was obviously contested but a *waqf* served mostly civic or public purposes. If church and synagogue authorities fulfilled these expectations and convinced authorities, they were eligible to establish these trusts or endowments. It is not surprising then that the use and allocation of sources devoted to churches and synagogues were often contested. Kenanoğlu argues that during the reign of Selim II (1566–1574), some monks attempted to get the approval of Şeyhulislam about the use of monastic or church *awqaf*. (Şeyhulislam was the highest-ranking member of the Ottoman *ulema* with juridical authority to issue fetwa.) Kenanoğlu documents that Şeyhulislam sent a *fetwa* to *Divan* and decreed that non-Muslim beneficence to *miri* (public) lands, vineyards, mills, gardens, houses, and cattle to churches is illegal and invalid (Kenanoğlu 271). This shows that these negotiations were played out on the Islamic legal field and must have challenged successive interpretations of imperial authorities. On the other hand, Kenanoğlu also contends that after the reign of Selim II, the Ottoman authorities were not that strict and they did not intervene in the allocation of *waqf* resources to churches or synagogues. The very idea that serving the poor and needy through *awqaf* would surely open up possibilities for establishing further rights as *awqaf* themselves, once founded, were relatively autonomous and autocephalous. Moreover, much like medieval European guilds, corporations, and cities, *awqaf* foundations such as orphanages, synagogues, churches, schools, and hospitals of non-Muslims groups were considered as juristic personas (Güneri 88–89). These possibilities enable us to establish some theoretical and empirical connections among *awqaf*, beneficence, and difference.

Awqaf and "Other" Subjects

There is limited but significant literature on the status of *awqaf* properties in conquered territories. Eugenia Kermeli demonstrates that monastic and church *awqaf* were already common institutions in the Balkans before the Ottoman conquest of these territories. Kermeli argues that the status of the properties owned by monastic groups was always a subject of controversy and negotiation between monasteries and the regional and central authorities. He also points out the scholarly literature is divided over how to interpret the struggles concerning these *awqaf* (Akgündüz; Fotić; Van Leeuwen). After outlining how these authors approach the status of monastic *awqaf*, Kermeli brings up the case of the monks of Mount Athos and Ebū's Su'ūd's (one of the mort important Şeyhulislams who served between 1548 and 1576) response to this event. For Kermeli, Ebū's Su'ūd's fetwa decreed to deal with that case calls into question some widely held assumptions about *awqaf* and religious groups. Kermeli argues that Ebū's Su'ūd was concerned with control of the misappropriation of land and its revenues. Since, according to the prescriptions of Hanefi jurisprudence, monastic *awqaf* were not permitted in Islamic law and they did not fall into the category of *waqf hayri*, these monasteries became the target of Ebū's Su'ūd's consolidation and confiscation attempts. As a result, Ebū's Su'ūd ordered (1568–1569) the confiscation of church *awqaf* in the Balkans (Kermeli 144–45). So far this sounds like a simple case of Ottoman jurists applying the letter of Islamic law. However, Ebū's Su'ūd, faced with the threat that the monks would evacuate monasteries in Mount Athos unless their demands were met, eventually produced a divergent interpretation of Hanefi jurisprudence on *awqaf*. Kermeli contends that Ebū's Su'ūd found a compromise solution that was acceptable to both sides. He defined them differently and categorized them as family *waqf*, treating the monks of a monastery as the offspring of the deceased monks. However, as Kermeli contends, Ebū's Su'ūd was aware of the pitfalls of this creative legal interpretation, and so hurriedly issued a fetwa restricting similar demands from other monasteries.

As a result, Kermeli rejects the argument that all monastic and church *awqaf* in the empire operated on the basis of an inflexible legal principle. On the contrary, he argues that the principle was much more flexible and responsive to the call of various groups and always allowed for negotiation. Therefore, he proposes further research on *awqaf* from different regions of the empire to have a broader and comprehensive view on the institution of *waqf*. Admittedly, it is very difficult to render broader judgment concerning the ways in which *awqaf* enabled "minorities" to negotiate their difference; however, it illustrates a possible research approach on *awqaf*, beneficence, and difference.

As illustrated by Ron Shaham, Christian and Jewish *awqaf* in Palestine, mainly in the towns of Jaffa and Nazareth, seem to exemplify this pattern. His investigation provides a detailed account of the nature of the founders, types of property involved, methods of administration as well as beneficiaries of the *waqf*, and determination of their gradual order. Shaham reveals that in some *awqaf* in Jaffa the *qadis* permitted exclusive endowments for the benefit of the monks and how these cases were negotiated (Shaham 462). He illustrates that Christians and Jews established *awqaf* not only because of legal and administrative compulsion, but also because of the practical advantages offered by these institutions. It is fairly straightforward to imagine that these practical advantages would involve the types of social services provided by *awqaf* as we have seen earlier.

Awqaf, Beneficence, Difference

When we recognize that "other" subjects not only were able to found *awqaf* but also were beneficiaries of services provided by them, a complex picture begins to emerge where *awqaf* as beneficence can be seen as a mediating institution of difference. A discussion of the everyday in Istanbul would shed some light on this concept (Ahmet; Bey; Işın). It is well known that while non-Muslim subjects in the empire were recognized with certain entitlements and rights, they were also differentiated. These forms of differentiation changed over time and were complex, ranging from vestiary and sumptuary to spatial regulation. To put it differently, Muslim and non-Muslim subjects of the empire have constituted each other via a whole gamut of orientations, ranging from strangers to outsiders to eventually involving alienation from each other resulting in violence. As strangers, non-Muslim subjects were differentiated via various sumptuary and vestiary regulations that stipulated dress, manners, and conduct in the everyday. Being on *awqaf* properties such as libraries, markets, or inns or benefiting from *awqaf* services such as fountains, soup kitchens, or hospitals, Muslim and non-Muslim subjects would easily recognize each other as strangers. In fact, throughout centuries sumptuary and vestiary regulation always attempted that that should be the case (Kenanoğlu 342–54). While these regulations were never consistent or intense, they nevertheless attempted to ensure that, for example, Muslim subjects were easily identifiable by their attire, whether by reserving certain colors for them or designating other colors for Jewish or Armenian subjects (Eryılmaz 54–55). More important, these regulations were also incorporated into social norms and were recognized as expected forms of conduct by both Muslims and non-Muslims (Eryılmaz 55–56).

There were also spatial regulations restricting settlement and movement of non-Muslim subjects in the city (Kenanoğlu 317–29). While these regulations never reached the level of stipulating virtual incarceration as in Jewish ghettos in medieval and early modern European cities, nonetheless there were ongoing problematizations of proximity of judges, for example, to synagogues and churches and proximity of non-Muslim subjects to mosques and masjids. These ongoing problematizations of proximity of

Muslim and non-Muslim subjects to each other were certainly consistent enough to would give each a sense of the strangeness of the other.

It is then possible to argue that difference was no stranger to Ottoman subjects. They well knew the difference between Ottoman, Jewish, Armenian, Christian (Orthodox or Catholic) subjects. Given these differences articulated in law and norms, I would suggest that *awqaf* properties and services might well be interpreted as mediating institutions of recognition and difference. Being able to found *awqaf* certainly enabled non-Muslim subjects to enact certain rights such as the freedom of conscience and religion that otherwise would have remained as abstract rights and freedoms. Similarly, being able to found *awqaf*, non-Muslim subjects were able to negotiate their difference via enduring rather than ephemeral institutions. It is important to recognize that non-Muslim subjects were founding *awqaf* understood as Islamic endowments and thus were negotiating their difference under the term of Islamic law in general and its interpretations under Ottoman government (Isin and Lefebvre). Moreover, as beneficiaries of *awqaf* properties and services, non-Muslim subjects were able to constitute themselves by benefiting from properties and services that were understood to be within Islamic and Ottoman law, and enacting their group rights and obligations through them. Their "difference" was neither given nor immutable but constituted through *awqaf* properties and services as both founders and beneficiaries.

All this is not offered as evidence of Ottoman "tolerance" or Ottoman "multiculturalism" (Gawrych). That would not only be an anachronism but also outright orientalism. Yet, when compared with how non-Muslim subjects begin to appear under universalizing attempts to construct an Ottoman identity during the nineteenth century and later during the collapse of that identity and the birth of nationalism in the late nineteenth and early twentieth centuries, one must recognize that indeed *awqaf* provided an integrative and accommodating, if not mediating, institution to recognize and negotiate the difference between Muslim and non-Muslim subjects such as Jews and Christians of the empire. The ethic that undergirded *awqaf* and other subjects can be called Ottoman cosmopolitanism not because Ottoman *awqaf* were symbols of liberal tolerance or because Ottoman *awqaf* bred pluralism or multiculturalism but because the Ottoman *awqaf* enabled the constitutive social groups to negotiate differences without succumbing to grand narratives of nation and nationalism. I shall return to the theme of "Ottoman cosmopolitanism" later but for now we need to attend to the emergence of the question of minorities and the rethinking of *awqaf* properties during modernization reforms of the empire in the nineteenth century.

NON-MUSLIM *AWQAF* AND *TANZIMAT*

It is important to focus on how Ottoman *awqaf* were approached during the modernization period in the nineteenth century when the grand narratives of nations and nationalism became gradually dominant. Nazif Öztürk (*Türk Yenileşme Tarihi Çerçevesinde Vakıf Müessesesi*) and Hasan Güneri have provided a glimpse of how *Tanzimat* reforms brought about important changes as to how the Ottoman authorities dealt with the non-Muslim *awqaf* and non-Muslim subjects.

As part of this broad transformation, reforms reconfigured the status of non-Muslim groups and their institutions including non-Muslim *awqaf*. As we have seen earlier, according to a widely accepted understanding in the millets in the empire, before the *Tanzimat* the Ottoman authorities governed the monotheist non-Muslim subjects of the empire, known as *dhimmis*, by recognizing their communal religious leaders (autocephaly) and ecclesiastical personnel as well as their relative judicial and fiscal autonomy. Thus, protected by the Ottoman authorities, these non-Muslim subjects were subject to poll taxes as their obligation. The Greeks, the Armenians, and the Jews were the main constitutive groups of the structure of millets. Throughout the *Tanzimat,* Ottoman authorities proposed a new conception of universal citizenship—Ottomanism—and attempted to transform the previous practices and principles, which organized the relations between Muslims and non-Muslim groups and their relations with the governing authorities. The Ottoman authorities introduced this principle in *Gülhane Hatt-ı Hümayun* in 1839 and took a step toward abandoning the principle based on what was then being perceived as "fragmentation" of religious groups and adopting the principle of universal Ottoman citizenship. In this conception, regardless of their religion, the subjects of the empire were considered all equal. In addition, it legalized the recruitment of non-Muslims in government services and their enrollment in both military and civilian state schools. These proclamations were reaffirmed in the Imperial Reform Edict of 1856 (*Islahat Fermanı*) and the constitution of 1876. The non-Muslims of the empire "were accorded the right to be represented in local and regional parliaments as well as in important state institutions such as the Council of State (Şura-yı Devlet), which served useful functions in legislative matters" (Aral). Simultaneously, the Ottoman authorities attempted to reform the institutions and regulate the practices of non-Muslim groups. To that end, they issued several legislative documents to restructure religious institutions of the Armenians, the Jews, and the Greeks (Eryılmaz 138–39). While maintaining the hitherto communal autonomy and rights in organizing civil and family affairs, new regulations limited the authority of the chief religious leaders and enabled members of newly found *cismani* (nonreligious) councils to become important actors within their groups. With this restructuring, the members of *cismani* committees became participants in decision-making processes regarding judicial and administrative affairs relating to their groups. More important, as part of the centralization of the state and its bureaucracy, the Ottoman authorities incorporated the non-Muslim *awqaf* into the *Evkaf-ı Hümayun Nezareti* along with the Muslim *awqaf*. As a result, the judiciary, the Ministry of *Awqaf*, and *Mezahip Nezareti* (Ministry of Sects) were put in charge of administering and controlling *awqaf* properties and services (Öztürk, *Türk Yenileşme Tarihi Çerçevesinde Vakıf Müessesesi*).

While the Ottoman authorities were undertaking these modernizing and centralizing reforms and endorsing the principle of universal Ottoman citizenship, the hegemonic states declared themselves as the guardians of the non-Muslim groups in the empire and non-Muslim groups as their "subjects." The hegemonic states intervened with the Ottoman affairs of the state and played a crucial role in the reforms concerning non-Muslim subjects in the empire. The hegemonic states—such as Russia, France, Britain, and the United States—problematized the social and political status of Ottoman non-Muslim groups in the empire as well as their "own" citizens residing in the empire. This is, at least, as old as the *Treaty of Küçük Kaynarca* of 1774 signed between Russia and the Ottoman Empire. With this treaty, the Russian authorities' intervention in the name of protecting the Orthodox Christian groups in the empire became legalized (Eryılmaz 96). This process gained momentum in the nineteenth century and after the empire signed the *Paris Peace Treaty* with the hegemonic states in 1856, each state imposed a reform program to benefit the empire's non-Muslim subjects. Despite the effort of the *Tanzimat* reforms to unite the Muslim and non-Muslim subjects under the rubric of Ottoman citizenship, the social, political, and legal status of the non-Muslims constituted a point of controversy between the Ottoman authorities and the foreign states. While the Ottoman authorities were attempting to create the image of universal Ottoman citizenship, the hegemonic states constantly put forward the status of non-Muslim subjects to the fore. By emphasizing their differences and distinct status among the subjects of the empire, the hegemonic states demanded extended privileges and special rights for the non-Muslim subjects. These events occurred at a time when the hegemonic states themselves were inventing and dealing with the problem of minorities in their own nation-states. During the eighteenth and the nineteenth centuries, the creation of homogeneous populations became a major, if not the primary, concern of the European nation-states. Undertaking these homogenization strategies, European states constituted certain groups as "minorities" and dealt with them through alienating strategies and technologies. Therefore, in order to understand how the Ottoman authorities oriented toward non-Muslim groups in the nineteenth century, we should acknowledge the link between the invention of the question of minorities in hegemonic nation-states and the concern for the status non-Muslim groups in the empire. The Ottoman authorities did not officially recognize the minority status of the non-Muslim subjects in the way the concept was constructed within the dominant European discourse of the nation. Nonetheless, the Ottoman authorities found themselves forced to engage with the dominant European orientation toward "minorities."

Through the modernization and centralization of the institutions in the empire, the situation of non-Muslims and the demands and policies of the hegemonic states posed difficulties for Ottoman authorities to accomplish reform projects. According to Öztürk (*Türk Yenileşme Tarihi Çerçevesinde Vakıf Müessesesi; Azınlık Vakıfları*), non-Muslim *awqaf* posed an important problem to the reform and centralization agenda of the Ottoman authorities. Öztürk contends that non-Muslim *awqaf* played a crucial role in the emergence of this problem. Öztürk argues that it was the *Islahat Fermanı* that allowed the European citizens to invest in real estate and the Ottoman authorities legalized these transactions in 1867 (*Türk Yenileşme Tarihi Çerçevesinde Vakıf Müessesesi* 319–21). For Öztürk, following the legislation of this law, many non-Muslim citizens of the hegemonic states invested in a considerable amount of real estate in the empire. These lands and properties were registered under either their names or the name of their relatives. Yet in other occasions, the Ottoman non-Muslims became citizens of hegemonic states in order to benefit from these privileges. To that end, Ottoman authorities enacted another law in 1869 to prevent the non-Muslims from changing their citizenship illegally. According to Öztürk, despite the legislative attempts of the Ottoman authorities to control the ways in which non-Muslims invested in real estate, the ministry of *awqaf* and other institutions fell short of controlling and regulating these processes outlined above (*Türk Yenileşme Tarihi Çerçevesinde Vakıf Müessesesi*).

Moreover, Öztürk (*Türk Yenileşme Tarihi Çerçevesinde Vakıf Müessesesi; Azınlık Vakıfları*) argues, missionary activities of the hegemonic states were influential in determining the structure of non-Muslim *awqaf* especially in the second half of the nineteenth century. Under the protection of the hegemonic states, especially France and the United States, non-Muslim groups and missionaries established a considerable number of social institutions. Schools, temples, hospitals, and churches were built to improve the situations of non-Muslims in various regions of the empire. Again, the Ottoman authorities were unable to control and monitor these institutions and activities. For Öztürk (*Türk Yenileşme Tarihi Çerçevesinde Vakıf Müessesesi* 328), in some cases, although there was no necessity to found a *waqf*, the Ottoman state nonetheless issued licenses to these buildings due to the intervention of the hegemonic states. In other cases, he argues, non-Muslims established churches, schools as well as factories without attaining license. Thus, Öztürk points out how non-Muslim groups contributed to the usurpation of *awqaf* properties near the buildings of religious, medical, and social institutions (*Türk Yenileşme Tarihi Çerçevesinde Vakıf Müessesesi* 329).

In 1912, the Ottoman state forbade the citizens of the hegemonic states to attain real estate in the empire under juristic personas. Only Ottoman citizens were allowed to establish a juristic persona and to invest in real estate. At the same time these regulations allowed non-Muslim groups to register the social, religious, and pious foundations under the name of communal juristic personas. As we have seen, *awqaf* foundations such as orphanages, synagogues, churches, schools, and hospitals of non-Muslims groups were considered as juristic personas (Güneri 88–89). The creation of juristic personas under the names of non-Muslim groups indicates that Ottoman authorities oriented toward these groups by applying modern legal codes and principles, which always questioned any group existence between the state and individual. In other words, this should be seen as continuation of modernization efforts of the Ottoman authorities.

After the Lausanne Treaty, signed in 1923 between the Turkish Republic and the Allied Forces, the Turkish nation-state—as the successor of the Ottoman Empire—recognized the minority status of the Greeks, the Armenians, and the Jews. This treaty approved the maintenance of the rights granted to the non-Muslim *awqaf* up until the Lausanne Treaty (Öztürk, *Azınlık Vakıfları* 132). In the following years, the republican state invited a Swedish expert, Hans Leeman, to join the committee preparing the *Awqaf* Law. The committee was organized in order to examine the situation of minority *awqaf* founded before 1926 and their compatibility with the new civil law of the Turkish republican state. According to Güneri (98–99), Hans Leeman prepared a report in 1929 and recommended the transfer of minority *awqaf* properties and institutions to the state along with those Muslim *awqaf*. However, rather than following the recommendation of Leeman and confiscating minority *waqf* properties and institutions, the Turkish parliament recognized the special status of minority *awqaf* with the new *waqf* law of 1936. The law charged the trustees and elected commissions with the administration of *awqaf* and thus the minority *awqaf* were incorporated into the state structure (Güneri 98–99).

In conclusion, from the first half of the nineteenth century, the Ottoman state authorities aimed to centralize and control *awqaf* institutions as part of broader transformation of the empire. Through these initiatives non-Muslim *awqaf* became the object of regulation for the reform movements. The authorities aimed to take them under the control of the Ministry of *Awqaf*. However, the Ottoman authorities had difficulties accomplishing this task. According to Öztürk, until the law of 1912, both the citizens of the hegemonic states as well as the Ottoman non-Muslims enjoyed the protection and privileges, and captured a considerable amount of *waqf* property and land in illegal ways. For the state authorities the *waqf* question was entangled with the question of the status of non-Muslim groups in the empire. Whether established by missionaries or built by non-Muslims groups, many *awqaf* went beyond the control of the state authorities. Seen in these terms, this question retained its relevance until the Turkish Republic—the successor of the Ottoman Empire—succeeded in completely controlling and incorporating non-Muslim *awqaf* into the new *waqf* legal structure, which emerged between 1929 and 1936.

ORIENTALISM, COLONIALISM, AND LEGAL HISTORY: THE ATTACK ON MUSLIM FAMILY ENDOWMENTS IN ALGERIA AND INDIA

It is instructive how non-Muslim *awqaf* became an object of regulation for the reform movements in the empire. Along with Muslim *awqaf*, non-Muslim *awqaf* were deemed as archaic structures in need of centralized control. Attempting to institute the society with the principles and discourses of modernization, the state authorities in the Ottoman Empire and the Turkish Republic targeted *awqaf*. As we have seen, as part of broader transformations, the non-Muslim *awqaf* became also a problem. We are told that under the protection of hegemonic states, non-Muslim subjects of the empire started to misuse these institutions and the state authorities. Depicted in this way, the incorporation and transformation of these institutions seemed inescapable. What is also at stake here is that the non-Muslim *awqaf* were situated in the constitution and problematization of otherness. As we have seen, the creation of minority groups and protected religious groups ran parallel to the problematization of non-Muslim *awqaf*. In other words, non-Muslim *awqaf* were implicated in the process of production of subjectivities such as legal and illegal, majority and minority, Muslim and Non-Muslim.

The case of Muslim *awqaf* investigated by David Powers and Alisa-Rubin Peled in colonial Algeria and India is useful for purposes of comparison. The colonization of Algeria and India created important conflicts between the colonized groups and the colonial authorities. Once the modern state and legal discourses diffused and attempted to transform premodern institutions, Muslim *awqaf* and practices became a problem. Although Algerian, Indian, and Ottoman experiences were different, similarities can also be drawn among them. While Ottoman state authorities adopted these modernization discourses and practices, in Algerian and Indian experiences it occurred through imposition and invasion. However, juxtaposition of these three trajectories and historical parallels may well yield important insights on how modern legal and state discourse came to perceive these nonmodern institutions and practices and legitimized their dismantling. Quoting Barnes, Powers and Peled state that "at the beginning of the nineteenth century, from one half to two-thirds of the landed property in the Ottoman Empire had reportedly been sequestered as endowment land" (537).

In Algeria, beginning in 1844, French property law began to replace Muslim laws controlling ownership of land. By 1873, the only area of Islamic law that remained under the control of Muslim judges was that of personal status—that is, marriage, divorce, and inheritance. Powers and Peled argue that Muslim religious endowments were a stubborn obstacle to the colonizers because these properties were inalienable in perpetuity according to the Islamic laws (540). The colonial government sought to mitigate the effects of this institution through a series of legislative enactments intended to bring all transactions and litigations involving land, including *habous* land

(land of family endowments), under the aegis of French civil law. According to Powers and Peled, due to the disagreement of French jurists on interpretations of these Muslim family *waqf*, these attempts became unsuccessful. However, as Powers and Peled contend, in the interest of colonial land policy, French orientalists invented a threefold interpretation of the institution according to which (1) public endowments were historically prior to family endowments; (2) family endowments were, from an Islamic perspective, an illegal and unethical means of circumventing the Koranic inheritance laws; and (3) family endowments and inheritance were mutually exclusive and incompatible (554). For Powers and Peled, orientalist discourses became dominant by the first decade of the twentieth century and displaced previous interpretations. Moreover, with this discursive shift, the structure of family *awqaf* in Algeria began a decline.

Powers and Peled argue that in British India, the government was in theory indifferent to family endowments, so long as land was productive and Muslims paid their taxes (563). However, eventually they became the subject of litigation in the imperial courts. They contend that British, Muslim, and Hindu magistrates, who were largely ignorant of Islamic law, undermined the status of Muslim family *waqf* as "charitable or religious" (563). As a result, between 1879 and 1893 the High Courts of India passed decisions that invalidated any endowment with the benefit of the founder and his family. As Powers argues, the British Indian experience takes a different path when Muslim political associations campaigned against policies nullifying family endowments. They had a considerable achievement in 1911 when Jinnah introduced the Muslim *Awqaf* Validating Act eliminating the ground on which the High Courts and Privy Council had refused to recognize family endowments as charitable and religious (Powers and Peled 561).

When we compare and contrast these three experiences—the Ottoman, Algerian, and Indian—we see similar effects of centralization and modernization on *awqaf* properties and services. Whether family or communal *awqaf*, we have enough evidence that in all three experiences the charitable and religious status of *awqaf* were questioned, contested, and negotiated. Modern legal and state discourses depicted them as archaic, uncontrollable, and unreasonable and interpreted them as threats to the state and its sovereignty. If we expand this comparative context, we can also argue that the attack on medieval European intermediate groups such as cities, guilds, and corporations that were able to negotiate rights to mediate differences was quite similar to the modern attacks on the *waqf* (Frug; Gierke; Isin, *Cities Without Citizens*).

CONCLUSION: ORIENTAL CITIZENSHIP

Modernity has instituted itself as progress in our imagination and our practices. The state with its twin principles of sovereignty and unity has become the bearer of that modernity. Modernization appears an inevitable and inexorable march toward progress guided by the state and its centralizing drives. As regards Ottoman *awqaf* I have attempted to illustrate some of the results of these drives. For centuries Ottoman *awqaf* had served as a mediating institution between and among various constituent Ottoman social and religious groups that enabled recognition and negotiation of difference via political strategies and technologies. In other words, the ways in which *awqaf* were utilized by millets to govern relationships of authority within these groups, between them and other millets and between imperial authorities indicate that *awqaf* provided grounds for negotiating and instituting group rights. That regime can be called "oriental citizenship." It had all the elements of citizenship understood as institutions of negotiating difference. That regime can also be broadly called "Ottoman cosmopolitanism" without reducing it to a romantic notion of "multiculturalism" or a proto-liberal regime of pluralism and tolerance (Armağan; Zubaida, "Middle Eastern Experiences of Cosmopolitanism"). I use "cosmopolitanism" here to describe an ethic toward the other that recognizes ecumenical or civilizational difference while engaging in negotiation, articulation, and affinity rather than assimilation, alienation, and absolute differentiation. In that sense, while Ottoman cosmopolitanism may not have been an explicitly articulated ethic, it was built into and embodied in various practices and institutions that made up the so-called millet system that responded to the need to recognize ecumenical religious differences: Islamic, Jewish, and Christian. Among these institutions the significance of Ottoman *awqaf* cannot be overestimated as both a citizenship institution (because it enabled negotiation of difference) and cosmopolitan (because it enabled negotiation of differences that were civilizational, ecumenical, and denominational). The Ottoman *awqaf* were also civic institutions. While some *awqaf* properties could be located in the countryside or just simply outside cities, they would still be related to properties located in cities. Moreover, and more important, the *awqaf* were by function and operation civic properties. As I have argued, they were built for civic functions such as public baths, fountains, and inns and they operated as civic properties involving the formation of civic identities by those who were either users or providers. As a gift-giving institution that was both cosmopolitan and civic, Ottoman *waqf* can and must be considered an "oriental citizenship" institution that was deeper and more inclusive than its modern version constituted as universal legal status.

As civic and cosmopolitan gift giving practices, Ottoman awqaf enabled various Ottoman subjects to institute their own practices of solidarity and sociability and negotiate their belonging to wider Ottoman government as citizens. That such recognition existed and that the terms of belonging were negotiated does not mean either harmony or absence of conflict. There were often conflicts but these conflicts found means for mediation in and through *awqaf*. Nor does it mean that such recognition and negotiation were open and available to *all* Ottoman social groups. The fact that the ecumenical religions of the book also constituted the main Ottoman social groups raises the question how other subjects were unable to constitute themselves as social groups and the attendant difficulties this may have created for them. As well, whether the difficulty to constitute themselves through the millet system meant a parallel absence in Ottoman *awqaf* is another issue. These matters await investigation, and the role of Ottoman *awqaf* as civic gift practices in negotiating difference and identity needs further research.

Yet, it can be argued that modernization of *awqaf* involved their centralization within the incipient Ottoman and then Turkish state and their removal from the institutions and practices of negotiating difference, identity, and belonging. To put it differently, without lapsing into a romantic image of Ottoman multiculturalism, it is possible to document *awqaf* as beneficence institutions enabling the negotiation of group rights within Ottoman law as Ottoman cosmopolitanism and their eventual destruction by the modern state. Modern law, being built upon the principle of sovereignty (indivisibility of power, unity of authority, and universality of status) made it impossible to negotiate group rights and thus made it impossible to find a workable system of "living together" of various Ottoman social groups that provided an autocephalous and autonomous order. Both modernization and centralization of *awqaf* illustrate this drama of the integration of Ottoman law and order in a rather poignant manner. All those properties and services that were endowed as *awqaf* throughout the empire were gradually squandered and dilapidated once the logic of *waqf* that sustained the negotiation of difference was displaced by the logic of the state and its inheritor, the nation.

ACKNOWLEDGMENTS

I would like to thank Erkan Ercel, Bora Isyar, and Ebru Üstündağ for their research assistance during various phases of this research. I am grateful to the Department of International Relations at Koç University, Istanbul, for hosting me in the Fall 2003 during which I undertook archival research on *awqaf* in the Prime Minister's Ottoman Archives (BOA). I am also grateful for the assistance I received from BOA staff. I would like to thank Fuat Keyman at Koç University for his hospitality in both 2003 and 2005. I cannot begin to express my gratitude for the assistance I received from various *sahafs* (antiquarians) in Istanbul in tracking down numerous rare books on Ottoman *awqaf*. I would like to especially thank Nedret İşli of Turkuaz Antiquarian and Ayhan Aktar, who himself is an antiquarian and scholar, for introducing me to Nedret. I would also like to thank Imtiaz Ahmad and Niraja Gopal Jayal for their close readings and immensely useful critical comments.

WORKS CITED

Ahmet, Refik. *On altıncı asırda İstanbul hayatı (1553–1591): İstanbulun düşünsel, sosyal, ekonomik ve tecimsel ahvalile evkaf, uray, beslev ve gümrük işlerine dair Türk Arşivinin basılmamış belgeleri.* 2nd ed. Istanbul: Devlet Basımevi, 1935.
Akgündüz, Ahmet. *İslam Hukukunda ve Osmanlı Tatbikatında Vakıf Müessesesi* [*The Institution of Waqf in Islamic Law and Ottoman Practice*]. Istanbul: Osmanlı Araştırmaları Merkezi, 1996.
Aral, Berdal. "The Idea of Human Rights as Perceived in the Ottoman Empire." *Human Rights Quarterly* 26.2 (2004): 454–82.
Armağan, Mustafa, ed. *Osmanlı'da Hoşgörü: birlikte yaşama sanatı* [*Ottoman Tolerance: The Art of Living Together*]. Harbiye, Istanbul: Gazeteciler ve Yazarlar Vakfı Yayınlari, 2000.
Barnes, John Robert. *An Introduction to Religious Foundations in the Ottoman Empire.* Leiden: Brill, 1986.
Bey, Ali Rıza. *Eski Zamanlarda İstanbul Hayatı.* İstanbul: Kitabevi, 2001.
Braude, Benjamin. "Foundation Myths of the Millet System." *Christians and Jews in the Ottoman Empire: The Functioning of a Plural Society.* Ed. Benjamin Braude and Bernard Lewis. New York: Holmes, 1982. 69–88.
———. 2001. "Millet Sistemi'nin İlginç Tarihi." *Osmanlı'dan Günümüze Ermeni Sorunu.* Ed. H. C. Güzel. Ankara: Yeni Türkiye Yayınları, 2001. 315–32
Braude, Benjamin, and Bernard Lewis, eds. 1980. *Christians and Jews in the Ottoman Empire: The Functioning of a Plural Society.* New York: Holmes, 1980.
Çizakça, Murat. *A History of Philanthropic Foundations: The Islamic World from the Seventh Century to the Present.* Istanbul: Bogaziçi UP, 2000.
Demirel, Ömer. 2000. *Osmanlı Vakıf-Şehir İlişkisine Bir Örnek: Sivas Şehir Hayatında Vakıfların Rölü.* Ankara: Tarih Kurumu Basımevi, 2000.
Ergin, Osman. *Türk İmar Tarihinde Vakıflar, Belediyeler, Patrikhaneler, Waqfs, Municipalities and Patriarchates in the History of Turkish Public Facilities.* Istanbul: Türkiye Basımevi, 1944.
———. *Türkiye'de Şehirciliğin Tarih-i İnkişafı, Historical Evolution of Turkish Urbanism.* Istanbul: Cumhuriyet Matbaası, 1936.
Eryılmaz, Bilal. *Osmanlı Devletinde Gayrimüslim Tebaanın Yönetimi.* 2nd ed. İstanbul: Risale, 1996.
Eyice, Semavi. . "Fatih Külliyesi." *Dünden Bugüne İstanbul Ansiklopedisi.* Vol. 3. İstanbul: Kültür Bakanlığı ve Tarih Vakfı, 1993. 265–70.
Fotić, Aleksandar. "The Official Explanations for the Confiscation and Sale of Monasteries (Churches) and Their Estates at the Time of Selim II." *Turcica* 26 (1994): 33–54.
Frug, Gerald E. "The City as a Legal Concept." *Harvard Law Review* 93.6 (April 1980): 1057–1154.
Gawrych, George W. "Tolerant Dimensions of Cultural Pluralism in the Ottoman Empire: The Albanian Community, 1800–1912." *International Journal of Middle East Studies* 15 (1983): 519–36.
Gierke, Otto Friedrich von. *Das deutsche Genossenschaftsrecht.* Berlin: Weidmann, 1866.
Güneri, Hasan. "Azınlık Vakıflarının İncelenmesi." *Vakıflar Dergisi* 10 (1973): 79–108.
Imber, Colin. *Ebū's Su'ūd: The Islamic Legal Tradition Jurists—Profiles in Legal Theory.* Stanford: Stanford UP, 1997.
Inalcik, Halil. "Istanbul: An Islamic City." *Journal of Islamic Studies* 1 (1990): 1–23.

Işın, Ekrem. *Istanbul'da Gündelik Hayat: Insan, Kültür ve Mekân Ilişkileri Üzerine Toplumsal Tarih Denemeleri, Istanbul dizisi; 15.* Cağaloğlu, Istanbul: Iletisim Yayinlari, 1995.
Isin, Engin F. *Being Political: Genealogies of Citizenship.* Minneapolis: U of Minnesota P, 2002.
———. *Cities Without Citizens: Modernity of the City as a Corporation.* Montreal: Black Rose, 1992.
———. "Citizenship After Orientalism: Ottoman Citizenship." *Citizenship in a Globalizing World: European Questions and Turkish Experiences.* Ed. Fuat Keyman and Ahmet İçduygu. London: Routledge, 2005. 31–51.
Isin, Engin F., and Alexandre Lefebvre. "The Gift of Law: Greek Euergetism and Ottoman *Waqf.*" *European Journal of Social Theory* 8.1 (2005): 5–23.
Karpat, Kemal H. "An Inquiry into the Social Foundations of Nationalism in the Ottoman State: From Social Estates to Classes, from Millets to Nations." Research Monograph no. 39. Center of International Studies, Princeton University.
Kenanoğlu, Macit. *Osmanlı Millet Sistemi: Mit ve Gerçek.* İstanbul: Klasik Yayınları, 2004.
Kermeli, Eugeina. "Ebü's Su'ūd's Definitions of Church Vakfs: Theory and Practice in Ottoman Law." *Islamic Law: Theory and Practice.* Ed. Robert Gleave and Eugenia Kermeli. I.B.Tauris, 1997. 141–56.
Kuban, Doğan. "Sülaymaniye Külliyesi." *Dünden Bugüne İstanbul Ansiklopedisi.* Vol. 7. İstanbul: Kültür Bakanlığı ve Tarih Vakfı, 1993. 96–104.
Öztürk, Nazif. *Azınlık Vakıfları [Minority Waqfs].* Ankara: Altınküre, 2003.
———. *Türk Yenileşme Tarihi Çerçevesinde Vakıf Müessesesi [The Institution of Waqf Within the Context of Turkish Modernization].* Ankara: Türkiye Diyanet Vakfı, 1995.
Powers, David S., and Alisa-Rubin Peled. "Orientalism, Colonialism, and Legal History: The Attack on Muslim Family Endowments in Algeria and India." *Comparative Studies in Society and History* 31.3 (1989): 535–71.
Reppetto, T. A. "Millet System in Ottoman and American Empires." *Public Policy* 18.5 (1970): 629–48.
Shaham, Ron. "Christian and Jewish *Waqf* in Palestine During the Late Ottoman Period." *Bulletin of the School of Oriental and African Studies* 54.3 (1991): 460–72.
Singer, Amy. *Constructing Ottoman Beneficence: An Imperial Soup Kitchen in Jerusalem.* SUNY Series in Near Eastern Studies. Albany: State U of New York P, 2002.
Soykan, Tankut T. *Osmanlı İmparatorluğu'nda Gayrimüslimler: Klasik Dönem Osmanlı Hukukunda Gayrimüslimlerin Hukuki Statüsü.* İstanbul: Ütopya Kitabevi, 2000.
Stefanov, S. "Millet System in the Ottoman Empire: Example for Oppression or for Tolerance?" *Bulgarian Historical Review* 2–3 (1997): 138–42.
Tanman, Baha M. "Hacı Beşir Ağa Külliyesi." *Dünden Bugüne İstanbul Ansiklopedisi* Vol. 3. İstanbul: Kültür Bakanlığı ve Tarih Vakfı, 1993. 469–73.
van Leeuwen, Richard. *Notables and Clergy in Mount Lebanon: The Khazin Sheikhs and the Maronite Church, 1736–1840.* Leiden: Brill, 1994.
———. *Waqfs and Urban Structures: The Case of Ottoman Damascus, Studies in Islamic Law and Society.* Vol. 11. Leiden: Brill, 1999.
Yediyıldız, Bahaeddin. "Müessese-Toplum Münasebetleri Çerçevesinde 18. Asır Türk Toplumu ve Vakıf Müessesesi." *Vakıflar Dergisi* 15 (1982): 23–53.
———. "Türk Kültür Sistemi İçinde Vakfın Yeri." *Vakıflar Dergisi* 20 (1988): 403–8.

———. "Türk Vakıf Kurucularının Sosyal Tabakalaşmadaki Yeri, 1700–1800." *The Journal of Ottoman Studies* 3 (1982): 143–64.

———. "Vakıf Müessesesinin 18. Asır'da Kültür Üzerindeki Etkileri." *Türkiye'nin Sosyal ve Ekonomik Tarihi (1071–1920)*. Ed. O. Okyar and H. Inalcık. Ankara: Meteksan, 1980. 157–61.

Zubaida, Sami. "Cosmopolitanism and the Middle East." *Cosmopolitanism, Identity and Authenticity in the Middle East*. Ed. Roel Meijer. Richmond, Eng.: Curzon, 1999. 15–33.

———. "Middle Eastern Experiences of Cosmopolitanism." *Conceiving Cosmopolitanism: Theory, Context and Practice*. Ed. Steven Vertovec and Robin Cohen. New York: Oxford UP, 2002. 32–41.

3 Living Together in Lhasa
Ethnic Relations, Coercive Amity, and Subaltern Cosmopolitanism

Emily T. Yeh

INTRODUCTION

Shrill warnings of an inevitable "clash of civilizations," and their invocation as justification for xenophobic patriotism and imperial invasion, have given renewed urgency to the search for emergent cosmopolitanisms, as practices of conviviality and forms of belonging and solidarity to a world community. The "cosmopolitan" ideals and projects necessary for the task do not refer to sophisticated world travel and cross-cultural expertise, the conventional sense of cosmopolitanism as no more than a "good ethical orientation for those privileged to inhabit the frequent traveler lounges" (Calhoun 112). Nor does it signal an inevitable return to Immanuel Kant's formulation; histories of colonialism and capitalism have long since discredited the benign potential of international commerce as a stable foundation for perpetual peace. Indeed, recent commentators have criticized the predilection to begin every discussion of cosmopolitanism with a return to European intellectual history: "[i]f it is already clear that cosmopolitanism begins with the Stoics, who invented the term, or with Kant who reinvented it, then philosophical reflection on these moments is going to enable us always to find what we are looking for. Yet [we could instead] try to be archivally cosmopolitan and to say, 'Let's simply look at the world across time and space and see how people have thought and acted beyond the local'" (Pollock et al. 585–86).

The search for cosmopolitanisms beyond elite border crossings and imperial universalisms animates Clifford's argument for "discrepant cosmopolitanism," exemplified by servants and migrant laborers who were and are also world travelers. These discrepant cosmopolitans are those excluded by Hannerz's insistence on the distinction between genuine cosmopolitans (who by his definition must be elites) and traders, tourists, migrants, and exiles, who travel but do not immerse themselves in another culture, or only do so out of necessity. The trope of travel is also taken up by Appiah, whose "rooted cosmopolitanism" of "cosmopolitan patriots" works against the presumed opposition between cosmopolitanism and nationalism, or patriotism. Cosmopolitan patriots are attached to a home of their own but also take pleasure in a world of others, and live in a world of movement, travel, and cultural hybridization. Hybridity is also important in Bhabha's "vernacular cosmopolitanism," which offers a view from the margins that is "culturally particularist" but also "linked to a transhistorical memory and solidarity" (41).

These interventions are significant in their emphasis on the nonelite, and in their refusal to dismiss postcolonial nationalism in the name of cosmopolitanism. Cheah argues that postcolonial nationalism is an ambivalent necessity, a double-edged sword made necessary as a defense against the predations of neocolonial capitalist restructuring and globalization. Cheah also critiques the celebration of travel and global flows that characterizes much of the work on nonelite cosmopolitanisms. In focusing so much on cultural flux and transnational mobility, they ignore those who cannot or do not migrate; for this majority the nation-state, whatever its problems, is a necessity "because postnationalism through migration is not an alternative" (Cheah 314). Similarly, Yeğenoğlu (103) argues that cosmopolitanism needs to be "less dismissive of the need for nationalism in the Third World, a nationalism that is capable of articulating the will of the excluded subaltern populations." Gidwani explicitly uses the term "subaltern cosmopolitanism" to describe a view that, like Cheah's is not based on flux and mobility, and that critiques the marginalization and exploitation brought about by economic globalization, understanding them as constituted by transregional and transnational processes. Subaltern cosmopolitanism refers, in this formulation, to practices that enable connectivity between the disenfranchised, practices that "are transgressive of the established order and that shame and expose its hermetic and de-politicized grids of Difference as political relations of difference"(Gidwani 16).

This essay takes as a starting point Pollock et al.'s suggestion to rewrite the history of cosmopolitanism by looking across the world in time and space and thinking outside of the box of European intellectual history; this, they suggest, would reveal an extravagant array of possibilities of cosmopolitanism. However, rather than follow the literature that takes translocal or transnational mobility as the key analytic for nonelite cosmopolitanisms, I focus on cosmopolitanism as a dismantling of the ideology of the clash of civilizations—as Mayaram (this volume) puts it: How have people of different cultural and ethnic groups lived together in a convivial, or at least indifferent, fashion, and when is it analytically useful, or not, to identify the fact of successful living together as a form of cosmopolitanism?

I explore the possibilities of non-Western and nonelite cosmopolitanism through a discussion of interethnic relations in Lhasa, Tibet's religious and political center and today capital of China's Tibet Autonomous Region. I examine continuity and change in these relations before and after the traumatic breaks of 1951, which marked the incorporation of Central Tibet into the People's Republic of China (PRC) and 1959, the uprising in Lhasa that led to the exile of the Fourteenth Dalai Lama and eighty thousand Tibetans. In both the pre- and post-1950s periods, Lhasa as a city differs from its popular image. First, Lhasa is imagined as having been historically isolated and exclusively Tibetan, when it had, in fact, been an important center of trade and a multiethnic city since at least the seventeenth century. I argue that Lhasa from the seventeenth to mid-twentieth century was characterized by a form of cosmopolitanism that preceded nationalism, was conducive to convivial living together across difference, and was at least partially informed by local interpretations of Buddhism. The first part of the paper discusses Lhasa as a multiethnic and multicultural city before 1950, and in particular the status and history of its Han and Muslim communities.

Second, contemporary Lhasa is often imagined as a site of ethnic conflict between the Han Chinese and Tibetans, a result of the Chinese annexation of Tibet and the struggle of Tibetan nationalism. However, the city has not witnessed forms of open violence between Han and Tibetans. Tensions do exist between Tibetans and the Hui (Chinese Muslims), but these too have only rarely been characterized by outright conflict. I argue that threads of an older cosmopolitanism based in Buddhism, reworked and given new meaning, partially inform these interactions. However, the primary reason for the smooth daily interactions among people of various ethnicities, especially Han and Tibetan, is not cosmopolitanism but rather the state's administrative practices, especially the use of "unity of the nationalities" (*minzu tuanjie*) as a hegemonic management device. *Minzu tuanjie* is a tool developed for the incorporation of Tibet into China, and continues to be used to mitigate the threat of Tibetan nationalism, and most recently to facilitate the social "stability" deemed necessary to attract capital investment for Tibet's economic development. I argue that this reorganization of interethnic life through coercive amity and the political, social, and economic domination of the Han, means that the current state of "living together with difference" cannot be described as the outcome of cosmopolitanism.

My argument is not that there is a fundamental clash between cosmopolitanism and nationalism (the unfulfilled nationalism of Tibetans who wish for their own nation-state) but rather that coercive harmony, which goes far beyond a disavowal of interethnic violence to guarantee the triumph of official, Chinese nationalism over Tibetan nationalism, is incompatible with subaltern cosmopolitan practices, which are instead transgressive of de-politicized orders of difference exemplified by the state's *minzu* (nationality) discursive practices. This part of the essay explores how practices of cooperation, ironic commentaries of conflict, imposed conviviality, and the threat of state violence come together in daily life. I employ ethnographic description of the complicated negotiations and pedestrian pathways of everyday life to write beyond the limitations of purely statist views, but without ignoring the ways in which state practices lay the ground for even the most mundane interactions.

LHASA IN HISTORY: MULTIETHNIC AND COSMOPOLITAN

Lhasa, "land of the gods," has long been represented in the West with oversimplified, one-dimensional images: Shangri-la, utopia, site of spiritual wisdom. Modern Chinese representations of Lhasa before the twentieth century have focused on its smallness and backwardness, its lack of technology and modernization, rather than its utopian, mystical qualities, but the images are similarly one-dimensional. Current Chinese development practices are premised on an image of Lhasa as having always been a backwater, lagging behind the rest of the world, in desperate need of modernization through urbanization. What these divergent narratives share is blindness to Lhasa's historical importance as a center of trade, as well as to its multiethnic mix of residents, and the ways in which they interacted across their differences.

Lhasa is said to have been founded by King Srongtsen Gampo, who unified Tibet and moved his capital to Lhasa in the seventh century. His Chinese bride, Princess Wencheng, recognized with her geomantic skills that the land of Tibet was constituted by a vast supine demoness who had to be subdued before Buddhism could be established. This unruly demoness was pinned down and controlled through the construction of a series of temples laid out in concentric squares, centered on the Jokhang temple, built over her heart. This account, which first appeared in the eleventh century, ties the founding of Lhasa to the rise of Buddhism over older religious traditions.[1] The presumption, often associated with this narrative, that Lhasa served continuously as Tibet's political capital from Srongtsen Gampo's reign onward, is not substantiated by the historical record. Only after the Fifth Dalai Lama rose to power as sovereign in 1642 did Lhasa become a true seat of government administration, and the major site of diplomatic activities (Blondeau and Gyatso).

Detailed information about Lhasa's lay population up until the twentieth century is scarce, as Tibetan historiographers were primarily interested in recording religious history. We do know, though, that neither the physical extent nor the population of the town grew very quickly. In 1904, the invading British Younghusband expedition estimated Lhasa's population at thirty thousand, including twenty thousand monks (Blondeau and Gyatso 26). Lhasa's 1950s population is also frequently estimated at around thirty thousand. At that time the city was a densely packed warren of alleyways branching off from the Barkor path, only three square kilometers in area. The Potala Palace and the village of Zhöl below it were considered separate from the city. Despite its miniscule size in comparison with other cities of the day, Lhasa was the largest and basically the only urban settlement in the Tibetan cultural world (Yeh and Henderson).

From at least the seventeenth century, though, the Barkor served as both a circumambulation path around the Jokhang and a bustling market for goods around the world.[2] At that time, Tibet was exporting, among other goods, musk, gold, medicinal plants, furs, and yak tails. The latter were exported not only for use as fly swatters and staffs, but also as ritual fans in Hindu temples, and as Santa Claus beards in Europe (Karan 7). Seventeenth-century imports included sugar, chilies, and tea, as well as glass bottles, copper, coins made in Nepal, Kashmiri saffron, Persian turquoise, European amber, and coral gathered from the Mediterranean and polished in workshops in Italy (Boulnois). Three centuries later, in the 1940s, Han traders sold silk and satin in Lhasa's Beijing Store, Kashmiri businessmen sold hats and pelts, and Newaris sold brocades, watches, and silk. Lhasa's wealthy residents could also afford to buy hats and cloth imported from Italy, Scotch whisky, Australian butter, and American corned beef. Heinrich Harrer, who lived in Lhasa from 1943 to 1950 recalled:

> There is nothing one cannot buy, or at least order. One even finds the Elizabeth Arden specialties ... American overshoes... sewing-machines, radio sets and gramophones and ... Bing Crosby's latest records.... we found an enormous store full of European felt-hats which are the *dernier cri* in Lhasa (126–27).

Just a few decades later, the markets and goods were gone, replaced by food rations and poorly stocked government stores (Goldstein, Siebenschuh, and Tsering 108). Only in the 1990s did internationally produced goods become available once more in Lhasa. As Barnett states, "It is one of the great tragicomic ironies of the Chinese presence in Tibet that since the new transition

Photo 3.1 Barkor, vegetable market, Lhasa. Photo by Emily T. Yeh.

point of 1980 Beijing's main claim to legitimacy in Tibet has been the fact that it has brought consumer commodities to the shops of Lhasa: until the Chinese arrived the shops of Lhasa had been full of them" (*Lhasa* 66). This "tragi-comic irony" parallels the ways in which ethnic governance and interethnic relations shifted from the pre-1951 period to now.

Multiethnic Lhasa

In addition to being a site of intense commercial activity, Lhasa was also a place where culture and arts from around Asia mingled. Jesuit missionary Ippolito Desideri, who reached Lhasa in 1716, encountered Mongol, Chinese, Muscovite, Armenian, Kashmiri, north Indian, and Nepalese merchants (Harris and Shakya; de Filippis 5). The city was also home to Ladakhis and Chinese Muslims. Merchants of different origin settled into distinct neighborhoods, with Nepalese living on the north side of the Barkor and the Kashmiri Muslims on the south (*Grong-khyer* 16–17). The Gorkhas had a strong presence in Lhasa since the seventeenth century; their office and military escort that functioned as a consulate was the oldest Nepali mission abroad.

An account by the Italian missionary Beligatti of the Monlam Chenmo celebrations performed in Lhasa in 1741 describes a celebration of difference:

> The cavalcade opened with sixty Newars on horseback, dressed up in their traditional costumes. They were followed by forty Indian merchants, also on horseback, but wearing clothes made of yellow Chinese brocade, followed in their turn by fifty-seven mounted Kashmiri Muslims . . . Eight mounted laymen, dressed up in Chinese brocade, carried four different pair of banners . . . On that occasion, the local Chinese community set up a magnificent Chinese-style garden in the square in front of the Dalai Lama's residence. (Bue 195–96)

Bue suggests that the magnificent festivals of seventeenth- and eighteenth-century Lhasa, together with feasts, patronage of art, and the flourishing of medicine, made Lhasa "a beacon for Tibetans as well as for their Buddhist neighbours" (197). However, the presence of Kashmiri Muslims and others in both the daily life of the city and the celebrations of festivals suggests that Lhasa welcomed and beckoned beyond the world of Buddhists to encompass multiple geographical origins and religious faiths.

This mix of ethnicities persisted through the first half of the twentieth century, during which Lhasa had a much more international flavor than it did during the century's second half. A British Mission operated in Lhasa between 1936 and 1947; there were also numerous Anglophile Tibetan aristocrats, educated in schools in England and India (Harris and Shakya). Lhasa was also home to a population of Sikh converts to Islam,[3] as well as Ladakhi merchants. An account by Abdul Wahid Radhu, a member of a family responsible for the caravan transporting offerings from the Ladakhi king to the Dalai Lama, suggests many close ties between Muslims in Leh and Lhasa; two of Radhu's cousins lived in Lhasa, including one who married a Chinese Muslim. Lhasa was also home to numerous Nepalese residents, who had certain extraterritorial privileges such as being tried by their own consul rather than in Tibetan courts (McGovern 446).[4]

The Chinese of Lubu

Though most Chinese living in Lhasa before 1950 were merchants and officials associated with the Amban, the Qing empire's representative in Tibet, the residents of the Lubu neighborhood, next to what is now the glittering pedestrian walkway of Yuthok Road, were descendants of Chinese settlers who farmed vegetables. They married Tibetan women, and their descendants speak Tibetan, dress in Tibetan style, and identify as Tibetan, even while holding onto their Han ancestry and, in some cases, surnames. The history of the Lubu neighborhood points to a possible future that did not come to pass: a way for Han and Tibetans to "live together" that is very different from the ways that seem natural and inevitable today.

Precise dates cannot be determined from available records, but interviews suggest that the ancestors of the current residents came to Lhasa from Sichuan as soldiers with an Amban around the 1840s–1860s. They married local Tibetan women, and the government allowed them to reclaim the marshy area around Lubu for vegetable cultivation. The Tshona family had the largest vegetable plot, land rent for which they paid to the Zhöl Laskhungs office; the women of the family also paid a yearly "labor release" (*mi-bogs*) fee to the Agricultural Office. One member of the family, born in 1918, recalled that her great-grandfather was Chinese; he married a Tibetan woman from Batang and settled in Lhasa. Her own grandfather was Chinese as well, and her Tibetan grandmother could speak Chinese well. However, she herself identified as Tibetan, and spoke primarily Tibetan. During the 1930s–1940s, a number of Lubu residents sent their children to attend the Guomingdang-run school in Lhasa, and her grandmother had wanted to send her. However, "other people said, 'why would a woman need to learn Chinese?'" Instead, she was sent to a private school in the Barkor, where she learned to read and write in Tibetan. She married a Tibetan official who, she claimed, was falsely accused of participating in the 1959 uprising, for which she suffered greatly, particularly during the Cultural Revolution.

Lubu residents often worshipped at Lhasa's *Guandi miao*, or *Gesar Lhakhang*, a temple that provides an interesting example of converging mythologies and cultural sharing. The Amban established the temple in 1792 after a victory over the Gorkha army, and dedicated it to Guandi, legendary Chinese warrior hero of the Three Kingdoms Period, often considered the God of War. Over time, it also became associated with the legendary

Tibetan warrior king, Gesar of Ling, who is also considered a protector deity. Thus, the temple was a place of worship for both Tibetan and Han residents of Lhasa, and the architecture of the temple reflects both styles.

Muslim Communities in Lhasa, Pre-1950

The Muslims who resided in Lhasa up through the mid-twentieth century were divided into two main groups: those of Chinese descent, referred to as Hebalin Khache (after the name of their neighborhood, Hebalin) or Chinese Muslims (rGya Khache); and those of Kashmiri, Ladakhi, or Nepalese descent, referred to as the Barkor Khache (they lived in the Barkor), the Kashmiri Khache (following the numerically dominant subgroup), the Lhasa Khache, or simply Khache. Their everyday lives in Lhasa up to the mid-twentieth century appear to have been rather similar, but the paths of the two groups diverged significantly after the 1950s.

Kashmiri Muslims first migrated to Lhasa during the rule of the Fifth Dalai Lama (1642–1682). According to the present-day leader of Lhasa's Barkor Khache community, seventeen boys and thirty men from Kashmir and Nepal came as merchants, and were invited by the Fifth Dalai Lama to stay as guests in Tibet. From that time, they received a stipend from the Tibetan government on the first, eighth, and fifteenth day of each Tibetan month, a custom that is said to have lasted until 1959.[5] A number of stories explain why the Fifth Dalai Lama granted these men land for a cemetery and a mosque in an area known as Khache Lingka, two kilometers west of town. According to one, the Fifth Dalai Lama saw the Muslim saint, Pir Yakup, praying and doing "prostrations" on a small rock shaped like a prayer carpet on Darga mountain, and asked that he be brought to him. When the Pir told him that he was worshipping on the hill because there was no mosque, the Dalai Lama sent a representative to shoot arrows to demarcate the land that he granted to the Khache both for prayer and to use as a cemetery (Cabezón).[6] Most of the Kashmiri Muslims lived in rented houses in the Barkor and made their living through commerce. For example, though Tibetans did not fish (for religious reasons), the nobility were not above covertly buying and consuming fish sold by the Khache (and others) in Barkor markets as "water turnips."

The Hebalin Khache began to settle in Lhasa somewhat later than the Kashmiris, in the eighteenth century. Their oldest mosque was built in 1776 (Moevus). Some Hebalin residents claim to be descendants of soldiers garrisoned in Lhasa, while others trace their ancestry to Chinese Muslims from Gansu, Shanxi, Qinghai, Sichuan, and Yunnan provinces, who arrived in Lhasa at the beginning of the eighteenth century during the reign of Kangxi. Still others are said to be descendants of soldiers of the Chinese army that fought against the Gorkhas in 1793 (Jest; Snellgrove and Richardson). These families, many of whom were surnamed Ma and Zhang, made their living in several ways: cultivating vegetables on the reclaimed sandy banks of the

Lhasa River, butchering, operating wheat-grinding mills, and selling meat and bread. Others owned small restaurants or were barbers and cobblers.

Over time, the Barkor and Hebalin Khache alike adopted Tibetan dress, language, and other cultural practices. The Barkor Muslims in particular were considered especially expert in the use of Tibetan honorific language (*zhe-sa*), a trait for which they are still admired today. Indeed, given the great difficulty many young Tibetans in Lhasa today have speaking Tibetan without code-switching with Mandarin, the Barkor Khache (now often called the "Tibetan Khache") are admired for their ability to speak pure Tibetan.

Many of the rights granted to the Kashmiri Muslims by the Fifth Dalai Lama applied to the Hebalin Muslims as well. Both groups were free to open shops and trade without the imposition of a tax or levy. Furthermore, both were exempted from restrictions on meat consumption during Sagadawa (Siddiqui). Muslim-Tibetan intermarriage was common, particularly between Muslim men and Tibetan women, with the Tibetans usually converting to Islam. Intermarriage between Kashmiri and Chinese Muslims was also common, though the two groups had separate burial grounds as well as mosques. The Khache had their own chief, the *Khache 'go-pa*, who judged offenses and chaired a council that advised the community on Islamic law (Jest). The Hebalin Muslims similarly elected their own leader, who was then approved by the Tibetan government. However, this leader was under the jurisdiction of the Department of Agriculture whereas the Barkor Khache leader was responsible to the Finance Office (Cabezón). Furthermore, Barkor Khache men were considered to some extent "foreign" despite generations of living in Lhasa, a designation that would work in their favor after 1959.

The Kashmiri and Chinese Muslims also seemed to have had a friendly rivalry about which group was more valued by the majority Buddhist Tibetans. The former make much of the fact that they lived on the Barkor, inside the boundaries of the Lingkor circumambulation path, whereas the Hebalin neighborhood was outside of the Lingkor. This, I was told by more than one Barkor Khache, "shows that we were more highly regarded than the Hebalin Khache." Though there may well have been hostility, there are no records–whether Western travelers' reports, residents' own written records, available archival material, or narratives of family history told by descendants now living in Lhasa—of interethnic violence or overt antagonism toward these Muslim communities. Both were governed through a different set of principles than other Tibetan residents vis-à-vis relationship to land and religious regulations. If they had grievances or felt unjustly treated, we have no record of it.

Buddhism and Cosmopolitanism

What might have been the sources of this prenationalist cosmopolitanism—including not only the stance of relating "self to non-self in . . . civility, compassion, indifference," but also deliberate celebrations of difference, as in the Monlam Chenmo festival witnessed by Beligatti in 1741? The role of the Fifth Dalai Lama in granting a place for the Kashmiri Muslims to worship, as well as the accommodations made for Hebalin Muslims and Lubu residents to cultivate land, suggests that pre-1950 Lhasa was multicultural and multiethnic through both contingency and to some extent, deliberate design. Even in the first half of the twentieth century, the Tibetan Buddhist religious establishment, by then characterized by extreme conservatism and an insular, isolationist orientation (Goldstein), accommodated the Kashmiri and Chinese Muslims and the residents of Lubu. Despite the ideology of combining religious and political affairs and the way in which commitment to Tibetan Buddhism had become the core of Tibetan national identity (Goldstein 2), neither the government nor society objected to allowing small non-Tibetan and non-Buddhist communities to thrive in Lhasa.

The long history of trade undoubtedly played a role in this ethic, but the Fifth Dalai Lama's deliberate creation of a space for these different communities, together with the central role of religion in Tibetan politics, suggests that Buddhism also had some relationship to the ideals and practices of living together. Indeed, the impermanence of reality and the inevitability of suffering lead, in the Mahayana tradition, to the principle of cultivating compassion (*nyingjé*) and the development of charity and self-restraint. Tibetan Buddhists pray for all sentient beings to have peace, freedom from suffering, and an escape from ignorance, attachment, and hatred (that is, to achieve enlightenment). The principles of fate and reincarnation also mean that any sentient being could have been one's mother in a previous lifetime, and should be treated accordingly. This ethical orientation is summarized in a teaching as follows: "Thinking of all living beings as the gracious parents of our past lives we should be compassionate to beggars and other unfortunates ... with love, compassion, and an enlightened attitude we should protect the lives of other living beings, give generously and without attachment ... be content, love others" (in Kapstein 218).

The wide acceptance in Tibetan culture of the cultivation of *nyingjé* as a basis for a proper life resonates with cosmopolitanism as ethical practices of living together peacefully and in solidarity. Of course, Tibetan Buddhists, like practitioners of all faiths, have not always put their ethical ideals into practice, and indeed have often violated principles in the name of religion. As Bielefeldt suggests, "Buddhists dupe, curse, seduce, oppress, and kill each other in the name of their religion ... Buddhists seem expert at finding ways to find the dharma in what they appear to do as a matter of their cultural course" (241). However, the fact that ethical ideals are not always practiced does not mean that they never are. It is difficult in the absence of more detailed historical records about the founding of various non-Tibetan communities in Lhasa to know the extent to which the cultivation of compassion may have deliberately shaped the way in which these communities were regulated and day-to-day interactions in the city conducted.[7]

Nevertheless, without romantically ignoring the economic deprivation of the Tibetan underclasses, or the occasional battles between monasteries, *nyingjé* can be posited as a partial basis for the peacefulness of coexistence in pre-1950s Lhasa, and one that as we will see still plays a role today. However, compared to pre-1950s Lhasa, the city today is multicultural and multiethnic in a very different way, and very much by the state's design.

LIVING TOGETHER IN LHASA TODAY

Lhasa, according to the Chinese state, is today a prosperous city, "home to the Tibetan, Han, and Hui peoples, as well as many other ethnic groups" who live together harmoniously, displaying in their everyday lives the "unity of the nationalities."[8] Indeed, Tibetan residents of Lhasa appear to do a disconcertingly good job of "living together" with their new Han neighbors. I discovered this when I lived for three months with a Tibetan family in Lhasa. Descendants of a family of wealthy merchants, their Barkor house was confiscated in 1959 and redistributed to poor urban residents. They lived in work unit housing until the mid-1990s when their salaries were suddenly raised and new policies encouraged them to build a new private "retirement house." The family moved to a neighborhood named "New Unity Village," bought land at a highly subsidized rate, and built a house in the "new *Simsha* [nobility]" style. Tibetan in appearance, but with many modern amenities, their two-story home is built around a large courtyard with a sunroom and a small lawn. Around the courtyard are the kitchen, the bathroom, the living quarters for the family and the Tibetan maid, and three other small rooms that the family rents out—to sex workers from Sichuan.

The heavy presence of Han sex workers is a common topic of conversation among Lhasa's Tibetan residents. One common theory is that the government not only has failed to stop prostitution, but has actively encouraged it, because it gives idle men something to do other than think about political protest. In addition to professing to subscribe to this view, my host also registered his dissatisfaction with the current political situation in many other ways. He sent one of his children at a young age to Dharamsala to be educated in schools run by the Tibetan government-in-exile. He complained frequently to me that Lhasa residents have "no freedom" and that, with the arrival of so many Chinese migrants, Lhasa has changed irrevocably for the worse. He rose every morning at 5 a.m. to circumambulate the Lingkor, though instead of praying, he took along his shortwave radio and listened secretly to Voice of America. Nevertheless, he and his wife were perfectly willing to augment their already generous retirement packages by renting out part of their home to the very people whose arrival they complained about on a daily basis. Though they never invited the migrants over for dinner, they shared a courtyard space, a water pump, and a common entrance. They crossed paths daily, said hello, and cordially lived their separate lives in close proximity.

A few kilometers away lived an elderly Tibetan woman whose family, like every other family in the village, had been subleasing their land to Han migrants for vegetable cultivation for about a decade. Although the Tibetan families earn more from leasing out their land than they do by growing barley themselves, their earnings are only one tenth of the Han farmers' net profits. Nevertheless, they quite willingly rent out their land. The Han and Tibetans mostly kept to themselves; the woman couldn't tell me where the Han renters of her family's land were from. "How would I know?" she said. "They're Chinese." One day, I mentioned that I had lived in Beijing some years earlier. "Tell me," she said, "are there any Chinese left in China?[9] I think there must not be, because they've all come to Lhasa!"

How should we understand these sorts of sarcastic comments and complaints about Han migration while also taking seriously the day-to-day fact that Tibetans and Han live together peacefully in the city, sometimes in lives that significantly overlap, and sometimes in very different, parallel lives? The daily, voluntary Tibetan-Han engagement in economic activities (rentals of land and courtyard space) seems to defy Tibetan resentment of Han migration, which emerges in sarcasm and bitter speech. The coexistence of these two phenomena can only be understood by examining how *minzu tuanjie* structures the lives and subjectivities of differently positioned ethnic citizens in Lhasa.

Administrative Autonomy and Minzu Tuanjie as Management Device

Sun Yatsen's theory of *minzu* ("nation/nationality") was adopted early on by the Chinese Communist Party, with each *minzu* allowed the right of self-determination, including the formation of an independent state. However, this was allowable only in theory, and not in practice, as Baba Phuntsog Wangyal, an early Tibetan communist revolutionary learned when he attempted to found a separate Tibetan Communist Party (Goldstein, Siebenschuh, and Tsering). Upon the founding of the PRC, the Party officially repudiated the option of secession and instead established a system of "autonomous" regions in areas where minorities predominated. Tibetans were divided into the prefectural-level Tibet Autonomous Region (TAR), and autonomous prefectures and counties in Yunnan, Sichuan, Gansu, and Qinghai provinces.

According to the State Council, "The Tibetan people enjoy, according to law, the equal right of participation in the administration of state affairs as well as the right of self-government to manage affairs of their own region and ethnic group . . . the full exercise . . . of the right of self-government." However, there is little meaningful political autonomy. In some cases, the exceptions made in the name of autonomy have been implemented, but

66   Emily T. Yeh

have little political consequence. In other cases, policies that would actually provide a measure of cultural and political autonomy remain unimplemented. And finally, in still other cases, policies implemented in the name of minzu autonomy in fact *increase* rather than decrease state control; the device of *minzu tuanjie*, or the "unity of the nationalities," is used to discursively transform measures that are administratively exceptional in their increased scrutiny and control into ones that pass as exceptions granted in the name of autonomy.

Within *minzu tuanjie* discourse, minorities' demands for greater autonomy than the state currently provides is interpreted as *minzu fenlie* ("national splittism"), the gravest threat to *minzu tuanjie*. Those accused of attempting to split the nation, and thus threatening the sovereignty of the Chinese state, end up losing their jobs, and sometimes in detention as political prisoners. In this way, *minzu tuanjie* works as a hegemonic device to manage a coercive unity (Bulag; Yeh, "Tibetan Indigeneity"). One of the most common forms taken by *minzu tuanjie* is the portrayal of China's fifty-six recognized *minzu* as one big, happy family, with the Han as the eldest sibling taking care of the others. A well-known political song about national unity was revived and set to pop music in Tibet in the late 1990s, when it became ubiquitous in karaokes, bars, and buses: "The sun and moon are daughters of the same mother / The name of the mother is

Photo 3.2   "Han Tibetans one family," Tolung Dechen, near Lhasa. People's Republic of China. Photo by Emily T. Yeh.

radiance . . . / The Tibetans and the Chinese are daughters of one mother / The name of the mother is China."

The long history of cultural and material interaction between Chinese and Tibetan civilizations is also marshaled to bolster the legitimacy of current political arrangements. The marriage of Chinese Princess Wencheng to Srongtsen Gampo in the seventh century was invoked after 1959 to prove Chinese claims of sovereignty over Tibet. (Srongsten Gampo's senior, Nepalese wife is absent from this narrative.) Since the 1980s, the date of Chinese sovereignty over Tibet has been moved in official history to the Sakya leaders' thirteenth-century submission to the Mongol Yuan dynasty, but Wencheng is still credited with bringing all manners of civilization to Tibet, including not only Buddhism, but also textiles, various technologies, music, and even (quite inaccurately) agriculture.[10] Her marriage is continuously used to symbolize *minzu tuanjie,* as Lhasa residents are frequently reminded, most recently by a twenty-part China Central Television series about Wencheng produced in 2000. Similarly, a recently commissioned report on ethnic unity in the TAR states:

> Princess Wencheng still lives on in the hearts of Tibetan people. [She] was a daughter of a Han family, but even more so, she is a part of Tibetan culture. Her name is like the water of the Yarlung Tsangpo River, gurgling and flowing in Tibetan hearts and minds . . . This is the true meaning of the very best kind of *minzu tuanjie* (Zhang, Luo, and Xu 60).

As a device that calls itself into being, *minzu tuanjie* makes expressions and behaviors that imply anything other than a familial relationship between the Tibetans and Han a sign of splittism, deserving of punishment. The entangled nature of Han nationalism with Chinese nationalism makes staying on the side of *minzu tuanjie* a tricky proposition (Bulag; Yeh, "Tibetan Indigeneity"). In Lhasa the most pressing issue today is the ever-growing number of Han and Hui migrants, leading to Tibetan fears of being outnumbered and marginalized. However, the view of the TAR as being Tibetan land is firmly rejected by the state; the TAR is always described in official documents as a "multiethnic region," inhabited not only by Tibetans, but also by Han, Hui, and other *minzu*. Thus, the TAR should be equally "home" to the Han as to Tibetans. To suggest otherwise, for example by objecting to the Han presence in Lhasa, becomes an offense against national unity, an attempt to split the motherland.

SPACE, ETHNICITY, AND PROTEST

I turn here to a brief examination of how the administrative and discursive practices of coercive amity have shaped spatialized, ethnic patterns in Lhasa from 1959 to the present. After the failed uprising in 1959, the state expropriated the houses of those who fled to India or had been sent to prison, dividing them into tiny apartments for poor residents. Young Tibetans were selected to attend schools in Shenyang and Beijing. These youth eventually returned to Tibet, many to Lhasa, to become cadres and today's new middle class. The urban area and population of Lhasa increased significantly after 1959, though available statistics have been both contentious and difficult to interpret (Yeh and Henderson).

Until the mid-1980s, most Han residing in Lhasa were cadres who had been sent to work in government offices. Of these, most returned home to inland China upon retirement. Little new housing was built, and much of the Tibetan population lived in the Barkor area. Of the 108,000 permanent residents counted officially in Lhasa in 1987, 27,500 native Lhasa residents lived in the old Barkor urban district; 37,800 Han and 33,300 Tibetans lived in work unit housing; and 8,000 Tibetans lived in nearby peri-urban villages. The Han constituted roughly 38% of the official urban population (Ma 822). Early Han migrant entrepreneurs, who began to arrive in Lhasa in the late 1980s, tended to live with their relatives in government work units. These patterns led demographer Ma Rong to remark on the fact that Han and Tibetans lived in separate spatial zones with little chance to come into contact with each other, leading to mutual lack of knowledge and misunderstandings (Ma 822, 835). As a foil to what he saw as Lhasa's problematic ethnic spatial separation, Ma pointed to Inner Mongolia, where "the relationship between Mongolians and Han . . . is reported to be generally good, they make friends from another group, live in the same . . . neighborhood, and have a certain level of intermarriage" (Ma 834), though by then the Han population of Inner Mongolia was already over 80%.

The unmentioned backdrop to the 1988 study that produced these findings was the one and only period since 1959 of open Tibetan antagonism toward Chinese in Lhasa. It began on September 27, 1987, when twenty-one monks and five lay people were arrested and imprisoned after they walked around the Barkor carrying a homemade Tibetan flag and shouting "Tibetan independence." Four days later, several thousand Tibetans besieged the Barkor police station after arrests and public beatings following another small protest; in response, police opened fire into the crowd. Over the next three years, there were three major independence demonstrations and dozens of smaller ones, all peaceful. They resulted in nearly a hundred deaths from police gunfire, some three thousand arrests followed by imprisonment and torture, and the imposition of martial law in Lhasa for more than a year (Schwartz; Barnett, untitled essay).

The target of the protests were apparatuses of the military and state, as when protestors set fire to the Barkor police station in 1987 in an effort to free those arrested inside. The only exceptions seem to have been during a riot in March 1988 when a Chinese restaurant and pharmacy were burned down; and on March 6 the following year, when Tibetans threw rocks at passing Han cyclists, forcing them to dismount and confiscating their bicycles. In both cases, some Tibetan protesters were concerned about drawing a distinction between their anger at the state from ethnic animosity. In the first case, a debate among protestors, essentially about the Buddhist principle of compassion and the equal moral status of all human beings, preceded the burning of the restaurant. According to a monk who was at the scene:

> The Chinese were chasing Tibetan demonstrators. The old people couldn't run away. They were beating them with the intention of killing them. So the Tibetans said, now we must chase away all the Chinese. Then there were two groups of opinion. One group said we should not fight all the Chinese since they are human beings also. The other group said that as long as they are Chinese we must struggle against them. At that time they burned down a Chinese restaurant and pharmacy (in Schwartz 83).

In the second case, individual Tibetans in the crowd protected the Chinese who had their bicycles taken, and helped them to safety (Schwartz 159).

In both cases, an ethic of *nyingjé*, or compassion for the Han as humans, as well as a rigorous distinction between resentment of the apparatuses of the state, and the individual migrants who unwittingly carry out state practice, can be seen as a form of subaltern cosmopolitanism, an ethic of living together with other humans in a way that runs counter to a clash of civilizations, but also is not incompatible with postcolonial nationalism. Buddhist compassion has, as indicated earlier, not always stopped those who profess it from engaging in violence, including in the name of Buddhism itself. However, what makes the debate (and ultimate resolution) over how to handle individual Chinese during the nationalist protests subaltern cosmopolitanism is precisely the invocation of religious principles, violently suppressed during the Cultural Revolution and still tightly controlled by the state, to argue the case for compassion. Insofar as religion has been both a form of resistance and a cause for which other acts of resistance to the state are undertaken, the forbearance shown toward individual Chinese is itself a form of resistance and thus a form of *subaltern* cosmopolitanism, one that shames and exposes the established order, while also transgressing it. This ethic of compassion has become increasingly prominent in the Fourteenth Dalai Lama's public statements about the need to separate actions of the government from those of individual Chinese. It is doubly ironic that such statements might encourage Tibetans in Lhasa to take such a stance even more seriously, as the Dalai Lama continues to be thoroughly denounced by the Chinese Party-state, which has promised to engage in a "fight to the death struggle" against him.

After the protests, the state responded with a two-pronged strategy, tightening political control while also implementing a rapid program of marketization. After 1990, security operations in Lhasa increased the use of surveillance technologies and informers, and expanded the role of the State Security Bureau (Barnett, untitled essay 187). Guaranteed prison terms for those caught advocating independence or otherwise practicing activities labeled "splittist," has served as an effective deterrent to other would-be protestors since the early 1990s. At the same time, Deng Xiao Ping's landmark 1992 Southern tour, combined with the declaration of Lhasa as a special economic zone, and the influx of migrants, dramatically altered Lhasa's ethnic landscape.[11] The TAR relaxed and simplified the acquisition of business licenses, relaxed intraprovincial border controls, and ordered government buildings to convert the ground floor of any property on main roads into spaces that could be rented out as shops (Barnett, *Lhasa*). Within one year, the number of individually run enterprises in Lhasa increased by 56%. A large number of Han migrants began to arrive in Lhasa, often through connections to cadres and soldiers.

By opening the way for a greatly increased presence of Chinese migrants, the declaration of Lhasa as a special economic zone has helped to consolidate state control. At the same time, marketization and a discourse championing free flows of people and goods has been accompanied by a new set of often extralegal rules that by default only apply to local residents. Indeed, they tend to be invisible to the migrants both because they are unwritten and because they are particular to Tibetan Buddhism as practiced by ethnic Tibetans. These new rules include a complete ban on display of photos of the Dalai Lama, and a prohibition against religious practice not just by Party members, but by all government employees (including teachers), their families, and students of all ages. Monks and nuns are banned from entering official spaces in Lhasa, including not only government offices but also the Tibet University campus (Barnett, "Modernity"). These rules, which violate both the Chinese constitution and the principles of autonomy, constitute a form of variegated sovereignty, but one in which migrants have more, not fewer, rights than locals.

As these changes took place, Lhasa continued to grow; by 2000, the urbanized area was reported at fifty-three square kilometers, with a population of roughly 170,000—tiny by world standards but vastly out of proportion to the rest of the TAR. Of the metropolitan population, 63% are reported as Tibetan, 34.3% as Han, and the remaining 2.7% mostly Hui (Yeh and Henderson). However, many outside observers have estimated that non-Tibetans account for 50–70% of the urban population (Erickson; Tibet Information Network; Hao). Sichuanese migrants I interviewed scoffed at the official statistics, telling me I should "use [my] own eyes and look around." As one put it, "Don't you know that *our* Lhasa is called 'little Sichuan'?" "Little Sichuan" is a common, affectionate name for Lhasa among Han migrants, evoking their radically different sense of place and imagination of the city than that of Tibetan residents.

At the same time as Han migration was taking off and new restrictions were being imposed on religious practices, the government also sought to mollify the Tibetan elite by dramatically increasing cadres' incomes—bringing urban salaries in the TAR to almost twice the national average, even while rural areas sank deeper into poverty. Altogether, about one half of the families of Lhasa's old residents are now employed by the government, and have become members of this newly enriched cadre class, while the rest are becoming the urban poor (Barnett, *Lhasa*). Han migrants continue to rent rooms in work units, but increasingly, they also rent living space in the courtyards of the spacious new homes of the Tibetan elite. Although the Tibetan residents of the Barkor and the Tibetan urban poor, in their cramped government apartments, may still live in rather separate spaces from the new Han migrants, it is now virtually impossible to conduct any economic transactions in Lhasa without interacting with the Han. The desired situation in Lhasa implied by Ma—in which the Han and Tibetan live intermixed with each other—has been achieved, through a set of administrative and discursive practices that are designed to stamp out any traces of Tibetan nationalism.

INTERPRETING HAN-TIBETAN RELATIONS IN LHASA

As a tool of coercive amity, *minzu tuanjie* structures the everyday processes through which people quietly make their lives in Lhasa. Han, Tibetan, Hui, and others who encounter each other on a daily basis at the office, school, market, on public transportation, and in stores, may not consciously think about *minzu tuanjie* as they interact, but their interactions are nevertheless shaped by it. Ignoring either the state's role in regulating interethnic relations or the deep entanglements of Han and Chinese nationalism leads to interpretations of Han-Tibetan relations that unintentionally mirror those of the state. I illustrate this through a brief examination of the narratives ordinary Han migrants offer about their relations with Tibetans and about the protests of 1987–1989.

Mr. Chen was one of the very first Han vegetable farmers in Lhasa. He was sent to Lhasa in January 1986 by an agreement between the Lhasa municipal government and the Shuangliu county government in Sichuan. At the time, urban neighborhoods still had collective farmland on the edges of the city; Chen subleased farmland first from an urban neighborhood and then in a peri-urban village. He recalled 1986–1987 as being a time of "very bad Tibetan-Han relations" compared to now, which he described as "no problem, no problem at all." When asked to elaborate on the 1987 problems, however, he gave as examples only the fact that the local police station removed the sign outside of its gate (out of fear of retaliation by Tibetans), and that the (Han) policemen were afraid to leave their office in uniforms. He reported that he himself spent some sleepless nights wanting to go home, but worrying that he could not do so because he had accrued too many debts to come to Lhasa. He avoided selling his vegetables in his Barkor during this period.

As for his relationship with the Tibetan villagers, however, "everything was fine." He portrayed a situation of cooperation, without papering over occasional, resolvable conflicts. Water scarcity led to a fistfight with a local Tibetan when he first arrived. Villagers were unhappy about his irrigation, and cut off his water supply. After he argued with them, one man stomped on his vegetables, leading to "lots of pushing and shoving." To resolve the conflict, he called upon the (Tibetan) village leader, who he described as "the type of person who can tell right from wrong" and who was very supportive of Mr. Chen. The leader talked to the other Tibetans, and the problem did not recur. Chen and other migrants like him told numerous stories of this sort: stories in which there is some Han-Tibetan conflict, but that is mild and can be easily resolved through a process of dialogue and cooperation.

Like some other rural Han migrants, Chen is relatively charitable in his assessment of local Tibetans, referring to them as "jovial" and "decent people." This assessment contrasts with the more typical view of Tibetans as being of "low quality" compared to local residents (Yeh, "Tropes of Indolence"). In recounting their experience, he and other vegetable-growing migrants stressed that their conflicts were minor and resolvable, and that the Tibetans are "people just like us; if you are good to someone, they are good to you too."[12] Many also claim that Tibetans "have affection toward us" and that "if you don't give them any trouble, the Tibetan people are very good to us." There are many examples of everyday cooperation and interaction; after harvest, Tibetans frequently help Han farmers collect vegetables, and in return take the unwanted stalks and leaves home for their livestock. Han migrants sometimes give some of their vegetables to Tibetan villagers, and more than one migrant recounted having trouble peddling heavy vegetables to market, and being grateful for a Tibetan who stopped on the street to help push their cart.

There is much evidence, then, of quotidian practices in which Han and Tibetan residents in Lhasa, while often living quite parallel and separate lives, also practice acts of reciprocity and sharing, seeing each other first and foremost as "people just like us." And yet Chen's views of himself and the Tibetans with whom he deals are structured by *minzu tuanjie*. In particular, his explanation of the 1987–1989 demonstrations strongly echoes the official narrative of these events. It was, he explained to me, the result of "a very small group of people" agitating for independence. Further, he said, part of the "problem" with the atmosphere of Han-Tibetan relations at the time, which has now been "fixed" was that "back then, all the Tibetans displayed Dalai Lama photographs" (now banned). Though he is in general no great admirer of the government, complaining about corrupt officials and taxes, he portrayed the government's work in Lhasa in the most conciliatory of lights:

... the Central Government tried very hard to use methods of unity to deal with the rioters. The Central Government strictly forbade the use of force against the rioters; instead, 3000 People's Armed Police and People's Liberation Army soldiers linked arms and encircled the rioters, isolating the few from the rest of the city, but without opening fire.

This account, diverging dramatically from the well-documented state-sanctioned violence toward the Tibetan protestors, fits well within the conventions of *minzu tuanjie* in Lhasa today, according to which the Han and Tibetans get along because the Han are like a protective elder sibling to the Tibetans. The protests can only be understood as the work of a few "splittists," blindly following the Dalai Lama, himself a dupe of foreign meddlers into China's sovereignty.

These accounts suggest that the imperatives of *minzu tuanjie* shape Han and Tibetan subjectivity and interactions with each other. For Tibetans, to do anything other than live peacefully together with the new Han migrants is to invite accusations of *minzu fenlie*. Though Tibetans and Chinese also lived peacefully together for centuries in Lhasa before 1950, the terms of ethnic interaction have fundamentally changed. Incorporation into the PRC introduced *minzu* not only as a conceptual category but also as an administrative one, which fosters certain kinds of interaction while discouraging others. Furthermore, the economic reforms enacted in the early 1990s, made in the name of economic liberalization but also implemented to address the protests of the 1980s, introduced Han migration on a large scale. These reforms put an end to hopes for a Tibetan-centered development by invoking the logic of the market; the most efficient seller of labor, services, and commodities would now be the winner, and the unlevel playing field for Han and Tibetans ignored. While the uneventful everyday interactions between Tibetans and Han in Lhasa that results thus cannot meaningfully be said to be a product of cosmopolitanism, the debates that took place during the nationalist protests of the late 1980s, and the continuing care with which most Tibetans in Lhasa separate their anxiety and anger about Han migration from the migrants themselves as human beings, can be understood as a form of subaltern cosmopolitanism rooted in both religious principles and the politicization of religion by the state.

TIBETANS AND MUSLIMS IN LHASA

Though *minzu tuanjie* refers to the unity of all nationalities in China, it has a special reference to the majority Han and their relationship with minorities, because of the strong association of the Han (*hua*) with the Chinese state through the notion of the Chinese (*Zhonghua*) *minzu* (Bulag). It has different effects on interethnic relationships among minorities, including between the Hui and Tibetans. In this last section, I examine the different trajectories of the Kashmiri and Chinese Muslim communities of Lhasa after 1951, and finally the implications of state ethnic policy for Tibetan-Hui relations today.

The Divergent Paths of Kashmiri and Chinese Muslims

In March 1959, the committee of Kashmiri Muslims asked the Indian Consulate to aid the entire community in migrating to India. The Chinese government at first refused, but the Indian government intervened and the families became the focus of a diplomatic dispute between India and China (Siddiqui). The result was that late in the year, 192 families—almost all of the Barkor Khache in Lhasa at the time—migrated to India and Nepal, and some farther on to the Middle East.[13] In 1962, some of the poorest families of the Khache community returned to Lhasa, and in 2004 there were fifty-two Kashmiri Muslim families living there. The Barkor Khache today express a deep sense of connectedness to Lhasa. Several community members spoke to me proudly about their long history in Lhasa (claiming that they had been there for five hundred years). Several also complained that "these days it's very hard to find real Lhasa Tibetans"—alluding to the influx of Han, Hui, and Tibetans from the eastern areas of Kham and Amdo into the city. "In the past," they bemoaned, "the Lhasa Tibetans knew that we are good people and respected us" but "now the Khampas and villagers don't know any better and so treat us Khache poorly."

The trajectory of the Hebalin Muslims has been very different. From 1951 to 1959, many became cadres, recruited to teach Tibetan to Chinese soldiers. Nevertheless, many members of the community, including those who had been cadres, asked for permission to leave in 1959 along with the Barkor Khache. However, as Siddiqui writes, the government "took revenge on those Muslims of Chinese origin . . . They were offered a choice by the Chinese—if they sold their properties to the Chinese, they would be allowed to go to any Muslim country. Seeing this as a way of saving their religion and faith, they sold their properties, but then were not allowed to leave the country . . . the Chinese government declared a social boycott of these Chinese Muslims—nobody was allowed to sell them food" (79–81). Many pulled out of their work units and were subsequently imprisoned for years.

Thupden Khatsun (296–301) offers a more detailed but somewhat less sympathetic account, according to which the "Hui troubles" began in 1961 when the Hebalin Muslims organized a scheme to leave the country as the Kashmiri Muslims had done. They left their jobs and moved in protest to their cemetery area in the Dogbde valley. Because they believed they would soon to be allowed to leave, they declined the grain and oil rations that were being distributed at the time. The government sent other Hui cadres to plead with them to stop protesting and trying to leave. However, the Muslims did not listen, instead telling the cadre messengers that they were "rotten inside" and beat them up. This led to the imprisonment of their leaders and severe hardship for the others, as they had no grain or oil rations. To survive, they were forced to buy grain and oil secretly at extraordinarily high prices. With no income, many were forced to send their children to Lhasa to beg.

The New Hui Arrivals

Since the mid-1980s, Lhasa's Muslim population has been dominated not by members of the former Hebalin and Barkor communities, but instead by a rapid influx of newly arrived Hui traders, who engage in a whole spectrum of economic activities, including running restaurants, driving rickshaws, butchering, and currency exchange. In 1991 there were officially three thousand Hui residents in Lhasa (Moevus) but Gladney suggests that even in 1985 there were some twenty thousand to thirty thousand Hui traders in Lhasa. Whatever the actual numbers, they have increased significantly since 1992. The newly arrived Hui are all the more visible given their heavy presence in services and trade.[14] Many have settled in Hebalin near the *Qing Zhen Si* mosque used for hundreds of years by the Hebalin Khache.

Gladney remarked that "the local 'Tibetan Hui' did not interact with [the new Hui traders], whom they regarded with suspicion, and preferred to marry their children to other Tibetans instead of to their co-religionists from outside Tibet" (34). My interviews and observations confirm both their preference for identifying with Tibetans over the new Hui, and the tension between the Hebalin Khache and the new arrivals. Despite sharing both ethnicity and religion, there is a significant difference between the two groups' identities, and the way they are perceived by Tibetan residents. The middle-aged brother and sister of the Zhang family, former Hebalin vegetable cultivators, were instructive in this regard. The siblings had retained their Chinese last names, and unlike some of the other families, could have passed as new Hui migrants. The sister wore a headscarf, and decorated their home with wall hangings depicting Mecca. However, they referred to themselves again and again as "we Tibetans," claiming a Tibetan identity that coexisted with, and was not subordinate to, their Khache identity. Another Hebalin Khache, a sixty-seven-year-old former vegetable cultivator, cadre, and prisoner, punctuated his life story with frequent assertions that he and his family were and are "real Tibetans." In the "old society," he said, he always wore a *chupa* (Tibetan robe). Today, his family eats Tibetan food and, he said, the only thing that distinguished them from other Tibetans was their religion. Otherwise, he stressed, he and his family were "the same as real Tibetans."

These assessments are reflected in the everyday talk of Tibetan Buddhists as well. In the course of other conversations, I frequently heard offhand comments such as those of an elderly Tibetan woman who said: "The

Hui are really bad. They do things that are much worse than the Han; they do all of the things that have *dikpa* [sin]. They're not like the old Khache at all. They didn't eat pork, and they wore head coverings, but otherwise, they're exactly the same as Tibetans. They eat tsampa and drink butter tea and speak Tibetan, and only speak Chinese now because they have to learn it in school." This attitude in turn affects the outlook of the remaining old Muslim communities in Lhasa. One complained, "These days the Hui from Xining [Qinghai] do bad things and give Muslims a bad reputation."

Until the expansion of the *Qing Zhen Si* mosque, there was considerable tension between the two groups of Chinese Muslims over use of the overcrowded space. In 2002, the mosque was significantly enlarged, with a prayer hall that can accommodate two thousand people. This resolved the conflict between the older Hebalin community and the newly arrived Hui, but has become the source of significant disgruntlement among Tibetans. Only 200 meters from the Jokhang temple, the mosque is also higher than it (though both buildings are two stories). Historically, the mosque was only allowed to be one floor high because, one Tibetan explained to me, "there is a saying that, 'The shoulder can't be higher than the head.'" However, this disgruntlement has not led to public protest; as a Tibetan cadre put it, "Of course Tibetans don't like it—but the mosque expansion was approved by the government's Religion Bureau. So what can we do? It would be a *minzu* problem." Here, then, *minzu tuanjie* was perceived as a threat to anyone who might protest the mosque, which was approved by the state. However, the issue for most Tibetans was what they saw as the state's purposeful belittling of Tibetan Buddhism, which came simultaneously with a battery of other new regulations restricting religious practice.

There have, however, been other types of conflicts between the newly arrived Hui and Tibetans. In 1995, an incident occurred in which Tibetans claimed that they had been served human flesh in a Hui restaurant. They subsequently smashed the restaurant's windows and broke its furniture. In retaliation, the owners threw bricks at the windows of nearby Tibetan restaurants. Police and People's Armed Police arrived quickly on the scene in large numbers, and there does not appear to have been extensive damage.[15] Though no other incidents of Hui-Tibetan violence or destruction of property have been reported in Lhasa, Tibetans there frequently complain about the Hui. Their complaints often take the form of allegations that "just recently" someone eating at a Hui restaurant "found a finger in their food" or found that bathwater was used for cooking. Quite a few Tibetan Lhasa residents refuse to patronize Hui restaurants, a stance unheard of for Chinese restaurants or for the services Chinese Muslim store owners before the 1950s.

This form of Tibetan-Hui antagonism is found across the Tibetan Plateau. However, as Fischer notes, the history of Muslim-Tibetan interactions is rather different in the east, particularly in Amdo, where military campaigns and the harsh rule of the Muslim Chinese warlord Ma Bufang in the Nationalist period killed thousands of Tibetans. In recent years, rural Amdo has been the site of a number of Tibetan boycotts of Hui restaurants. In Golog, a 2003 clash between Tibetans and Hui led to the stabbing of a Tibetan, rioting, and destruction of Hui-owned property. This was followed by the poisoning of three Tibetans in a restaurant in 2004, leading to a Tibetan boycott of Hui business. Within a year, the number of Hui restaurants in the entire prefecture reportedly fell from seventy to twenty (Fischer).[16] The small nomadic township of Thangkor in Zorge, Sichuan, also recently organized a successful boycott leading to the closure of all Hui-owned restaurants. Such boycotts have not, however, been conducted in Lhasa.

Fischer argues that the conflictual Tibetan-Hui relationships in the east are more representative than the harmonious relationships between Muslims and Tibetan Buddhists in pre-1950s Lhasa, which he argues are of little importance. However, I argue that thinking about Lhasa's exceptionalism in this regard can be quite suggestive and important, pointing as it does both to the possibility of cosmopolitanism (and its relationship to a city), and to the power of the sedimented histories of place. Memories of the Hui in Amdo are those of the depredations of the Ma Bufang years, whereas among Lhasa's Tibetans, the magnanimity of the Fifth Dalai Lama in granting land to the Khache community still plays a role in how Tibetans imagine themselves, and thus how they interact with others.

When I have asked Tibetans in Lhasa and elsewhere to look beyond purported incidents of provocation to underlying reasons why Tibetan-Hui relationships seem more strained than Tibetan-Han relationships, they often responded, "It's a clash of religions. Buddhism and Islam aren't compatible." Yet, a history of amicable living together in Lhasa before the administration of *minzu tuanjie* makes this an unsatisfying explanation. Instead, what seems to be at stake in contemporary Tibetan-Hui antagonism across most Tibetan areas of China is the perception that the Hui have taken jobs away from Tibetans, contributing to the latter's economic marginalization since economic reform. Indeed, Gladney has shown that Hui across China have since economic reform prospered at an astounding rate through small private businesses and industry, often far surpassing their Han neighbors. While the Hui, the Han—and indeed, the Tibetans—argue that the Hui predisposition toward trade is an inherent ethnic feature, a historical analysis shows instead that "it was state policy that encouraged and stimulated entrepreneurialism among the Hui, while at the same time restricting it as still antisocialist among the Han" (Gladney 284). Chinese minzu discourse specifically identified "entrepreneurialism" as a defining nationality trait of the Hui; this in turn created preferential policies to further support their entrepreneurialism.

Thus, Gladney argues, government policy encouraged ethnic entrepreneurialism among the Hui, while encouraging much more ambivalence toward capitalism and economic prosperity among the Han. This ambivalence toward entrepreneurialism that Gladney finds in the Han is even more pronounced among Tibetans (Yeh, "Tropes of Indolence"), who have been defined as an even less entrepreneurial group by the state, despite the long history of trade in Lhasa. Most Tibetans in Lhasa who are wealthy today are so because of their relationship vis-à-vis the state, not their independent business ventures. State minzu discourse has preslotted Tibetans and Hui into opposing discursive categories, making it conceptually safe to invoke economic antagonism between the two groups, despite the fact that by sheer number it is Han migrants who pose the much greater threat to Tibetan livelihoods.

Finally, one other important factor distinguishes Han-Tibetan from Hui-Tibetan relationships. The identification of the Han with the Chinese state through the conflation of Han and Chinese nationalisms means that overt discontent against Han presence is politically much riskier than public displays of anger at the Hui. The latter is treated as a pesky problem between two minorities, both of whom need to mature and learn the lessons of national unity through the guidance of the big-sibling Han, but is not interpreted as a threat to state security. The former, on the other hand, is immediately translated into an attempt to split the motherland. Thus, public frustration over the presence of the Hui can be a politically relatively benign surrogate toward which the state indirectly funnels Tibetans.

CONCLUSION

The peaceful coexistence of peoples of different cultures, religions, and ethnic groups has characterized Lhasa from at least the seventeenth century to the present. The "clash of civilizations" is far from inevitable. However, in Lhasa, the terms through which everyday practices of living together have been structured have changed dramatically, and not all can be considered cosmopolitanism.

Before the 1950s, the Barkor and Hebalin Muslim were outside of the Tibetan social hierarchy and governed through a different set of rules and institutions than other residents. Though they practiced their own religions and lived in distinct neighborhoods, they also adopted local dress and language, while also retaining their own languages. The Barkor Muslims were treated as "foreigners," but because Tibet was not a modern nation-state, this had rather different implications than it would now. Calhoun writes that cosmopolitan sensibilities seemed to have thrived, without explicit effort, in market cities, imperial capitals, and court society such as those of Ottoman Istanbul and old regime Paris "partly because in neither were members of different cultures and communities invited to organize government together" (111). In pre-1950s Lhasa, Chinese and Kashmiri Muslims had their autonomy within their communities, but no role in the governance of Lhasa as a whole.

Minzu tuanjie promised to rectify this by officially making Tibetans, Han, and Hui equally valued citizens of the PRC as a multinational state—whether or not they wanted to be, as shown by the case of the Hebalin Muslims' failed attempt to leave in 1959. This has created very different grounds for multiethnic living today. The script of *minzu tuanjie*, while ostensibly liberating in its provision that Tibetans, as minorities, have a role in the government, puts Tibetan officials in the unenviable position of always having to prove their loyalty to Chinese nationalism by showing, for example, that they unreservedly welcome Han brothers and sisters to come to Lhasa, for Lhasa belongs to China, and not just to Tibet.

Unlike the ancestors of residents of the Barkor, Hebalin, and Lubu neighborhoods, who migrated to Lhasa and settled down for good, the vast majority of today's Han and Hui living in Lhasa are short-term migrants, who stay for several years or a decade, but have no intention of settling permanently. Despite this, the demotion of Lhasa from political center of the Tibetan world to capital only of the TAR, a geopolitically strategic but economically trivial provincial-level unit of the PRC, has meant that today it is Tibetans who learn to speak Chinese, not the other way around; young Tibetans in Lhasa are increasingly unable to read and write Tibetan, or to speak it without code-switching. A number of terms exist to describe this new hybridity among residents of Lhasa, of which the most popular is *ramalug,* "neither goat nor sheep." This hybridity is the subject of black humor, not uncritical celebration; hybridity is not the foundation of subaltern cosmopolitanism such as it exists in Lhasa.

With the deepening of marketization efforts, the availability of commodities and the delivery of a consumptive lifestyle to a privileged stratum of Tibetan citizens in Lhasa has been increasingly used as a justification for Tibet's inclusion in the PRC. Ironically though, before 1950, Lhasa's shops were already overflowing with goods from across the world. Similarly, under *minzu tuanjie,* the peaceful living together of all of Lhasa's different ethnic groups is said to be proof of the rightness of rule. But this too is no great leap forward, as peaceful coexistence was the norm half a century ago. Indeed we can argue, without romanticizing pre-1950s Lhasa, that the city has undergone a process of decosmopolitanization. An ethic of living together, only partially deliberate, was dislodged by the incorporation of Tibet into the PRC, which introduced both minzu as a way of governing ethnic life and a large Han presence in Lhasa, the questioning of which is not tolerated.

Ironically, the imperatives of coercive amity can also unintentionally heighten ethnic sensitivities, creating boundaries even as it purports to erase them. Ordinary conflicts that have no ethnic motivation are subject to being defined by fiat as ethnic problems, if both Han and Tibetans are involved. However, Han-Tibetan ethnic violence is not, in fact, bubbling up beneath the surface, submerged only by state violence and ready to erupt at any time. There are cross-ethnic friendships, particularly in the

80 Emily T. Yeh

case of government workplaces, and over the past two decades all Tibetan lives in Lhasa have become increasingly economically intertwined with those of Han migrants. Nevertheless, peaceful interethnic coexistence and interaction in Lhasa today is grounded on a hegemonic discursive practice of *minzu tuanjie*, which is both premised upon and seeks to continually impose an always already existing state of unity. Although there is much evidence of long histories of cultural and material exchange and shared religious traditions between Han and Tibetans, their marshaling to bolster the legitimacy of the state's claims to the contemporary political status quo is not in the spirit of cosmopolitanism. The ethical ideals and practices of living together that define cosmopolitanism need to be disentangled from neoliberal discourses on the one hand, and state-sponsored official nationalism (masquerading as unity) on the other. Whereas a prenationalist cosmopolitanism grounded in both trade and religion characterized Lhasa as a city before 1950, it no longer does today.

At the same time, though, there is a subtler subaltern cosmopolitanism at work. It is grounded in religion through multiple valences, calling upon principles that have long been interpreted as Buddhist, as well as new meanings for Tibetan Buddhism in China forged in the present political moment. Drawing on the principle of compassion, it suggests that all humans should be treated as equal. At the same time, the very fact of drawing

Photo 3.3 "National culture belongs to the world," Lhasa, People's Republic of China. Photo by Emily T. Yeh.

on Tibetan Buddhism, and especially any principled association with the Dalai Lama and his public statements about compassion, becomes itself an act of resistance. This form of subaltern cosmopolitanism is opposed to official nationalism but not to postcolonial nationalisms. Its existence in Lhasa today, together with historical evidence of a long earlier period of multiethnic and multicultural conviviality, shows the promise of being archivally cosmopolitan, of looking across world history and geography beyond Kant for arguments against both primordial ethnic conflict and theories that cosmopolitanism belongs only to the Western elite.

EPILOGUE

This chapter was completed before March 2008, when antigovernment protests erupted in more than forty sites across Tibetan areas of the PRC, calling for religious freedom, human rights, and a return of the Dalai Lama, often through the idiom of independence and the Tibetan national flag. The protests were unprecedented both in their geographical scope and in the broad spectrum of participants, including not only monks and nuns, but also nomads and farmers, cadres and university students. They began in commemoration of the March 10, 1959 uprising and as a specific reaction against intensified "patriotic education" campaigns in which monks are required to denounce the Dalai Lama.

After four days of peaceful protests came a day marked by unprecedented Tibetan violence in Lhasa toward Han and Hui property and persons. This turn to violence was unexpected and shocking to most Tibetans; the Dalai Lama threatened to step down as Tibetans' political leader if it continued. The Chinese media quickly took control of all information, kicking out foreigners and restricting phone and Internet service. Thousands of heavily armed paramilitary troops, including elite combat units, were quickly deployed to Lhasa, where according to currently available accounts, Tibetans have been subject to arrests, intense surveillance, house-to-house searches, and restrictions on movement.

After a deliberate news blackout, the Chinese media repeatedly broadcast selected images of Tibetan violence in Lhasa against Han and Hui, while not reporting dozens of peaceful protests or the violent state responses, including the firing of live ammunition at unarmed demonstrators, in Lhasa and elsewhere. The fact that there was ethnically marked violence in the first place can be seen as a tragic victory for a biopolitical logic of sovereignty, in which the targets of anger were successfully displaced from symbols of state power onto the bodies of the Han and Hui. Even more tragic is the way in which state media has successfully whipped up Han nationalism against Tibetans, calling forth old stereotypes of Tibetans as lazy, barbaric, and ungrateful, and justifying discrimination anew. Against reason and evidence, the state has rejected the Dalai Lama's calls for negotiations in the context of meaningful autonomy, and blamed all acts of violence on the Dalai Lama, calling him a jackal in monk's robes.

As of this writing it is too early to know the details of what has happened or the shape of things to come. One thing does, however, seem unfortunately clear from official reactions to date. In demonizing the Dalai Lama and his call for what is effectively Buddhist cosmopolitanism, through a targeted crackdown of bodies marked as Tibetan, and by encouraging its Han citizens to be angry at "ungrateful" Tibetans, the state reinforces the coercive nature of amity, fosters a hardening of ethnic boundaries, and calls into being a terrain more conducive to future interethnic violence.

—March 23, 2008

ACKNOWLEDGMENTS

My thanks to all of the participants of the Workshop on Communities in Interaction for convivial exchange, and to Aihwa Ong and Shail Mayaram for detailed comments on an earlier draft. The fieldwork on which this paper is based was made possible through funding from the Ford Foundation, Social Science Research Council, and the John D. and Catherine T. MacArthur Foundation Research and Writing Grant.

NOTES

1. Bön is the conventional name for the pre-Buddhist religion of Tibet. However, many scholars argue that in its contemporary, institutional form, Bön is better thought of as a variant of Buddhism that began to take shape in the tenth century. Other autochthonous beliefs, such as cults of local protector deities associated with particular mountains and lakes, have been absorbed by both Buddhist and later Bön traditions (Kapstein).
2. Until the mid-twentieth century, the city of Lhasa was defined by three nested ritual circumambulation circuits, centered on the Jokhang: the Nangkor, "inner circuit" within the Jokhang; the Barkor; and the Lingkor, the outer path encircling the old city and the Potala Palace.
3. Known as Singpa Khache, they were descendants of prisoners taken during the Dogra wars (Cabezón 15)
4. The *Kazara,* as descendants of mixed Nepali-Tibetan marriage are known, are Nepalese citizens but have the right to live in Lhasa, where some own the most popular tourist hotels today. In 2003, there were 338 official Nepali residents of the TAR (Turin and Schneiderman, n.d.); their children may attend either local Chinese schools or the Nepalese government-sponsored Gorkha Primary School. Kazara today often speak Newari, Nepali, Tibetan, and Chinese.
5. Cabezón (17) was told a very similar story, but with slightly different numbers: "the Fifth Dalai Lama . . . is said to have given official patronage to the fourteen elders and thirty youths . . ."
6. According to another version, when the Khache arrived, they first settled in a place just southwest of the Potala but were moved given concern that they

were using a site inside the Lingkor to bury their dead and butcher livestock. This story, however, is quite different from the ones recorded by Cabezón and by Gaborieau as well as those I was told in Lhasa, all of which emphasize that it was the Kashmiris who had trouble with their cemetery, and the Dalai Lama's proactive role in granting them new space. The area today is site of a mosque and cemetery, as well as a community gathering area.
7. What is often interpreted as Tibetan Buddhist ideals in the West today is necessarily quite different, especially in its universalism and lack of specific ritual elements, from what Tibetans in specific times and places believed and practiced. My argument is thus not about a universal Buddhism but rather about the ways in which locally grounded interpretations of what it means to be a proper Buddhist were mobilized in a possibly cosmopolitan way.
8. http://zt.tibet.cn/tibetzt/lasa/index.htm.
9. Here she used the term *rgyanag,* which nowadays refers to the Han-dominated, eastern areas of the PRC.
10. See for example *Lhasa, Tibet: A Bright Pearl on Snowland.* Beijing: China Tourism Press, 2002.
11. The declaration of Lhasa as a Special Economic Zone serves a very different function from similar zones in China's coastal regions. The latter are, according to Ong, neoliberal exceptions to socialist rule in China, and examples of technologies "of a form of market-driven rationality that demarcates spaces . . . in order to capitalize on specific locational advantages of economic flows, activities, and linkages"(103). The zoning of Lhasa, however, was designed not to take advantage of flows, but to encourage them to begin, to overcome what the central government claims is a deficit in development compared to coastal China because "Tibet had very little to start with in terms of social development, and because of its high-altitude oxygen deficiency and other harsh natural conditions" (State Council). Rather than global economic competitiveness driving a move to variegated sovereignty, the declaration of Lhasa as a special economic zone uses neoliberal discourse to consolidate state control.
12. This is not universally true, of course. Some Han migrants I interviewed describe the Tibetans as being "barbaric" and "low quality."
13. According to Naik, "One day the Chinese commanded that all the Tibetan Muslims of Kashmiri origin should stand in line. There they were warned that they would be shot if they were heard repeating any words indicating their desire to leave Lhasa." However, the Indian government intervened, arguing that the Tibetan government had always treated the Kashmiris as foreigners, exempting them from compulsory levies and local courts.
14. According to the 2000 census, 7.7% of those involved in "wholesale and retail trade, catering services" were neither Tibetan nor Han (and thus presumably Hui).
15. TIN News Update, 7 Feb. 1995.
16. Also Sue Costello, personal communication.

WORKS CITED

Appiah, Anthony. "Cosmopolitan Patriots." *Cosmopolitics: Thinking and Feeling Beyond the Nation.* Ed. Pheng Cheah and Bruce Robbins. Minneapolis: U of Minnesota P, 1998. 91–116.
Barnett, Robert. Untitled essay. *The Tibetans: A Struggle to Survive.* Ed. Steve Lehman. New York: Umbrage, 1998. 178–96.

———. *Lhasa: Streets with Memories*. New York: Columbia UP, 2006.
———. "Modernity, Religion and Urban Space in Contemporary Lhasa." Association of American Studies meeting, San Francisco, 6–9 April 2006.
Bhabha, Homi. "Unsatisfied: Notes on Vernacular Cosmopolitanism." *Postcolonial Discourses: An Anthology*. Ed. Gregory Castle. Oxford: Blackwell, 2001. 38–52.
Bielefeldt, Carl. "Practice." *Critical Terms for the Study of Buddhism*. Ed. Donald Lopez. Chicago: U of Chicago P, 2005. 229–44.
Blondeau, Anne-Marie, and Yonten Gyatso. "Lhasa, Legend and History." *Lhasa in the Seventeenth Century: The Capital of the Dalai Lamas*. Ed. Francoise Pommaret. Boston: Brill, 2003. 15–38.
Boulnois, Luce. "Gold, Wool and Musk: Trade in Lhasa in the Seventeenth Century." *Lhasa in the Seventeenth Century: The Capital of the Dalai Lamas*. Ed. Francoise Pommaret. Boston: Brill, 2003. 133–56.
Bue, Erberto F. "Scholars, Artists and Feasts." *Lhasa in the Seventeenth Century: The Capital of the Dalai Lamas*. Ed. Francoise Pommaret. Boston: Brill, 2003, 179–98.
Bulag, Uradyn. *The Mongols at China's Edge: History and the Politics of National Unity*. Boulder: Rowman, 2002.
Cabezón, José. "Islam in the Tibetan Cultural Sphere." *Islam in Tibet—Tibetan Caravans*. Ed. Gray Henry. Louisville: Fons Vitae, 1997. 15–54.
Calhoun, Craig. "The Class Consciousness of Frequent Travellers: Towards a Critique of Actually Existing Cosmopolitanism." *Debating Cosmopolitics*. Ed. Daniele Archibugi. London: Verso, 2003. 86–116.
Cheah, Pheng. "Given Culture: Rethinking Cosmopolitical Freedom in Transnationalism." *Cosmopolitics: Thinking and Feeling Beyond the Nation*. Ed. Pheng Cheah and Bruce Robbins. Minneapolis: Minnesota UP. 290–328.
Clifford, James. "Traveling Cultures." *Cultural Studies*. Ed. Lawrence Grossberg, Cary Nelson, and Paula A. Treichler. London: Routledge, 1992. 96–116.
de Felippis, Jeanne. "The Western Discovery of Tibet." *Lhasa in the Seventeenth Century: The Capital of the Dalai Lamas*. Ed. Francoise Pommaret. Boston: Brill, 2003. 1–14.
Erickson, Barbara. *Tibet: Abode of the Gods, Pearl of the Motherland*. Berkeley: Pacific View Press, 1997.
Fischer, Andrew. "Close Encounters of an Inner Asian Kind: Tibetan-Muslim Co-Existence and Conflict in Tibet Past and Present." Working Paper. London: Crisis States Research Centre, 2005.
Gaborieau, Marc. "Power and Authority of Sufis Among the Kashmiri Muslims in Tibet." *Tibet Journal* 20.3 (1995): 21–30.
Gidwani, Vinay. "Subaltern Cosmopolitanism as Politics." *Antipode* 38.1 (2006): 7–21.
Gladney, Dru. *Dislocating China: Muslims, Minorities and Other Subaltern Subjects*. Chicago: U of Chicago P, 2004.
———. *Muslim Chinese: Ethnic Nationalism in the People's Republic*. Cambridge: Harvard UP, 1991.
Goldstein, Melvyn. *A History of Modern Tibet, 1913–1951: The Demise of the Lamaist State*. Berkeley: U of California P, 1989.
Goldstein, Melvyn, William Siebenschuh, and Tashi Tsering. *The Struggle for Modern Tibet: The Autobiography of Tashi Tsering*. Armonk: Sharpe.
Goldstein, Melvyn, Dawei Sherap, and William R. Siebenschuh. *A Tibetan Revolutionary: The Political Life and Times of Bapa Phuntso Wangye*. Berkeley: U of California P, 2004.
Grongkhyer Lhasa'i lorgyus rig-gnas deb drugpa: Kreng Kon Chus [*The History and Culture of Lhasa City, Book Six: The Chengguanqu*]. Lhasa Municipal Political Consultative Committee. Lhasa: Tibet, Xinhua, 1998.

Hannerz, Ulf. "Cosmopolitans and Locals in World Culture." *Global Culture: Nationalism, Globalisation and Modernity.* Ed. Mike Feathersone. London: Sage, 1990. 237–51.
Harris, Clare, and Tsering Shakya. *Seeing Lhasa: British Depictions of the Tibetan Capital 1936–1947.* Chicago: Serinda, 2003.
Harrer, Heinrich. *Seven Years in Tibet.* 1953. Delhi: HarperCollins, 1992.
Hao, Yan. "Tibetan Population in China: Myths and Facts Re-Examined." *Asian Ethnicity* 1.1 (2000): 11–35.
Jest, Corneille. "Kha-che and Gya-Kha-Che: Muslim Communities in Lhasa (1990)." *Tibet Journal* 20.3 (1995): 8–20.
Kapstein, Matthew. *The Tibetans.* Oxford: Blackwell, 2006.
Karan, Pradyumna P. *The Changing Face of Tibet: The Impact of Chinese Communist Ideology on the Landscape.* Lexington: U of Kentucky P, 1976.
Ma, Rong. "Han and Tibetan Residential Patterns in Lhasa." *The China Quarterly* 128 (1991): 814–36.
McGovern, William. *To Lhasa in Disguise: A Secret Expedition Through Mysterious Tibet.* New York: Century, 1924.
Moevus, Claude. "The Chinese Hui Muslims Trade in Tibetan Areas." *Tibet Journal* 20.3 (1995): 115–23.
Naik, Yusuf. "Memories of My Father, Abdul Ghani, in Tibet." *Tibet Journal* 20.3 (1995): 31–35.
Ong, Aihwa. *Neoliberalism as Exception: Mutations in Citizenship and Sovereignty.* Durham: Duke UP, 2006.
Pollock, Sheldon, Homi Bhabha, Carol Breckenridge, and Dipesh Chakrabarty. "Cosmopolitanisms." *Public Culture* 12.3 (2000): 577–89.
Radhu, Abdul Wahid. *Islam in Tibet: Tibetan Caravans.* Trans. Jane Cazsewit. Ed. Gray Henry. Louisville: Fons Vitae, 1997.
Schwartz, Ronald. *Circle of Protest: Political Ritual in the Tibetan Uprising.* New York: Columbia UP, 1994.
Sheikh, Abdul Ghani. "Tibetan Muslims." *Tibet Journal* 16.4 (1991): 86–90.
Siddiqui, Ataullah. "Muslims of Tibet." *Tibet Journal* 16.4 (1991): 71–85.
Snellgrove, David, and Hugh Richardson. *A Cultural History of Tibet.* 1968. Boston: Shambala, 1995.
State Council. *Regional Ethnic Autonomy in Tibet.* 2004. <http://www.china.org.cn/e-white/20040524/index.htm>.
Tibet Information Network. Reports from Tibet 1998. *News Review* 27. London, 1999.
Thupden Khatsun (*Thubbtan mkhasrtshun*). dk'asdug 'oggi byungba brjodpa [*The events that happened under suffering*]. Unpublished memoirs, 1998.
Turin, Mark, and Sara Schneiderman. "Yams in Boulderland." n.d. <http://www.digitalhimalaya.com/projectteam/turin/abstracts/j_yamsboulderland.html>.
Yeğenoğlu, Meyda. "Cosmopolitanism and Nationalism in a Globalized World." *Ethnic and Racial Studies* 28.1 (2003): 103–31.
Yeh, Emily. "Tibetan Indigeneity: Translations, Resemblances, and Uptake." *Indigenous Experience Today.* Eds. Marisol de la Cadena and Orin Starn. Oxford: Berg, 2007. 69–97.
———. "Tropes of Indolence and the Cultural Politics of Development in Lhasa, Tibet." *Annals of the Association of American Geographers* 97.3 (2007): 593–612.
Yeh, Emily, and Mark Henderson. "Interpreting Tibet's urbanization: administrative scales and discourses of modernization." *Journal of the International Association of Tibetan Studies.* Forthcoming.
Zhang Zongxian, Luo Shujie, and Xu Jieshun. "Xizang Minzu tuanjie Kaocha Baogao" ["Report on an Investigation of the Unity of Nationalities in Tibet"]. *Zhongguo Minzu Tuanjie Kaocha Baogao.* Ed. Xu Jieshun. Beijing: Nationalities Press, 2004. 49–123.

4 Intelligent City
From Ethnic Governmentality to Ethnic Evolutionism

Aihwa Ong

INTRODUCTION

The paper is about the emergent global Asian city and its reliance on a rescaled ethnic formation as a mechanism for producing a new biopolitical architecture of intellectual accumulation. I am not talking about new moves to be more friendly to strangers, such as the introduction of legal prohibitions against ethnic discrimination and racism in Hong Kong. Rather, my concern is with the new kind of entrepreneurial political thinking behind the rise of high-tech centers in Asia—Singapore, Kuala Lumpur, Bangalore, and so forth—and the quest for knowledge workers. Specifically, I want to identify how urban authorities reconfigure relations among expatriate and local populations through techniques that re-ode de-territorialized ethnic populations as essential to the growth possibilities that cannot be solely met by territorialized ethnic communities.

Increasingly, as *foreign Asians*, Indians from South Asia and Chinese from the People's Republic of China (PRC) are becoming associated with the kind of intelligence and expertise marketable to global industries, the very institutions of knowledge and wealth making that Asian cities seek to attract. Given the multicultural makeup of a city like Singapore, the influx of ethnicized professionals has a destabilizing effect on the territorialized mode of ethnic governmentality. Furthermore, the intensive recruitment of mainly Asian expatriates as "global talent" engenders an evolutionary view that they possess greater intellectual capital or are more intellectually evolved than local ethnics. At different scales of ethnic differentiation—the city, the group, the individual—ethnicity as a mechanism of biopower also exercises the right to disqualify less evolved ethnic groups long territorialized in the city.

It is estimated that by 2015, Asia will account for twelve of the world's twenty-one megacities (over ten million inhabitants)—Karachi, Delhi, Dhaka, Beijing, Tokyo, Shanghai, Jakarta, Manila, Kolkata—and 267 cities with one million or more.[1] The sheer scale of such growth is mind-boggling, and one result is that different cities move to claim a "global" status beyond the mere demographic, or the explosive mix of cultures and ethnicities.

What effects are there on the ethnic majority of the city, previously tied to the founding of the postcolonial nation? In struggles for independence from foreign colonialism, Asian capital cities materially and symbolically stood for the ethnic-racial majority. A series of reconstructions ensued, to erase dominant traces of other pasts and other founding groups, in order to attest to the racial majority of the nation. Kuala Lumpur, the capital of Malaysia, is a prime example of the capital city as an anchor of national ethnic domination. The town had been founded by immigrant Chinese mining camps and for decades was populated by an ethnic Chinese majority. In the aftermath of racial riots that betrayed deep-seated anxieties of the Malay majority that claims its political domination from its status as *bumiputera* or "princes of the soil," the postcolonial Kuala Lumpur city-profile became systematically transformed as new mosques and stunning skyscrapers designed with an Islamic cast overshadow the earlier Chinese urbanscape, now shrunk to a lower-class Chinatown, alongside a working-class Indian neighborhood aptly called Brickfields. The ethnically marked landscape was further enhanced as social clubs that serve the recreational needs of the middle classes are also divided along ethnic lines. Thus the reimagined Asian city in the aftermath of colonialism is busily reinscribing a more politically correct ethnic asymmetry onto the cityscape (Bishop et al 3).

Elsewhere as well, the impulse to remold the identity of key cities after a political transition is strong, as a kind of indigeneity reclaims building and real estate for local control. Recently, authorities in Kunming, China, imposed new guidelines to erase foreign-identifying names ("Ginza Office Tower," "California Island," "Paris of the East Plaza," etc.) from major buildings and malls. By renaming these urban structures with Han Chinese names, the authorities seek to preserve and showcase "our local characteristics." One assumes that the urban government would also welcome monikers representing indigenous peoples such as Dai, Yi, or Hui Muslims in the province of Yunnan. Thus, beyond the multicultural vibrance of contemporary Asian cities, political strategies such as mechanisms of architectural governance mentioned above should be part of our study of cultural and ethnic diversification.

The political strategies I am interested however are not about the structuration of ethnic differences and asymmetry onto the cityscape. My approach therefore goes beyond the conventional study of ethnic diversity as territorialized or contained within the borders of the city or the nation. Rather, I am concerned about how the mobilization of flows of capital, technology, and knowledge have exceeded the geographical limits of the city. Increasingly, like a spider, the agile global city weaves around itself an ever-widening web of capital, knowledge, and actors. This up-scaling of urban networks also involves a recoding of ethnic populations in relation to intellectual capital, or a shifting from ethnic governmentality to ethnic evolutionism. There is a recoding of de-territorialized ethnic populations as essential to urban growth possibilities that cannot be solely met by territorialized ethnic communities.

The outline is as follows. I begin by discussing a new metropolitan thinking of the Asian city as an ecosystem constituted by the traffic, exchanges, and interactions of diverse populations, thus exerting a fragmenting effect on stabilized ethnic modes of governance.

I then turn to an analysis of the workings of biopolitical distinctions that depend on a kind of ethnic evolutionary reasoning, or the premise that elite foreign nationals are more developed kinds of intellectual beings. Finally, I refine the suggestion of multiculturalism as "living with strangers," by describing a metropolitan milieu where various regimes of cosmopolitan living are linked and juxtaposed in a fluid urban ecosystem.

THE URBAN ECOSYSTEM

There is a theory that global cities are defined by their functions in managing the crucial services of key trade, technology, finance, and multilateral networks (Sassen). But among the dozens of emergent Asian cities, the claim to globality is less one of sustaining existing global functions, but rather to resituating themselves more centrally in global flows and networks. Hong Kong tries to do this by repositioning itself as "Asia's World City." Besides its gateway role to China, the city has belatedly passed laws reining in Chinese cultural chauvinism by banning discrimination against multi-Asian populations. In contrast, other Asian cities are seeking to transform themselves into high-tech centers that plug into highly global lucrative industries. Hyderabad and Bangalore are famous as cybercenters that attract the displacement of high-tech jobs from Western sites. Singapore and Seoul, already high-tech manufacturing centers, have turned to biotechnology as a way to become Asian hubs for biotech research and drug companies.

The reimagining of the Asian city as a high-tech hub is the latest version of this strategy of "urban entrepreneurialism" to promote conditions for global economic competitiveness. This strategy to reposition the city at the center of crucial circuits of capital and knowledge relies on the differentiation of spaces, but not merely, as David Harvey has suggested, along conventional scales of the national, the regional, and the urban. Rather, the rescaling practices of metropolitan authorities like Singapore rely on assembling an array of global and situated elements that will interact in a new way, thus crystallizing a new set of conditions for optimal growth. Singapore as a city-state is an interesting case for investigating how an entrepreneurial intervention can respatialize the metropolitan as an extended space of heterogeneity in cultures, values, and ethnicity. Or to put it slightly differently, the multicultural populations and technological diversity are crystallized within the space of the assemblage of interacting global forces and situated factors.[2]

In the late 1990s, Singapore technocrats crafted a strategy to radically break from the geographical, demographic, and intellectual limits of the island. "We aim to build a vibrant and effervescent enterprise ecosystem, where large and small companies can thrive and leverage on [sic] innovation and intellectual property to create value."[3] This program entails a reimagining of the nation as a platform in a chain of knowledge production. Instead of being confined by given geography, there is a re-envisioning of the Asian city spinning into being an ecosystem for knowledge flow, accumulation, and knowledge production. At a recent symposium, the Singaporean minister of defense considers this the core program that will attract and retain "the finest regional talent, along with the generation of an exciting ecosystem of research and idea creation."[4]

By providing the institutional forms (see below) for such "an ecology of expertise," Singapore can assemble diverse flows of actors who interact to create a particular synergy for accelerated growth in intellectual and economic capital (Ong, "Ecologies of Expertise"). The institutional elements in this network include the establishment of two kinds of hubs, a state-financed Biopolis research center, and an educational cluster that is linked with overseas research institutes. We will focus on the latter "global schoolhouse" project as a mechanism for drawing in overseas students whose presence changes the ethnic dynamics of the city.

ETHNIC GOVERNMENTALITY

Heretofore, Singapore as a nation-state was administered through an implicit biopolitics of ethnic hierarchization, with the majority Chinese as an ethnic majority that is treated as distinct from the smaller Indian and Malay populations. While the state policy is officially against ethnic rule (official languages include Chinese, Hindu, Malay, and English), in practice, a mode of ethnic governmentality pervaded society as well-educated Chinese were consistently contrasted with less educated Malays. There is an interesting symbiosis between race-blind, pro-multicultural state policies on the one hand, and persistent forms of ethnic differentiation in the exercise of power relations.

Singapore has always been an immigrant society, inflows regulated to maintain a population distribution that is over 75% ethnic Chinese, the remainder mainly composed of ethnic Malays and Indians. From independence from Great Britain to the 1970s, the island received ethnic Chinese and some Indian immigrants from Malaysia across the narrow causeway. Many former Malaysians were professionals who suffered from some form of ethnic discrimination in Malaysia under its native regime of bumiputra-ism or native-first rule that privileges Muslim-Malays. The inflow of educated Chinese, especially, augmented the domination of ethnic Chinese in all domains of Singaporean life. During the 1980s, the Asian values discourse added a new dimension to ethnic differentiation as a mechanism of power. The prime minister Lee Kuan Yew famously articulated a theory of "hard" (read Chinese) versus "soft" (read Malay) cultures to explain the marked differences in economic success between Chinese-dominated Singapore and less developed nations such as the Philippines and Indonesia. The axis of ethnic differentiation thus pivots not only on ethnic cultural differences but also on the right to disqualify soft or underperforming ethnic groups from a merit-based society.

The biopolitics of ethnic disciplining was also revealed in the regulation of population growth. During the first postindependence (1965) decades of development, a family-planning policy sought to achieve eventual zero population growth in this small island. But when the fertility rate dropped below replacement level by 1986 and Singapore had become an affluent country, measures and tax incentives were introduced to encourage couples to have "three or more children if they can afford it." This pro-natalist policy has failed to stem falling birthrates (still at 1.5 in 1999) especially among the middle-class Chinese and Indians (Yap). Efforts continue to induce the urban middle classes to reproduce at a higher rate. The growing resistance to marriage and parenthood among young professionals spurred a "baby bonus" program that supported the second and the third child in the family. The state also played matchmaker by arranging dating services and courtship venues to induce college-educated women to marry and make babies (Heng and Devan). Meanwhile, tens of thousand of Singaporeans study or live abroad, adding to the shortfall in skilled labor. Nevertheless, the calibration of ethnicity to skills made Singapore an appealing city made of hard-working professional Chinese and low-cost Malay labor. Multinational companies set up factories and located their regional offices in Singapore. Ethnic governmentality coded as Asian values—stress on strong families, diligence, education, and loyalty—was associated with the rise of Singapore as a "tiger economy."

In the late 1990s, the Asian financial crisis crippled this tiger model of low-cost manufacturing and disciplining through ethnic hierarchization. Suddenly, there was the recognition that ethnic scheme frozen in a fishbowl situation was not the model for maintaining city growth, especially when jobs were flowing to China's gigantic labor markets. The governing logic shifted from territorialized ethnic hierarchy to a more fluid and dynamic mixing of populations in an expanded metropolitan space. A Singapore official remarked: "Competition is a fact of life. This is an open economy in which global links predominate." The old ethnic governmentality was represented by the Chinese merchant figure who drew on kinship- or ethnic-based relations (*guanxi*) to conduct business. This figure, he argued, must be buried once and for all. What is needed, he stressed, is "the international risk-taking entrepreneurial figure who is beyond the Chinese merchant model. In the post-industrial society, the need is for a Western attitude of risk-taking, a need to mix guanxi with Western global practices." The statement thus combined the ethnic element of Chineseness with global values of risk taking and professional skills. The more educated, entrepreneurial, and mobile figure—ideally of Asian ancestry—is increasingly to be found not within the city itself, but from overseas.

ETHNIC EVOLUTIONISM

> "The specificity of modern racism, or what gives it its specificity . . . is bound up with . . . a mechanism that allows biopower to work."
> —Michel Foucault

Singapore's rise as a global biotech center requires an accelerated acquisition of scientific knowledge and experts not available locally. Thus, an "adding value" strategy mobilizes a dozen joint collaborations with overseas scientific institutions. For instance, there are collaborations between the National University of Singapore and MIT; Johns Hopkins University; the University of Illinois; the University of California; Stanford University, Duke University; University of Munich and Eindhoven (Netherlands), among others, for training programs in chemical engineering, biomedicine, environmental sciences, advanced technology, and so forth. While the aim is to upgrade the skills of Singaporeans, the most immediate goal is, in the words of an educator, to "build-up the talent pool" by attracting "better talents" by recruiting what is vaguely referred to as "global talent."

Global talent is a code word for preferred expatriates, that is, mainland Chinese and Indians who are identified by headhunting programs and recruited through the offer of expensive scholarships to enroll in the newly upgraded Singapore university programs. The expectation is that they will furnish (Asian) skilled labor for the Biopolis, thus attracting more pharmaceutical companies to develop therapies and drugs in Singapore.

For instance, over the past five years, approximately seven hundred MA graduates from the MIT-Singapore (MITS) program were made available to work in research labs in the Biopolis, for private companies, especially in the areas of electronics, and biological and chemical systems. Their availability as a relatively cheap Asian labor force has attracted major firms such as Lilly's, GlaxoSmithKline, Schering Plough, Pfizer, and other companies in molecular engineering, and drug delivery. At the Department of Johns Hopkins Singapore (DJHS), where the focus is on experimental therapeutics, they are recruiting and hiring target scientists and students from the PRC. The goal is to build up a mainland Chinese talent base for work in the Singapore research labs. To this end, DJHS has forged links with scientific institutes in Central China such as Wuhan University.

Other joint university collaborations also engage in recruiting mainly foreign Asians (from India, China, Taiwan, Southeast Asia, as well as Western countries) to form a concentration of "global talent" in the city.

Furthermore, the policy—through ease of obtaining residency permits, special taxation schemes, housing perks, and so on—is to eventually embed foreign experts, especially Indians and Chinese, as permanent residents or citizens in the city.

What are the implications of this concerted strategy to recruit, train, and employ foreign Asians for the preexisting scheme of ethnic governmentality? First of all, the ethnic composition based on territorialized claims is unraveling as the broad sweep of expatriate recruitment is creating an upper layer of privileged foreign Asians. Huge amounts of state money have been pumped into the biotech field, which is currently employing mainly to foreign workers and students. There is general resentment among Singaporeans against foreigners who are suspected of getting jobs local citizens can perform. A few local students are also being groomed for high-tech jobs, and sent for expensive training overseas (to the tune of half a million Singapore dollars each), and bonded for up to six years to return and work in Singapore. More locals are prodded to go into the scientific fields, not least in order to ensure the future relevance and security of their city in a globalized world. Over the past ten years alone, the life sciences have attained a mass appeal among the public, which is becoming more inclined to send their children to science rather than business programs. There is also the sense that if bioscience is becoming the "fourth pillar" of the metropolitan economy, "the government cannot fail" and should be supported by loyal citizens.

There is a reconfiguration of ethnic privilege that exceeds the terrain of the city and is increasingly rooted in transnational knowledge circuits. The association of scientific skills and excellence with foreign Indians and Chinese has decentered the territorialized scheme of ethnic privilege. Instead of historically entrenched forms of ethnic ranking, de-territorialized subjects are setting new standards of prestige and value to the city. These expatriates are also racialized in that their nationalities (Indians or PRC citizens) are assimilated into racial terms of Indians and Chinese, a kind of foreign version to ethnic counterparts in Singapore. It appears that by focusing on smart people from India and China, the implicit policy is to build up the intellectual capital of the city-state that can racially blend in with the preexisting population. But clearly, this move of blurring territorialized and de-territorialized and racialized groups cannot conceal the mechanisms of a new biopolitics for sustaining this urban ecosystem. An evolutionary view allows this kind of racially discriminating biopower to do its work.

Many Westerners including Alan Colman of the "Dolly" sheep fame are recruited to lead research institutes. But the main focus is on assembling a "world-class" scientific labor force—that is, overseas Asians—who can be employed in research factories that will serve drug companies. This mobilization of an elite "Asian" labor aristocracy is based on the premise that they are more intellectually capable and evolved intellectual workers than their local ethnic counterparts.

An earlier tendency to evolutionary thinking in city politics was first applied to policies urging university graduates (i.e. middle-class Chinese and Indians) to make more "graduate babies." As fertility rates among the more fecund and less educated Malay minority outstripped that of other classes, a major campaign focused on "graduates," itself an informal category of social prestige, to marry and reproduce at a higher rate in order to ensure more future Singaporeans who can be identified as graduates.[5] The whiff of eugenics thinking is unmistakable, since ethnicity becomes conflated with probabilities of class and education achievement; only graduates are assumed to be capable of reproducing future graduates.

Current evolutionary reasoning is remapped onto a wider scale of Asian populations. An ethnicization of intellectual heredity is now merged with an expanded conflation of ethnicity and race across a spectrum of countries. "Asian values" discourse has given way to a discourse of "global talent" that is drawn mainly from foreign Asians. There is the suggestion that overseas, less coddled Indians and Chinese possess greater brain power needed to drive the city situated in Southeast Asia. The cluster of evolutionary ideas include ethnic or racial genealogy, struggle of the fittest, adaptability, resilience, global technological competition. The cluster of joint academic programs, a university professor told me, is an "incubator" that generates a synergy between smart Asians and foreign entrepreneurs so that "commercializable ideas that are technology-related" can spur the rise of start-up companies in Singapore. By nurturing a group of entrepreneurial scientists, the city will become "a hub for international talent, while remaining socially cohesive and nationally resilient,"[6] not least in broad ethnic strokes that include Asian expatriates/races.

Clearly, a preferred citizenry defined by value-added intellectual capital suggests that not all citizens are intelligent enough, or adaptable enough, to be similarly valued. The effort to concentrate the presumed intellectual superiority of foreign Asians also seems to disqualify underachieving local co-ethnics. For instance, the leader of a research institute was reported to have said that "if Singaporeans have only basic degrees, they might as well wash test tubes." As lesser, territorialized versions of foreign Asians, locals can become lab janitors to their foreign ethnic counterparts. A media official reminded me that Singaporeans are accustomed to being told that they are to compete with foreigners on their own home turf. It's a matter of merit, not race or ethnicity, she claims. "If you're no good, you're no good. The job goes to better educated people," no matter where they are from. But where the majority of expatriates are from is major Asian countries, the foreign co-ethnics who are assumed to be more talented and competitive. The moral calculus in this knowledge ecology requires a worthy citizen to excel at self-management, and to be at once globally competitive and politically compliant.

Thus in the name of the growth, competitiveness, and security of the city-state, a kind of evolutionary thinking makes calculations about intellectual capital in relation to assumed racial competence and ethnic ranking. A distinctive ethnic ecology is being shaped by technologies of immigration and recruiting foreign talents. Even among foreign Asian experts, PRC Chinese students are considered more intellectually competent and adaptable than their counterparts from India. Initially, there was great interest in recruiting Indian students because of their fluency in English and their training in excellent technical institutes. But over time, recruiters found that there was unevenness and unpredictability in the Indian student pool. Institutions cannot guarantee uniform excellence of selected students, some of whom were not as well trained as expected.

Other students had used fake academic documents in their applications for Singapore fellowships. Given this uncontrollable element in the recruitment of Indian candidates from India, the authorities have turned more and more to Chinese institutes of science and technology. The claim is that the recruitment of bona fide excellent students is more controllable from Chinese universities, and that heretofore, the PRC will be the main source of Asian candidates and experts. In other words, the biopolitical strategy discriminates among transnational flows of intellectual brainpower that become racialized in relation to the urban ethnic composition. There is the implicit belief as well that mainland Chinese science workers can blend more easily among the majority ethnic Chinese population, and intellectual links with China will contribute to the emergence of Singapore as a global hub of biotechnology.

REGIMES OF COSMOPOLITAN LIVING

I have approached the question of multiculturalism in an emerging Asian city by focusing not on the spontaneous influx of diverse populations, but on the social engineering of the flows of specific kinds of subjects and the coordination of their presence with the preexisting ethnic populations. In a recent speech, the prime minister justified the new Singaporean discrimination in favor of foreign nationals: "Today, wealth is generated by new ideas, more than by improving the ideas of others. . . . That is why we have to bring in multi-national talent . . . Like MNCs [multinational corporations], multi-national talent, or MNT, will bring in new expertise, fresh ideas and global connections and perspectives. I believe that they will produce lasting benefits for Singapore."[7] Particular kinds of foreigners will be the biopolitical tool for securing the rise of the city-state.

Singaporeans will have to learn to live with these chosen talented strangers, and to compete with them in their own city. While Singapore is a city-state, there is clearly the realization that by becoming a "multinational city," claims and prestige are less derived from territorialized citizenship than from possessing or the perception of possessing relevant intellectual skills. A new mix of territorialized natives and a de-territorialized intelligentsia in the would-be global city suggests a historicized reframing of the multicultural phenomenon in Asian metropolitan spaces.

There is a popular assumption that ideals of "living together with strangers" can emerge spontaneously, somehow outside the space of the global market place. The argument is that cross-cultural encounters formed through exchange, reciprocity, and sharing produce a process of mutual recognition. The moral economy of multiculturalism draws its sociality from the multiple sources of traditions and religions. But if we rephrase the ideals of living together as cosmopolitanism, then there is the necessity to discuss how living among strangers in an ideal condition of conviviality is frequently shaped by encounters in the marketplace. Kant's notion of cosmopolitanism derives from the encounters and exchanges among strangers interacting in ever-expanding institutional networks created by markets. From such promising beginnings, he suggests ideals of market-driven hospitality to strangers can give rise to allegiance to the worldwide community of human beings, an ever-rippling effect of goodwill and solidarity across the world that will bring about perpetual peace (Kant). Applying some of Kant's insights to contemporary discussion of Asian cities, we notice that he identifies two elements that I have sought to bring to the fore in the above discussion.

To become global cities, citizens whether in Bangalore or Bangkok are expected to rethink their deepest affiliations to the nation, ethnicity, culture, and religion in order to generate a human consciousness at a broader level. In the case of Singapore, older particularistic attachments to ethnic identity and culture must coexist with new connections with foreigners linked to other places now interconnected by global markets.

It seems necessary that discussions of multiculturalism should be unpacked as a concept and as an ideal we are searching for in Asian's great cities. In these dynamic metropolitan situations, we cannot claim a uniform kind of multiculturalism rooted only in traditional ethics. It may be more appropriate to talk about a variety of small cosmopolitanisms, or what I have called cosmopolitanisms with a small "c" (Ong, *Flexible Citizenship*) or particular kinds of multiculturalism that are based on a wide range of practices—consumerist lifestyles, managerial-professional skills, human rights activism—rather than the Kantian notion of universal solidarity. In Singapore, a socially engineered form of evolutionary cosmopolitanism underlies the strategy to increase the density of marketable expertise in the city. It is ironic indeed that an evolutionary mechanism of urban biopolitical calculation is fused with an evolutionary mode of ethnic discrimination. The regulatory mechanism to fix preferred ethnicities to urban space produces an enforced cosmopolitanism that drives the city's quest to be "global."

There are of course, other kinds of "actually existing cosmopolitanisms," (Ong, "A Bio-Cartography") including less market-driven ones than those based on voluntary affiliations with strategic others. We can, for instance, point to the religious communities and their global interconnections, such as a newly vibrant form of cosmopolitan Islam. There is also the proliferation of NGOs that forge a transnational public beyond the state but remained connected to grassroots issues.[8] Despite its self-branding as an intelligent city, multiple regimes of cosmopolitan living—international business people and experts, jet-setting professionals, middle-class consumers, religious groups, regional migrant workers, a micro NGO group—coexist in Singapore. These parallel zones of cosmopolitan sociality—elite, middling, and grassroots—articulate and disarticulate in the fluid landscape that seeks to harvest and produce global expertise, but cannot entirely control other political agendas. Cosmopolitanisms are multiply-rooted here and there, existing together and yet apart because they are partially embedded in politically designed ethnic spaces as well as in transnational modes of identifications that remain open to broader affiliations of markets, knowledge, and ethics. The constant rearticulations of transnational and urban relationships continually unmake and remake governmentalized configurations of multiculturalism, ethnicity, and human value.

NOTES

1. "Boom Towns: How an Urban Explosion Is Transforming Asia," *Newsweek* (Asia), 20 Oct. 2003: E8–9.
2. The concept of "global assemblage" is developed in Ong and Collier.
3. Singapore Economic Development Board, *Into the Fifth Decade*, 2001, 9.
4. Tan Kong Yam et al., "Has Foreign Talent Contributed to Singapore's Economic Growth? An Empirical Assessment," report by the Singapore Ministry of Trade and Industry, 2002.
5. See Heng and Devan.
6. Lee Hsien Loong, Speech at the launch of Manpower 21, 31 Aug. 1999.
7. Goh Chok Tong, "New Singapore," National Day Rally 2001 Speech by the Prime Minister at the National University of Singapore, 19 Aug. 2001. Ministry of Information and the Arts, Singapore.
8. See, e.g., Aihwa Ong, "A Bio-Cartography: Maids, Neo-Slavery, and NGOs."

REFERENCES

Bishop, Ryan, John Philips, and Wei-Wei Yeo. "Perpetuating Cities: Excerpting Globalization and the Southeast Asia Supplement." *Postcolonial Urbanism*. Ed. R. Bishop, J. Philips, and W.W. Yeo. New York: Routledge, 2003. 1-36.

Foucault, Michel. "Society Must be Defended." *Lectures at the College de France 1975-1976*. Trans. David Macey. New York: Picador, 2003.

Harvey, David. "From Managerialism to Entrepreneurialism: The Transformation in Urban Governance in Late Capitalism." *Geografika Annaler*, B 71/1 (1989): 3-18.

Heng, Geraldine and Janadas Devan. "State Fatherhood: The Politics of Nationalism, Sexuality and Race in Singapore." *Bewitching Women, Pious Men*. Ed.

Aihwa Ong and Michael Peletz. Berkeley: University of California Press, 1995. 195-215.
Kant, Immanuel. "Perpetual Peace: A Philosophical Sketch." *Political Writings.* Ed. Hans Reiss. Cambridge: Cambridge University Press, 1991. 93-130.
Malcolmson, Scott L. "The Varieties of Cosmopolitan Experience." *Cosmopolitics: Thinking and Feeling beyond the Nation.* Ed. Pheng Cheah and Bruce Robbins. Minneapolis: University of Minnesota Press, 1998, 233-45.
Ong, Aihwa and Stephen J. Collier, eds. *Global Assemblages: Technology, Politics, and Ethics as Anthropological Problems.* Malden, Mass.: Blackwell, 2005.
Ong, Aihwa. "Ecologies of Expertise: Assembling Flows, Managing Citizenship." *Global Assemblage: Technology, Politics, and Ethics as Anthropological Problems.* Ed. Aihwa Ong and Stephen J. Collier. Malden, Mass.: Blackwell, 2005. 337-52.
Ong, Aihwa. *Flexible Citizenship: the Cultural Logics of Transnationality.* Durham: Duke University Press, 1999.
Ong, Aihwa. "A Bio-Cartography: Maids, Neo-Slavery, and NGOs." *Neoliberalism as Exception: Mutations in Citizenship and Sovereignty.* Durham: Duke University Press, 2006. 195-218.
Nonini, Donald and Aihwa Ong. "Introduction." *Ungrounded Empires: The Cultural Logics of Modern Chinese Transnationalism.* Ed. Donald Nonini and Aihwa Ong. New York: Routledge, 1997. 3-36.
Sassen, Saskia. *The Global City: New York, London, Tokyo.* Princeton: Princeton University Press, 1991.

Section II
Cosmopolitanism Compromised/Denied

5 Impossible Cosmopolises
Dislocations and Relocations in Beirut and Delhi

Yasmeen Arif

Cities struck by sectarian/communal violence carry their scars in many ways. Geographies of fear and suspicion, cultures of hate and hostility, halted or transformed personal and group biographies are some ways in which the social fabric of such cities are changed into times far beyond the event or era of the events themselves. My intent in this essay is to explore two such urban -contexts, both damaged during specific episodes of ethnic violence or civil warfare, in Delhi and Beirut respectively. The overall theme under which I bring together Delhi and Beirut is as follows—what futures do these events produce in urban horizons that have been marked by violence? What kinds of socio-spatial formations appear which work towards the fragmentation or integration of everyday spaces and relationships in these cities?

The answers to these queries are explored and interrogated through notions of cosmopolitanism or as I will argue, through the idea of "mundane" cosmopolitanisms. For the most part, (I am simplifying here, but nonetheless) the meaning of cosmopolitanism is suggested as an attitude, an openness to the other, to the stranger as well as an ability to imbibe, sustain and manifest a tolerance for difference. It is also a disposition towards balancing one's ethnocentric loyalties or patriotisms with global cultures and universal ideals. The classic space for such relationships was the urban, the city. This link between cosmopolitanism and the dynamic of the urban has been a hallmark of urban experience articulated in the writings of Walter Benjamin, Georg Simmel, Robert Park and Louis Wirth among many others. In another paradigmatic sense, cosmopolitanism is also often associated with a consumption aesthetic, an elite consciousness and practice, often associated with a transnational, global population who has the consumption power and access to dabble in multiple, global cultures, places and worldwide trends. In both the above senses, cosmopolitanism is an urbane experience where it is the urban environment that provides not just plurality and difference within "local" limits, but also a positioning in a global network of multiple symbols and practices. However, in the wide grand canvass of historical cosmopolitanism existing among and between civilizational groups and epochs, or in the finer poetics of worldly cosmopolitan experience that transcends local selves to encompass many others, some other humbler, ordinary activities of plural experience, gets overshadowed. These are the mundane give and take of work and livelihood, of trade and exchange in homes, neighborhoods and across city spaces that both fleeting and sustained encounters of interaction and exchange are experienced, encounters that cut across a spectrum of social identities.[1] These are not necessarily attitudes built from a conscious cognition of cosmopolitanism as a desired ideal but rather, they occur as conditions of life that are generated because of the spatial and temporal density of urban life. These close proximities, in the everyday spaces of urban life condense a compelling form of interaction in which cosmopolitanisms can be either inculcated or thwarted.[2]

I would particularly endorse the crucial dynamic of space in understanding the densities of urban life where most social abstractions (of identities, for instance) turn into practices made corporeal in space.[3] If the workplace, the school, the hospital, the market, the neighborhood park allows for a constant flow and mixing of different peoples bearing variegated identity markers, the encountering of these "others" becomes a highly spatialized experience. On the other hand, a temple, a church, a mosque, a wedding or a funeral heightens the sense of a singular community interaction, thus, spaces outside these instill another kind of experience, that of multiplicity.[4] At the same time, these sorts of experiences are also about the temporal in the spatial because just as space localizes events/experiences that occur in time, time also inscribes itself in the formulation of any given locale. Moments of identity contestation and conflict often turn condensed spaces of interaction into arenas of fear, suspicion or hostility that can escalate into brutal violence. Even without manifest events of conflict, experiences generated in personal biographies or by larger historical processes and social formations contour individual or collective orientation in ways can make for realms of threat or comfort in different kinds of spaces. Thus, in my exploration, the theme of mundane cosmopolitanisms is primarily an exploration of cosmopolitan spaces, their possibilities or their suspensions over varying temporal spans.

Through narratives set in Beirut and Delhi, in the particular circumstances of recovery/rehabilitation that I describe below, I argue that processes of ordinary, practiced mundane cosmopolitanisms come to be threatened among groups and in situations where ethnic strife has already grievously undermined any existing cosmopolitan living. While examining these contexts, my intent is to separate the exploration from certain existing discourses. For instance, ethnic re-territorialization of city spaces under conditions of civil hostilities is a known and investigated phenomenon. The crystallization of signifying identities and their mapping onto neighborhoods or localities often brought about by violent exclusions and protected inclusions, has been one of the ways in which such urban spaces are understood. In my argument here, however, I intend to shift the focus to some hidden processes which often remain silent and invisible in the discourse that surrounds the communal/ethnic inscriptions on social formations in urban locations. Towards this aim, my explorations moves away from the macro processes of identity crystallization, their violent mobilizations and their mappings on city space to a very specific circumstance, i.e., to an afterlife of reconstruction or rehabilitation. In effect, the frame that is used here does not set the limits in terms of immediate consequences of the events themselves, nor in terms of the strategies of reconstruction or rehabilitation per se. Rather, they are about the terrains that these measures of recovery can lead to, over long durations, into the social and material landscape of cities.

In her analysis of critical events, Veena Das shows how events of violence have a transformative effect in people's lives where they get "propelled into new and unprecedented terrains," (*Critical Events* 5, 6)—terrains which come into being in the interstices of family, community, bureaucracy, legal institutions and the state. My focus is on a similar afterlife of violence where I will aim to describe certain strategies of recovery, which eventually generate terrains that reinforce, directly or in unintended ways, the fragmentation of social fabric much in the way that civil hostilities had done. These are terrains that are formed in the interstices of state practice, of communities and families, bureaucratic and legal injunction and not least of all, in the material compositions of place and property.

My ethnographic exploration of the two separate cities of Delhi and Beirut, their different contexts, and the disparate groups of people that I have encountered have been persuasive in posing the above problem. The groups of people that I will discuss here are those collective biographies that articulate trajectories of movement within a cityscape, spatial biographies that emerge from a violent past and find their way into a "relocated" future. The guiding queries in both situations are, in a city that has been scarred by devastating violence, what kind of mappings and movements occur in the lives of those whose personal places of living and being disappear or are taken away? What are the factors that influence these movements? Given this ethnography, my analysis then uses notions of everyday cosmopolitanism, for instance, what forms of social inclusions and exclusions do these ethnographies reveal, how do these rearranged personal mappings negotiate the formulations of social identity? In answering these queries, as I will describe, I have found that the continued reinforcement of certain insular social boundaries in city spaces bear a compelling relationship to the logic of "recovery." In another way, the aspirations of a cosmopolitan city and the repeated rhetoric of the importance of promoting harmony in ethnically disturbed cities come to be arrested by the very logic of recovery.

One final introductory point that requires mention here is that I do not pose this essay as a comparative study with common criteria of evaluation over two cities; rather it is the reading together of two contexts with similar concerns. The Civil Wars in Beirut cover a 15 year span,[5] whereas the event of the Sikh carnage in Delhi lasted for some days, the morphology of these two situations in terms of "causes and consequences" are vastly different. In the specific matter of relocations, in Delhi, the colony I explore has been the result of a formal rehabilitative measure to provide adequate housing to the survivors of the carnage. In Beirut, the people that I write about were given monetary compensation and limited options in housing with which to relocate themselves. However, both narratives, Delhi and Beirut, lie in the same frame of issues through which they have been brought together. They are both particular instances of how urban space comes to be reconfigured in lived experience through disruptive occasions of violence. In the same instance, they are also about how such re-configurations come to have an influence on everyday urban socialities particularly among groups of people whose place in the city, in the first place have been contested by issues about identity. It is the anthropological encounter with these two sets of representations and experiences that bring about simultaneity, a sameness in difference that allows for an analytical perspective.[5] The conceptual anchoring that this requires could come from what Marc Augé writes about in the introduction to his Anthropology in Contemporaneous Worlds. Referring to certain global categories such as liberal capitalism, nationalism, fundamentalism and so on, he suggests (x),

> The movement of planetarization and individualization is not making itself felt everywhere with equal force, but it is a general condition and it is creating singular particular resistances of various forms around the earth. Intuitively we feel that the development and expansion of liberal capitalism, nationalism, particularism, fundamentalism are contemporaneous in the full sense of the word: they belong to the same time and space and they are connected to one another—they hang together.
>
> The title of this volume combines a singular noun—anthropology—with a plural one: contemporaneous worlds. It is meant to register the double movement of universalization and particularization that is simultaneously affecting the entire planet. Social Anthropology has always taken into account the context of the groups and phenomena it studied. Today, while multiplicity is being maintained, or more exactly, renewed, that context has become, for all cases, planetary.

In my argument here, Beirut and Delhi "hang together," because of the way in which they suggest plural instances of a fairly singular condition—that of personal and community socialities rearranged through conditions of displacement in urban spaces. Of course, Augé refers to another set of planetarizations—nationalism, fundamentalism and so on. The contexts in this essay are at another level, however, the conceptual framing and the analytical intention remains the same. This intention is about bridging the gap between absolute relativisms (where each context remains insularly trapped within its own particularities) on one hand and forced homogenizations/

uniformizations (where contexts become blurred under the forced criteria of simple comparison) at the other.[6]

In the following, I first sketch the background to the contexts in Beirut and Delhi and in each I discuss and trace the maps through which the rearranged spatialities take form. Second, I read these empirical expressions together with a focus on how reconstruction or rehabilitation activity together with limited personal options lead to a special kind of dispersal and re-organization of social identities in an already frayed urban social fabric.

BEIRUT 1975–1989

During July-August 2006, Lebanon and Israel were at war. Towards the middle of August, a UN resolution brought in an uncertain cease-fire. The circumstances under which lives have once again been lost remains outside any syntax of language I could articulate, however, in my own range of affairs, the devastation in South Lebanon in both life and property raises once again the questions of rehabilitation and reconstitution. Hezbollah, the Shi'ite militant political party and primary protagonist in the war with Israel has taken on the task, with extreme expediency and effectiveness to reconstruct most kinds of property damage especially housing and other public buildings like schools, hospitals etc. within its domain of functioning. They are involved in similar activities in the city of Beirut as well, particularly in the southern suburbs, the locality that a substantial part of my discussion in the following is based in.

During the JulyAugust 2006 war, the southern suburbs of Beirut were the targeted Shi'i locales for the Israeli assault, leaving other parts of the city virtually untouched, attacks that effectively pulverized various residential pockets in these areas. The mapping of a circumscribed Shi'i locality in the southern suburbs of Beirut has been the result of a historical process of both internal migrations and sectarian politics of space management, lasting almost five decades. In the last 15 years or so, one predominant factor in the formation of these sectarian locales has also been the rehabilitative efforts of the Hezbollah in providing appropriate housing options especially to those displaced by the Civil Wars of 1975—89. After the July wars, they have continued this role in providing relief in times of crisis in a fairly unprecedented way. In fact, the Hezbollah, in various forms and modalities, had been actively and strategically building up a formidable support structure for the Shi'is of Lebanon, who are now the single largest demographic group in the country, as well as the least privileged.[7] To say the least, the Hezbollah presence in Beirut is a profoundly socio-spatial one with the southern suburbs identified as marked Hezbollah territory, a fact that has come tragically alive in the recent War. In my tracings below, the trajectories of people who move towards these southern suburbs in Beirut are linked, however, with earlier processes of rehabilitation, not the recent devastation. My intent in following these trajectories was to explore how certain kinds of community activity aimed at rehabilitation had profound influence in the ways in which sectarian identity and practice comes to be reinforced onto city geography. The recent devastation of the southern suburbs of Beirut in the July Wars was what I had hoped not to witness, but expected as a possible extreme that predictable hostilities of the region and their spatial outcomes could lead to.

The narrative in Beirut starts in Downtown Beirut, a place that has been the pivotal center of the city. Almost five thousand years of antiquity has layered this atmospheric heart of the city with historic diversity and vivacity. Beirut, mirroring Lebanon, is like a patchwork quilt where every patch on the territory of the city/nation is designated to be of a given sectarian denomination, its location determined by various historic forces. Confessionally defined neighborhoods, laying side by side in close proximity make up the social, religio-political profile of the city, places where primordial identity connections guide the ebb and flow of social and political relationships. The west was largely Sunni Muslim, East Beirut was Maronite Christian, the southern suburbs largely Shi'i with interspersed pockets of distinct quarters of the Druze, the Greek Orthodox, the Armenian and in addition, the Palestinian camps. These pockets were social and political spaces bounded in with clear identities whose boundaries could turn into friendly frontiers in peacetime and protective/hostile barricades during conflict. Downtown Beirut, the historic core stood out in this milieu of the city as a genuinely mixed public space where Lebanese of all hues mixed together in the everyday rhythm of urban life.[8]

Most important government buildings, financial centers—banks, insurance companies and other commercial services were located here. The hotels district within downtown Beirut boasted the finest hotels; the neighborhood also provided the city's popular as well as sophisticated entertainment. The social mosaic that described the area had its own brand of appeal. The *souks* (local marketplaces) here were not only a tourist attraction but also a significant public space for the natives of Beirut. Economic co-operation enhanced a sense of co-existence and at the same time resisted the specter of sectarian difference. In the same square mile, along with the souks there were other public spaces—Martyr's Square, Place de L'Etoile (also known as Nijmeh square) and the country's central transport terminal, all of which were meeting points for the people of the city. Pocketed in the midst of all this were little residential zones that housed Lebanese of all sects and confessions. Inter-communal mixing in Beirut was at a high pitch in the center. Before the Civil Wars of 1975—89, at least for the period that it lasted, the city center was a place resonant with its environment, atmosphere and historic legacy. It was embedded in the memory of the city as a shared space. Downtown Beirut was a "quality," a characteristic of a nation that Lebanon desired to be.

Following the initial outbreak of sectarian clashes in 1975, Downtown Beirut, in the first two years of the war came to be the primary battlefield.

This was the time when the infamous Green Line dividing Beirut into a Muslim West and a Christian East came to be, cutting right through downtown Beirut from the east to the west. Militias on both sides of the city, east and west, in cycles of attack and retaliation, expelled or killed those different from their own, gradually creating homogenous territories on either side. Throughout the war till 1989, violence organized itself around the city in typical sections of inside/outside formations and across various front lines. The first two years of the war effected a near complete devastation of the city center and a total abandonment of the Green Line interface. All that remained was a virtual noman's land that sported a line of barricades, occasional snipers and other forms of artillery warfare. Through the later years of the Civil Wars, although downtown Beirut was not a direct target of warfare, yet its initial devastation was enough to start an irreversible decline of the area.

Violence, in Beirut, as an event or as a collection of events had produced its own spatial topography, which was not only about the dismantling of the plural space of downtown Beirut, but also the reified crystallization of socially bounded spaces. The gradual demise of downtown Beirut had begun to carve out a new urban geography in the city. The dispersal of residents, businesses and services associated with the downtown area brought about changes that remained far beyond the time of the Wars. Nabil Beyhum, a sociologist at the American University of Beirut, commenting on these phenomena observes that the city was partitioned into "unconnected islands" of "single community ghettos" made doubly acute by the fact that any existing public spaces were completely erased. The indirect effects of violence achieved a new assemblage of urban spaces that was far from a desired alternative in a city beleaguered by civil hostilities.[9] In the years following the wars, downtown Beirut is remembered as an iconic place of mixed, cosmopolitan living; a nostalgic ideal that remains as a social desire in a devastated city.

My interest in downtown Beirut, earlier and in this project,[10] has been anchored around the idea about how a neighborhood, once known for its cosmopolitan appeal is experienced by its residents over the different war phases and the stages of reconstruction. Between my earlier visit during 199798 and the later visit during September 2004, downtown Beirut had undergone a sea change. Nearly a decade of reconstruction had created a wholly new locale, not only in terms of its spectacular visual profile but also in terms of its social makeover.[11] It has indeed become a new city center—slick, glossy and powerful with its grandly renovated government buildings, multinational business offices, branded stores, all of which blend into the pristinely renovated "traditional urban villages" that surround the inner core of the city center. These quaint little neighborhoods complete with antique lighting and street furniture, cobbled pathways etc. are now some of most highly priced residential addresses of the city with apartments valued at upwards of a million dollars. The new city center has also become a very popular spot, a veritable crowd puller going by the number of tourists and local visitors who flock there for trendy leisure and entertainment options. Clearly, a new kind of popularity has come to be associated with downtown Beirut, the older ebb and flow of an urban core has given way to a new set of users, the cash heavy local consumer or the moneyed tourist from the Gulf, the global businessman and the elite residents as also the everyday visitors from around the city taking in the sights and sounds of a glamorous new neighborhood.[12]

The spectacular facelift of downtown Beirut has been owed to SOLIDERE, a real estate company who is responsible for the whole sale reconstruction, conservation and management of all real estate, old and new, located roughly within one square mile of the downtown area. The creation of SOLIDERE in 1995 has been credited to a masterful blend of state power and private capital engineered by the then Prime Minister, Rafiq Hariri (assassinated during February 2005), who used his own billionaire status and political office to bring about this project. SOLIDERE has the distinction of owning the square mile of property on which reconstruction was to take place, making the reconstruction of downtown Beirut one of the world's first private capital based post war rebuilding projects. Political will combined with enormous private capital had created a formidable force of change that appeared to completely upstage any presence of the state to the extent that, in the words of Saree Makdisi, "capital had become the state." Of course, built into the plan was an ostensible blend of public accountability combined with private efficiency, for example, the Master Plan was to be debated publicly, the state was to maintain control over all the public spaces, SOLIDERE, in exchange for exclusive land rights and development in certain concentrated areas was to provide for the entire infra-structural over hauling of the area.

Among the challenges facing SOLIDERE during the initial stages of their operations, a significant one related to the complicated tangle of property rights, which created an immense obstacle for the clearing away of private owners, tenants or migrants/squatters before SOLIDERE could lay claim to their ownership of the area. A legal solution to this problem was written into the making of SOLIDERE as a joint stock company, where shares were allotted in exchange for property and all pertaining rights. Government appointed committees were given the task of fixing the values of the properties under consideration. On the ground, an overwhelming reaction to this has been that the evaluation procedures for most properties were grossly out of proportion. Most agree that their properties were undervalued and a significant number of these evaluations were under litigation. Thus, the general speculation was that if any property owner in downtown Beirut has been offered a certain amount in shares in lieu of his/her property and if s/he expects to regain the property by buying it back, the new prices will be far higher, given the increased development premium by the time the property is up for sale again. In this situation, the possibility of some of the original owners returning to their businesses or properties in downtown Beirut would be very dim.

However, that is not all. It is now evident that Solidere's modes of appropriating property went far beyond the mere issue of disproportionate compensation. The ways in which most of these people have been forcibly evacuated has become an issue around which organized effort was under way during the time of my fieldwork. One of these groups was "The Coalition of Rightful Owners of Downtown Beirut," who claims that since Solidere started operation, only about 100 of more than 5000 families remain among those who used to reside in the area, and the number of businesses has fallen from more than 15,000 to about 950. As they vehemently maintain, not all of these moved willfully. Among the many property holders in Downtown Beirut were people who had also declined compensation, opting instead to stay on in the area. Solidere is believed to have used a number of unlawful tactics in order to forcibly evacuate those who refused the company's offer of compensation. Water and electricity were cut off, trash services were suspended and some were even overtly threatened. Some had even been physically moved out.

As I made attempts to trace some of these movements, perhaps find families who would be willing to share their stories with me, one of the first avenues I found was the coalition of Downtown Beirut property owners mentioned earlier. Connected across different locations in the city, these were people and families who had moved out to other areas during the war, relocations influenced largely by help from family or community. During October 2004, they were attempting to garner both local and international support for a daylong demonstration and public campaign against Solidere, which was going to be the first public protest since the company's inception. Avedis Hammelian, an elderly Armenian gentleman, was one such Downtown Beirut resident we met in one of the group's meetings. His story ran as follows, during the 1940's, he had bought a beautiful historic building for his home in the downtown area and had lived in it since, raised his children and also ran his business in a store close by. During the war he was forced to close down his store, but he managed to live on in his home through the war years, as he said, without any fear or harm. Once Solidere started activities, he opted for $15,000 compensation in shares for his store, whose value he said, had currently fallen to about $6000. Soon, he was informed that the area in which his home was also going to be included in Solidere's plans and his house was listed as a historic structure. Unwilling to part with his home, he started negotiations with Solidere in 1994, who agreed to allow him to retain his property on the condition that he take on the renovation work himself. Solidere had in fact also made this a part of their regulations, those choosing to hold on to historic or other property would have to renovate it according to Solidere's stringent guidelines after they furnished bank statements guaranteeing the availability of resources. Avedis followed all the rules and provided a $2.5 million guarantee but three years later, as he told us, his troubles started. Using a very minor legal ploy in his ownership agreement, Solidere sued him, to which he responded with an appeal and during August 1998, while his appeal was still pending, nearly two dozen soldiers and construction workers appeared at his doorstep and proceeded to make him leave at that very instant. Avedis who was 76 at the time, and his wife were forced to move out without anything to a relative's house in Gemmayze, a neighboring area. Ever since, Avedis has been fighting a protracted battle with the company, spending his resources and quite evidently, his health as well.

Like Avedis, there have been many who have left their homes in Downtown Beirut. For some like Avedis it was a home of many years, a place where his life had taken shape. For some others, it also was about losing generations worth of business enterprise. Clearly, this was a pattern unfolding over most of Downtown Beirut. During the first round of my fieldwork in 1997–1998, I had worked in one of the residential neighborhoods in downtown Beirut called Saifi which was located close to the Green Line and associated with the Christian Eastern side of the city. The area was undergoing massive reconstruction at the time, habitation was very sparse, but nonetheless I met with a number of families, or business owners who were people who had either remained in their original locations throughout the war years; or had returned to their original homes and businesses after the cease-fire. In the course of my visits, many of them mentioned emphatically that the war years were tough, but they managed to survive. However, it was the reconstruction that was seriously challenging their tenacity. During the war, in spite of the ostensible danger of snipers, militia takeovers of property, and even the basic lack of amenities like water and electricity, most, who could not or did not choose to relocate found ingenious strategies of survival. However, it was only when reconstruction formally started in 1995, I was told, that these people found their locations seriously threatened. Speaking from various positionings of confession (although the area was allegedly homogenized) and social class, they articulated experiences that seemed to express a profound loss and this loss was about their memories, their lives in an ambience they represented as a genuine mixed space of Beirut.

I met with a Druze hotel owner whose popular lodging establishment was closed because he did not have resources to renovate it according to the company stipulations. At the time, he was planning to move away to a known Druze village in the mountains and start a new business. Another Armenian gentleman and his son showed me their once prosperous garage which had been taken over by the militias. Having no capacity to set up their business again, they reluctantly accepted Solidere's compensation, handed over the property rights and moved their efforts to the Armenian quarter. When I asked, why they specifically wanted to return to downtown Beirut, the elderly gentleman said, " . . . it was the *ruh-al-wataniye* (the spirit of the country), people mixing together from all religions, involved together in work. What more can I tell you, there was the true spirit." A similar question was posed to another former resident of Downtown Beirut, who had moved from his original home to a rented accommodation in Hamra and then on to another locality called Tayyouneh in search of cheaper rent. He compared Hamra, another famously cosmopolitan center of pre-war Beirut to Tayyouneh and said, "[Hamra is] civilized. I like mixed areas, without a human mass where sectarian disease can spread. (Tayyouneh . . .) I don't feel part of that area. There are people from mountains. There is no civilized life. We know them from villages. We do not build open relationships . . . (they are) different kinds of relationships."

For yet some others, Downtown Beirut had provided a refuge from volatile situations in places where they belonged. One distinct group that occupied a significant number of abandoned buildings in the downtown area were Shi'i Muslims fleeing from southern parts of the country because of Israeli occupation and other localized regimes of militia violence. These predominantly rural Muslims were often the most resented group among some of the city dwellers, particularly those in Ras Beirut and downtown Beirut, as being the "polluting" outsiders who have progressively invaded not only their homes but also their cherished cosmopolitan ideals of mixed living.[13] Once dislocated by violence, these were people who, in 1995—96, had to move out of their make shift homes once again, this time because of reconstruction efforts.[14]

Given their apparently already homogenized, insular and politically volatile profile, it seemed obvious that they should move on to locales within the city that offered similar socialities. My interest was in trying to find the trajectories of these people—where did they go, what kinds of practices or choices were evident in terms of the localities or areas they moved to? Clearly, as squatters they had no legal rights to the properties they occupied. SOLIDERE, nonetheless, tackled the "problem" by offering compensation to them to abandon their make shift homes. My initial queries led me to understand that a large number of these families evacuated from Downtown Beirut had moved to part of a southern suburb called Hey-us-Sellum.

Mona Fawaz's work on the housing patterns in Hey-us-Sellum shows that the latest wave of newcomers to the area was young families who had been displaced by the reconstruction projects, mostly Downtown Beirut and some other highway projects in other suburbs of the city. Her survey shows that a large number of this group were people who chose this area because of the lack of any other affordable option in the city, in fact, this is a factor which is mentioned as more significant than the attraction of one's kin or village group members. Interestingly, Fawaz also mentions that although living close to family was considered an important factor in the apartment buying process, "many reported increasingly individualized processes that responded to tight economic conditions and strict religious lines." As per my information, two apartment blocks in Hey-us-Sellum, the Abbas and the Jawad complex, had a number of residents who had bought their apartments after their relocation from Downtown Beirut. In the Jawad complex six apartments were known to have been bought by members of an extended family who had moved from Downtown Beirut.

I was able to visit a few families in these buildings during September 2004. From these conversations in Hey-us-Sellum, I could decipher that choice was determined by a sense of moving to a place that one could be rightful part of, as one young couple put it, " . . . everyone comes to his own area," implying not so much voluntary choice but rather the narrowed down option of having to move to a sectarian locality mostly because of no other available housing possibility as wells as for reasons of community and existing kin networks. The actual choice of the apartment came about because of chance information by friends or kinsmen. The second feature was of course, affordability within the area. The couple mentioned that their family was given $12,000 in compensation by Solidere and the prices in Hey-us-Sellum could range from $30,000 to $100,000, given location, so the lesser money you had the farther you had to move. When I asked, how different life was in the new place, I was told, "There, we were happy. People were also close to each other. Here it is OK . . . everyone has his own apartment," indicating a somewhat insular everyday life. In response to a query about what most seemed to be a distinguishing factor between Downtown Beirut and Hey-us-Sellum, the quick answer from the man was, "Friendship, there we were seeing each other daily, now, every one month or two."

Hiba Bou Akar's work details how, during the negotiations between the squatters, Solidere and Ministry of the Displaced, representatives of the Hezbollah and Amal[15] were part of the Councils set up for the fixing of compensation and allocation of funds. Allegedly acting for the displaced Shi'is, the Hezbollah were also effectively including these people in a large network of housing properties and loan options on one hand and on the other, building up a powerful socio-political territory within the city. Once again, it is worth mentioning that Hezbollah is indeed the most visible political identity of the area. One significant and interesting aspect of their pre-eminence in Hey-us-Sellum is the NGO activity and its reach into the everyday life of local residents. Although registered as "charity" organizations, these organizations have openly proclaimed religious political ideologies, they are rather, "Islamic resistance NGO's" as Mona Fawaz describes them, modeled along "mother" NGOs based in Iran. Organized principally to meet the complete lack of government services, these NGO's also cater to specific needs and target groups; the three who are most active among the poorest of those affected by the war are *AlShaheed*, *AlJareeh*, and *Al-Imdad*—all of which provide health care, food subsidies, education and training. A couple of these are also involved, in devising self-sufficiency programs. Accordingly, bread making, sewing, cooking, carpet making, mini stores, etc are activities sponsored by these. The incredible outreach added to the fact that all volunteers are local residents, help in spreading the message very effectively. For instance, a group of "volunteer sisters," *Al-Akhawat al Moutatwe*, dedicated to maintain links between the NGOs and their beneficiaries and activate further outreach in the area, were originally screened so as to ensure only those volunteers who prescribed strictly to Islamic values and strongly believed in the resistance and social justice movement. Their attire conforms strictly to the dress code—covered head/chin and long formless clothing; they also practice strict segregation from men and choose prescribed language habits and so on. At one time, the zeal of these ideological goals had found resistance among those who did not wish to conform to strict codes of allegiance or who did not want to be associated with the obvious political image. However, with the near complete homogenization of the area after the war, that no longer poses a problem.

Returning to the ordinary social experiences of the "relocated," it will be important to end the Beirut narrative with a sketch of the neighborhood that the people we met in Hey-us-Sellum had relocated from in Downtown Beirut, an area called Wadi Abu Jmeil, a small residential quarter once known to be made up of Jewish refugees and migrants. Once the war broke out in 1975, the Wadi found itself on the Green Line, towards the Western side, almost mirroring Saifi's location on the eastern side, especially in terms of SOLIDERE's jurisdiction. During the war years, a number of complicated developments dispersed its original Jewish residents, sometimes under the generic threat of a warring city, and eventually because of a perception that they were somehow linked to the Israeli invasion of 1982. During this time, under the actions of the Kataeb, a leading Christian militia, many Jewish families were escorted out to "safer" Christian sections in the city. However, what is also known about the Wadi was that there were several Kurdish families, Christians and Muslim as well, who had continued to live in the area along with one last Jewish resident. During the war and in the few years after the cease fire, Wadi Abou Jmeil's profile came to be added upon by some more relocations, when various groups of people, from different confessions found their way to the neighborhood as a result of displacements from other parts of the city and country. These were Shi'i Muslims evacuated from the Christian East of the city, even Christians from East Beirut with wrong political connections, all of whom came to share the buildings and alleyways of the Wadi with all the others.

During 1995 -1997, with SOLIDERE and their clearing activities, several of these families had to move out, in patterns I mentioned above, the Shi'is to the southern suburbs, Christians to Christian areas and so forth. Once again, the responses to our queries about these choices were mainly about the financial considerations and not about confessional connections. Very eloquently, some of these families talked about their recollections of the neighborhood that had taken shape around them even when the war raged on, connections that lasted well beyond. A Kurdish housewife and the last remaining Jewish lady talked about their warm relations with the

Shi'i neighbors who had to move to the southern suburbs. And in the southern suburb, one of these relocated women said, "When" I come back after visiting my friends in the Wadi, I feel I have come into a "camp." The significant point made was that, through the travails of the war and beyond, this group of people could find ways of supporting each other and building up a community, as they said, " . . . we were seeing our friends more than we even saw our families." We were told about how little gathering places began to be formed, football in a yard, a coffee shop, a liquor shop and so on. Wadi abou Jmeil, during my visit in 2004, was on its way to becoming a "traditional urban village," some charmingly restored apartment blocks much like Saifi, a carefully guarded athletics club and a pristine park were already in place. The overall gloss and exclusiveness of the streets, new walkways, the immaculate facades of the buildings was already very clear.

The point I would like to underscore in the sketch above is about how certain movements within the city abetted by displacements and relocations, break down and dissipate very fragile bonds of interaction. These fragile bonds are those that had appeared as rare moments of mundane cosmopolitanism that occurred in the fraught times of a city under duress. The space in which these bonds had happened, i.e. Downtown Beirut resonated with a nostalgic force of a cherished cosmopolitanism that worked to reinforce, at least in the remembered memories of these people, a desire for an urbane existence different from what the cloistered community neighborhoods could offer.

DELHI '84

The carnage against the Sikh community, during October-November 1984, following the assassination of Prime Minister Indira Gandhi by her Sikh bodyguards, has remained one of the most horrific events of civil violence in the capital city of independent India.[16] With genocidal intensity, several Sikh localities in Delhi were targeted and particularly men, both young and old were annihilated through some of the most grotesque methods of mass murder. Places of worship were vandalized, entire blocks of Sikh homes and business establishments were razed to the ground; enormous amounts of looting and property damage also occurred during the same few days. While attacks on Sikhs were spread across the city, the worst affected areas were working class neighborhoods in Sultanpuri, Mongolpuri in West Delhi and Trilokpuri in East Delhi. Several relief camps had been set up around the city, many of which wound up operations after a few weeks. By late 1984 and early 1985, faced with the destitution of a large number of widowed Sikh women, relevant State authorities made a decision to relocate these women and their remaining families in a newly built colony originally meant for lower level government employees. Named as the Tilak Vihar Widows Relocation Colony (hereafter the Colony), this is a relatively small neighborhood, composed of three storied, single room apartment blocks,[17] tucked away beyond the edge of a bustling, fairly prosperous neighborhood in West Delhi. From March 1985, about 950 families, brought together into relief camps from various parts of the city were relocated to this neighborhood. Most of these families were widows and their remaining children. Around 250 other families were surviving sons and daughters of men who were killed.[18]

The references to the Colony in the following discussion are largely limited to my fieldwork conducted during 2004, by which time there was a slight change in the demographic profile in so far that few families had sold their apartments and moved out of the neighborhood, while the existing families had changed in size because of other relatives joining them over the years or because of usual family changes by birth, marriage or death. The community identity here is singularly Sikh with perhaps a few, fairly negligible exceptions. Interestingly enough, the larger neighborhood, Tilak Nagar, which practically surrounds the Colony, is also a predominantly Sikh, business oriented, middle class neighborhood. I cannot sufficiently determine whether this factor was in any sense influential in the choice of this colony when the relocation efforts were being made.

The particular nuance that I would like to emphasize in this Colony is a sense of "cast away-ness" that the residents articulate, a sense that produces a social identity that congeals over time around an acute community experience. Elsewhere, I have discussed how this identity comes to be constituted by a sense of exile, as a group conscious of their transformed lives, bound together by solidarity of failed justice.[19] As I have described in that context, the Sikh killings of 1984 continue, after twenty years, to be one of the singular instances of judicial failure in India because the number of convictions as against the killings remain absurd. Official and public enquiry commissions continue to delve into the matter where political involvement and police culpability, among other factors are regularly pointed out, but the fact remains that for the families in the Colony, the deaths of their men folk remain without retribution. Material and monetary compensation have been granted in various categories, the allocation of flats in the Colony has been a part of the rehabilitative effort of the state. In some consequence of this effort, I would like to reiterate one aspect, namely, the production of a social identity profiled overwhelmingly as a "victim" community, which then comes to be parenthesized by space and a place in the wider horizon of a cityscape.

The naming of the Colony as a "Widows" Relocation Colony, apart from the affect of taboo and exclusion that it immediately signals in Indian society, has another kind of import when attached to widowhood that emerges from community violence. It is a group, identified as all widows, not simply by a common community identity (Sikh), or by a positioning in a social structure (widow) but rather as a group produced by communal violence, whose coherent identity[20] is to be reproduced over time in the spatially confined segregation of a locality, seemingly produced by statecraft. As victims living in a city who could not exercise the option of returning to or finding shelter in some other refuge like a family home in order to remake their lives, they became a constructed group within the larger beleaguered community.[21] Among the families we interacted with in the Colony, most do not express the desire to go back to their earlier homes, a sentiment that is underlain with the trauma not only of the killings, but also the fact that, as Uma Chakravarty mentions, for most of these women, " . . . what stood out in their consciousness was the dramatic transformations of their homes from a space they regarded as inviolable and protected from 'outsiders' to the very site of their killings." A relentless memory of these transformed spaces was also the fact that most of these widows or mothers could not recover the bodies of their kinsmen in order to accord them a proper burial. Apart from the geography of fear that follows such pogroms, for those who might have liked to return, they would have had little or nothing to come back to, so complete was the devastation wrecked by the attack. For instance, our work in Tilak Vihar also included an ethnographic mapping of Sultanpuri, one of the worst hit areas of 1984, particularly the blocks where most of the Sikh families had originally resided. As our findings show, perhaps predictably, there is little or no trace of the fact that 20 years ago, this area was indeed a vibrant Sikh locality.

For the widows, the movements towards this colony starts from different locations of the city, leaving behind ordinary lives to a circumspect colony that over a period gets produced and reproduced as a "community space." It is a corporeal crystallization, precisely because these are lives that come to be formulated in trajectories that cross over and move away from their experiences of other city spaces, and come to settle in a segregated space. In other words there is an actual address of "exile" in which the widows inhabit. I have elsewhere argued[22] that the Colony works as a space of circumscribed "emplacement" whereby a set of people when bound together by their apparent similarity, find themselves inscribed into a space of victimhood. No doubt, the bureaucratic act of placing these "victims" together in a single space has its own rehabilitative logic, however, over a temporal span, the congealed limits of the Colony also act as a boundary of exclusion (or inclusion, as the case may be) for its residents which has its own repercussions into the possibilities of ordinary life. As described in the following, these repercussions translate into realms of private and public manifestation, which extend from an initial act of rehabilitation into a social destiny for its residents. In one sense, the Colony inscribes an enclosed geography of mourning. One of our informants had been a very young widow in '84 and had spent the last twenty years in the Colony where she was successful in putting together a reasonable life for her family (the children were educated, one had a job). When I asked whether she ever thought of leaving the colony to a better place, she said, "Here I can talk everyday about '84. I can share my burden everyday. But anywhere else, people will just be tired of me the mad woman who only talks about one thing." [23]

On the other hand, the very nature of this enclosed space predicts and eventually realizes a future of crisis. Soon after the widows were relocated here, it became necessary for almost all of them to leave their homes in order to find some form of livelihood. For some, the state offered jobs in offices that required them to travel long distances away from home. Some others found sustenance in a community organization that had set up their operations in the Colony to support the residents. This organization (their activities will be discussed further later) set up a sewing center that allowed these women to earn some money from sewing garments for sale. In the course of this, most of these women had to leave their children (a large number of whom were very young at the time), either in the care of neighbors or other elderly, largely female relatives that the household consisted of. Some older children had to fend for themselves. A predominant theme that ran through most of our conversations with the people in the Colony was about the fate of these children, who in their perception, grew up without proper parenting implying "male" parenting which led, especially the boys to fall into the predictable cycle of drug abuse, petty crimes, gambling etc. usual to conditions of poverty and deprivation.[24] During our visits in 2004, we were told that even within the first half of that year, drug related deaths were as high as 200. It is quite likely that, in other comparable colonies in the city, similar profiles among young men will be fairly common. The striking point here is that in the Colony this profile has another kind of interpretation, one that is overwhelmingly about the special character of their neighborhood rather than about the usual challenges. Some of the young men in the Colony told us how the bad name of the Colony has in fact severely tainted the efforts they make in finding jobs, sometimes the mention of where they come from is enough to dissuade any potential employer. A group of young men told us the following,

> A: A friend of ours had learnt the work of Air Conditioners. He went to an interview and everything was fine. At the end they asked him, where do you stay? And he said, Tilak Vihar. They said you have to go, we cannot take you. Because you are from Tilak Vihar. Just because of this word. They say, everybody is a deviant here, we are disreputable. Someone is a pickpocket, someone is a thief—you catch them and they say they are from Tilak Vihar.
>
> ... They say you are from '84. There is such dirt there (in the Colony), you must also be doing the same. We can only say that five fingers are not the same. If along with four bad ones here there is another, he will also be considered bad.
>
> C: Shahpura[25] is even worse than Tilak Vihar. All bad things happen there—chain snatching, kidnapping but only Tilak Vihar is considered disreputable.[26]

The fixing of a social identity to a place makes the Colony not only internally coherent but simultaneously spatially parenthesizes it into a marked location. This ascription then has implications into the way the world outside, the city at large, comes to negotiate with this place.

Another way in which the Colony becomes a marked location is the way in which, over the years, it has become the iconic place with which to represent any ongoing reference to the events of 1984. During the times when the more controversial inquiry commission reports are made public, the media uses the Colony for their mandatory visuals, sound bytes etc. Organized protests predictably emerge out of the Colony. The appointment of a Sikh Prime Minister has also been a reason for the public gaze to revisit the Colony. On the whole, public reference to the events of 1984 makes the Colony the necessary and easy way to "locate" the community, especially the "victimized" part of the community. When we started our work in the area, the initial responses to our visits were that " . . . people like you come to us all the time. Whenever there is any discussion about '84, media people reach here with their cameras and microphones. Many foreigners have also come, they take our stories, but we don't get anything out of this. Never, not even a shawl to cover ourselves with." Obvious in such utterances–it is the persistence of a channeled public gaze, which contributes heavily to making the social identity a peculiar burden to bear. On one hand, it is this identity itself which is required to keep their coherence as a political group seeking redress for failed justice or compensation for loss. On the other, in a more interior plane, it becomes a label that becomes also a stigma when negotiation with a larger social universe is concerned.

Another nuance to the community identity is related to the non-governmental activity that is practiced here. Apart from state compensation, one of the main sources of long-term relief was the Delhi Sikh Gurudwara Management Committee which had provided a monthly pension to these widows, that was subsequently discontinued since 1999. However, the organization that is permanently located in the Colony and has been providing services since 1985 is a non-governmental community establishment called Nishkam Sikh Welfare Council. Nishkam started as a loosely organized group of Sikh individuals of Delhi who were involved in relief activities during the initial days after the carnage. Some opening statements of their website are,

> Nishkam was entirely a community effort, Nishkam Sikh Welfare Council (Regd.) in India was founded by a group of 11 key founders in 1984. These "Founder Members"/ "Permanent Members" were all Sikh gentlemen, residing in New Delhi, India. They shared a common passion for charity work and felt the urge to reach out to the dispossessed in their immediate environment. These volunteers believed in the one of the key tenets of Sikhism, to serve all of God's children, regardless of color, religion or caste. Nishkam today is an NGO that has an established track record. It is also trying to make a long lasting

difference in the lives of students by raising educational standards in Punjab, India. Nishkam is also assisting members of the Sikh faith that are outside of Punjab, but residing in India in the re-discovery of their roots. In addition to this it is making educational and material investment in such communities. The Sikligar Sikhs of Karnataka are one such community.

In Tilak Vihar itself, they maintain the sewing, training and production Center which was aimed mainly at the widows and their daughters. Additionally, there is the typing and shorthand center, computer education classes, other child and adult welfare activities—English speaking, placement services, and fairly extensive polyclinic cum diagnostic center. In spite of the ostensibly secular aims, Nishkam is a strong community organization funded largely by generous contributions from the Sikh diaspora as well from local Sikhs. Running through their activities are obvious indications of the commitment to community identity, for instance, the Library holdings in Tilak Vihar, apart from school textbooks and computer aids, are mostly about Sikh history and religion. Educational programs are predominantly constituted of learning *Gurmukhi* (the script used in Punjab, the ethnic state of origin for Sikhs), *Gurbani* (reading of the scriptures), *Gur-itihas* (history of the Gurus) and Sikh history. The appeal to volunteers is also worded significantly in the cosmology of the community. For example, quoting from the website again,

> Humanitarian service is the Sikh ideal of *seva* (service). Sri Guru Nanak (the first Guru of the Sikhs) has said: "Truth is above everything but higher still is truthful living." Thus *seva* is the first step to achieve the final goal of eternal peace.
>
> Therefore, Nishkam is on the look out for such volunteers, who subscribe to the above ideology and are not looking for power, position or money. As of today, Nishkam Sikh Welfare Council (Regd.) has a total of about 50 volunteers in India. The members and volunteers devote their evenings and week ends to Nishkam. None of the founders (and none of the current volunteers) ever drew/draw any salary or any kind of compensation from Nishkam.

Nishkam's presence in the Colony is overwhelming. In our meetings with the residents, a common topic of conversation was Nishkam which included elaborate descriptions of their activities, the volunteers and their changing profile, their honesty and dedication or lack of it and so on. The young men we met where also involved in the training programs, a large number of the widows we visited were regular members of the sewing Center. In fact, for most of them the Center's sewing activity was the sole source of livelihood. For some of the very poor families, there was no other option because traveling out of the Colony to find work elsewhere was too difficult considering the expenses of traveling by bus. Many residents were also aware that it was because of Nishkam that the charity efforts of many could reach them in an organized manner. Clearly, the relations between the organization and the Colony had changed overtime, sometimes becoming strained because some of the local residents feel that their motivation has changed from charity to profit making. But others do make the point that, however the perception may be, Nishkam as compared to state support has been present and available.

An interesting twist to the double bind of community in this situation is when the community becomes the site where both betrayal and succor are apparent. The proximal relations within a neighborhood, the shared burden as it were, brings out one sort of identity consciousness, but at the same time in terms of wider connections with the community at large, there is a perception of betrayal by the Sikhs as a political group. A statement by an elderly woman eloquently shows this,

> Whatever has happened to us was very bad. What can we do now? What has happened to us has happened. But then, even our Guru Granth Sahib has been sacralized. What has been done to our men has been done. Our Sardars have always been martyred. We are a community of martyrdom, but Durbar Sahib has been burnt—it has been vandalized. What fault did it have? Many Gurudwaras have been burnt. The people who had done this, their killings, nothing has been done. Nobody has been caught. There are these hearings and then our people say, "Well, this government is supporting us." No government is supporting us. We are just sitting peacefully, waiting for when God will Himself act.
> ... We do not want anything from them, the justice we should have been given has been denied to us.
> Whatever has happened in whatever way, the Sikh Community has forgotten everything. They garland those people, today our murderers have won and come back and our brothers our garlanding them. There is no one to listen, no justice. They gave us jobs but with the jobs our children were left behind, no one to look after them. The children kept going wrong without us . . . when women leave their children behind, what can happen, they will go wrong, under whose care could we have left them. No one child here has been reformed, some are drug addicts, some gamble. Our community should have settled us, the Gurudwara has stopped our pension, they say, your children are now earning, they have done nothing for us. They have done whatever they wished. They might go on making Prime Ministers, but till we get justice we will remain tormented like this.

The neighborhood identity becomes the entity of reference where most negotiations, internal or external take place; in a sense there is a near complete erasure of a civic society which can transcend community symbols and formations, in its place there are tightening holds of community consciousness, whether it be in positive terms or negative. This, of course, is enhanced by the perceived or real impotence of the state in according justice or even in providing enough support towards the generation that grew up in these conditions, all features that speak of a failure in the rehabilitative intent of state practice.

My intent in the above sketch has been to highlight the ways in which a heightened community consciousness can intricately and immutably get tied to the lived experience of a locality, one that congeals identities over time, identity formations that go beyond "primordial community connections." These then are trajectories of lives traced out by violence, and then relocated by rehabilitative strategy to addresses rendered thick with community coherence and marked out in city space as bounded and homogenous.

IMPOSSIBLE COSMOPOLISES

In conclusion, the ethnographic descriptions I have made above highlights two kinds of processes manifest in the afterlife of violent events in two cities. In Delhi, it is the homogenization of a "victim" neighborhood with a straight jacketing of community identity, i.e., a somewhat centripetal movement. In Beirut, the description is about a centrifugal force that has disassembled heterogeneous spaces, whose fragments then congeal together again in homogenous social formations.[27]

It has been established in urban discourse that neighborhoods are indeed always formed by networks of kin, community and social identity and as such homogenous pockets in city spaces are common. In Delhi, the original homes of the survivor families would have been fairly homogenous, if not as large conglomerations but certainly as small pockets within larger heterogeneous masses. In fact, why should a similar cohesion in the circumstances outlined above elicit further probing? The primary answer to that is, while such primary neighborhoods can have social identities signified by ethnic identity among others, these formations have been formed organically, as "natural" growth processes of urban expansion. Community cohesions and corresponding urban socialities in identifiable city spaces have been established outcomes of rural-urban connections, kinship networks, professional groupings and related factors.

However, in the circumstances I describe above, the inscription of community identity on space, in the first instance, has been the outcome of violence. They are constituted by community hostilities and by overt conditions of suspicion and hatred. This is a definite difference from the kind of social interactions and formations of multi-community locales where several identity groups coexist; or from the balance, however fragile and uneasy that exists among proximal but separate community neighborhoods and locales. However, spaces marked by violent homogenizations get thickened with meaning in a way that surpasses any earlier or other social coding. Cognitive maps, geographically and socially, for both those inside and outside, operate to mark out differences in clearer terms than before, and are often doubly strengthened by political mobilization that make the public face of these identities more visible. Allen Feldman's discussions of spatial formations in Belfast bear a striking resemblance to the kinds of processes I have described in Beirut and Delhi. He uses the notion of an "interface" to "explain, . . . the topographic-ideological boundary sector that physically and symbolically demarcates ethnic communities in Belfast from each other. The "interface" is a spatial construct pre-eminently linked to the performance of violence. . . . during periods of residential retrenchment along sectarian lines, the proliferation of interfaces, the dissemination of margins, the formalizations of boundaries can be expected.

In different ways, both in Beirut and in Delhi there are compelling re-mappings where those lines that had previously served to trace the social map of the cityscape now became formalized as antagonistic boundaries. My frame, however, extends beyond these formations to another set of temporal and spatial processes where rehabilitation or reconstruction becomes instrumental, in two separate ways, in either context of Delhi and Beirut. Illustratively, in Delhi, I have described the way in which the rehabilitative gesture of statecraft has contributed towards creating a space for a "society of victimhood," as it were, creating a lasting emblematic marker for a given community. There is no denying the fact that, either by profession or ethnic identity, this group may have occupied community spaces even before the event. In fact, that is how a systematic attack could take place given that the Sikh concentrated neighborhoods were easily identifiable. Yet, earlier, they did not possess the singularity, the parenthesizing that is now ascribed to them. In our conversations with the women in Tilak Vihar, we were often told about how their men folk took their services and businesses far out of their neighborhoods, sometimes even abroad, to places where they built up connections with other city dwellers. Some others, told us about how poverty had been a common burden, which had made peaceful, supportive neighbors out of each other. Uma Chakravarty writes of a widow who struggles to make meaning of their fate where she sees herself as part of ordinary men and women trying to eke out a living, living under the protection of leaders common to all. They remember that the assassinated Prime Minister Indira Gandhi was as dear to them as for any other group. The question they ask is—How is it that the action of a few made everyone in the community become substitutable for the killers' guilt, separate from all others? Clearly, this is the kind of sharp contouring that marks out the Colony, a process that concentrates the burden of an event onto a circumscribed group, shifting the public gaze onto a set of people who now substitute for an identity emblem.

In Beirut, in another version of a related process, a recovery provision legitimated by the state contributes towards the undoing of an already existing mixed space, Downtown Beirut. It may be argued, that given Beirut's already fragmented city spaces and strong primordial socialities, how does the factor of reconstruction of a select area matter so much. Second, given that Beirut has been and is continuing to be divided up into circumscribed community localities, it is highly likely that with or without reconstruction, in post-Civil War Beirut people may have automatically chosen to live in neighborhoods of their own kind. However, given the ethnographic articulations described earlier, my contention would be that such assumptions endorse the discursive power of divided publics, simultaneously denying the possibility of ordinary cosmopolitan experiences of everyday citizens, as also their desire for the same, especially in prolonged hostilities. The preoccupied stressing of hostility in fraught situations effectively disallows or ignores those processes, experiences and conscious aspirations of those who seek to move past the disruption. Downtown Beirut, for instance, was one of the few cosmopolitan spaces of pre-war Beirut. It was a quality and an attitude manifested and sustained by its residents and participants in a society that has historically maintained primordial priorities. Even the temporary social arrangements, for the while that they lasted did not prevent the building up of a small, but sustainable cosmopolitanism. The expulsion or dispersion of these very groups disconnects some fragile connections and destabilizes an already frayed social fabric. The spatial aspect of this is fundamental, the perceived distances between older connections, the need to spatially enclose one's quotidian existence in homogenous locales destroy the cohesion that was once felt among a multiplicity.

How do these sorts of remapped city spaces or re-emphasized social identities measure up to a notion of cosmopolitanism? A combined reading of the above contexts seems to indicate that certain arenas that manifest "mundane cosmopolitanisms" somehow fall outside the paradigmatic frames of discourse. Often, in the lofty discourse of global cosmopolites, the potential of local intermixing is undermined or read as a very different sphere of discourse of multi-cultural relations rather than as something akin to the cosmopolitan "aesthetic." Here, I indicate the everyday city spaces of streets and alleyways, bazaars and neighborhoods where the common citizens, migrants or refugees of modern metropolises live their lives, build their relationships and, in effect, manifest a powerful cosmopolitanism. I would like to emphasize my earlier point that in the multiculturalism of cities, the everyday social experience of these environments spatially concentrates cosmopolitanism to a ground level, to a density that can be volatile as it can be powerfully constructive. In the discursive constructions of urban sectarian violence, while the potential of violence is often re-iterated and rightfully so, given the number of worldwide episodes of contemporary urban violence, the possibility of a constructive social energy that could be a resource, particularly in post-conflict situations is frequently overlooked.

Downtown Beirut, in its glorious past, was in fact an iconic presence on the city horizon, as a mixed space where all confessions worked, entertained, consumed and also lived side by side. In the historically fragmented city spaces of Beirut, this was the spatial embedded logic of a common area that translated into iconic practice. The denizens of the area who chose to cling on to their precarious existences in the area may have stayed on because of a lack of alternatives, but their representations indicate considerable impact of an experience of cosmopolitan living. Memory as a resource may have even fuelled a new desire, perhaps inspired by a nostalgic recollection of a harmonious past. This is evident from the enthusiasm displayed by those who wanted to return to the area even after having "settled" for many years into their own kind of neighborhoods. These acts of social intent, particularly after deep chasms of belligerence need to be recognized and given adequate place in the planning towards recovery or in measures of "reconciliation."

Similarly in Delhi, most of the earlier homes of those relocated to the Colony had been in pockets defined by community, kinship or ties of place of origin. Yet the daily meeting and interactions with either proximal others or those in the wider city necessarily instilled a sense of heterogeneity and multiplicity of experience, perhaps available only in the density of urban life. This is the crucial dynamic of ordinary cosmopolitanism that becomes inevitable in the "urban" experience of sustaining livelihoods, work and in patterns of everyday contacts that makes for a tolerance of the other. The sense of fear and insularity that genocidal attacks impose upon a community takes away, among other things, this ground level of openness to others. When insularity generated in the moments of violence gets sustained over long durations that cross over into future generations through further ghettoizing processes, there is damage created to the social fabric that may grow deeper roots in the social landscape.

At the same time, I would hasten to clarify that in the contexts I describe and perhaps in others as well, the critical factor is not that the established past experience of cosmopolitanism and its reclamation is the only way to ensure its future revival. By offering another reading, I would suggest that the reinforcement of identity constructs and their circumscribed carving out of city maps inevitably curtails the strength of those ordinary aspirations which seek to step out (or need to step out of) of homogenizing experiences to far more anonymous conditions of existence, at least in certain arenas of everyday life. Ironically, these mundane cosmopolitan experiences and aspirations have found expression in those very spaces that are undermined by processes that are ostensibly aimed at reparation, but some how remain shortsighted about the social connectivities that may result into the future.

Discursive cosmopolitanism most often focuses on imaginaries that ranges from the national to transnational frameworks, or on cultural multiplicities that span global flows in order to interrogate notions of identity and belonging. The focus, when moved to include micro processes, display very different sorts of movements across boundaries and frontiers, those that imply a "vertical" depth rather than a "horizontal" expansion, or in other words, the multiple layerings that appear within cities. For instance, intra city neighborhood experiences that do not necessarily imply the original paradigmatic identity categories of the global imagination, rather they produce and reproduce localized identity terrains and their contestations or equilibriums, and significantly for the argument here, they identify mundane cosmopolitanisms that need to be recognized as having equal place and potential with the rhetoric of a global, often elite dynamic of cosmopolitan. These internal compositions, the localized values and lived notions of everyday cosmopolitanism deserve particular attention in post-violence landscapes precisely so that the attempts at reconciliation and reparation can be better substantiated through an understanding of an existing dynamic as social resource or as the case may be, as social deterrent.

In conclusion, I would conjecture that if our understanding of the urban form can be suggested as the logical spatial outcome of multiple relations of exchange and connectivity, social identities being one of these, then one of the results of cities remapped by violence is the territorialized realms of identity space. What we may need to keep in mind, through our investigations of the strategies of recovery measures—are these territorializations being given further form in a way that a silent but tenacious link is forged between property, work, commerce on one hand and ethnic identity, on the other? In these cities, like the nuances of Beirut and Delhi, could identity mappings be transformed from registers of fluid difference to concrete urban densities that overrides the logic of mundane cosmopolitanism to produce impossible cosmopolises?

ACKNOWLEDGEMENTS

My deepest gratitude is to all the people in Delhi and Beirut who took the time to share their stories with me, undoubtedly at great personal distress. My appreciation of Zeina, Michelle, Amr, Harpreet and Simi's support, is I hope, expressed by my continual attempts at giving some shape to our bewildering experiences in the field. I am also grateful for the funds that both IDPAD (for Delhi) and the Ford Foundation (for Beirut) provided with which fieldwork for this essay could be conducted.

NOTES

1. Steven Vertovec and Robin Cohen mention the historically granted notion of cosmopolitanism as an elite practice and discourse. However, they also add, the contemporary world and its dynamics has led to "the necessity of cheek-by-jowl relationships between diverse peoples at work or at street corners and in markets, neighborhoods, schools and recreational areas. Some of the most fascinating social research in the field is now generating countless examples of so called 'everyday' or 'ordinary' cosmopolitanism." (5)
2. Hiebert locates a kind of everyday, ordinary cosmopolitanism in a study of his own neighborhood in Vancouver's East Side. In his understanding of cosmopolitanism as a way of living based on "openness on all forms of otherness," he states, "This lifestyle is exemplified in the vignette of my back lane, where men

and women from different origins create a society where diversity is accepted and rendered ordinary." He relates this to the basic contexts of social life, " . . . the home and neighborhood, work, consumption, and social interaction" where mono-cultural and mixed cultural experiences mingle together through everyday spans (Hiebert, 212). While Hiebert's example deals with people coming from different nations, my examples are confined to multi-ethnic groups that, by and large, relate to the same "nation." This introduces an element of difference between northern and southern notions of cosmopolitanism or multi-ethnic living in urban conditions. This essay does not necessarily require that exploration but the factor remains important.

3. Reiterating the importance of space in urban epistemology would only mean covering well established ground. The works of Henri Lefebvre, Michel de Certeau along with Edward Soja among many others, have eloquently demonstrated the analytical position of space in urban experience.
4. The fluidity and subversion of boundaries between such spaces have to be constantly reiterated, to mention just one obvious example, sufi shrines are well known examples of places that carry community inscriptions but are places experienced by many beyond the limits of community identity.
5. The possibility of casting the ethnographic/anthropological encounter between two locations, particularly in a "south—south" frame, by privileging a contextual "sameness in difference" is an idea developed in my essay titled, "Anthropologies of Difference: The Making of New Encounters."
6. As I have mentioned in note 6, this essay is also about the possibility of reading contexts in the "south" together. Although I do develop this essay along that trajectory, it will be useful to see how far the reading of urban conditions, specifically in the south carve out a distinct epistemological space that may stand separate from urban perspectives based predominantly in studies of northern cities.
7. No formal census has been conducted in Lebanon since 1932, when the shared scheme of government was first installed (since the end of the French mandate), whereby a Maronite Christian was to be the President, a Sunni the Prime Minister, a Shi'i speaker of the house to be followed next in office by the Druze. Sharing of power was based on demographic strength of the time, the figures have since changed drastically, but the elected scheme of government remains the same. The challenges to a democratic government and the conflicts within are intrinsically generated by these demographic dynamics. As a consequence of this, no official figures are available. Territorial control, therefore, also becomes a central part of the power dynamic that operates in Lebanon whereby political leaders not only lead their sects but also those designated spaces that they occupy. The growing strength of Hezbollah, in the present context and their entry into government has been a development fueled along by the existing patterns of Lebanese statecraft.
8. The western district of Ras Beirut, particularly the Hamra quarter is the other recognizably mixed space of Beirut, especially before the war. Where Hamra is associated with a sophisticated cosmopolitanism generated by the American University of Beirut, well placed expatriates, bohemian artists and intellectuals, Downtown Beirut was more about a popular, vibrant culture of intermingling.
9. For a succinct appraisal of how the social geography of Lebanon has changed in the post-war years, see Salim Nasr. Very little research or statistics is available about post-war Beirut, however, Nasr's essay provides basic indications.
10. My initial fieldwork in the Downtown area, as part of my doctoral work was conducted in 1997–1998. I revisited Beirut for fieldwork associated with the "Cities in Interaction" project during September-October 2004. I was assisted by Amr Saeddedine, graduate student at the American University of

Beirut (AUB), in my research in Beirut during the months of September and October, 2004. Zeina Misk and Michelle Obeid, also graduate students at AUB at the time, helped in my doctoral fieldwork.

11. The reconstruction of Downtown Beirut has been a highly controversial and debated event in Lebanon. Conducted under the aegis of a private real estate company called SOLIDERE (more detail below), this was a historically singular event of post-war rebuilding where a single company took on the ownership and management of a highly symbolic place in the city. In my work, I have held that the spectacular rebuilding of a completely destroyed core as a flagship project for a recuperating nation could only have been achieved with a vehicle like SOLIDERE. However, this does not discount the fact that in a war devastated country there are a host of other concerns of housing, health and livelihood as well as other economic, political and social rehabilitative measures that require as much if not more, attention. Prioritizing the glamorous renovation of one square mile, with limited range of effect, cannot be evaluated without critique.

12. An important recent event within the Downtown area, in early 2005, has been the demonstrations after the assassination of ex-prime Minister Rafiq Hariri, who was one of the key figures in engineering the alliance of political will and financial clout in the reconstruction of downtown Beirut. Overwhelming crowds came together in the downtown Beirut area, with participation of a very visibly mixed group of people from across the various denominations in Beirut (except for the Hezbollah , the Shi'i political wing) to assert their solidarity with Hariri's anti-Syrian stand (which is alleged as one of the primary reasons for his assassination). This event perhaps marks the return of Downtown Beirut as a new, reformulated public space that reflects the contemporary pulse in Beirut's socio-scape. See Sune Haugbolle for a related description.

13. A part of my doctoral research explored the neighborhood of Hamra to map the range of social transformations experienced by its residents. The statement I make here is largely based on my own ethnographic work during 1997, based on about 35 extended interviews with a variety of people associated with Hamra.

14. Hiba Bou Akar describes some of ways in which these relocations happened both during the initial phase of warfare and later, during the phase of reconstruction. Her description and analysis makes it amply clear how homogenizing identity politics were dominant in all stages of these processes. Finding appropriate empty homes in the abandoned houses of downtown Beirut, eventually getting adequate compensation during eviction etc. were situations where political parties like Hezbollah had almost total influence.

15. The Amal are the second political body of Shi'is in Lebanon. Although older in years than the Hezbollah, they lag behind in popularity or visibility. See Lara Deeb for a discussion of the relationship between Hezbollah and Amal.

16. The assassination of the Prime Minister by her Sikh bodyguards was connected to the prevailing Sikh militancy of the time. The days from 1st to 4th November 1984 are considered to be the worst 72 hours of the carnage, an event unparalleled in the city since the partition of 1947. Some other parts of the country were affected as well. Official figures estimate the dead to be 2733, most of which were men in the age group 20–50, although other sources place the figure at 4000 or above. There are still no official figures on the numbers of injured, of raped women or on estimates of property damage. For an anthropological insight into the immediate experiences of Sikh women after the riots, see Veena Das ("Our work to cry, your work to listen."). For a compilation of narratives collected from the survivors of the Sikh carnage, see Uma Chakravarty and Nandita Haksar as well as Madhu Kiswar for accounts of sexual violence against women in the same event.

By way of a brief background—the '84 events were related to the movement (particularly from 1981), propagated by Sikh leaders with the express motivation of establishing Sikh sovereignty, possibly as a separate nation. For the present discussion, it is interesting to note a few themes of the militant discourse of the 80's that led to the carnage of '84. Veena Das (*Critical Events*) notes how the modern discourse of the state aids in the making of a Sikh crisis produced by their leaders by way of which past and present events are collapsed to produce the Hindu nation/state as the threatening powerful "other" whose overarching "Indian" claims endanger their existence. This same discourse of victimhood in the hands of the Hindus is made to extend to the Muslims, who are, in the same vein, equal victims, thereby selectively forgetting the earlier histories of oppression or violence related to Muslims. In this new context, the massacre in Delhi validates the threat felt from the ruling Hindu majorities. Although it is important to keep the Hindu or Muslim relations with Sikhs and their genealogies in perspective, it is also important to note that explaining away the '84 carnage with pre-existing tensions does not allow adequate discussion of the role of the state and its unmitigated use of violence in the name of law and order. Nor does it allow a sufficient consideration of the long afterlife of such events, especially in the confines of everyday city spaces. See J.P.S. Uberoi for a discussion of Sikhism's historical hostilities with Hinduism and Islam. Also see Brian Axel for the spread of Sikh militancy. Dipankar Gupta, W.H. McLeod and Harjot Oberoi provide discussions about contemporary Sikh identity.
17. The ethnographic information in this essay is based on our interviews with approximately 30 households in the neighborhood. I was assisted by Simi Bajaj and Harpreet Kaur from the ISERDD research team in conducting these interviews and funding for this part of fieldwork came from IDPAD. A majority of the original allottees in the Colony came from Sultanpuri and Mongolpuri, two of the worst hit colonies of the city. Differences within the Colony in terms of economic status was significant ranging from poor to lower middle class, caste hierarchies were also evident.
18. Figures quoted from information available at www.nishkam.org.
19. See Yasmeen Arif ("The Delhi Carnage of 1984"). Sections of narratives from the widows and other informants in the colony which have appeared in that essay have also been included here. I thank Vrinda Grover for allowing me to use her work on the failure of justice in the Sikh carnage.
20. I am privileging the *community* identity over other features such as gender, age, or profession that could equally constitute social identity, mainly for the sake of analytical simplicity in the arguments presented here.
21. I would emphasize the fact that while it is indeed the Sikh community at large that suffered this attack, the burden of its afterlife is different within different sections of the community depending on a variety of factors of social and economic class, spatial location or degree of loss, for instance, matter or/and life.
22. See note 20 above.
23. Dori Laub psychologically analyses similar sorts of repetitions in her work on the Holocaust testimonies. She writes, "Trauma survivors live not with memories of the past, but with an event that could not and did not proceed through to its completion, has no ending, attained no closure, and therefore, as far as its survivors are concerned, continues into the present and is current in every respect.... To undo this entrapment is a fate that cannot be known, cannot be told, but can only be repeated, a therapeutic process—a process of reconstructing a narrative, of reconstructing a history and essentially, of *re-externalizing the event*—has to be set in motion. This re-externalization of the event can occur . . . only when one can articulate and *transmit* the story, literally transfer it to another outside oneself and take it back again,

inside."(69) The geographical proximity within the colony could allow for such a movement of therapeutic externalization-internalization.
24. In our current fieldwork we came across some male members in certain household who did not belong to the category of fathers or sons. Their relationship to the widow was hard to establish, at any rate this was not information that was easily forthcoming. We sensed that it would be very detrimental to broach the topic of remarriage, nonetheless, if pursued it could have lead to further analysis on how the constructed nature of this community of widows influences the engagement with the usual social sanctions and taboos of widowhood.
25. A similar neighborhood, not too far from the colony.
26. The narratives from the colony are verbatim translations, retained here in that form so as to convey the expression. They are, thus, not grammatically correct.
27. Constraints of space here do not allow a fuller discussion on the extent of relocations and dislocations in the biographies of those I mention here. Just as the Shi'i families who had made a second home in downtown Beirut measure their move to the suburb as a second round of relocation, some of the Sikh families we have met register their move to the colony as a second displacement because a number of them had originally been moved to Sultanpuri from elsewhere as part of internal relocations in Delhi during the phase known as the Emergency (1975–1977) in India during which controversial slum clearance and resettlement programs were imposed.

WORKS CITED

Arif, Yasmeen. "Anthropologies of Difference: The Making of New Encounters." *The Journal of the World Anthropologies Network* 1.2 (2006): 41–57.

———. "The Delhi Carnage of 1984: Afterlives of Loss and Grief." *Domains, The International Journal for Ethnic Studies.* Special Issue on Riots Discourses. (2007) 3: 17–40.

Augé, Marc. *An Anthropology for Contemporaneous Worlds.* Trans. Amy Jacobs, Stanford: Stanford UP, 1994.

Axel, Brian. *The Nation's Tortured Body: Violence, Representation and the Formation of the Sikh Diaspora.* Durham: Duke UP, 2001.

Beyhum, Nabil. "The Crisis of Urban Culture: The Three Reconstruction Plans for Beirut." *The Beirut Review* 3 (1992): 43–62.

Bou Akar, Hiba. "Displacement, Politics, and Governance: Access to Low Income Housing in a Beirut Suburb." Unpublished Master's Dissertation, Massachusetts Institute of Technology, Cambridge, MA, 2005.

Chakravarty, Uma. "Victims, 'Neighbors' and Watan: Survivors of the Anti-Sikh Carnage of 1984." *Economic and Political Weekly,* 15 Oct 1994: 2722–2726.

Chakravarty, Uma and Nandita Haksar, eds. *The Delhi Riots: Three Days in the Life of a Nation.* New Delhi: Lancer International, 1987.

Das, Veena. *Critical Events: An Anthropological Perspective on Contemporary India.* Delhi: Oxford UP, 1995.

———. "Our Work to Cry, Your Work to Listen." *Mirrors of Violence: Communities, Riots, Survivors in South Asia.* Ed. Veena Das. Delhi: Oxford UP, 1990. 345–98.

Deeb, Lara. *Hizballah: a primer.* Middle East Report Online. http://www.merip.org/mero/mero73106.html 2006.

de Certeau, Michel. *The Practice of Everyday Life.* Berkeley: University of California Press, 1984.

Fawaz, Mona. "Agency and Ideology in the Service Provision of Islamic Organizations." Unpublished Discussion Paper. UNESCO conference on NGOs and Governance in Arab countries, Cairo, Egypt, 29–31 March 2000.

Feldman, Allen. *Formations of Violence: The Narrative of the Body and Political Terror in Northern Ireland*. Chicago: U of Chicago P, 1991.

Haugbolle, Sune. "Spatial Transformations in the Lebanese 'Independence Intifada'." *Arab Studies Journal* (Fall 2006): 60 -77.

Grover, Vrinda. *Quest for Justice: 1984 Massacre of Sikh Citizens in Delhi*. Mimeo, 2002.

Gupta, Dipankar. *The Context of Ethnicity*. Delhi: Oxford UP, 1997.

Hanf, Theodor. *Co-existence in Wartime Lebanon*. London: I.B. Tauris, 1993.

Hiebert, Daniel. "Cosmopolitanism at the Local Level: The Development of Transnational Neighborhoods." *Conceiving Cosmopolitanism: Theory, Context and Practice*. Eds. Steven Vertovec and Robin Cohen. Delhi: Oxford UP, 2002. 209–23.

Kiswar, Madhu. "Gangster Rule." *Manushi* 25 (1984): 10–34.

Laub, Dori. "An Event without a Witness: Truth, Testimony and Survival." *Testimony: Crises of Witnessing in Literature, Psychoanalysis, and History*. Eds. Shoshana Felman and Dori Laub. New York: Routledge, 1992.

Lefebvre, Henri. *The Production of Space*. Oxford: Blackwell, 1991.

Makdisi, Saree. "Laying Claim to Beirut: Urban Narrative and Spatial Identity in the Age of Solidere." *Critical Inquiry* 23.3 (1997): 661–705.

McLeod, William Hewat. *Who Is a Sikh? The Problem of Sikh Identity*. Delhi: Oxford UP, 1989.

Nasr, Salim. "The New Social Map." *Lebanon in Limbo: Postwar Society and State in an Uncertain Regional Environment*. Eds. Theodor Hanf and Nawaf Salem. Badan-Baden: Nomos Verlagsgesellschaft, 2000. 143–57.

Oberoi, Harjot. *The Construction of Religious Boundaries: Culture, Identity and Diversity in the Sikh Tradition*. Delhi: Oxford UP, 1994.

Vertovec, Steven and Robin Cohen, eds. *Conceiving Cosmopolitanism: Theory, Context and Practice*. Delhi: Oxford UP, 2002.

Soja, Edward. *ThirdSpace: Journeys to Los Angeles and Other Real-and-Imagined Places*. Los Angeles: U of California P, 1996.

Uberoi, Jit Pal Singh. *Religion, Civil Society and the State: A Study of Sikhism*. Delhi: Oxford UP, 1999.

6 Limiting Cosmopolitanism
Streetlife "Little India," Kuala Lumpur

Yeoh Seng Guan

Despite its lack of history, Kuala Lumpur has a vibrant culture. This is a city in which the train station looks like a Moorish/Malay palace. This is a city filled with cultural performances of all kinds. This is a city where even the most modern buildings, even skyscrapers, make use of Islamic and Malay motifs. This is a city where Chinatown is as good as Chinatown in San Francisco and Little India is a smaller, cleaner version of bright, towering, artistic mosques, eye-catching Chinese temples, colourful Hindu temples and cathedrals that come straight out of Europe. If you've never been a people watcher, and I've never really been, Kuala Lumpur will change that. If there's one thing Malays seem to love it's colour. You can see it in their brightly painted houses, colourful dances, treasured kites, famous weaving and most of all, clothing. Most Malay women wear bright colours wherever they go, often with elaborate decorations. In fact, Malays are famous for a type of woven cloth that actually uses gold thread. Not gold-coloured thread, but thread made from gold. I'm not kidding. Fewer Malay men wear traditional cloths, but those who do are just as colourful. Kuala Lumpur's many Indians also wear colourful sarongs. Only the Chinese prefer western clothing, which seems drab in comparison. All this makes any crowded street seem like a kaleidoscope of people.

That description certainly fits Little India. The Indian part of town is full of the sights and smells of India, but only the more pleasant smells. You can smell the aroma of incense, Indian spices, and Indian food cooking as you look at the prayer rugs and jewelry for sale in the Muslim part of Little India. In the rear of that area stands a mosque that combines Moorish and Malay designs and stands at the convergence of rivers that gave Kuala Lumpur its name. In the Hindu part, you can see small jasmine garlands hanging from kiosks as you look through the shops selling Hindu statues and colourful pictures of the Hindu gods. By 6.00 pm, the Hindu and Muslim parts of town converge in the Indian night market, conveniently located on the street that more or less divides the two communities. The Indian night market is a welcomed assault on the senses, assuming you're not too easily overwhelmed. Any number of bizarre things can be found, even leeches. No, I don't know anyone would be in the market for leeches. Muslim women with their bright head scarves do business with Hindu women wearing bright sarongs, and curious Malays drop by to add even more colour.[1]

INTRODUCTION

The project—"Communities in Interaction: Discourses of Conflict, Conversion, and Coexistence in Cosmopolitan Contexts"—behoves its collaborators to elucidate the contours of "subaltern cosmopolitanism" that striate and animate the Asian cities constituting the foci of this publication. The analytical quest set for us is to examine and clarify the ethical idea of living together with strangers and to explore the kinds of coexistence between ethnic groups that have a history of collective interethnic violence. Borrowing from Michel de Certeau's suggestive imagery of "intertwined pedestrian pathways" that are obscured by the panoptic (and statist) view of the city, we are asked to "identify aspects of shared-ness in multi-cultural contexts that are defined by difference, by the politics of separate and parallel ethnicities."[2]

In the specific case of Malaysia, scholars in the critical tradition have over the years conventionally focused on elucidating the divisive dynamics of ethnic politics in general and exclusivist Malay nationalist politics in particular. A dialectical binary is usually set up between an indigenous Malay community—constitutionally imbued with political supremacy—and immigrant non-Malay communities that have pragmatically gained economic control of the country's resources. Beginning in the early 1970s, the twin powerful forces of Islamic revivalism coupled with the social engineering motif of the New Economic Policy (1971–1990) and its later mutations have further provided additional empirical fodder for a critique of the racial and class dimensions of Malaysian polity and society. Following this tack, the central argument commonly advanced is that the interplay between statist and nonstatist actors has lent itself to a competitive ethnicized and uncosmopolitan compartmentalization of everyday life, and the subsequent deterioration of interethnic and interreligious relations over the past three decades. More recently, however, following interventions in postcolonial, poststructuralist, and postmodern scholarship, attention is being redirected to the analytical categories deployed in putatively explaining the discursive prevalence of political and social primordialism in the country. For instance, historian Sumit K. Mandal argues that critical scholars have not been vigilant enough in developing a more precise cultural language of politics as they map the country's regime of ethnicity and political economy. Despite the questionable salience of racialized categories in everyday life, Mandal laments that "scholarship persists in deploying them" (60). As a counterpoint, he turns to historical antecedents in party politics as well as the work of various contemporary cultural activists to suggest that hybrid cultural politics and transethnic solidarities and cosmopolitanisms have continued viability in relation to the race-based polity of the nation-state (see also Farish).

In this essay, I recast and refract the differently positioned concerns expressed in the preceding paragraphs into urban spatial terms. More specifically, I anchor them in the particular locality of "Little India" situated near to the heart of old Kuala Lumpur. As the lengthy (but inaccurate) travelogue Internet entry quoted above by a foreign tourist connotes, street life "Little India" is today a place benevolently euphemized for things "Indian" and "Muslim."[3] But, as my ethnography will suggest, the colorful imagery portrayed—like much of the state-sponsored rhetoric of celebratory multiculturalism—glosses over and oversimplifies much more convoluted and complex historical processes. In explicating the kinds of quotidian and transquotidian flows that constitute this locale, I address the contradictions of a technocratically driven version of "cosmopolitanism" set in motion by state imaginaries as well as situate its contrapuntal other, "subaltern cosmopolitanism," as they are played out in "Little India."

As a point of departure, perhaps a compelling imagery for the politics and poetics of subaltern cosmopolitanism might be spoken of along the contours of positionality. Here, a symbiotic binary needs to be set up between the lofty regime of codes, symbols, and strategies "from above" and the labyrinthine trajectories of commonsensical knowledge and tactics "from below." While strategic thinking works to limit the multifarious number of variables affecting people by creating a protected zone in which the environment can be rendered predictable, tactics refers to the set of practices that strategy has not been able to domesticate (Buchanan, *Michel de Certeau* 89). Famously enunciated in an exegesis of the city planner's towering gaze of Manhattan from the 107th floor of the (now annihilated) monumentalist World Trade Centre, Michel de Certeau depicts the erotics of knowledge embodied by omni-visual power as essentially translating "the city's complexity into readability" and "freezing its opaque mobility into a crystal-clear text" (de Certeau 94). In opposition to the "fact" of the city, de Certeau argues that the concept of a city established by urbanistic discourse operates along the "basis of a finite number of stable and isolatable elements, each articulated to the other" (94). These elements consist of a threefold operation—the creation of a rationalized clean space, the substitution of a synchronic system for the ambivalence of tradition, and the creation of a universal and impersonal subject. It is in contrast to the "authorized" organization of life that street pedestrians on the ground "write without reading" or have oblique forms of reading. As the official nonproducers of culture, the *modus operandi* of ordinary people is opportunistic, furtive, and tactical. Not unlike the *raison d'etre* of this project, it is the possibility and the elaboration of a critical heterology as opposed to a sterile monology in theoretical terms that de Certeau seeks to convey. A related idea that de Certeau draws our attention to is that of "sensitive zones," characterized as indeterminate spaces pregnant with conflictual possibilities that are beckoned into being as disciplinary power and instrumental technologies attempt to grid, striate, and enframe space. When anthropological everyday space is displaced by managed functional space, he sees the production of antitexts by ordinary people as an inevitability. The manner in which these notions are translated, negotiated, and embedded in spatial practices over time in a particular enclave in old Kuala Lumpur constitutes the basic thrust of this essay.

"THE WORLD-CLASS CITY"

In local history books, tourist brochures, and city-day annual celebrations (on 1st February), canonical narratives of the genesis and evolution of Kuala Lumpur from a tin-mining trading outpost to an aspiring world-class, cosmopolitan, and multiculturally vibrant city are rendered unmistakably clear to Malaysians. Comparatively speaking, Kuala Lumpur is a young Asian city. Its origins is conventionally traced to the middle of the nineteenth century when joint business ventures between local Malay royalty and immigrant Chinese entrepreneurs in search of valuable tin ore farther upstream from the royal port settlement of Klang led to a mixed congregation of Chinese and Sumatran Malay traders springing up near to the muddy confluence of two rivers (namely, the Gombak and Klang rivers). Later, recognizing the growing commercial and strategic importance of Kuala Lumpur, the British decided to relocate their state administrative capital some thirty-five kilometers upstream from Klang in 1880. By 1884, the British Resident of Selangor, Frank Swettenham, decided to rebuild Kuala Lumpur. The reconstruction program sought to replace *attap*-roofed wooden houses with rows of two-story brick and tiled buildings following building regulations. Ostensibly, these permanent structures were to mitigate the threat of fires—a hazard that had destroyed much of Kuala Lumpur during the Selangor Civil War in the early 1870s—but European urban aesthetics also came into play. A new kind of spatial formation thus became gradually discernible in the town's layout. Government offices were built at a strategic location away from Malay and Chinese communities. For this purpose, Tamil and other Indian laborers were brought in elsewhere from the Empire to construct government buildings and the Kuala Lumpur-Klang railway line. Their dwelling houses were congregated mainly to the north and south of the town boundaries where the railway workshop and brick kilns were sited—in Sentul and Brickfields respectively. Europeans, by comparison, built their residential bungalows on hills safely overlooking the town.

Kuala Lumpur became the *de facto* capital of British Malaya as control over the entire peninsula was eventually secured by the beginning of the twentieth century. The colony was administrated through an amalgam of direct and indirect rule—the Straits Settlements comprising the older beachhead possessions of Malacca, Penang, and Singapore, the Federated Malay States, and the Unfederated Malay States. Of the many urban centers located on the peninsula, the historic entrepot of Malacca, in particular, possessed the most political and cultural valence. As the strategic seat of the expansive and illustrious Malacca Sultanate, which drew in traders from near and far and which was a base for Islamic missionary activities before it fell to successive European empires beginning in the early sixteenth century, the British administrators were sanguine in sidestepping this site as the colonial capital city. Kuala Lumpur was not only geographically central but was also a desirable *tabula rasa*. By the same measure, when the road map for political independence were worked out with the British, Tunku Abdul Rahman (who became the first premier of the country) chose Malacca to make his maiden public announcement (in February 1956) of the date of the historic handover while brandishing an unsheathed *keris* (traditional Malay sword) to dramatize the country's symbolic link to the Malacca Sultanate. In more recent times, the Malacca Sultanate of old has continued to be an overdetermined charter myth to plot the grand trajectory of the nation-state, glossing over other antecedent and subsequent empires and migratory histories as aberrations or incidentals.

In short, the discursive strategies of valorization and mystification continue to be integral in localizing a collective imaginary of a shared place and destiny in the postcolonial milieu. To be sure, the current project, indexing the translation of Kuala Lumpur's continued insertion into the nexus of a globalizing capitalism, perpetuates a trajectory begun during the colonial era. The globalizing repositioning of cities also inhere the familiar theme of differential socioeconomic development. Saskia Sassen, for example, discerns two emergent trends in this scenario—an increase in economic inequalities between nodal cities and others in their own countries, and a hierarchy in the worldwide network of global cities. Thus, current self-conscious state-capital collaborative ventures to transform Kuala Lumpur into the iconic and commoditized attributes of a "world-class city" entails making this space both recognizable and different in the face of a universalizing and competitive cosmopolitan and developmentalist marketplace. Still, these strategic globalizing endeavors at reconstituting space, time, and subjectivities do not unfold in a *tabula rasa* but are also inflected by a whole range of mediating agents, not least of which are local cultural logics and historical contingencies. Thus, the manner in which governments negotiate processes of urbanization and urbanism do not necessarily manifest in identical and monolithic ways. The specific conditions in which urbanization take root are important distinguishing frameworks that produce variations. Evers and Korff, for instance, have detailed the variety of urban forms as well as the different ways in which urban spaces are politically, economically, and religiously articulated in a sample of Southeast Asia cities.[4] In the case of Malaysia, the pattern of urbanization has been conventionally posed in terms of the volatility of the race problematique. Some thirty years ago, human geographer Terry McGee noted that urbanization in Peninsular Malaysia took root in "an unstable setting," making reference to the communalistic structure of the country as framed by John Furnivall's influential tripartite "plural society" thesis, and the urban-rural economic disparity between migrant ethnic Chinese and native Malays.[5]

From the vantage point of history, we now know that the attempt to hold down ethnic Malays in the "rural sector" through substantial government investment in agriculture has been abandoned in the aftermath of the watershed Kuala Lumpur "racial riots" of 1969, largely between Chinese and Malays. The affirmative action New Economic Policy (NEP) that was subsequently crafted and enforced for two decades after 1971 opened up a range of possibilities for ethnic Malays to "modernize" in the towns and cities that they gravitated to and in the process address the colonial legacy of an ethnicized spatial divide. A major destination of migrants has been the Klang Valley encompassing the capital city of Kuala Lumpur. In the absence of the availability of affordable and adequate public housing, migrants turned to self-help vernacular housing on vacant and unused land, considerably swelling the already substantial squatter population residing within the capital city.[6] Most visibly salient to planners and academics were that these settlements were disturbingly segregated along ethnic lines. At the same time, heightened by security concerns in the aftermath of the Kuala Lumpur "race riots," a number of slums situated near to the flashpoints were demolished under the quickly promulgated Essential (Clearance of Squatters) Act 1969.

Following a Foucauldian perspective, Aihwa Ong has characterized this milieu as marked by an ethnic-based governmentality buttressed further by an Islamic governmentality—"an extensive system of graduated sovereignty has come into effect as the government has put more investment into the bio-political improvement of the Malays, awarding them rights and benefits that are largely denied to the Chinese and Indian minorities" (214ff). Ostensibly, the overriding objective of the NEP was to create a sizeable middle and entrepreneurial Malay class to offset the perceived economic imbalance of wealth hitherto held by foreign companies and ethnic Chinese, an endeavor that former prime minister Mahathir Mohamad was to appropriate as his trademark project.[7] Moreover, during his twenty-two-year-long premiership, the country's economic and social orientation was realigned toward the neoliberal (and cosmopolitical) project of "privatization," "pro-growth," and "efficiency" beginning from the mid-1980s. Commensurate with the country's rising GNP, embarking on numerous large-scale and flagship infrastructural (particularly transportation and communications) and construction projects required large reserves of cheap and seasonal foreign workers sourced largely from Southeast Asian and South Asian countries. In many cases, the successive waves of cheaper foreign migrant labor displaced Malaysian Tamil laborers who had worked in plantations for decades into town centers, particularly Kuala Lumpur, to seek alternative livelihoods in the lower rungs of the urban economy.[8]

Cross-border labor flows of this nature coincided with a concerted effort by City Hall (placed directly under the purview of the Prime Minister's Department) to rationalize and plan more comprehensively the city's morphology through the introduction of a structure plan in 1984. It was from this period that civil society groups have noted that the forced eviction of urban squatters became comparatively more intense and unrelenting as the authorities labored to contain and manage their spatial expansion. By the 1990s, the notion of a "squatter-free city" as a signifier of modernity entered into the official discourse and everyday linguistic currency. It worked interchangeably with another teleological, utopic, and additive discourse of transforming Malaysia into a "fully developed" nation by the year 2020 ("Vision 2020") launched by Mahathir Mohamad in 1991.

On a similar key, the unveiling of the second Kuala Lumpur Draft Structure Plan (in 2004) was deemed necessary because, as its authors noted, most of the policies of the first plan had been rendered obsolete by unanticipated developments such as the setting up of the Multimedia Super Corridor (MSC), the Kuala Lumpur International Airport (KLIA), and the creation of a hypermodern federal government administrative complex outside the city boundaries called Putrajaya.[9] Another change stemmed from the high outmigration of the working population to many residential areas situated just outside the city limits and covering an extensive region of Selangor state, including westward all the way to the former capital of Klang. The fluid mobility of peoples across administrative boundaries necessitated the creation of the notion of a "Kuala Lumpur and its conurbation" (or "KLC" in short) to encapsulate new spatial realities. Details spelled out in the KL Structure Plan are explicitly anchored around the grand plan of morphing Kuala Lumpur into attaining the cosmopolitan and infrastructural attributes of a second-tier "world-class city" in the first instance, and positioning itself favorably to be "global city" in the near but, as yet, uncertain future.

Socio-spatial engineering of this kind overlaps with the discursive cultivation of a patriotic kinship-type imaginary appropriated by the Mahathir administration, and that reinterpellates various "fault lines" in the history of Malaysian race and class relations, itself an interesting departure from his earlier explicit racialist reading of the Malay economic and political dilemma. Mohan Ambikaipaker (12), for instance, has characterized the neoliberal and cosmopolitan discourse of *Bangsa Malaysia* ("Malaysian race") as essentially a departure from an overt tone of Malay-centric ethnonationalism and toward a developmentalism hinged on transracial national identity formation. Another oft-used slogan, *Malaysia Boleh* ("Malaysia can do it/is capable"), typifies this "benign discourse of race and ethnicity" (Lee 133) and signifies the "capabilities of individuals with special racial identities" (Lee 137). Following Homi Bhabha's lead, what these kinds of projects suggest are that they are not necessarily foreclosed but are relational and contingent realities, viz., "as the rhetoric of globality becomes more vaunting and all-embracing, there emerges an indeterminate, uncertain discourse of community, that, nevertheless, provides a moral measure against which trans-national cultural claims are measured" (42).

The economic, political, and cultural ramifications of the developmentalist transformation of Malaysia over the past three decades have been a subject of much critical study and debate.[10] Most salient of these changes is the rise of "exclusionary populism and clientelist patronage made manifest in a stream of state positions, licenses, contracts, generous lending, and, in the 1990s, a skewed privatisation of state assets, followed by re-nationalisation amounting to bailouts" (Case 32). Intense contestations over the political largesse and for patronage inevitably gave rise to endemic "money politics" within UMNO (United Malay National Organisation), the dominant political party of the National Coalition (*Barisan Nasional*) and replicated to a lesser extent in its other partner parties. In the later years of his premiership, the extent of the phenomenon compelled Mahathir Mohamad to make repeated histrionic references in his keynote speeches to the annual UMNO General Assemblies. These admonitions notwithstanding, many local commentators have argued that there is a strong correlation between these kinds of entrepreneurships and the rise of a triumphalistic and self-conscious Malay-Muslim public persona that, in accentuating the centrality of a range of Islamic jurisprudence, beliefs, and practices, has also impinged the sensibilities and mundane spaces of non-Muslims in unsettling ways. These range from prohibitions of the use of certain words like *Allah* and *doa* ("prayer") in non-Islamic literature, the difficulties of non-Muslims in obtaining land for the construction of places of worship and burial grounds, the widespread removal of old Hindu roadside shrines and small temples ostensibly for urban redevelopment to the requirement for non-Muslim dog owners securing letters of consent from their Muslim neighbors before they could apply for licenses. Urbane Muslims in cosmopolitan Kuala Lumpur have not been spared from punitive actions as well. Several amendments in *Shari'a* criminal laws since the 1990s have strengthened the moral surveillance, enforcement, and punishment of Muslims who have transgressed a range of Islamic rulings—straying from obligatory fasting during the holy month of *Ramadan*, consuming *haram* (forbidden) substances like alcoholic beverages, exposing one's *aurat* (modesty) in public, and being deemed to be in close physical proximity (*khalwat*) to members of the opposite sex who are not relatives. In the case of *khalwat* involving a non-Muslim, he or she can be detained by the police for further questioning, an action that is problematic from the standpoint of civil rights (Yeoh, "Managing Sensitivities"). Though arguably muted in the past, the advent of the Internet has fomented stronger public expressions of dissatisfactions with the rise of ethnic and religious supremacy, and the undermining of civil liberties as enshrined in the Federal Constitution. This, in turn, has attracted thinly veiled threats of ethnic-based recriminations from various politicians and religious leaders should the status quo be challenged.

"LITTLE INDIA"

I now turn to my fieldwork site to explicate a particular articulation of "cosmopolitanism" that simultaneously partakes of and departs significantly from the disparate and multiscalar kinds of processes discussed earlier. By heuristically viewing "Little India" as a prismatic site, I show that the *habitus* in evidence at the street level refracts various trajectories that have been brought to bear on the place over several decades. This is not to argue that a geographical locality acquires their particularity from a positivist sedimentation of various elements but rather from specific interactions and articulations of different processes, experiences, encounters, and understandings that converge and overlap in that space.

The locality now commonly denoted in tourist brochures of Kuala Lumpur as "Little India" is both an orientalist-like artifact of recent place-marketing endeavors by the tourist authorities as well as of more diverse and temporally stretched out bundle of localized place-making activities. Slippages and collisions between these differentially constructed worlds are readily apparent to longtime locals and perhaps to the discerning outsider. To cite just one example for now, not only is the putative geographical location of "Little India" deemed imprecise but it is also strenuously contested by some of my informants who have an older stock of memories of the locality, and who also spoke from a position informed by the kinds of larger developments discussed earlier. For instance, Mr. Maniam, a veteran Tamil-Hindu lawyer whose office has been anchored in the locality for over two decades, contended that "Little India" should be confined to the historic street called *Lebuh Ampang* ("Ampang Street") situated across on the other side of the Gombak river, and where the row of Chettiar-owned shops and Tamil-Hindu restaurants are sited and whose fortunes have dipped because of changes in the vehicular traffic flow into no-parking, one-way streets. For him, the current designation, centered around the iconic *Masjid India* ("Indian Mosque"), has a more recent, unsavory and inauthentic past.

Indeed, the locality is more commonly known as "Masjid India." The spine of the locality, as it were, consists of *Jalan Masjid India* ("Masjid India road") flanked by rows of modern shophouses. Three landmark high-rise structures—*Wisma Yakin* (built in the early 1970s) and the pair of housing towers ostentatiously called Selangor Mansion and Malayan Mansion (built slightly earlier by private concerns)—punctuate the skyline. At first glance, the signages of shop fronts confirm the "Little India" tourist-promoted persona of the locality. They denote a spectrum of South Asian provenances like "Madras Textiles," "Ajuntha Textiles,"

"Peerbhai Trading," "Jai Hind Restaurant," "Mydin Emporium," "Al-Amnah Restaurant," "Little India Jewellers," and "Haniffa Textiles" among others. However, less overtly conspicuous are vestiges of a more historically hybrid past as embodied in a range of businesses owned by individuals of Malay, Sumatran, and Chinese ancestries. Most are found lodged inside the buildings just mentioned or tucked away on side roads branching off *Jalan Masjid India*.

A closer historical rereading of the locality would be pertinent at this juncture. As suggested earlier, eyewitness accounts chronicled by British administrators and travelers note that segregated ethnic enclaves were the dominant visible feature of the fledging tin-mining settlement of Kuala Lumpur. Thus, Chinese pioneers (of predominantly Hakka and Hokkien linguistic groups) were reported as congregating largely to the east of the confluence of the Gombak and Klang rivers, eventually forming the spatial template of "Chinatown," which is popularized today in travel guide books as a haven for an array of imitation consumer goods. By comparison, the northern part of the town near to Bukit Nanas ("Pineapple Hill") just across the Klang river from present-day "Little India" was largely occupied by Sumatran Malays, and called *Kampung Rawa* ("Rawa village"). Additionally, many also constructed small trading posts along the banks of the river. Apart from Sumatran Malays, the colonial archives note that other villages comprised settlers of Malaccan and Pahang Malay geographical origins (Gullick, *A History of Kuala Lumpur* 49). Later (circa 1880), after Kuala Lumpur was chosen to be the new colonial capital of Selangor state, the British Resident decided to strategically build government offices on high ground west of the Klang river as a bulwark against the twin threats of floods and native uprisings.

Apart from rivers, various constructed thoroughfares also provided convenient boundary markers of ethnic enclaves as well as mute testimonies of changing political and economic fortunes. For instance, the key historic thoroughfares that encapsulate present-day "Little India" are "Batu Road," "Java Street," "Malay Street," and "Dickson Street." While "Java Street" has been renamed twice—first to "Mountbatten Road" and then to *Jalan Tun Perak*—"Batu Road" has become *Jalan Tuanku Abdul Rahman* (after the first king of a newly independent country), and "Dickson Street" has morphed into *Jalan Masjid India*, "Malay Street" remains significantly static as *Jalan Melayu*.[11] In the 1870s, "Java Street" was observed to mark the boundary between the Chinese and Malay quarters. Later, contemporary British records (circa 1903) lamented that while "Java Street" was "the slum of slums of our local paradise" it was also a busy commercial hub for "native businesses." Because the road was a short walking distance to the British spatial complex of church-court house-cricket ground, it was subsequently favored for the siting of a row of European emporiums (such as Robinsons, Whitaways, Laidlaw, and John Little). By contrast, *Jalan Melayu*, situated immediately to the rear and consisting of a crescent-shaped row of comparatively nondescript two-story shophouses, has continued till today to be the favored site for non-European business merchants. By the 1940s, most of these lots were taken over or rented by Punjabi-owned businesses dealing in textiles, sundry provisions, and restaurants, probably because of the proximity of a sizeable Punjabi settlement in Gombak Lane. Certainly, by the 1950s, in the recollection of Mr. Hacharan Singh, who grew up in one of the shoplots along *Jalan Melayu*, the place attracted a lot of Indian customers so that it had the feel of a "mini India" with bicycles as the main mode of transport. Today, the complexion has changed and the *Jai Hind* ("Victory to India") Restaurant is the oldest surviving reminder of this milieu.[12]

At least until the 1960s, the area beyond *Jalan Melayu* (to the cardinal north) was largely "undeveloped." Although a road reserve had been notionally charted on the municipal plans, "Dickson Street" was for many decades an unmetaled earth track, running parallel to the main thoroughfare, "Batu Road." At an early stage of the history of Kuala Lumpur, the marshy vacant land on both sides of the road reserve was rehabilitated by pioneers to set up an assortment of small businesses housed in wooden shacks that doubled up as their homes as well. While there were subsequent infrastructural improvements, the sight of modest wooden shophouses along *Dickson Street/Jalan Masjid India* was still prevalent until a series of urban redevelopment initiatives radically transformed the local land/ethnoscapes beginning in the 1970s. In the words of one of my key informants, the area was "like a desert with no big buildings except for the Selangor and Malayan Mansions, and plenty of wooden shops, many of whom were Chinese businesses who left after the disturbances of May 13."[13] Closer to *Jalan Melayu* is the original site of an array of "Malay & Sumatran" (and other ethnic) businesses—merchants in textile goods and garments (like head scarves, prayer garments, *sarongs, songkoks,* etc.), tailors, barbers, and cobblers. Although housed in modest environments, the *Jalan Melayu* tailors, in particular, gained a reputation for possessing a stock of specialized knowledge in the making of a diverse range of traditional attire from the different Malay states in the peninsula. Their clientele included various high-ranking Malay government ministers and other "VIPs" who needed signature clothes and headgear for official functions. As we will see later, their privileged position has also been rendered precarious by recent redevelopments. Indeed, in comparison to its current "developed" status, there was a certain rustic and chaotic charm associated to the place. For instance, Mary Joseph, a veteran social activist for migrant workers who has worked in the locality since the 1970s, recollects:

> Previously, the place had shops where people were free to earn their money. There was no hassle. The stalls were mixed and many. . . . It was a happy place. People would come, shop and hang around. In the early 1970s, there were no migrant workers yet. There were maybe a few Indonesian traders but there were more Malaysians around.[14]

Ironically, some of those displaced were the result of the construction of a high-rise office tower, *Wisma Yakin,* by state authorities to catalyze Malay capital accumulation in the city. A small group—those involved in tailoring, textile, and garments—were subsequently relocated back on the ground level of the modern office block. Others, like the barbers, moved to cheaper replacement wooden shops sited slightly farther away. Soon afterward, the vacant space in front of *Wisma Yakin* became reappropriated again as a gathering spot for purveyors of traditional Malay medicine (including foot and body massages) plying their wares and knowledge on the streets with only simple paraphernalia as their stock-in-trade. According to a representative of the Association of Traditional Medicine Traders, the locality is now portrayed as the birthplace of the trade in modern and cosmopolitan Kuala Lumpur.[15] In later years, they were joined by street vendors selling an array of Islamic and political literature, some of which were of a perceived heterodox *Shi'i* and pro-*Reformasi* slant.[16] For much of 2004, these vendors were forced to ply their trades elsewhere as they were displaced by the construction of a highly contentious modernistic "Malay Bazaar" championed by City Hall.[17] With the completion of this structure (by the Islamic fasting month of *Ramadan* 2004), not all vendors could return to their favored place of commerce. Indeed, some claimed that they were selectively denied the opportunity to rent one of the gridded small lots because of their perceived oppositional political and religious inclinations.

At the other end of *Jalan Masjid India,* a similar story of contesting, albeit incommensurate, appropriations of the locality over time can be narrated. Where a large shopping complex, ironically called *Semua House* ("Everybody's House") now stands, a sprawling squatter colony of notorious repute peopled predominantly by ethnic Chinese once occupied the site. Elderly Kuala Lumpur residents know this locality generically as the "Batu Road area" or, more colorfully, as *Blakang Mati* (literally, "dead end"). *Blakang Mati* was the haven where many criminals and prostitutes lived and plied their trade. When the settlement was demolished as part of the large-scale slum clearances of the late 1960s, much of the prostitution activities were displaced to the newly constructed Selangor and Malayan mansions that quickly became well-known more for their nefarious nocturnal activities than the legitimate businesses found in the lower floors. Long-time residents of the buildings recollect that the prostitution dens attracted mostly a working-class clientele that "came from all races—Malays, Chinese, Indians." Despite frequent raids by the police, the activities and stigma stuck on. As Mary Joseph recollects:

> In the 1970s, everybody knows that this place is a sex and drugs area. I remember we were told not to come here after 6.30 pm because people will think you are a sex worker or they will come and disturb you.

Today, however, a new generation of prostitutes ply their flesh trade elsewhere, in the nearby back lanes of "Chow Kit Road" and "Petaling Street," and occasionally the new three-star hotels found within the *Little India/ Masjid India* locality itself, not because of the success of policing activities but more of the outcome of changing economic fortunes that require better commercial use of the buildings. The range of sexual choices in the form of racialized bodies has also considerably widened to cater for the increasingly cosmopolitan and mobile crowds that gravitate to the locality. As elsewhere, human trafficking of young and impoverished women, mostly from the neighboring Southeast Asian and South Asian countries, has become more unrelenting because of differential economic prosperities and easier cross-border mobility in the region (e.g., see Blair).[18]

While both the Selangor and Malayan mansions continue to have a small number of tenants, particularly in the upper floors, who have lived there since the 1970s, many flats have now been taken over by recruiting agents, restaurant owners, and other business owners to become functional and transit dormitories for waves of South Asian migrant male workers, largely of the Muslim faith.[19] To increase the use of premium space, the original three bedrooms in the mansions have been partitioned into smaller cubicles for subletting and to be able to accommodate up to ten persons per room. Tenants range from workers on long stays to those on transit who pay 5 *Malaysian Ringgit* (about US$1.30) per day for a temporary place to rest for the night as they try to secure a job in the city. In case of businesses that operate twenty-four hours daily (like the numerous Malaysian *mamak*-owned restaurants close by), workers take turns recuperating in the same cubicles outside of their shift hours. In the lower floors, offices and businesses—like tour and recruiting agencies, association offices, restaurants, barbers, video/audio cassette vendors, and sundry shops—and even a madrasa for schoolchildren are the anchor occupants because of higher rental charges. In many respects, the mansions now mimic a more familial (albeit verticalized) "Little India" enclave providing a significant space for face-to-face sociality and intimacy, and as a point of referral for the thousands of South Asian males who have successively inhabited these buildings.

Their daily routines are dominated by long hours of labor, and it is not often that they have disposable resources or time to go on holidays or to seek sexual liaisons in the back lanes of Chow Kit Road or Petaling Street. Many also conceded that friendships with local Malay-Muslims are uncommon as they feel that they are "viewed differently" even though they might share the same faith. Indeed, a stereotype of the male foreign migrant worker is one that draws from vague images of criminality and sexualized danger requiring in turn caution and disciplinary surveillance.

Informants usually spoke glowingly of the "developed" status of Malaysia, and of the high stature of Mahathir Mohammad in the Muslim world. They explained that they were drawn to Malaysia believing that as a prospering

Islamic country it would be easier for them to find good-paying jobs or that they would be treated well. Subsequently, many quickly became disappointed with the disparity between what was promised by recruiting agents and the harsh reality of being part of an anonymous large pool of cheap and seasonal migrant labor. For "undocumented" ("illegal") informants, narratives of deception and mistreatment by employers and authorities were even more stark and despairing. Despite these difficulties, remaining to find work in Malaysia was rationalized in terms of the comparative worsening economic conditions of their own countries, earning for their dependents back home, and to settle debts incurred in coming over to Malaysia. With few exceptions, the network of male migrant sociality in the mansions largely embodied the conditions of their respective places of origins and by the parameters set up by recruiting agents. Friendships (and rivalries) were thus aligned according to their own religious, linguistic, and regional groupings while at the same time allowing diasporic opportunities to come into face-to-face contact with more of their fellow countrymen. Relationships pursued with other migrant worker women was difficult and complicated given their terms of employment, long hours of work, and uncertain status. For the few that persisted and succeeded, offsprings produced faced the formidable obstacle of legal recognition by Malaysian authorities and thus easy access to basic amenities like health and education.

Innovations in communicational technologies have partly helped to mitigate the palpable feelings of loneliness and alienation undoubtedly experienced by these migrant male workers. The numerous international call centers situated here (and elsewhere) provide plentiful lines of communication with families and loved ones back home at comparatively cheap rates. Simple and functional paper posters advertising the costs of prepaid cards for a range of South Asian and Southeast Asian countries abound in the locality and provide an indication of the range of migrant workers' clientele.[20] More commonly, on weekends the streets of *Masjid India* are transformed into one of a range of popular venues of congregation for predominantly South Asian migrant male workers based within and around Kuala Lumpur.[21] The usual routine is to have a simple communal meal in one of the many coffee shops or restaurants in the locality, and then retreat to the side pavements to sit, converse, and gaze at the changing streetscape until it is time to return to their abodes by public transport or by buses provided by their respective companies. In particular, after the receipt of monthly salaries, the former colonial entertainment landmark of Coliseum cinema on *Batu Road/Jalan Tuanku Abdul Rahman* nearby—which in the past had only screened American Hollywood and British films but now offers a constant diet of the latest Hindi and Tamil Bollywood movies—is jam-packed with predominantly male viewers. For a few hours, the cinematic experience rejuvenates the migrant workers' spirits and allows a tangible imaginative reconnection with their distant homelands. The presence of a large migrant South Asian clientele in search of the periodic cinematic connection also accounts for the rejuvenation of some strategically located abandoned old cinema halls in central Kuala Lumpur, which had earlier lost out to modern cineplexes housed in shopping malls. Now screening only a menu of Hindi and Tamil movies on the first floor, there is usually a *mamak* restaurant set aside on the ground floor as well to enhance these recuperative stints.

As noted earlier, the locality is synonymous with *Masjid India,* a place for spiritual sustenance and solace for both Indian-Muslim migrant workers and local Malay-Muslim residents alike. Less known to outsiders and even to a number of shop tenants whom I spoke to is the presence of a small Hindu shrine dedicated to the goddess Kaliamman farther up *Jalan Masjid India* and near to Semua House. While the shrine has recently received eviction orders because of the construction of a high-end condominium next door, the trustees of *Masjid India* have no such anxieties. First erected as an *attap*-roofed wooden hut in 1863 to cater for the Muslim migrant population that congregated in early Kuala Lumpur, it has since been rebuilt twice according to the South Indian style, and today can accommodate around thirty-five hundred worshippers. Its religious and ethnic significance today is that it is the only extant South Indian-Muslim mosque of the Hanafi school sited inside central Kuala Lumpur. Despite its current architectural prominence, the mosque has a more bucolic and modest past. For instance, Mr. Hacharan Singh, recounts that as a young boy:

> The *pondans* ("trans-sexuals") prostitutes used to hang around the corner here where the *lorong* (lane) is (behind his father's shop). We used to disturb them. We used to call them *pondans* and they would chase us. We used to disturb the *imam* as well. He refused to let play on the mosque grounds. The mosque was beautiful. There was a small wooden mosque with a big sandy compound and a few coconut trees. It had a unique green bush that used to cover the whole back of the fence. I have never seen that bush ever again in my life. There was also a pond where people came to wash their feet and hands before prayers. It was a man-made pond with fish inside. That was our playground. We used to play hide-and-seek, *kunda-kundi* ("stick game"), marbles, chopping board, slippers and cards on the five-foot way of the shophouse. If we became too noisy, the *iman* would come out and chase us![22]

Today, the mosque continues to aurally punctuate the routines and rhythm of life in the locality through its powerful public address system. Muslim businesses pause for prayers at the five temporal nodal points of the day. On Fridays, there is a striking scene around midday and perhaps not visible elsewhere in central Kuala Lumpur. All business activities—including aural fanfare from a Hindu-Tamil owned music shop in proximity to the mosque—would cease activity for about an hour as a Tamil *khutbah* (sermon) is broadcast followed by ritual prayers. Because of insufficient floor space within the mosque, the large congregation of Muslims from the surrounding offices and businesses who converge here pragmatically convert the road and street pavements temporarily into an extended praying area with an assortment of prayer mats, cardboards, and newspapers. The faithful who congregate here in large numbers on Fridays comprise not only local Malay and Indian-Muslims but also Muslims drawn from countries like Indonesia, Bangladesh, Pakistan, and India, and more recently from the Middle East, who work and live in the locality. For an outsider/tourist, the cosmopolitan Islamic ambience of the locality would appear obvious. However, as I have discussed earlier, the texture of the place as indexed by changing ethnic and religious compositions is not monologic but entailed a negotiated process over time. Thus, as characterized by Mr. Hacharan Singh:

> In the 1950s, the place was already like a "Little India." People who would want to go back to India or go on Islamic pilgrimages would come here first to buy their metal trunks . . . When the *Masjid India* area was developed, a lot of Indian business opened up—textiles, food, everything. The whole area captured the Indian market. This was the most significant change. . . . From 1980s onwards, this area was totally Indian, so much so that the property here was worth more than Batu Road. . . . All the Indian shops in *Jalan Melayu* and Batu Road felt that they lost their customers. This place became phenomenal. . . . [23]

Even when the winds of urban change portended of possibly unfavorable conditions, the specter of racialized difference was still optimistically accorded some value.

> When did this place become less Indian? [pauses for a few seconds]. I think it was during the mid-1990s. The first thing that started was the construction of the arcades near to Batu Road selling batik cloth. That was the first inroad made by the Malays. Before, it used to be controlled by the Indians. That business started mushrooming. Instead of Indians going to Indians, we have something else happening. Some of the traders had Indonesian relatives, so they also started. But that was good because the area became more cosmopolitan. Yes, it was still good. There was nothing bad about that because it was all money.[24]

Indeed, for many of the neighboring Indian-owned businesses whom we spoke to, the greater influx of an assortment of entrepreneurial Malay small businesses and petty traders in *Masjid India* was generally seen as a boon to other businesses in the locality as well as they drew in more Malay customers who would also occasionally patronize their stores. But all agreed that it was the setting up and marketing strategy of the landmark Indian-Muslim-owned Mydin Emporium that dramatically changed the shopping demographics of *Masjid India*. Initially known for purveying only Islamic religious paraphernalia for pilgrimages and everyday use, the owners decided to include a host of low-priced secular consumer items that appealed as well to the Malay masses. As a local businessman put it, "Mydin has been the major push factor here. Ever since he came in, the ethnicity of the crowd is easily 85 percent Malay." Over the years, by word of mouth and by concerted advertising, the enclave has developed a reputation for a range of bargain "ethnic goods." Local shopping myths have it that even comparatively affluent Singaporean and Brunei Malays find the place appealing if not irresistible. Rocketing ground rental charges and the changing customer ethnic profile are also reconfiguring the spectrum of businesses along *Jalan Masjid India*. At the time of fieldwork, increasingly more jewelry, textiles, garments, VCD/DVD shops, and trendy restaurants have taken over the streetscape at ground level, and displaced a broader and ethnically diverse range of older businesses.[25] Some newer businesses starting up in the locality adopt a niche marketing strategy in order to keep up with the competition. For instance, an Indian-Muslim gold jeweler explained that unlike his bigger competitors he not only sells items that would selectively appeal only to Malay customer sensibilities but also employs young Malay women staff to cater to their queries. Even some established businesses have diversified beyond their original target Indian customer base in terms of the kinds of items on display. Thus, a well-known Tamil-Hindu store purveying Hindu religious and cultural paraphernalia (like brass oil lamps and an assortment of pots for prayers) in addition to a wide range of South Asian garments and textiles has now shifted the former to a higher floor in order not to offend perceived Muslim sensitivities. In short, paraphrasing the insights of one of my informants, the trajectory of *Little India/Masjid India* is that it is fast becoming a destination for *halal* goods and cuisine in general and for a predominantly Malay clientele in particular. The manner in which this trajectory has impacted upon local-level relations and, perhaps more important, of outsider perceptions of what these changes portend for the country as an imagined whole form the subject of discussion in the next section.

SACRED MOMENTS AND COMMERCIALIZED SPACES IN "MASJID INDIA/ LITTLE INDIA"

Periodically, the sacred moments of different religious calendars would temporally coincide with or be proximate one another. In multireligious Malaysia, this is a periodical occurrence given the significant presence of the adherents of the major faiths of Buddhism, Christianity, Hinduism, Islam, Sikhism, and Taoism. These festivals are accorded as national public holidays that translate as not only into state-recognized opportunities to fulfill religious obligations in the first instance but also, for those not of the same faith, a welcome reprieve from work because of the possibility of authorized extended rest. Arguably, these sacred temporal conjunctions have also been particularly opportune for distinct but related kinds of entrepreneurship by different social actors. On the one hand, it has become commonplace for key political leaders of *Barisan Nasional,* the ruling government, to capitalize on these occasions to buttress a regime of patriotic tropes through the state-controlled media.[26] This bundle of imaginaries usually include exhortations to Malaysian citizens to cling to traditional "Asian values" in the face of an excessively materialistic and Americanist-type globalization, to practice interracial harmony and religious tolerance, and to maintain transethnic loyalties to ethnic-based consociational political parties. As routinely depicted in the Malaysian media, performing national unity is singularly euphemized in the ritualized practice of carnivalesque government-sponsored "open houses" where political and business dignitaries welcome crowds of friends, allies, and strangers into their homes (or other rented public venues) for the expressed purpose of building up a stock of multicultural social capital for interethnic and interreligious conviviality. However, as suggested earlier, secularized nation-state projects do not always cohere with religiously inflected sensibilities. While one trajectory counsels an appreciation of multicultural difference for the purpose of social cohesion and collective developmental well-being, the other draws from the specter of irreconcilable differences to maintain and patrol essentialized purity.[27]

On a less fractious note, commercial businesses (particularly those housed in locally owned shopping complexes) have also sought to latch onto these joint celebrations with the enticement of "special festival sales" coupled with a range of glossy visuals that suggest unproblematic commensurability in the marketplace. In the specific case of the Islamic fasting period of *Ramadan,* the increasing volume of Muslim city dwellers has provided a strong catalyst for a range of business—hotels, restaurants, and street traders alike—to garner higher than average earnings in providing sustenance when fasts are ritually broken in the evenings for up to a month. Various outdoor sites for "Ramadan Bazaars" selling food and festive items are usually earmarked, identified, and publicized by City Hall to streamline these celebrations.

At *Masjid India/Little India,* in particular, the presence of a mosque within a commercial enclave makes the locality a highly popular destination for Muslims working nearby to congregate and break the day's fast. With packages of purchased food at hand, they wait expectantly at food courts and along street pavements for the *azan* to be broadcast at the appointed time through the powerful public address system of the mosque. However, as I will illustrate shortly, in the context of a temporal conjunction of sacred moments not only is there a phenomenal increase in the volume of human traffic in the locality, certain fault lines that hover in the background come to the foreground, throwing into sharper relief the ambivalent character of a technocratic version of cosmopolitanism.

Limiting Cosmopolitanism 149

In November 2004, the religious climax of Hindu *Deepavali* and Muslim *Hari Raya Puasa* were only four days apart.[28] In the weeks preceding the climax of the festive celebrations, many local businesses sought to capitalize on the economic opportunities through colorful and innovative advertising spins. One of the more arresting images conjured up by the tourist industry consisted of huge colored plastic banners bearing the catchphrase "Deepa-Raya" to signify this auspicious conjunction.[29] The streetscape along *Jalan Masjid India* was also transformed to take on a carnivalesque atmosphere with giant decorative iconic street lamps representing Islam and Hinduism—a *ketupat* (rice wrapped with coconut leaves) and an oil lamp respectively—strung overhead. For shop keepers, emporium owners, and street traders alike, the monthlong prefestive season was eagerly awaited as an exceptionally lucrative period in their respective business cycles.

In the recent past when such a temporal conjunction was not made significant and the locality relatively "undeveloped," it was common practice for Indian-Hindu traders to set up temporary stalls along *Jalan Masjid*

Photo 6.1 Deepraya festival sales, Kuala Lumpur. Photo by Yeoh Seng Guan.

India for the festive season of Deepavali. Radical changes were prominent, however, in 2004 and the subsequent two years. At the end of September 2004, City Hall officials had invited petty traders keen on taking up stalls at *Masjid India* to ballot for temporarily gridded lots carved out of the public spaces of street pavements and roads. Indian petty traders present at the draw became dismayed to learn that of the 556 bazaar lots to be made available for street trading, only 66 lots (12%) had been officially reserved for Indian traders.[30] City Hall officials explained that the allocation formula was based on indicators like the size of the Indian population and the nature of business in the locality. To appease the aggrieved Indian-Hindu petty traders, the mayor of City Hall ordered the additional allocation of one hundred bazaar lots elsewhere in the city—in the colonially created Indian enclaves of Brickfields and Sentul. In response, the chairman of the *Federal Territory and Selangor Indian Petty Traders Association* voiced their disappointment with City Hall, claiming that in previous years 350 lots in the *Masjid India* area was the norm. The replacement lots were deemed unsuitable because they could not guarantee the desired economic returns honed out of routinized familiarity—"we had carried out business during Deepavali festivals in *Jalan Masjid India* for 15 years, and our customers have come to know us."[31] Another reason for their reluctance to

Photo 6.2 View of Jalan Masjid India during Deepa-raya festival. Photo by Yeoh Seng Guan.

move to Brickfields was explained to me in terms of not desiring to create ill feelings with established traders in that locality through the real (and imagined) threat of undermining their accustomed profit base. Those who did eventually take up the lots felt compelled to do so by the harsh economic reality of having to pay for large quantities of goods already ordered in anticipation of windfall sales.

A field survey conducted between October and November 2004 revealed that only about 4% of all stalls eventually set up in *Masjid India* comprised Indian-Hindu traders. Many had decided to relet their lots to other traders (including Malay-Muslims) in the face of intractable logistical problems. Being spatially fragmented and demographically outnumbered by Malay-Muslim stalls posed a challenge in creating a festive aural atmosphere through a mixture of devotional Hindu and Bollywood music without the nagging fear of creating ill feelings with their neighboring vendors. Almost without exception, all those we spoke to chose to explain the loss of an eagerly awaited business opportunity along racialized terms. For them, City Hall had explicitly not taken into consideration the economic welfare of Hindu-Indian traders and once again had continued the perceived trend of marginalizing Malaysian Indians in the country.[32] Others additionally directed their frustrations at certain well-placed Hindu-Indian leaders based in various trade associations, and who had opportunistically used their positions to obtain the prized lots for their own network of acquaintances only and to the detriment of their wider ethnic Indian kin.

The advertised rental rate for the trading lots created by City Hall was 306 *Malaysian Ringgit* (US$80). But it was also common knowledge that better organizationally connected vendors resorted to paying additional *wang kopi* (literally, "coffee money") of several thousand *Malaysian Ringgit* in order to increase their possibility of getting the desired lots. Knowledgeable vendors explained to me that the lots were artificially inflated because of the profiteering rentier logic and political connections between certain UMNO-linked businessmen and key City Hall officials. They claimed that these individuals were not interested in street vending at all but rather in making quick turnovers from the rerenting of these lots. For this reason, strategically situated lots were reserved for these individuals and not open for competitive balloting. Some vendors also confided that they were not the original beneficiaries, and that they had taken over the lots with higher rentals (of between 3,000 and 12,000 *Malaysian Ringgit*) calculated on the basis of the particular kinds of trade they were engaged in and expected profit margins.

To buttress these kinds of investments authorised by legislative rationality, surveillance and policing by City Hall officials in the locality were intensified. A number of City Hall green trucks and a caravan office were conspicuously stationed along *Jalan Masjid India* ostensibly to take immediate action against street vendors who did not possess the required permits. City Hall had also come up with an ingenious and profitable way of easily identifying errant vendors. Apart from underwriting rental fees, all legitimately recognized vendors were also required to pay for large red and white umbrellas embossed boldly with City Hall initials, and which they were required to use as additional proof of their status. However, despite heavy policing, a number of individuals who were unsuccessful in the balloting or who were unable to come up with enough *wang kopi* decided to take calculated risks. Nicknamed "Rambo" by licensed vendors, they were constantly on the alert for roving City Hall enforcement officers, and darted off with their wares whenever the situation required. Those who were not fast enough had their wares confiscated or, if the particular officers concerned were willing, parted with some cash as temporary inducement to inaction. Throughout the first few weeks, Rambos played out an exhausting cat-and-mouse game with the City Hall officers. Despite numerous cases of these stalls dismantled on a daily basis in full public view, there were many others quick to take over their places. Nearing the end of the prefestive period, however, when policing by City Hall enforcement officials petered off, the number of Rambos increased exponentially, and congested further the legion of stalls in the locality. Because they did not have to pay any inflated rentals, their wares were priced lower than legal vendors. Although sympathetic to their plight of having the opportunity to *cari makan* (literally, "find food"), legal vendors felt that City Hall enforcement officials should be more diligent in getting rid of their competitors. In the context of the spectacularly commodified space of *Little India/Masjid India,* expressions of an idealized comradeship with Rambos easily became ambivalent as the days wore on. In fact, a number of street vendors were convinced that most Rambos were actually Indonesian foreigners and thus should therefore face punitive action.

By contrast, medium- and large-size businesses anchored in permanent shophouses along *Jalan Masjid India* were dissatisfied with street vendors, Rambos, and City Hall alike. Their grievances were largely framed in terms of spatial and practical inconveniences—the haphazard arrangements of the stalls blocked easy access into their shops, the unloading/loading of goods rendered an impossibility, and in the event of a fire, the congestion of stalls was a potential safety hazard. Most important, the imagined army of mobile and anonymous street vendors represented a serious threat in undermining their profitability during the festive season. They chided City Hall for practicing double standards and disregarding their interests as (more) legitimate and law-abiding citizens. In comparison to street traders who paid only license fees for the festive period, they had high overhead costs—rental, assessment fees and income tax—to bear.

In the fierce contestation over commodified and gridded spaces, migrant workers also featured prominently in the drama. Unlike in the past, when street business closed earlier in the night, the exorbitant rentals and the greater intensity of competition prompted many vendors to keep their stalls open for twenty-four hours. While family members, close relatives, and friends continued to form the core of labor, in many cases, additional help was sought in the shape of migrant workers. They provided much needed reserves of stamina in moving goods around and keeping a watchful eye over the valuable wares for the duration of an exhausting month. As noted earlier, migrant workers, however, did not escape the politics of blame either. Working-class migrant workers (particularly Indonesians in this case because of their physical and linguistic similarities with Malays) were generically perceived to form the predatory coterie of Rambos in *Little India/Masjid India*, and hence the most likely cause of heightened tensions with both street vendors and shop keepers alike. As a migrant stranger, their insertion into the local *habitus* was comparatively weak, and this pragmatically translated into a tactical license to flaunt routinized practices in the locality.

In the following year, alerted by the developments of 2004, the *Masjid India Action Committee* was in a heightened state of preparedness. On the first day of the fasting month of Ramadan (5 October 2005), they decided to stage a public demonstration. About five hundred shop owners and traders led by Datuk Ameer Ali Mydin, the chairman of the committee (and the owner of the landmark Mydin Emporium), marched along *Jalan Masjid India, Jalan Tuanku Abdul Rahman,* and *Jalan Raja Laut.* What catalyzed their public show of dissatisfaction was the disturbing sight of City Hall peons marking the street pavements for temporary stalls a few days earlier. The committee promptly investigated and found out that 150 temporary hawker licenses were approved in the locality for the period of Ramadan. Although their demand to withdraw these licenses was primarily directed at the City Hall mayor, the media also reported that the deputy prime minister of Malaysia would be looking into the matter as well.[33]

The pointed lobbying of the shop owners achieved their desired effect. In comparison with the spectacle of the previous year, local residents commented that streetlife "Little India" during the Ramadan of 2005 was comparatively tame as reflected in minimalist decorative lights and banners. Although street vending was permitted by City Hall, they were now fragmented into smaller pockets of space. More tellingly, the five footways fronting the shophouses were kept vigilantly clear of vendors. Once again, surveillance of the legal status of vendors was easily visually ascertained via custom-made City Hall umbrellas (of a different color from the previous year) that they had to purchase together with their permit. And, as before, an army of City Hall enforcement officials were conspicuously camped at various key sites to wage spatial warfare against would-be illegitimate Rambos. What was particularly striking was the relative diminution of Hindu-Indian vendors in the locality. Many had decided to shift their activities to the enclave of Brickfields or even farther away to add numbers to the "Little India" quarter of the neighboring town of Klang, some thirty kilometers toward the coast, and in the process reconstituting different spatial trajectories to the localities.

CONCLUSION

As elsewhere in Kuala Lumpur, I suggest that the ethnographic site of "Little India" is an index of various processes of uncanny cosmopolitanisms in motion over the years. Although its geographical space has been successively structured, shaped, and enlivened by the historically changing spatial and hybrid flows of capital, people, desire, and ideas, it belies the kind of magical gloss that has been constructed over it in recent times. Not all the people who occupy that particular space have been able to enjoy and celebrate the benefits of the emergent cosmopolis in equal measure even if "refugees, peoples of the diaspora and migrants and exiles represent the spirit of the cosmopolitical community" (Breckenridge et al. 6).

Primarily through Michel de Certeau's analytical notions of "sensitive zones," "strategies," and "tactics," I have explicated aspects of the diverse, disparate, and overlapping processes played out in the commercial enclave. On the one hand, I have noted the historically evolving technologies of governmentality that speak to reinvent and reposition the postcolonial city with the globally marketable marks of magical "cosmopolitanism" and "multiculturalism." To be sure, the rearticulation of a collective imaginary for Kuala Lumpur with wider networks of meanings draws their recognizability and durability from earlier grammars of colonial urban practices of rationality and social order. On the flip side, I highlighted as well evidence of agonistic everyday interreligious and interethnic encounters anchored around a loosely cohesive community of local Indian-Muslims in the first instance but that also includes an ecumenical and significant mix of migrant Muslims from South Asia, the Middle East, and beyond, a demographic feature that is of recent provenance. The local mosque, enjoying a greater symbolic prominence than before, facilitates a gathering of a wider cosmopolitan range of Muslims working and living in the locality for regular prayers and face-to-face encounters. New opportunities for heterologic cultural exchanges and the opening up of pathways that might differ from state-defined political and religious orthodoxies have thus become an emergent possibility. Social differentiation along class, racial, and religious lines do not, however, disappear from view altogether. In particular, the wider spectrum of non-Muslim business groups that had inhabited the locality for many decades have diminished and been displaced elsewhere through a convergence of state imaginings and market forces. Consequently, while a Muslim-inflected cosmopolitanism is arguably thriving, the diminishing zones of direct contact and quotidian social interactions with those outside of the Muslim fold has not fomented wider cosmopolitical trajectories in *Little India/Masjid India*.

Notwithstanding official discourses of the Malaysian brand of multiculturalism, in my portrayal of the official management and local responses toward street trading activities during the temporal conjunction of two religious festivals, I gave attention to the disjunctures that unfolded in the locality during my fieldwork period. In the conceptualization and mobilization of rationalized and commodified spaces in promoting a vibrant ethno-religious enclave, these planning actions raise critical questions about what they index about the health of "intertwined pedestrian pathways" and creolized cultural difference in multiethnic and multireligious Malaysia.

Although my fieldwork data does lend limited support to the notion that ordinary (and mobile) people do labor to seize the opportunities thrown up in these "sensitive zones," there is a nevertheless a substantive limit to their tactical "successes." Stating it differently, the current keen contest (symbolic and material) over the control, use, and meaning of street-level *Little India/Masjid India* is of comparatively recent provenance. Arguably, it is more ominous in the light of recent inter- and intrareligious tensions and contestations unfolding elsewhere in the country in the current milieu of globalization and neoliberalism.[34] In short, while "intertwined pedestrian pathways" of the kind that Michel de Certeau speaks of continue to exist and morph over time in *Little India/Masjid India*, the range and diversity of pedestrians who traverse them as far as this particular enclave is concerned, is rapidly shrinking.

ACKNOWLEDGMENTS

Intermittent fieldwork in "Masjid India/Little India" was first conducted between June 2004 and August 2005. Occasional follow-up visits, especially during the "Deepa Raya" festivals of 2005 and 2006, were also carried out. I am grateful to Dr. Shail Mayaram and the Ford Foundation for making this fieldwork possible. I also owe my appreciation to Mr. Sevan Doraisamy for his enthusiastic, able, and insightful research assistance. Finally, I am thankful to the many individuals who shared generously their experiences and memories of "Masjid India/Little India."

NOTES

Note on currency: US$1= 3.8 Malaysian Ringgit (RM)
1. Robert Wilson, "Finding Religions—Plenty of Them–in Kuala Lumpur," http://www.jadedragon.com/archives/travel/religions01.html. First accessed on 30 Aug. 2005.
2. See http://www.communitiesininteraction.org/theproject.html.
3. In popular parlance, Malaysian South Indian-Muslims are called "mamaks," which arguably carries derogatory and lowly working-class associations. More recently, the icon of the *mamak* tea stall/shop/restaurant imagery has been promoted by the tourist industry to be a convivial culinary meeting point for Muslims and non-Muslims alike. Correspondingly, a new class of *mamak* restaurants complete with staff uniforms, open air-conditioning, big TV screens, and a more sanitized environment have cropped up all over the

country. They usually operate twenty-four hours a day and are staffed by a small army of South Asian migrant workers.
4. See also Bunnell, Drummond, and Ho; and Bishop et al.
5. See McGee, "Reconstructing 'The Southeast Asian City,'" for an accounting of his earlier work on Southeast Asian cities. For recent criticisms of the primordialist and essentialist categories deployed in examining race relations in Malaysia, refer to Mohan 2004 and to Sumit 2004.
6. During this period, it was officially estimated that the squatter population occupied some 30% (3,000 acres) of the Kuala Lumpur municipality land area, and comprised about a third (156,000 people) of the town's population. The first major influx of urban squatters was during "The Emergency" (1948–1960). Several thousand rural settlers gravitated to Kuala Lumpur to escape the counterinsurgency strategy of forced resettlement into barb-wired hamlets euphemistically called "New Villages." For a critique of the "squatter problem," see Yeoh, "Creolised Utopias."
7. For analyses of the involvement of key political parties of the ruling coalition (Barisan Nasional) in corporate business, see Gomez 1990, 1994; and Gomez and Jomo. See also Khoo, *Paradoxes of Mahathirism*; Khoo, *Beyond Mahathir*; and Yao for discussions of Mahathir Mohamad's palpable imprints on the Malaysian polity.
8. For a classic study of the manner in which early migrant Tamils were configured into the capitalist development of the country in the colonial and postcolonial era, see Stenson. See Nadarajah and Loh for more recent updates. In recent years, Malaysian-based Tamil activists have turned to the communicative powers of the internet to reach a wider English-educated and diasporic audience (http://www.tamilnation.org).
9. See *Draft Structure Plan Kuala Lumpur 2020: A World Class City*, p. 1.
10. See Gomez 1994, 1990; Gomez and Jomo; Khoo, *Beyond Mahathir*; and Loh for critiques.
11. During the course of the interview, the same Tamil-Hindu lawyer informant mentioned earlier underscored twice that "there is not a single Malay shop along there despite its name."
12. Elderly informants remember Punjabi-Hindu cobblers working along its five footways, a rare if not nonexistent sight today. For many elderly Punjabis, the "Jai Hind" restaurant along Jalan Melayu continues to be a popular meeting place. The settlement in Gombak Lane was demolished in late 1969 as part of the squatter clearance activities of the government in the aftermath of the May 13 riots ("Two More Squatter Areas to Be Cleared," *Malay Mail*, 7 Jan. 1970). The City Hall building occupies a portion of the site of the former Punjabi settlement.
13. Interview with John Lourdes (pseudonym), a Tamil-Catholic business resident in Malayan Mansion since 1972, on 10 June 2004.
14. Interview with Mary Joseph (pseudonym) on 22 Apr. 2005.
15. "Bigger Crowds Expected," *Star Metro*, 25 Oct. 2004.
16. The "Reformasi" is a political renewal slogan coined by the former deputy prime minister of Malaysia, Anwar Ibrahim, after he was unceremoniously sacked from office by Mahathir Mohamed in 1998.
17. A full account of this episode is provided in Yeoh, "Kuala Lumpur."
18. According to Mary Joseph, there continues to be discreet sex trafficking of Nepalese women in these mansions as well as in the numerous hotels and lodges situated nearby to cater to both migrant workers and traveling businessmen. In the past, prostitution activities in the mansions were controlled by Chinese secret societies but some recruiting agents have allegedly taken over this function.

19. Non-working-class Muslims comprising a host of nationalities (e.g., India, Pakistan, Middle East, etc.) by contrast, reside in the upmarket One-City Condominium in the locality.
20. A call center operator situated within Malayan Mansion estimated there were about thirty-five call centers in the locality. About 60% of his customers were "regulars."
21. During national public holidays in Malaysia, the numbers gathering in these places increase exponentially. Many travel from other states to meet for a few hours to exchange letters and home newspapers and to converse. See "Foreigners Crowd KL Shopping Centres," *The New Straits Times*, 11 Feb. 2005. In comparison to Singapore's "Little India," the nodal points for these weekly congregations are more spatially dispersed and therefore less easily monitored by the authorities through CCTV cameras.
22. Interview with Harcharan Singh (pseudonym) on 23 Dec. 2004.
23. Ibid.
24. Ibid.
25. In mid-2006 for instance, one of the oldest Chinese coffee shops in the locality had to make way for a *mamak* restaurant because the owners could not afford the new inflated rental charges.
26. By contrast, a few years earlier there had been a similar conjunction between Hari Raya Puasa and Chinese New Year. The occasion provided a safe space for political leaders to plot the improvement of Chinese-Malay interethnic relations over the years since May 13, 1969.
27. A case in point (in 2006) was the charge of deviant "unIslamic" behavior by members of the National Fatwa Council to the government proposal of having joint celebrations of Islam and Hindu festive events. See "Top Cleric Says No to Deeparaya," *Malaysiakini*, 17 Oct. 2006 (http://www.malaysiakini.com/news/58313).
28. It was pointed out to me that the temporal conjunction of Deepavali and Hari Raya Puasa, which covers the years during my fieldwork period, occurs only once every three decades.
29. Mydin Emporium is one of the landmark businesses in the locality, and probably employs the largest cohort of South Asian migrant workers as well.
30. For the fasting period of Ramadan 2004, City Hall approved a total of 4,718 temporary lots for street trading in Kuala Lumpur. Of this, 1,307 lots were given out to different ethnic-based trading associations.
31. See "Indian Petty Traders Association Unhappy with Scant Allocations," *Malay Mail*, 4 Oct. 2004.
32. Where human agency failed, suprahuman intervention was sought for solace in leveling inequities. For instance, an irate Hindu-Indian street trader whom I spoke to wished that "it rains every day so that all the businesses would be badly affected—not only the minority but also the majority." In late 2000, I had serendipitously found my way into *Masjid India* close to the Deepavali period to discover a much more overt display of displeasure. Uniformed City Hall officials were in the process of carting away the tables and goods set up by Indian traders who did not possess the relevant permits. A few traders had hastily scribbled messages on manila cardboards to bear witness to their anguish—"*Kita orang India tapi rakyat Malaysia*" ("We are Indians but also Malaysian citizens"); "*Hari Deepavali tak bersimpati*" ("No sympathy during Deepavali"); "*Satu tahun satu kali saja*" ("Once a year only"). Additionally, a group of irate traders were making angry press statements to a journalist—"*Malaysia boleh tapi orang India tak-boleh*" (literally, "Malaysia can but Indians cannot"); "Malaysia's economy go down because of this"; "Those fuckers [City Hall

leaders] are hiding. Their faces blue already"; "Our Member of Parliament is sleeping." Unsurprisingly, this incident was not reported in the mainstream media.
33. "Uproar Over Hawkers at Doorsteps," *The New Straits Times online*, 5 Oct. 2005.
34. In late November 2007, the Hindu Rights Action Force (Hindraf), a coalition of thirty Hindu-based NGOs, staged a street demonstration in Kuala Lumpur with an estimated thirty thousand in attendance after a series of smaller gatherings and activities. Police crackdown on the rally was widely covered and debated upon especially in cyberspace. Hindraf has accused the Malaysian government of allegedly practicing "ethnic cleansing" through discriminative policies against Malaysian Indians as evidenced by the destruction of "illegal" Hindu temples, disproportionate incidence of poverty, and the lack of educational and business opportunities. The government responded by calling these claims "seditious" and that the group has links to the "Tamil terrorists" in Sri Lanka. To date (January 2008), key Hindraf leaders are still being imprisoned under the Internal Security Act (1960), which allows for detention without trial. For more information on Hindraf, see http://en.wikipedia.org/wiki/HINDRAF.

WORKS CITED

Ambikaipaker, Mohan. "Race and Globalisation in the age of Bangsa Malaysia." Conference on Overcoming Passions: Race, Religion and the Coming Community in Malaysian Literature. 11–12 October, National University of Singapore. 11–12 Oct. 2004.

Bhabha, Homi. "Notes on Vernacular Cosmopolitanism." *Postcolonial Discourses: An Anthology*. Ed. Gregory Castle. Oxford: Blackwell, 2001. 39–52.

Bishop, Ryan, John Phillips, and Wei Wei Yeo, eds. *Postcolonial Urbanism: Southeast Asian Cities and Global Processes*, New York: Routledge, 2003.

Blair, Thomas, ed. *Cross Border Mobility and Sexual Exploitation in the Greater Southeast Asia Sub-Region*. Nakhon Pathom: Southeast Asian Consortium on Gender, Sexuality and Health, 2006.

Breckenridge, Carol A, Sheldon Pollock, Homi Bhabha and Dipesh Chakrabarty, eds. *Cosmopolitanism*. Durham: Duke UP, 2002.

Buchanan, Ian. *Michel de Certeau. Cultural Theorist*. London: Sage, 2000.

———, ed. *Michel de Certeau: In the Plural*. Spec. issue of *The South Atlantic Quarterly* 100 (2002): 2. Durham: Duke UP.

Bunnell, Tim, Lisa Drummond, and K. C. Ho, eds. *Critical Reflections on Cities in Southeast Asia*. Singapore: Times Academic Press, 2002.

Case, William. "Testing Malaysia's Pseudo-Democracy." *The State of Malaysia: Ethnicity, Equity and Reform*. Ed. Edmund Terence Gomez. London: RoutledgeCurzon, 2004.

de Certeau, Michel. *The Practice of Everyday Life*. Berkeley: U of California P, 1984.

Dutton, Michael. *Streetlife China*. Cambridge: Cambridge UP, 1998.

Evers, Hans Dieter, and Rudiger Korff. *Southeast Asian Urbanism: The Meaning and Power of Social Space*. London: St. Martin's, 2000.

Farish, Noor. *The Other Malaysia*. Kuala Lumpur: Silverfish, 2002.

Gidwani, Vinay K. "Subaltern Cosmopolitanism as Politics." *Antipode* 38.1 (2006): 7—21.

Gomez, Terence. *Political Business. Corporate Inolvement of Malaysian Political Business.* Townsville: James Cook University of North Queensland, 1994.
———. *UMNO's Corporate Investments*, Kuala Lumpur: Forum, 1990.
Gomez, Terence, and K. S. Jomo. *Malaysia's Political Economy.* Cambridge: Cambridge UP, 2000.
Gullick, John M. *A History of Kuala Lumpur, 1856–1939.* Kuala Lumpur: Malaysian Branch of the Royal Asiatic Society, 2000.
———. *The Story of Kuala Lumpur, 1857–1939.* Singapore: Eastern Universities Press, 1983.
Harper, Tim. *The End of Empire and the Making of British Malaya.* Cambridge: Cambridge UP, 1999.
Khoo, Boo Teik. *Beyond Mahathir. Malaysian Politics and its Discontents.* London: Zed, 2003.
Kuala Lumpur Structure Plan 2020. City Hall, Kuala Lumpur,
Lee, Raymond. "The Transformation of Race Relations in Malaysia: From Ethnic Discourse to National Imagery, 1993–2003." *African and Asian Studies* 3.2 (2004): 119–43.
Lefebvre, Henri. *The Production of Space.* 1974. Oxford: Blackwell, 1991.
Loh Kok Wah, Francis. "The Marginalisation of the Indians in Malaysia: Contesting Explanations and the Search for Alternatives." *Southeast Asia Over Three Generations: Essays Presented to Benedict R. O'G. Anderson.* Ed. James T. Siegel and Audrey R. Kahin. Ithaca: Southeast Asian Program, Cornell UP, 2003.
Mandal, Sumit. "Transethnic Solidarities, Racialisation and Social Equality." *The State of Malaysia: Ethnicity, Equity and Reform.* Ed. Edmund Terence Gomez. New York: Routledge, 2004. 49–78.
McGee, Terry. "Beach-Heads and Enclaves: The Urban Debates and the Urbanisation Process in Southeast Asia Since 1945." *Changing Southeast Asian Cities: Readings on Urbanisation.* Ed. Y. M. Leung and C. P. Lo. London: Oxford UP, 1976. 60–75.
———. "Reconstructing 'The Southeast Asian City' in an Era of Volatile Globalization." *Critical Reflections on Cities in Southeast Asia.* Ed. Tim Bunnell, Lisa Drummond, and Kong-Chong Ho. Singapore: Times Academic, 2002. 31–53.
Milner, Antony. *The Invention of Politics in Colonial Malaya: Contesting Nationalism and the Expansion of the Public Sphere.* Cambridge: Cambridge UP, 1999.
Nadarajah, M. *Another Malaysia Is Possible and Other Essays.* Kuala Lumpur: NOHD, 2004.
Ong, Aihwa. *Flexible Citizenship: The Cultural Logics of Transationality.* Durham: Duke UP, 1999.
Sardar, Ziaduddin. *The Consumption of Kuala Lumpur.* London: Reaktion, 2000.
Sassen, Saskia. *Cities in a World Economy.* Thousand Oaks: Pine Forge, 1994.
Schneider, Jane, and Ida Susser, eds. *Wounded Cities: Destruction and Reconstruction in a Globalised World.* Oxford: Berg, 2003.
Smith, Michael Peter. *Transnational Urbanism: Locating Globalization.* Oxford: Blackwell, 2001.
Stenson, Michael. *Class, Race and Colonialism in West Malaysia: The Indian Case.* St. Lucia, Queensland: U of Queensland P, 1980.
———. *Paradoxes of Mahathirism: An Intellectual Biography of Mahathir Mohamad.* Oxford: Oxford UP, 1995.
Ward, Graham, ed. *The Certeau Reader.* Oxford: Blackwell, 2000.

Yao, Souchou. "After the Malay Dilemma: The Modern Malay Subject and Cultural Logics of 'National Cosmopolitanism' in Malaysia." *Sojourn* 18.2 (2003): 201–29.

Yeoh, Seng-Guan. "Creolised Utopias: Squatter Colonies and the Postcolonial City in Malaysia." *Sojourn* 16.1 (2001): 102–24.

———. "Kuala Lumpur: 'Truly Malaysia, Truly Asia'?" Conference on Living Capital: Sustaining Diversity in Southeast Asian Cities. Phnom Penh, 10–11 Jan. 2007.

———. "Managing Sensitivities: Religious Pluralism, Civil Society and Inter-Faith Relations in Malaysia." *Roundtable: Commonwealth Journal of International Relations* 94.382 (2005): 629–40.

———. "Quotidian Peace (and Violence) in a Squatter Colony in Malaysia." Unpublished essay. 2005

7 Invisibility and Cohabitation in Multiethnic Tokyo

John Lie

In the twenty-first century the world seems awash with ethnic, racial, and religious hatreds and conflicts. Communities are said to be in tension and contention; peoples argue, bicker, and compete with other peoples. Pundits and scholars scribble endlessly on the nature, causes, and consequences of such disputes. Indeed, group conflict—often ending in mayhem and murder—seems like a natural state of affairs, a default human condition. The Hobbesian situation appears especially prevalent in cities. As different sorts of people—who are often unequal in terms of power and wealth—live in propinquity, urban areas are rife with minor miscommunication and mass mobilization. The received assumption is that difference and inequality generate misunderstanding and conflict: the larger and more complex the urban demographics, the greater and more intense the group conflicts appear to be.

What then should we make of contemporary Tokyo? Indisputably a great megalopolis, it is virtually devoid of visible racial or religious contention. Whether we turn to the urban centers—the great agglomeration around Shibuya or Shinjuku Station—or the suburbs and exurbs, one would be hard-pressed to document any major manifestations of confessional or ethnic tension. The commonsensical explanation would be that there are no minority groups and very insignificant religious diversity in contemporary Japan. Yet the population of non-ethnic-Japanese people is far from being transient or trivial (Lie, *Multiethnic Japan*). As the Aum Shinrikyo Sarin incident suggests, there are also religious-based diversity and dissent in Japan.[1] I argue that the very presumption of nonexistence provides the condition of possibility for invisibility and hence "peaceful" coexistence and cohabitation.[2] More generally, the virtual absence of interethnic conflict is overdetermined: the collapse of prewar imperial ideology, persistent residential and occupational segregation, rapid post–World War II economic growth, the prevalent norm of civil indifference and public harmony, and the absence of ethnic-identified organizations.

MULTIETHNIC TOKYO

Tokyo is by any criterion or definition a major megalopolis. Already with over a million denizens by the eighteenth century when it was called Edo, Tokyo and the conurbation around it have grown continuously, constituting nearly a fifth of the total Japanese population by the beginning of the twenty-first century.[3]

Tokyo is also a global city. By the eighteenth century Edo featured people from across the Japanese archipelago and beyond, creating a culture of cosmopolitanism.[4] Even in the post–World War II period when the foreign influx was virtually absent, Tokyo featured notable aggregations of minorities ranging from Ainu and Burakumin to Koreans and Chinese (Lie, *Multiethnic Japan*). If we add the steady influx of rural migrants and foreign workers, Tokyo was indisputably a multicultural and multiethnic city by the 1990s. Although this influx did not match in size and scale the influx into New York, London, or Paris, Tokyo should be classified as a "world city" based on the heterogeneity of its population and the linkages they maintained with the world outside.

In spite of the pervasive perception inside and outside Japan that Tokyo is a monoethnic city, Tokyo has long been a complex conglomeration of distinct peoples, whether we define them as old-timers versus newcomers or Japanese versus non-Japanese. In the early twentieth century, amidst industrial transformation and rural exodus, Tokyo not only grew—both extensively in area and intensively in density—but also became more complex in at least two ways. The establishment of urban centers—usually around a railway station—generated identifiable locales and neighborhoods. These specific places often became associated with particular functions or features, whether the traditional association of Yoshiwara with sexual entertainment or Jinpō-chō with bookstores. These commercial and cultural divisions of labor were overlaid by definable loci of peoples, whether the long-standing Burakumin hamlets in Kyoto or the new towns for recent Okinawan or Korean immigrants in Osaka and Tokyo.

Far from creating a generalized anomie of homogenized Tokyo-ites, then, Tokyo comprised matrices of modular, identifiable places: the formal surface similarity among places, whether the jumble of narrow alleys or the dispersal of commercial establishments, did not erase local particularities and peculiarities. These places were, moreover, not merely diverse but also unequal. Indeed, in pre–World War II Tokyo, one's place of origin and the place of residence were largely conflated and provided a principal means of social classification and identification. Denizens of the city's low-lying "downtown" areas (*shitamachi*) were almost uniformly working class or poor, whereas residents of the high areas (*yamanote*) surrounding the Imperial Palace lived in bourgeois comfort. There were also ethnic neighborhoods, such as "villages" of Burakumin or Chinese, which conflated neighborhood and identity. Someone was thought to be a Burakumin precisely because she lived in a Burakumin area. Place became a master signifier of class, ethnic, and other forms of social identification.

Beyond social geography, an explicit ethnic hierarchy existed. In the urban labor market, ethnic status determined one's wage level. In the 1920s, for example, Korean construction workers earned 70% of what their Japanese counterparts made (Ishizaka 193; cf. Iwamura 35–36). Lower-paid ethnic workers also lived in poorer neighborhoods. Labor organization, for example, often occurred along ethnic lines (Ishizaka 209–13). Not surprisingly, tensions and disputes often flared up along ethnic lines, entrenching ethnic identification more deeply. Whether the coalminers in Hokkaido or the construction workers in Osaka, Japan in the 1940s witnessed a series of labor agitations by low-paid Korean workers. The conflation of class fractions and ethnic constitution fueled the spiral of conflicts that rendered ethnic difference and hierarchy an indisputable fact of urban life even as the state sought to integrate the Korean population into mainstream society (Miyata 150–56). Toward the end of World War II, in fact, the dominant government discourse declared the isogeny of Japanese and Korean people, and promoted their isogamy. The imperial ideology in the 1930s and 1940s projected a vision of multiethnic Japan that encompassed much of East and Southeast Asia. Though most took it for granted that the Japanese race was superior, Koreans and Chinese—and at times peoples as far away as in India and Indonesia—were regarded as integral members of the Japanese imperial family-state.

The prewar reality of multiethnic Tokyo—replete with interethnic tensions and conflicts—became a faded and fitfully recalled memory for the vast majority of the population by the 1960s. The overarching context for the prevalence of harmony in postwar Japanese life is rapid economic growth. Visible improvements in ordinary lives squelched potential of labor-based conflicts. Although Tokyo's multiethnic population generated tensions, rapid economic growth overshadowed and diffused them. More specifically, economic growth stifled ethnic tensions by virtually eliminating the possibility of labor movements and conflicts organized along ethnic lines. Furthermore, economic growth also set the stage for the new self-image of "monoethnic Japan" by creating a sense of national pride or a sense of "Japaneseness" increasingly defined in contradistinction to the West. The postwar era ushered in a distinct self-image: the idea of Japan as a homogeneous, monoethnic society.

THE RISE OF MONOETHNIC IDEOLOGY

The collapse of imperial ideology effaced the prewar reality of multiethnic Japan. Instead, Japanese people envisioned postwar Japan as a homogeneous country: without status or class inequality and without ethnic diversity.

The end of the empire rendered Japan smaller and more homogeneous. Having lost extensive territory in Asia and the Pacific, the country had shrunk down to the four major islands of the Japanese archipelago, which constituted roughly a fourth of the landmass of the empire at its most extensive. While expatriate Japanese returned "home," there was a simultaneous exodus of "foreigners" from the Japanese archipelago. Stripped of citizenship rights after the 1952 San Francisco Peace Treaty, the majority of Korean, Chinese, and other non-Japanese nationals departed the Japanese archipelago.[5]

Nonetheless, not all "foreigners" left Japan. Most immediately, there were indigenous minority groups, including Ainu, Burakumin, and Okinawans, who remained. How did such ethnic heterogeneity dissolve in the ideological melting pot of Japanese homogeneity? As I argued in *Multiethnic Japan*, a concatenation of factors facilitated the prevalence of monoethnic ideology by the 1960s. In addition to the actual reduction in the number of foreigners and ethnic minorities that the postwar exodus caused, both the right and the left in Japanese politics promoted the ideal of a "small" Japan that was at once democratic, egalitarian, and homogeneous. The idea of homogeneity extended well beyond the ethnic dimension to encompass social inequality and regional diversity. Immediately after the end of World War II, pervasive poverty and the elimination of status hierarchy created a much more egalitarian society, in terms of both income inequality and political identification. Rapid cultural integration—facilitated greatly by industrialization, urbanization, and militarization in the first half of the twentieth century—accelerated in the 1950s and 1960s. Here the expansion of the mass media—not only the media of radio and television but also the messages conveyed—relentlessly reduced dialectal diversity and promoted cultural unity. Japanese intellectuals not only contrasted monoethnic Japan with the multiethnic United States—the foil for all comparisons in the postwar era—but they also sought the Japanese *differentia specifica* in Japan's cultural and ethnic homogeneity. Here we should not downplay the significance of Western, and especially American, commentators on Japanese society who insistently portrayed Japan as a homogeneous society. The convulsive churning of all of these forces within the postwar Japanese body politic spread the belief that homogeneity is the defining quality of Japaneseness. Indeed, the belief in Japanese homogeneity became a defining characteristic of Japan. The fact of ethnic heterogeneity became expunged from the elementary knowledge about Japanese society (Lie, *Multiethnic Japan*).

THE VISION OF INVISIBILITY, THE SOUND OF SILENCE

The expunction of ethnic heterogeneity in the dominant discourse is only one side of the story. If there were indeed a significant population of ethnic minorities, then why were they invisible and silent?

Invisibility was a fact of life: out of sight, out of mind. The vast majority of the ethnic minority groups were residentially segregated prior to the 1960s. Furthermore, most of them worked in distinct occupations, usually far apart from ethnic Japanese people. As neighbors and colleagues, then, non-Japanese people were virtually nonexistent to ordinary Japanese people, living and working in parallel societies.

By the 1960s, however, the ethnic minorities became indistinguishable from the majority population. This occurred precisely at a time when regional cultures (including speech and sartorial signifiers) became integrated into the relatively homogeneous, normative Japanese language and culture. Burakumin[6] were defined by their origin and residence in Burakumin villages. Just as significantly, they looked distinct and lived differently from the non-Burakumin majority. The stereotype of Burakumin—stereotypes are far from being false as sociological generalizations—included their distinct clothing items such as straw sandals and culinary items such as entrails. That is, many Burakumin looked, talked, and ate the way outsiders presumed they did. Yet by the 1980s, differences had virtually disappeared. Whereas the prewar common sense was that Burakumin constituted a distinct race, by the 1980s most Japanese regarded them as part of the majority population. For Koreans, ethno-national cultures manifested themselves in everyday life, perhaps most viscerally in speech and food. Yet the preponderance of second-generation Korean Japanese by the 1970s meant that the majority of Koreans in Japan were in no obvious ways distinguishable from ordinary Japanese people. By the twenty-first century, the tests of Koreanness frequently failed to distinguish the two peoples. The consumption of *kimch'i*—a type of pickled vegetables—was long regarded as the master signifier of Koreanness. Yet it has become a mainstream Japanese food item, readily available in supermarkets. Today, a person buying it is much more likely to be Japanese than Korean.

Appearance, in any case, is highly ambiguous and subject to conflicting interpretation. When surface markers were readily apprehensible, they became part and parcel of naturalized differences that were at once congenital and incorrigible. Thus, Burakumin were long considered a distinct race from the majority Japanese population in the prewar period; now almost everybody regards them as culturally—and racially—indistinguishable from the mainstream Japanese people. When I have asked Japanese people to identify a Burakumin or a Korean person from a group of five or six people, they have consistently failed to do better than the statistical likelihood (i.e., of being right more than once in five or six tries). Curiously, the proportion didn't improve appreciably even when I included recent arrivals from East and Southeast Asia or those with one non-Japanese parent. Passing, in any case, has long been a possibility for Burakumin who seek at once to transcend the dual stigmas of racism and classism (Cornell 349–52). Given the length of the Japanese archipelago—and the multiple geographical origins on the Eurasian mainland of those who have populated the Japanese archipelago over the millennia—the mainstream Japanese population itself is highly hybrid and incorporates distinct phenotypes. Hence, it is not surprising that someone from Southeast Asia (who may very well have a great deal of Chinese ancestry) may look more Japanese than a self-identified Japanese person. Once when I was walking in Tokyo with my daughter, whose mother is British, an elderly Japanese couple began a friendly conversation. When I told them that I lived in the United States, they marveled at how long I had stayed away from Japan, all the while not suspecting that I may not be Japanese, whether by my own or any other basis of identification. After several minutes, they decided that they could detect my American accent. When they realized that my daughter could only talk in English, they looked at her very closely and the woman said that living in America made my daughter look American as well!

Invisibility is not simply a matter of the majority group's inability to differentiate non-Japanese from Japanese people. It entails a conscious and persistent effort on the part of the minority population to pass as mainstream or ordinary Japanese people. To be sure, cultural integration should not be understood as either enforced or voluntary; there is always a mixture of constraint and choice, the proverbial carrot and the stick. Be that as it may, we shouldn't underestimate the minority population's desire to assimilate into the mainstream, whether lured by higher income, greater prestige, or the sheer avoidance of prejudice and discrimination. The reality of invisibility is thus partially a consequence of camouflage and silence: the unwillingness to identify publicly as a member of a minority and the willingness to play the part of an "ordinary" Japanese.

The structure of silence goes beyond this simple dialectic. The Japanese ideology of monoethnicity was not imposed forcefully from above by conservative ideologues or government bureaucrats. Rather, minority groups actively embraced and promoted it. In the case of the Burakumin, the 1955 formation of the Burakumin Liberation League crystallized the strategy of assimilation. The primary political tactic of the League was to denounce people who demean and defame Burakumin. However, the definition of "demeaning" or "defaming" Burakumin included those who asserted their ethnic difference from the mainstream Japanese population. Because the League situated Burakumin as fundamentally Japanese, the organization sought not so much to promote Burakumin identity as much as to deconstruct it and render it part of the Japanese population. The Korean case differs somewhat. The Korean minority population has long been represented by two organizations with divided allegiance to the two Koreas. What has united them, however, is their steadfast refusal to link the fate of the Korean population to that of the Japanese archipelago. That is, if the desirable outcome of Burakumin activism was total assimilation, the ultimate goal of Korean agitation was to return to the Korean peninsula, whether to North, South, or a unified Korea. In spite of these distinct political desiderata, Burakumin and Korean organizations in Japan both accepted the ideology of monoethnicity. That is, Burakumin are Japanese, Koreans are Koreans who should be in Korea, and only Japanese people in principle live permanently in the Japanese archipelago.

Invisibility and silence, then, leave the ideology of monoethnicity unscathed. This was the unquestioned reality of Japanese ethnic constitution in the late twentieth century. Although individual-level interethnic interactions are common, almost all of them are misrecognized (by the majority population at least) as intraethnic interactions. In the ethnic syllogism of monoethnic Japan, then, there can be no interethnic tensions and conflicts because there are only Japanese people living in Japan.

AD LIB AND AD HOC: THE UNSCRIPTED ENCOUNTERS

There are, however, millions of non-Japanese people living in Japan, who recognize themselves and would be identified by others as non-Japanese. Given that they may be neighbors and colleagues or celebrities and superiors, inevitably and systematically interethnic encounters and interactions occur in everyday life. Let me adduce four ethnographic examples.

1. After a typically overextended academic seminar, several scholars retired to a nearby bar for a recap and a nightcap. Besides me, there was one man who passed himself off as Japanese but was in fact of Korean ancestry and another man who was married to a Japanese citizen of Korean ancestry (who explicitly identified herself as "Korean"). After a round of drinks, one of the scholars derided a presenter for his academic shortcomings and used the derogatory term for Koreans "Chon." Curiously, perhaps out of deference to his seniority, none of the others intervened to "correct" his racist language. Even more curiously, the "racist" was someone who took some pride in his progressive attitudes, especially on matters of ethnic and foreign inclusion in Japan. Afterward, I asked the Korean-Japanese scholar about the incident and he shrugged it off by saying that it didn't mean much, being at worst a reminder and a legacy of the colonial era (though the "racist" scholar was not even enrolled in elementary school at the end of World War II). The man with a "Korean" wife merely observed that the "racist" was a decent person. The enforced politeness of public encounters in contemporary Japan effectively made the utterance of improper language in public a logical impossibility. The very articulation of racist terminology was understood as informal talk—as evidence of camaraderie, of exposing the backstage (*honne*) instead of the formality of the front stage (*tatemae*)—and was translated as being virtually devoid of any racist intent or content. To underscore this point, the Korean-Japanese man pointed out that the "racist" scholar was very friendly to me during

the bar-time conversation and engaged in neither explicit nor subtle efforts to disparage me. Divorced from any substance, then, the racist terminology had merely a phatic function—or so it was taken by two people who should be sensitive to manifestations of racism against Koreans in Japan. The matter never came up again, though I saw all three of them in question several times in the course of that year. The irruption of the racial epithet became a nonevent, smoothed over by the polite patina of everyday academic interaction.

2. Easily the closet thing to an interethnic conflict I observed in over two years of residence in Tokyo during the 1980s and 1990s was the forced evacuation of foreigners—predominantly Iranians—from Yoyogi Park in Tokyo in 1993. In response to complaints about the noise and the mess that the Iranians made at their weekly gathering, the police pushed them out of the park premises. Several Iranians whom I interviewed expressed anger against the police in particular and Japanese society in general. Yet none of them staged any sustained resistance—undoubtedly in part to prevent deportation. The only visible expression of police resistance was a group of Japanese people who claimed to be upholding the rights of the foreign workers (as the Iranians were labeled). One middle-aged woman said that it was very important for Japanese people to "protect the rights of foreigners" as part of the imperative of promoting human rights in general. A college student felt that it was a blight of Japanese society that so many Japanese people lived with pervasive racial prejudice. Yet the whole affair approached nothing like the ferocity of the clash between riot police and radical students in the 1960s and 1970s, or the labor agitation of the immediate postwar decades. After an hour or so, the police force dispersed, along with the Iranians and the Japanese demonstrators. Returning to Yoyogi Park later in the day, there were no visible remnants of police action. There were even some Iranians selling telephone cards (one of the major occupations of Iranians who lived in Tokyo in the late 1980s and early 1990s). Nor was there much mass media coverage. The seemingly large congregation of Iranians disappeared altogether soon thereafter, driven less by police surveillance or brute force and more by the Japanese economic downturn. The end of the "bubble" economy, in other words, ended the "problem" of foreign workers in Japan. When I sought to contact the Japanese demonstrators several months later, only one of them had sustained their links to foreign-worker-related organizations.

3. At a rally to support foreign workers, speech after speech included ringing denunciations of Japanese society, replete with allegations of historical wrongdoings and present problems. The polite but aroused audience clapped enthusiastically. The afternoon ended with a collective arm raising—in contradistinction to the raising of both hands and shouting "banzai" that marks a normative Japanese expression

Invisibility and Cohabitation in Multiethnic Tokyo   169

of solidarity—and a collective affirmation of their movement. Except for the continuation of quotidian assistance to individual foreign workers—ranging from visa-related inquiries to workplace dispute resolutions—the rally didn't result in any political initiative, media campaign, or collective movement, whether among concerned Japanese themselves or non-Japanese residents. The collective effervescence of the rally was like a bubble that dissipates right after the event, not unlike the evanescent confrontation of the Yoyogi Park incident. One young man was actually present at both occasions. When I asked him about the lack of sustained activism, he shrugged his shoulders and said: "That's the way it is and I am not sure that there's much one can do about it. It's just the way Japanese people are these days, pursuing their individual desires and separate lives." More relevantly, this relatively long-term activist himself didn't connect his work to parliamentary politics. When I asked him about his connections to political parties or government bureaucracies, he responded that conventional politics was useless. He went so far as to deny that they had any real relevance to the lives of the foreign workers or ethnic-minority members. Without much hope for change, then, he was content to blow bubbles.

4. At the loudest event I experienced, Burakumin Liberation League members used megaphones to denounce a writer whom they deemed to be denigrating Burakumin. Yet, as I argued above, the activists were adamant that they are in no ways different from ordinary Japanese people and categorically denied that they were members of an ethnic-minority group. When I suggested that external discrimination and internal identification made Burakumin fit the basic definition of an ethnic group, they interpreted my argument as a casuistry that revealed my ignorance of Japanese history and culture. When I conveyed my conversation to several Japanese sociologists, they generally agreed with the Burakumin activists. An eminent social scientist added that the very act of classifying Burakumin as an ethnic minority would incur the Burakumin activists' wrath. That is, she feared that public advocacy of my position might very well generate the kind of public denunciation I witnessed earlier. She told me that academic freedom is illusory for scholars of Burakumin history and culture. The consequence of Burakumin activism was effectively to silence all discussions of Burakumin, thereby rendering them invisible to a public that persists in believing in essential Japanese homogeneity. Loud, mechanically amplified speeches of Burakumin activists not only silenced dissident voices but also added to the nationwide chorus that, unthinking, insisted on the fact of Japanese monoethnicity.

All these encounters are unscripted; they occur outside of the Japanese cultural repertoire. In the dominant script, because there aren't ethnic-minority members in Japanese society, there shouldn't be interethnic encounters. Put differently, instances of interethnic tension or conflict lack relevant interpretive frameworks or conceptual schemes. Whether a racial epithet or an interethnic tension, they evaporate into the hurly-burly of metropolitan life and in no way threaten the patina of Japanese homogeneity. They are therefore invisible to the vast majority of the population, and the few who speak out are ignored or silenced. I once observed a Southeast Asian man screaming loudly at a politician who was campaigning. The angry foreigner was saying in English that the politician was a racist and a fascist. The politician smiled, politely bowed, and thanked the Southeast Asian man for his support: "I am very pleased that even our foreigner friend is supporting my candidacy!" The very fact of multiethnicity can be neither seen nor heard. When interethnic encounters do emerge in everyday life, they evaporate soon thereafter.

The facts of the matter are indisputable. Interethnic conflicts do occur. In Tsukiji Fish Market where many foreigners work, Bestor (*Tsukiji* 233–35) discusses a brawl between a Chinese and a Japanese worker and describes a Japanese account of why interethnic misunderstanding and conflict arises. The account is no different from many interviews I conducted and focuses on foreigners' failure to understand Japanese cultural repertoire. The point, however, is that as prevalent as the discourse is, it coexists with the ideology of monoethnicity and the concomitant notion that there are no significant ethnic populations in Japan, much less interethnic conflicts. In Bestor's account, the brawl was quickly forgotten, and remains the only reminder of the large presence of foreign workers in the Tsukiji Fish Market in his book.

The dissipation and dissolution of interethnic tensions and conflicts are not simply cognitive or cultural lacunae. The general tilt toward homogeneity and harmony—assiduously reproduced in interpersonal interactions as well as by the major organizations and institutions ranging from school to work—provides the master cultural backdrop against which these specific instances of ethnic tensions and conflicts are silenced and squelched. The ideology that collapsed after the war included not only the Emperor system but also the valorization of martial violence. Almost overnight, Japan became a "peaceful" society. Informal social controls that animate all social life continued to stifle conflict in face-to-face settings (cf. Bestor, *Neighborhood Tokyo* 208–14), but with the additional overlay of harmonious civil indifference. That is, the dominant mode of urban interaction operated under the mantra of "not bothering others" (*meiwaku o kakenai*). Indeed, in postwar Tokyo, civil indifference and informal social control both work to suppress interpersonal conflicts and emotional outbursts to maintain a veneer of civility and harmony. Japanese and non-Japanese alike learn of the prevailing harmony ideology such that the Japanese are said to have a distinct way of interacting among one another. Whether in the classroom or the workplace, historical facts of contention are expunged and present instances of disharmony are disavowed. The culture of consensus is a highly stylized interpretation that fits neither the past nor the present of Japanese society. Yet there are psychological, interpersonal, and organizational mechanisms that render the generic expressions of diversity and dissonance insignificant in the discourse of Japaneseness and in everyday interactions in metropolitan Tokyo.

THE ABSENCE OF ESCALATION AND THE ABSENCE OF ORGANIZATION

Nonetheless, why don't these individual instances of altercation, bickering, and conflict spiral into newsworthy interethnic tensions and outbursts? After all, Japanese people are far from being brainwashed into submission or living under totalitarian surveillance. Engaged conversations often reveal an awareness of ethnic diversity in Japanese society. Everyone I talked to at any length could recall an ethnic Korean person as a firsthand acquaintance and even report what might be interpreted as interethnic tension and conflict, a permutation of one of the anecdotes I narrated above.

Beyond rapid economic growth and harmony norms, what ensures the sublimation of interethnic conflict is ultimately the absence of organizations that propagate the evanescent facts and that prolong them to constitute a recorded reality. In other words, there are precious few people or organizations that generate any discussion of the fact or meaning of interethnic conflict. Simultaneously, very few organizations organize the voices of discontent to generate sustained mobilization.

Consider two classic arguments on political mobilization. V. I. Lenin argued that without a revolutionary party the workers would only promote a reformist agenda. That is, intellectuals, broadly conceived, project a particular vision of current reality and future possibilities that leads the masses to think of themselves as members of the working class. The theory may become so robust that reality cannot be understood apart from that particular framework. The Stalin-era Soviet Union used class categories as the master scheme of political identification and social classification (Fitzpatrick). Hence, eager scholars begin to observe class consciousness and class conflict in the unconscious manifestation of suboptimal work performance. Conversely, the absence of a class-analytic frame may misrecognize class-based expressions of social reality. In the post–civil rights United States, for example, ethnicity and race became master categories of social analysis. Hence, many instances of individual altercations or class-based conflicts came to be seen indisputably as instances of interethnic conflict (Lie, "The Black-Asian Conflict?"). Put differently, I am suggesting that the diffusion of ethnic categories and identities in contemporary Japanese society may very well lead Japanese people to reinterpret my first anecdotal case as manifestations of well-entrenched Japanese racism.

Another way to think about the phenomenon is in a choice-theoretic framework. Albert O. Hirschman argued that there were three fundamental individual responses to organized life: exit, voice, or loyalty. Living in a society that at once discriminates against and denies the very existence of ethnic minority, the discriminated and invisible minority may very well choose to exit. Certainly, that was one common solution among Koreans, whether they migrated to the United States or returned to Korea. Alternatively, they may learn to live with monoethnic ideology and society. As I have suggested, both Burakumin and Korean activists complemented and strengthened the dominant ideology of monoethnic Japan. Yet there is the third possibility: voice. Only when individual voices meet the possibility of collective expression and social transformation can the voice option become viable. In the absence of organized opposition to the prevailing interpretation of social reality, individual voices become marginalized and ignored, as we saw in the ethnographic examples I adduced. Social movements shift the interpretive framework and acknowledge the hitherto neglected reality, whether one thinks of the prevalence of poverty in the Cold War United States or the existence of Palestinian peoplehood in Israel.

Whether we follow the lead of Lenin or Hirschman, discourses and ideas that are embodied in political organizations or social movements are crucial for framing and making sense of political and social reality. In postwar Japan, there were no sustained organizations or movements to dispute the dominant ideology of monoethnicity or to sustain the claims of discrimination against minorities. In the inauspicious climate of opinion, individuals and instances remained marginalized.

Finally, the spatial structure of Tokyo is resistant to public action. As I suggested earlier, Tokyo is a composite of urban centers. Though commercially vibrant, they are almost inevitably devoid of open, public spaces: the space of the public sphere. The principal exceptions are sacred spaces—most important, the Imperial Palace—but they are by definition resistant to host public protest. The Imperial Palace in particular is well fortified, an island in the center of a metropolis with very few and well-defended bridges. Thus, large urban parks in the prewar era and college campuses in the postwar era provided the loci of public protest. The salient point is that the rare public displays of ethnic activism cannot take place in visible space; they are inevitably held in large auditoriums or local parks that are by and large invisible to the larger urban population.

Thus, the absence of interethnic tension and conflict is overdetermined in contemporary Japanese society. Rapid economic growth stunted class- or material-based movements. Remnants of occupational and residential segregation minimize actual interethnic interactions. In the dominant understanding of social reality, in any case, there are no minorities in particular and hence no conflicts in larger society. Indeed, the dominant mode of urban interaction effectively eschews the very possibility of public conflict. Even the actually existing organizations of ethnic minority groups work assiduously to sustain the social myth and channel individual energies away from voice and contention. Therefore, individual instances of resigned frustration or heroic expression become marginalized incidents that at best articulate a highly unorthodox view. Given the virtual absence of ethnic-based activism and of public protest, the belief in monoethnicity becomes tenable.

SUBPOLITICS AND SUPRAPOLITICS

The reality of multiethnic Japan and the myth of monoethnic Japan exist in an uneasy relationship that occludes and obfuscates interethnic tension and contention. What is indisputable is that postwar Tokyo has generated very few overt instances of interethnic conflict. A more careful scanning of newspaper articles or a more scientific survey will not uncover the overlooked reality.

The missing conflict among ethnic groups reflects not only the strength of monoethnic ideology, the structural diffusion of minority groups, and the absence of ethnic-identified organizations that advocate ethnic-identification agenda but also the overarching character of postwar Japanese politics. The postwar era produced a classic division between the left and the right that reproduced the supranational politics of the Cold War. The Liberal Democratic Party aligned itself closely with the United States in particular and the "free world" in general. Especially after the 1955 formation of the Liberal Democratic Party, the sheer dominance of the one-party system effectively squelched subnational political concerns, whether the rights of women or the demands of minority groups. The fundamental fact of rapid economic growth precluded systematic expressions of discontent and protected the entrenched power of the ruling party and the national government.

Subpolitics—defined broadly to include concerns about subnational groups—remained very much marginalized in postwar Japan. As we saw, the activists for Burakumin or Koreans advocated a universalistic agenda that was broadly leftist and socialist in orientation. The particular expression of the left, however, was radically circumscribed by the nationalist mind-set. Squeezed among class politics, nationalism, and the Cold War, subpolitics remained submerged and sublimated in the more epic struggles of global and national political ideologies and movements.

Nonetheless, the submerged reality of subpolitics is far from being an inevitable feature of contemporary Japanese society. Already there are indisputable signs of ethnic mobilization across the archipelago, from the Ainu of Hokkaido to Okinawans. Second- and third-generation Koreans in Japan are increasingly aware of their entrenchment and embeddedness in Japanese society. The influx of indisputably foreign peoples continues. The demographic bases exist, in other words, for greater ethnic mobilization and interethnic conflict. Simultaneously, we no longer have the suprapolitics of the Cold War or the nationalist myth of monoethnicity to prevent the expressions of ethnic contestation.

In the twenty-first century, Japanese politics totters along with the fluctuating fortunes of the half-century rule of the ruling party. The belated emergence of subpolitics—including interethnic contention—is a looming possibility that may very well explode, whether because of a "foreign" terrorist attack, a war in East Asia, or a fresh increase in the influx of foreign workers. In this regard, the past is by no means the best guide to the future, even the immediate future. Those who persist in studying the past are doomed to be surprised, caught unaware by the dynamic nature of social reality.

ACKNOWLEDGMENTS

I wish to thank Asef Bayat, Ryan Calder, and Shail Mayaram for their helpful comments.

NOTES

1. The Aum Shinrikyo sarin incident refers to the detonation of deadly poison gas in the Tokyo subway train in March 1995 that killed twelve people and injured thousands. The perpetrators were the followers of Aum Shinrikyo, a charismatic cult. For the purposes of this paper, however, I focus on the matter of ethnic and racial diversity.
2. In this paper I will draw on my observations over the past four decades, supplemented by research that culminated in *Multiethnic Japan*. My ethnographic observations are drawn principally from the Tokyo metropolitan area, including my extended stay in Shibuya in the late 1960s, Tsukishima and Kawasaki in 1985, and Mita and Hiyoshi in 1993. For this paper, I made several trips to the Tokyo metropolitan area in 2003 and 2004.
3. See, in general, Machimura, esp. chap. 2. Cities are perforce hybrid and heterogeneous entities. An autochthonous development that may ensure homogeneity is incompatible with the vibrancy of urban life. Whether immigrants from the countryside or other countries, the outsiders are inevitably part and parcel of the urban constitution.
4. Needless to say, the extent of cosmopolitanism was limited in comparison to the twenty-first-century world cities, such as Manhattan or London. However, in spite of the claim that Japan was "closed" (*sakoku*) to foreign contact, both non-Japanese peoples and commodities circulated around the archipelago. It is also worth emphasizing that the extent of national identity was at best very weak. Thus, Edo was cosmopolitan precisely because there were "different" peoples residing in the city.
5. The U.S. military authorities explicitly endorsed Wilsonian nationalism and internationalism that eschewed ethnic or national heterogeneity. Thus, Koreans were to be relocated to Korea; Japan was to be for Japanese ethnics and nationals.
6. Burakumin comprise descendants of prewar outcasts and low-status people, such as *hinin* (literally, nonpersons). The new Meiji state in the late nineteenth

century squelched most manifestations of status inequality and decreed *hinin* and other low-status groups to be "new" citizens.

WORKS CITED

Bestor, Theodore C. *Neighborhood Tokyo*. Stanford: Stanford UP, 1989.
———. *Tsukiji: The Fish Market at the Center of the World*. Berkeley: U of California P, 2004.
Cornell, John B. "Individual Mobility and Group Membership: The Case of the Burakumin." *Aspects of Social Change in Modern Japan*. Ed. R. P. Dore. Princeton: Princeton UP, 1967. 337–72.
Dore, R. P. *City Life in Japan: A Study of a Tokyo Ward*. 1958. Richmond, Eng.: Japan Library, 1999.
Fitzpatrick, Sheila. *Everyday Stalinism: Ordinary Life in Extraordinary Times: Soviet Russia in the 1930s*. New York: Oxford UP, 1999.
Hirschman, Albert O. *Exit, Voice, and Loyalty: Responses to Decline in Firms, Organizations, and States*. Cambridge: Harvard UP, 1970.
Ishizaka, Kōichi. *Kindai Nihon no shakaishugi to Chōsen*. Tokyo: Shakai Hyōronsha, 1993.
Iwamura, Toshio. *Zainichi Chōsenjin to Nihon rōdōsha kaikyū*. Tokyo: Azekura Shobō, 1972.
Lenin, V. I. *What Is to Be Done?* 1902. Harmondsworth, Eng.: Penguin, 1988.
Lie, John. "The Black-Asian Conflict?" *Not Just Black and White*. Ed. George Fredrickson and Nancy Foner. New York: Russell Sage Foundation, 2004. 301–14.
———. *Modern Peoplehood*. Cambridge: Harvard UP, 2004.
———. *Multiethnic Japan*. Cambridge: Harvard UP, 2001.
Machimura, Takashi. *"Sekai toshi" Tokyo no kōzō tenkan: Toshi risutorakuchuaringu no shakaigaku*. Tokyo: Tokyo Daigaku Shuppankai, 1994.
Miyata, Setsuko. *Chōsen minshū to "kōminka" seisaku*. Tokyo: Miraisha, 1985.

Section III
Cosmopolitan Microprocesses

8 Cairo Cosmopolitan
Living Together through Communal Divide, Almost

Asef Bayat

INTRODUCTION

What does the modern city do to ethnos? In what ways does urban geography contribute to reinforcing communal belonging or fostering cosmopolitan experience? How far, if at all, does modern urbanity diminish communal strife by blurring ethno-religious divide, by facilitating mixing and mingling, and establishing interpersonal trust? "Primordialists" would expect that ethno-religious groupings would persist over time, because members are born into their natural ethnic or religious formations. In this perspective, ethnic groups are seen as primordial, permanent and bounded entities with clear lines of cultural demarcation, and identified by such objective characteristics as a common ancestry, language, physical features, and religion (Geertz). This way of thinking has been seriously challenged by "instrumentalists" who suggest that an ethnicity, rather than being a natural group, is constructed by members' invariable reference to an imagined common kinship origin. This means that ethno-religious groups are dynamic beings, which are subject to continuous deconstruction, shifting boundaries, and reconstruction,[1] a process that has direct bearing on inter- and intracommunal interactions. In other words, "communities" are not simply introverted and exclusive collectives whose relation with others is defined merely in terms of conflict. Rather, communities also attempt to overcome their differences and live together. They have done so through the lived experience of sharing histories, misfortunes (wars, crises, and natural dangers), work environment, and living space—as well as undertaking mutual institutions. In short, humans have historically exhibited a capacity to coexist and cooperate across religious or ethnic divides. Yet coexistence and sharing do not take place in a vacuum. They take shape under specific structures and possess particular geographies.

My purpose in this essay is to explore how the intricate dialectic of both diminishing *and* reconstituting ethno-religious identities takes place, and how in particular modern urbanity contributes to this complex dynamics. The debate about communal life under modernity is as old as the history of modernity itself (Delanty). The classical perception in the nineteenth century regarded "community" as an ideal to be achieved, a social unit that stayed in opposition to the state. The early twentieth century coincided with the crises of world wars and anomies, and the "iron cage of bureaucracy" altered the notion of community. Perceived as the embodiment of "thick" values, community stood as the alternative arrangement to "society" as the harbinger of "thin" and superficial values. Thus, the Chicago School of Urban Sociology and its late-nineteenth-century precursors such as Tonnies, Durkheim, or Simmel all observed and regretted with great dismay how modernity undermined "community"—a social organization they characterized by interpersonal relations, locality, informality, flexibility, and solidarity (Redfield). Later proponents of modernization theory also believed that modernization and homogenization would wreck the foundation of traditional communal life. But they saw the process in positive light. For them, individualism, mobility, and cosmopolitan life were to furnish the foundation for a more democratic social order (Gellner). As the experience of Cairo shows, urban change and modernization have unquestionably contributed to a dramatic shift in communal life, but they have not led to its disappearance.

One consequence of modern urbanity has been the possibility of everyday cosmopolitan life, one that is distinct from, and in my view favorable to, the inward-looking and closed-knit ethnic or religious community that espouses narrow, exclusive, and selfish interests. By everyday cosmopolitanism I mean the idea and practice of transcending self (at the various levels of individual, family, tribe, community, religion, ethnicity, and nation) to associate with agonistic others in everyday life. This notion of cosmopolitanism is not limited merely to elite lifestyle, but is extended especially to include the subaltern experience of intercommunal coexistence. It concerns the way in which members of different ethno-religious groupings mix, mingle, and intensely interact; and how such interactions affect the meaning of "us" and "them" and its dynamics, which in turn problematizes the meaning of group boundaries. Modern urbanity contributes to this arrangement by facilitating geographies of coexistence between members of different religious or ethnic groups. This is so not simply because people of different religions come to live and interact together. After all neighbors might dislike and distrust one another. Rather, proximity and interaction can supply opportunities for religiously divergent parties to experience trust (as well as mistrust) between them.

On the other hand, my line of thinking differs from the evident evolutionist tendency present in Chicago School of urban sociologists such as Park and Burgess who viewed the disappearance of "community" as an inescapable outcome of modernity (Park; Burgess). The logic of "urban ecology" would compel such enclosed communities as "ghettos" to eventually get assimilated into the mainstream urban society. The truth is that "community," in new forms and dispositions, may be reproduced precisely due to the exigencies of modern work and lifeworlds, on the part of those who cannot afford the cost of modernity. Thus, extended family and close-knit territory-based urban communities are likely to re-emerge in the conditions where people are unable to survive as individuals in the competitive and cut-throat urban political economies (Bayat). In addition, the spread of "moral communities" in modern urban landscapes to counter anomie and alienation has already been the subject of much scholarly research (Kepel; Giddens). Indeed, as some observers have contended, globalization, instead of eliminating ethnic communities, may in fact reinforce and revive them. Here ethnicity, whether national or transnational, embodies cultural groups' resistance against the homogenizing forces of the postmodern world (Melucci; Appadurai).

My argument is that a modern city like Cairo tends, on the one hand, to differentiate, fragment, and break down the traditional face-to-face ethnic or religious-based communities by facilitating the experience of sharing with other cultural-religious groupings. At the same time, however, religious-ethnic identities may persist or get reinvented not necessarily through face-to-face interactions, but through the construction of imaginary or "distanciated" communities. My reading of Cairo shows that the modern city has the tendency to differentiate, individualize, and fragment its inhabitants, to weaken the traditional ties, break down extended family (among people who can afford to go autonomous), and increase geographical mobility. The logic of land use, cost of housing, and jobs often determine where families settle. Spatial congregations based on ethnic or religious affiliation give way to class segregation so that the ethno-religious communities based on intense interpersonal interactions get undermined as their members break up into clusters of individual families dispersed across the vast expanse of the city, where they are compelled to connect to the "larger society," and where religious members may experience real interactions and sharing with other city dwellers with different religious or ethnic affiliations. But deep association and sharing between members of different communities does not mean the end of religious or ethnic identities. On the contrary, the breakdown of faith-based local collectives can, in conditions of general feeling of uncertainty and threat, give rise to different—"virtual" or "distanciated" religious—communities. Here identity is based not on real cooperative experiences, but on imagining ties with distant, faceless, and unknown "brothers" or "sisters," whose general whereabouts are shared through modern networks of daily papers, through TV, or through heresy and rumor. This dialectic of both communal identity, on the one hand, and the real day-to-day cooperation with people outside, on the other, generates a more complex intra-communal dynamics than simply harmony or conflict. For individuals are likely to test their imaginary and abstract view of the "other" (resulting from, for instance, prejudice or provocation) against the experience of real association they develop with them. This is how I see Muslim-Christian relations in today's Cairo.

In what follows I will elaborate on these propositions by focusing on the city of Cairo where historically diverse ethnic and religious communities lived often in their respective quarters with a good degree of in-group bonds up until the early twentieth century. The essay investigates the relationship between Cairo's Muslim and Christian (Coptic) residents, by drawing on ethnographic data collected from Shubra, a historic section of Cairo where both Muslims and Christians have been living together for over a century.

MAPPING COMMUNAL DIVIDE: A HISTORICAL SKETCH

Today, Egypt represents primarily a Muslim majority nation. Yet a substantial proportion of the population, some 8 to 10% or six million are Coptic Christians.[2] Christianity came to Egypt by the Roman conquest of Egypt, but it spread largely from the mid-first century AD. It has been suggested that the oppressive rule of the Roman Empire created a sort of nationalistic Coptic, or Egyptian, Christianity that stood in opposition to the Byzantine authorities. With the Arab conquest in 639 AD came Islamization and Arabization of Egypt, so that by the tenth century Muslims became the majority population (Staffa 37). Conversion to Islam was not smooth. Some embraced Islam voluntarily for its promise of justice, many did so to avoid special taxations (*karaaj* or *jizya*), while still others to acquire equal social and political status with Muslims (Marsot 1–3). In the meantime, Arabic gradually replaced the "Coptic language"; since the government diwan (bureaucracy) used Arabic, it compelled the Coptic elite (who continued to work in the administration) to learn Arabic, and teach it to their children who would then pursue similar occupations as their fathers. When in the twelfth century the Pope Gabriel decreed that the Church use the Arabic language in their sermons, lay Copts also began to speak in this language. So in the end, Arabic became the language of Egyptians, both Muslim converts and the remaining Christians, with the Coptic language dying out sometime between the fourteenth and eighteenth centuries (Chitham 18).

Under Muslim rule during Umar (717–740), Copts became a *dhimmi* (non-Muslim) "minority," denied both of serving in the army and of high political positions, and subject to special poll tax, *jizya* (in exchange for their protection), for centuries. Only as late as the reign of Said Pasha in 1856 was the *dhimmi* status dropped, *jizya* lifted, and Copts became full citizens. Mamluk rulers (1250–1517) had already attempted to create a balance between the Copts and Muslims by recruiting the former into bureaucracy and trade, so that Copts became a counterpoint to a growing educated Muslim "middle class," which also aspired to diwani positions. Modern times brought formal equality between the two communities. Muhammad Ali's Hamayouni Decree in 1856 established Coptic personal status laws, allowed to them into the military, removed *jizya* tax, and promised freedom of religion, equality in employment, and removal of all discriminatory terms and symbols, even though the construction of churches remained a contested issue even until today.

The "Liberal Age" was the hallmark of Coptic public presence and citizenship. Elite Copts and Muslims developed almost identical liberal lifestyle and taste, informed by French Enlightenment and English liberal trends. In the early twentieth century, two Christians became prime minister (Boutros Ghali Pasha, 1908–1910, and Youssef Wahba Pasha, 1919–1920). Wafd, the political party of independence, was so close to Copts that Islamists and ultranationalist Misr-al-Fitah labeled Wafd the "Party of Copts," and the king as the "protector of Islam." Although the Revolution of 1952 treated both Copts and Muslims equally in welfare dispensation and educational attainment, it inflicted disproportionate economic loss on the Coptic community. Being excessively richer than Muslims, Christians lost more to Nasser's nationalization policies than Muslims (some 75% of their work and property) (Ibn Khaldoun Center 16). Following the dissolution of political parties, their presence in politics and parliament drastically declined. These developments led to the first wave of Coptic emigration, to Canada, the United States, and Australia in the 1960s and 1970s. The continuing outflow of educated Copts together with the rise of Islamist militancy in Egypt since the 1970s has cemented a strong identity politics among the vocal Coptic community in exile and to a lesser degree among Copts living in Egypt.

In the past three decades, the status of Coptic Christians in relation to the Muslims in Egyptian history has become the site of contention. Both the reality of Christian-Muslim relations and its representation have been deeply politicized. In this contestation, "history" as usual has become the battleground. One view expressed mainly by the militant Copts in exile and at home, considers Christian Copts as a distinct ethnicity with distinct ancestry, religion, and way of life, but one that has been relegated by the Muslim majority and the Egyptian state to the status of an oppressed "minority" (Labib 140–41). The very meaning of the term, Copt, rooted in the word *Aegyptos* or *Egypt*, suggests Christians to be the "true original Egyptians," a distinct racial group. Their perception is of having over time been turned into a "second class" population (Atiya).[3] Interestingly, militant Islamists in Egypt likewise attribute a distinct ethnic character to Coptic Christians, albeit not as an "oppressed" minority, but as the stooge of crusaders and Western interests. As Christians, the militants say, Copts have no place in the Egypt of daar al-Islam. In contrast, most Coptic intellectuals and the Church leaders as well as Muslim elites inside Egypt view Muslim-Coptic relations in a unique fashion that does not resemble any other interethnic or interreligious dynamics. Such Coptic figures include Samir Mosrcos, Hani Labib, Ghali Shukri, and Milad Hanna, and along with Muslim counterparts such as Tariq el-Bishri, Salim el-Awa, and Gamal Badawi view Egyptian Christian Copts not as a sociological "minority," but as players and partners in the unique Egyptian-Arab-Islamic civilization. The Coptic population is seen as integral element in the category of "Egyptian people" at par with their Muslim counterparts; while Egypt is constituted as a "unique entity," a "land of inherent pluralism and mélange" owing to its pharaonic, Greco-Roman, Coptic, and Islamic heritage (Hanna cited in Purcell 432–51; Badawi; Labib; El-Bishri). In Gamal Hamdan's words, most of today's Egyptian Muslims are yesterday's Copts. In fact Egyptians are made partly of Muslim Copts and partly of Christian Copts, considering that the word *Copt* means "Egyptian" (Hamdan cited in Badawi 15). According to a Christian, Hani Labib, although Islamists may consider Copts as second-class citizens, the Egyptian Constitution rules for equality, and the modern state renders the concept of *dhimmi* status redundant (Labib 121–22). While the former view insists on "minority" status, "discrimination," and conflict, the latter underlies "citizenship," "equality," and accommodation. Yet, both seem to characterize Coptic reality in terms of certain "objective," historical and cultural "facts," a long-standing meta-narrative. There is little reference to everyday life processes, to interpersonal relations and agency, to specific episodes of conflict, to the intricate marriage of both clash and coexistence, nor especially to the spatial dimension of these processes.[4]

NARRATIVES OF CONFLICTS

Notwithstanding claims about the "unique historic affinity" between Egypt's Christians and Muslims, evidence of episodic sectarian conflict, clash, and violence abound. In modern times, three episodes of sectarian clash stand out: British colonial period, the presidency of Anwar Sadat, and the Islamist era. During its colonial rule, Britain deployed the usual divide-and-rule strategy to separate Copts from the national movement. She recognized the Copts as an "ethnic minority," stressing their anthropological "distinctiveness." Encouraged by British support, groups of Copts, notably wealthy families, pursed a sectarian line, demanding in 1911 special Coptic representation in councils and the legal system, proposing a "Sunday holiday" instead of on Friday. Muslims responded with dismay rejecting the demands. Yet the majority of Copts seemed to disprove British emphasis on "Coptic distinctiveness," discarding her attempt to insert in the 1923 Constitution a clause recognizing a special status to "foreigners" and "minorities," including the "Coptic community." Copts in general seemed to desire not a "minority" status, but citizenship. Indeed the "liberal era" (1923–1952) through the 1960s during the rule of Nasser, somehow fulfilled that desire as Christians and Muslims exhibited a good measure of national unity and cooperation at societal and governmental levels up until the 1970s.

The presidency of Anwar Sadat in 1971 marked a turning point in Muslim-Coptic relations. Sadat wanted to take Egypt out of the Nesarist system associated with socialism, populism, and nationalism; he wished to open up to the West, foreign capital, and market forces. To undermine Nasserists and communists, Sadat gave a free hand to the growing Islamist movement, both the reformist Muslim Brothers and the new Gamaiyyat, Islamist students associations, which dominated most universities, and which later turned into the violent Gama'a el-Islamiyya organization. In addition, Sadat himself assumed a pious posture, speaking the idiom of Islam, and passing religious laws. He changed the Constitution to enshrine the shari'a as the main source of law, the measures deemed to undermine the status of the Christians. There were even signs of provocation to undercut Coptic authority. In 1972 a report was said to be circulated in which the Coptic pope allegedly had called for an increase in the Coptic population in order to return Egypt fully to Christians (Badawi 13–15). In addition, measures were taken to restrict new church construction by placing many conditions on it. Such pressures instigated the fury of the Coptic community, forcing Sadat to back down by passing laws on national unity and freedom of belief.

Yet, the opportunity for sectarian strife remained. In 1972, Muslim youths in Beheira clashed with Copts, burning shops and houses on the grounds that a Christian shop owner had shot at the provocative youths. Then in 1977, Al-Azhar called for passing laws to implement Hodoud, Islamic penal codes, and to implement the execution of apostles. The measures, which would have brought Christians under the Islamic laws, caused the fury of the Coptic community and the Church. The ensuing protests, statements, and hunger strikes, however, were overshadowed by the 3rd February 1977 mass urban riots; the laws went ahead and only the exiled Coptic community followed up the campaign. Yet the new measures were bound to create communal strife. A year later in the Upper Egyptian towns of Menya and Assiut, priests were attacked and churches were set on fire, while officials renewed their threat to implement apostasy laws in an attempt to silence the Church. With the pope retreating to the desert as a gesture of protest, the Coptic Church and Sadat's regime entered a head-on collision.[5] Although a compromise and relative calm were established, they failed to abate sectarian violence. In June 1981, Egypt witnessed particularly bad Coptic-Muslim violence. Reportedly a personal dispute between two individuals in Cairo's poor community of al-Zawaya al-Hamra turned into an armed confrontation between groups of Christians and Muslim neighbors. The violence ended with the intervention of the state. In 1981, the regime arrested twenty-two priests and bishops and deposed Pope Shenouda, as part of a large-scale crackdown on internal dissent arose following Sadat's peace deal with Israel and his new Open Door economic policy.

President Sadat ironically was gunned down by an Islamist group to which he had given lip service support. His successor, President Mubarak, amended relations with the Christian community and the Church, but could not stop sectarian conflict. On the contrary, the 1980s and early

1990s, the height of Islamist movement in the country, witnessed the most frequent and spectacular sectarian violence in Egypt's history. In March 1987 the Islamist groups instigated a band of youth to burn the Church of Virgin Mary in the southern town of Sohag on the grounds that some Christians had set a mosque (Kotb) on fire. September saw violent clashes in Assiut between militant Islamists and police, in which Coptic shops were destroyed. In the meantime, Muslim militants in Menya attacked a private party given by a wealthy Copt and threw explosives into a church, after which followed violent clashes between Muslims and Christians. In the next two years churches were assaulted in Rowd al-Farag and, in Cairo's Masara, a wedding party was attacked, and more skirmishes ensued in Menya and Assiut. In March 1990, Menya's Abu-Kersas became the scene of forty-eight burned shops belonging to Copts and bomb attacks on more churches took place. Violence, largely against Coptic Christians, continued in the early 1990s in Bani Sweif and Menya, and in Cairo's Ain al-Shams, Zeitoun, and Shubra. In 1992 alone dozens of shops were destroyed, twenty-two people were killed, and homes and places of worship were attacked. For every one Muslim killed two Copts were murdered (Ibn-Khaldoun Center 21). The most dramatic sectarian violence took place in the southern village of al-Kosheh in January 2000 in which at least sixteen people died. A dispute between two traders spread into the surrounding villages where scores of businesses and homes were destroyed and residents were killed in the course of three days of violence. Police regained control only after the violence had already escalated (Labib 178–80; *African Research Bulletin* 138–39).

The conflicts were not confined to these isolated acts of sabotage by some professional activists. Undoubtedly, they left their imprints on communal sentiments, reviving a new identity politics in Egypt. The hegemony of Islamism had altered the political mood in the nation; had generated a more inward-looking religious nativism, manifested in defensive selfhood and communalism. As Muslims became more Muslim, Copts likewise became more Christian. Muslims grew beards, put on the veil, massively attended mosques, and chose more and more religious names for their children; and similarly, Copts showed off their crosses, displayed Christian icons, paid much greater attention to Church activities, and called their offspring with the names of Christian saints. The two communities continued to compete in, what Zeidan calls, the "war of stickers" on cars. As they felt threatened, Coptic Christians moved more and more into themselves. College students found their own sectarian groupings, with some calling for the establishment of a Coptic political party (Zeidan 53–67). Meanwhile occasional sectarian outcries spread from the pulpits of mosques; slanderous books, pamphlets, and cassette tapes unleashed sentiments of communal suspicion and mistrust often disproportionately against the Copts. These developments were to ascertain the claim of Copts as an "oppressed minority," whose dissenting sentiments the Church leadership tended to appease. An absence of collective actions had earned them the description of a "passive minority." Thus, when thousands of angry middle-class Christian youths took to the streets of Cairo in June 2001 to express outrage against a slanderous report in a newspaper against the Coptic Church (about a defrocked priest allegedly having sex with a woman in the premises of a church), the political elite was shocked. Similar collective outrage was expressed only a year later at the screening of the film *Bahib al-Sima* (*I Love Movies*) made by a Copt, which had allegedly "misrepresented" the Christian way of life in Cairo. Significantly, in both cases protesters refused to seek state protection but resorted to direct protests from the nucleus of their own community, the Church.[6] These represented communal protests, directed not against other religious members, but against a particular newspaper and a filmmaker.

What do these forms of incidents tell us about the nature of interreligious relations in Egypt? Violent clashes occur in particular political conditions, for example, the reign of President Sadat and the rise of Islamism. Accordingly, they originate less from the large mass of the community than from elites and political activists. Significantly, most of the incidents took place in rural areas or provincial towns of southern Egypt, rather than in large cities, such as Cairo where a large concentrated Coptic population lives. Finally, these narratives of conflict are of the vocal, the noise, the shouting, burning, and killing, which are often reported, recorded, and which we hear. They are real and require serious attention. But they conceal the more intricate dynamics of communal interactions; they tell us little about how "separate" communities have nevertheless so profoundly merged into a cultural fabric that drawing boundaries between them becomes a challenge. The tales of the "mainstream" often obscure the way in which Christian and Muslim families live their lives on a daily basis, interact with one another, merge and diverge identities, and continue to share longstanding lifeworlds, and also experience moments of mistrust and suspicion. To highlight the spatial moments of coexistence, I will focus on the Cairo district of Shubra, unique for its cosmopolitan history and high concentration of Copts (currently 30%) located in the largely Muslim megacity in which the Christian population is dispersed in small pockets or individually in the vast urban landscape.

CAIRO'S SHUBRA: GEOGRAPHY OF COEXISTENCE

For centuries after Cairo's construction, Shubra remained the summer residence of the notables and the elites. In fact, the word *Shubra* is a Coptic term referring to "Djebro" or "Sapro" meaning "countryside" (Viand). Since the nineteenth century the area expanded, developing especially after World War I. In 1947 Shubra had 282,000 residents, increasing to 541,000 by 1960. The natural population growth and migration turned the surrounding areas into Coptic neighborhoods. So in the current administrative division, Shubra constitutes only a segment of the adjacent districts of Rod al-Farag, Ezbekiya, and Sahel, which accommodates the highest concentration of Christians in the city. In its modern expansion, Shubra developed new European-style streets and buildings, including churches, clinics, missionary schools, and cinemas. Mohammad Ali Pasha's summer palace, modeled on the Parisian Versailles, crowned Shara Shubra, the fashionable carriage promenade, regarded as Egypt's Champs Elysee. With the settlement of elite families originating from the Levant, Ottoman Syria and Lebanon, who were escaping from the bustle of old Cairo, Shubra assumed an exceptionally cosmopolitan character, attracting a host of artists, singers, writers, and poets (Viand).

Twentieth-century Shubra, an extension of Ezbekiya, has been the residential area of middle-class urbanites, with a 40% Coptic concentration. However, in current form Shubra looks in many ways like hundreds of other lower-class areas in the city. The district has lost its past glory, style, elitist cosmopolitanism. From Egypt's Champs Elysee, Shara' Shubra has now turned into a congested, crowded road, darkened and depleted by the city's traffic fumes. The run-down remains of its old-style homes, two- or three-story villas, are now choked by scores of tasteless, boxy and flimsy buildings, struggling to emerge out of layers of dust and pollution. Its urban form, shops, people, and rhythms are not radically different from comparable neighborhoods. Yet, Shubra represents a distinct urbanity, reflected in its history, memory, in its urban "footprints," in social space, in manners.[7] It is perhaps the only "baladi" area in the city, where one can see a larger number of unveiled women shopping, walking, or working in the public space. Some of them stand behind store counters as salespersons, while older ones may be sitting in the front-door chairs on the sidewalks. More striking is perhaps Shubra's skyline. Minarets of cross and crescent conjoin sometimes in juxtaposed proximity, staring at one another in resolve and rectitude. From these structures emanate the echoes of evening prayers filling the sky of the neighborhoods.

Indeed, for Muslim passersby, Shubra's small churches are not estranged places; they look remarkably like Muslim zaways—small single-room and simple structures with male worshippers usually sitting on the floor, reciting the holy book, which is simultaneously broadcast on rooftop loudspeakers. The large churches, such as Maar Gurgess in Khalawafi where worshippers are seated on chairs, are more complex. They often act as community centers, places of prayer, recreation, education, interpersonal relations, and spaces of communal identity and association. Both male and female Copts attend large churches but, as in mosques, they pray or attend religious classes in segregated halls. Similarly, the informality that characterizes Coptic churches (the apparent disorder, screaming children, men and women chatting, sipping tea and nibbling on sandwiches) resembles that of mosques. Both institutions of faith share in their regard for one another. During Muslim festivals and Ramadan, for instance, Shubra's churches illuminate with colorful, green lights to express solidarity with mosques.

The experience of sharing in the public space encompasses common use of many different institutions. Coptic and Muslim children attend the same government schools, where they play, fight, form peer groups, and experience almost identical youthfulness. There are plenty of stories of Muslims attending Christian schools, of Copts joining Islamic *awqaf* schools. Educated Copts from an older generation took courses in Al-Azhar; the poet Wahbi Tadross studied the Qur'an and Francis al-Eter attended classes by Muhammad Abdu, who decried sectarian divide and saw nationalism as the cooperation of all citizens irrespective of religion (Badawi 166). In the localities, Muslims and Christians build deliberately nonsectarian organizations such as community associations to improve the neighborhood. Coptic and Muslim businesses and shops are invariably adjacent, with almost no way for an outsider to know which belongs to whom, except by religious names of their owners. This integrated work world structures daily personal interactions, for instance, cleaning up the sidewalk in front of the shop, watching each other's businesses, lending and borrowing, and neighborly chatting and discussing. I did not see an indication suggesting that Christians refer only to Christian businesses and Muslims to Muslim businesses.

Business personnel of Shubra are likely to live in the vicinity, in the typical three- or four-story boxy apartment buildings, where each floor is usually tailored to enclose two or three flats, within each residing a Muslim or Christian family. The proximity of buildings across the narrow streets and alleyways is such that neighbors cannot avoid seeing or hearing one another. In such an interfaith spatial arrangement, few things remain private. For residents who have a shared common life, apartment doors do not remain closed. Umm Yahya may enter into Abla Mary's flat just across the hall without knocking on her door and engage in small talk for several hours, a practice not to the liking of the more autonomous new generations. If a neighbor does not hear the usual buzz in the next-door apartment, she might wonder what has gone wrong. Safa, a Christian resident of Shubra, recounted to me a story about her neighbor, Umm Yahya. Umm Yahya had not heard Safa's mother's usual "good mornings" because the mother had fallen ill. Upon hearing the news, Umm Yahya "came back, before lunch, with two big chickens and lots of macaroni," a visit that was followed by frequent calls to make sure that the children were fine.[8] "It is not clear in your story if Umm Yahya was a Christian or Muslim," I commented. "She was Muslim, God bless her; she was a neighbor," she replied. "You see at the time," Safa went on, "we did not know [notice] religion. We were not just aware if this person was Christian or that one Muslim. Actually my father kept both the Qur'an and Bible at home. We had both; we didn't know the separation." In fact, there is little that distinguishes a Christian home from a Muslim one in middle-class Shubra. Apart from the religious icons, the home decor and interiors are almost identical—small rooms packed with heavy furniture, big and bright chandeliers, and walls filled with religious calligraphy. So, a Christian entering a Muslim home would find not a strange but a familiar habitat.

Neighborly relations widely involve the customary practice of borrowing things from one another—money, tools, or more frequently a cup of oil, sugar, rice, or beans. For those who have scarce cash, it is essential, as part of survival strategies, to secure access to foodstuffs by lending and borrowing. The practice follows attendant rationalities of keeping the accounts, including the frequency of transfers and the time of returns. The tradition also means that food culture in both communities is essentially similar. "Coptic food and Muslims' diet is exactly the same," according to Safa, only Muslims avoid pork and Copts camel meat. Otherwise, the main Egyptian dishes—molukhiya, kushari, ta'miya, and the like—are an integral part of food culture in both communities. Even such Muslim delicacies as ashura (a special sweet made of milk, rice, and sugar) is widely consumed by Christians and given on special occasions to "important" members of the family, particularly men. Muslim and Christian male neighbors may get together in the evenings to socialize, play tawla, and talk, while women serve them with tea and delicacies, which reflects similar patterns of gender relations in the two communities.

The Orthodox Church stipulates that it is the man's duty to house, feed, clothe, and shelter his wife who, in return, is obliged to obey her husband and not to leave home without his permission. Women are denied the right to make major decisions in the Church or to become deacons or priests, even though they may be involved in charity and service work. Both in mosques and in churches, men and women sit separately during the prayer. Early marriage is condoned and female circumcision is practiced in both communities. Christians share, more or less, moral codes similar to Muslims' in terms of family relations, respect for elders, sexuality, and marriage. "Conservatism is not just a Muslim thing," Coptic Maged commented. "The Church is also saying TV or films are haram."[9] However, while the conservative piety of Muslim women is often judged by their public appearance in veil (as opposed to "modern" unveiled ones), lack of veiling among Christian women often veils their conservative ethos. What in principle determines the cultural and behavioral patterns in Egypt is not religion, but class. Muslim and Coptic middle classes share by far more than what poor and middle-class Copts share. No distinct dress codes separate members of the two faiths. Gone are the nineteenth-century days when the Copts were compelled to wear colored turbans, belts, or heavy crosses around their necks as reported by Edward Lane (554–57), even though the use of some religious symbols (such as crosses and tattoos, which in the past largely peasants used to get protection from evil spirits) seems to be back. The growth of veiling among Muslim women is a very recent phenomenon, largely since the 1980s. It is mainly religious names (such as Mohammad or George) that distinguish between a Christian and a Muslim. Yet with the growing use of neutral names (such as Farid or Mona) this identity marker has drastically diminished.

Followers of both faiths invariably stressed the deep interfaith friendships, in particular among youths of the same sex. Beyond the schools where peer groups are formed, neighborhoods and apartment buildings are places where youngsters establish deep affinity. Male youngsters spend a great deal of time in the street corners to stroll, chat, see movies, sit in coffee shops, or play soccer games, sometimes during the very late hours of night. But young females, both Muslim and Christian, are likely to join together in the privacy of homes to build close association. Even when Fatma, a Muslim friend of Christian neighbor, Lilian, went through a new religiosity by putting on the veil, their deep affinity was not affected.[10] Muslims in Shubra attend churches for marriage and religious festivities, while Christians may partake in Muslim weddings and such festive occasions as Eid-al-Fitr, or Eid al-Adha, and Ramadan iftars. National ancient holidays such as Shamm Nasim are shared by both religious members.

It is true that intermarriage is rare, but cross-religious love is not. Every novel and film on Shubra has stories about love affairs between Christian and Muslim youths, highlighting secret romances between neighboring teens. The virtual proximity of homes, windows, and balconies makes eye contact, personal interactions, and emotional exchange between neighbors—in their ordinary or "natural" states, their T-shirts or pajamas—an order of life. Yet such tales of interfaith love often entail unhappy endings, in sad realization that legal union will not be possible.

Venturing in Shubra neighborhoods on Friday midday, one cannot escape the reverberating sound of Qur'an recitation and adan (call for prayers) from the bustling mosques, large or small. The mosques soon are packed with young and old men, often extending into the surrounding alleys and streets. In the Western mainstream media, the groups of bending, praying men are the most eye-catching marker of Islam—note the images in books on Islam or daily papers—representing a clear religious pointer that separates "us" from "them." For the Christians of Shubra, however, the scenes are neither novel nor an issue, expect perhaps for the traffic congestion they might cause; otherwise, they are just how things are in the neighborhood. People simply "do not see them." Indeed, the lack of awareness about many identity markers, which readily stand out for an outsider, is remarkable. For over a month that I lived in Shubra's neighborhood of Khalafawi, I would be wakened often abruptly by the thundering noise of morning adans, the calls for prayer, which blast from the loud speakers hooked on to the front door of neighborhood mosques. Almost every night I would wonder how the Christian neighbors would feel about such piercing sounds in the middle of the night. "We don't hear them," they usually respond. They seem to be used to the sounds. This discourse of "not seeing, not hearing,

Photo 8.1 Church, Khalafawi, Shubra, Cairo. Photo by Asef Bayat.

or not noticing," in a sense, points to a state of unconsciousness about "difference" in Shubra's daily life, indicating the dissipation of boundaries in some domains of social and cultural life among Muslims and Christians.

DIALECTIC OF CONFLICT AND COEXISTENCE

There is no romantic picture of harmonious sectarian relations in Cairo. What good does such sharing do if it suddenly turns into episodes of violent confrontations, of killing, burning, and destroying in the name of religious difference, it might be asked? What if these members do not invoke their shared lives when the overarching image of communal divide hunts them? We have already seen how Egypt experienced three decades of frequent violent conflicts between members of Muslim and Christian communities, with dozens of people killed, mosques and even more churches attacked, and scores of properties destroyed. But as we indicated earlier, the violent clashes were instigated primarily by militants, occurred in specific geographies, and escalated not simply out of sectarian difference but also due to the Upper Egyptian "culture of vendetta," of "revenge killing" (or Tha'r), which in essence serves to strengthen the patriarchy of lineage or tribe (Hopkins and Saad 13–15). More important, incidents of conflicts took place, not within the large modern cities, but overwhelmingly in villages or provincial towns.

Yet, interreligious clashes do arise in everyday interactions. Conflict between the Christians and Muslims is as common as within a religious group. Further, tensions arising from secular roots are often given a religious color as a way of cultivating support or opposition in an urban locality. Radical activists of both sides attempt to highlight religious differences in their quest to build popular backing. We know how militant Islamists have often "othered" Copts as a nonreligious people in order to create a more exclusive religious identity among their potential constituencies. National politicians at times exalt one faith over the other to nurture support. Thus Christians often feel a profound insensitivity when political leaders or soap operas project "Egypt as an Islamic nation," a posture that subtracts the Coptic population from the national membership.[11] Yet other tensions arise directly out of difference in religious traditions, for instance, when churches ring their bells simultaneously with the mosques' calls for prayers (adans).

Lay people of the faith, as in Shubra, time and again try to find solutions to their differences. Many Shubra residents remain indifferent to the divisive tactics of national politicians. Thus, during the parliamentary elections in 2000, in the mostly Muslim district of Al-Weili in Shubra, the Muslim candidate of the ruling party (NDP), Ahmad Fouad Abdel-Aziz, used the sectarian card against his Christian opponent, Mounir Fakhri Abdel-Nour from the Wafd Party. He propagated the idea that a Christian Member of Parliament could not represent Muslims. Yet Muslims went ahead to elect the Christian candidate as their deputy (*Cairo Times*, 23–29 November 2000). In general, Cairo has seen the prevalence of more sectarian coexistence than conflict. The reason cannot be attributed simply to some natural tendency of humans to cooperate, for we have also seen periods of conflict even though humans also possess the capacity to coexist, largely when the "right conditions" are at their disposal. Nor can the general interreligious calm be reduced to Copts' minority position, their "passivity" and tolerance of discrimination, or their subordination to the hegemony and cultural power of the majority. We have seen also episodes of disquiet, protest, and the expression of collective identity. Although Copts constitute a distinct group in terms of shared historical memory, religion, a "proper name," or a "myth of common ancestry,"[12] undoubtedly their shared traits, homeland, history, and culture with the "larger Muslim society" play a major role in Muslim-Christian coexistence. Yet there is a need to transcend generalities and abstract images of commonality, by exploring the concrete ways in which people of different ethno-religious groupings experience interconnectedness in daily life. In other words, we need to highlight the geographies within which sharing is experienced (or conflict fostered). The modern city severely undermines the "traditional" pattern of immediate, local, interpersonal and territorial ethno-religious communities. It mixes people with various primordial imaginings, facilitating experiences of interpersonal interaction and sharing; it destabilizes total and indiscriminate images of sectarian community and solidarity. Muslim-Coptic relations in Shubra are a function of the transformation of urban space in Cairo in the twentieth century.

Social change and the modernization of Cairo in the past one hundred years has led to the breakdown of the traditional Coptic community—that is, from a relatively bounded religion-based group localized in a particular urban territory with regular day-to-day interpersonal relations into a mostly fragmented population loosely tied together through a "virtual" or "distanciated community." These Copts with a broad Christian identity simultaneously share and experience life with different and diverse non-Coptic individuals and groups. Janet Abu-Lughod has shown how the ecological organization of the preindustrial city in medieval times has in many ways shaped the ethnic and religious distribution of the population in today's Cairo. Built in the tenth century by the Fatimids, the walled city of Cairo did not expand considerably until the French expedition in the early nineteenth century and the ensuing process of modernization. During this period its population did not exceed some 200,000 inhabitants. Until the nineteenth century, the Muslim majority largely lived inside the walls, while some twenty thousand religious minorities—Greek sects, Jews, Armenians, and some ten thousand Copts—resided outside, in the northwest corner of Cairo, were "excluded by and in turn excluded the majority" (Abu-Lughod, *Cairo*, 60). It was not only the religious minorities but also the Muslim majority who were ethnically divided into distinct groupings including Egyptian Arabs, foreign Muslims, Mamluks, Black Nubians, and Ethiopians. The ethnic and religious groups, irrespective of class and status, lived in distinctive shared quarters, where workplaces stood traditionally in close proximity to homes. Only Jews typically lived in the walled city, since their major occupation, money changing and goldsmithing, were located inside the walls, and because they lived close to and under the protection of the ruler who crowned the walled city. The Coptic quarter was located just north of the modern Azbakiya, the site of the port town of al-Maqs, and within the Qas al-Sham'a portion of old Cairo. What determined their spatial location had to do with Copts' mainstream occupations, as scribes, account keepers, and customs officials who resided close to their work site, the port (Abu-Lughod 59–60). These were the urban occupations that the early Arab conquerors (warriors) were neither interested in nor had the skill to perform (Chitham 78–79).

The rapid modernization process transformed occupational structure and changed many spatial features of Cairo, including the walled quarters; it created new architectural styles and institutions, a class-based spatial division, distinction of workplace and living areas, land use separation, and ethnic and religious mixing. The modern industry, education, and administration generated a new class of professionals and businesses among both Muslims (effendies) and Coptic alike. Yet Copts remained disproportionately more urban, more professional, and better-off. Coptic tradition of secular education emphasizing professionalism seems to have contributed to the higher percentage of teachers, doctors, and engineers among them. One estimate in the 1970s stated that some 80% of all pharmacists and 30–40% of all doctors in Egypt were Copt (Chitham 82–86). They have also been involved in businesses such as moneylending or wine and pork production, in which Muslims express less interest. As modernization swept through the nation, such wealthy and professional Copts did not hesitate to move out of traditional Coptic neighborhoods to spread and merge into the newly established middle-class areas across the city. What added to a further fragmentation of ethnos and dilution of ethnic communities was that many ethnic and religious minorities, especially Jews, some middle-class Copts, and foreigners (Greek and Italian entrepreneurs, British civil servants, troops, and businessmen), left Egypt after the 1952 Revolution. By the late 1960s, close to 300,000 Egyptians were living abroad (Chitham 30). Although, the walled section of contemporary Cairo has maintained some aspects of its traditional spatial organization, it has been strangled by the encroaching modern neighborhoods and their feeble buildings devoid of any memorable character.

Thus, the Coptic population—some 10% of the total inhabitants (Abu-Lughod *Cairo*, 211)—are dispersed individually or in pockets of families across the vast terrain of this megacity. It was largely Shubra, an extension of the Coptic quarter in Azbakiya that maintained its historic legacy of relatively higher (40% and 30% respectively) Christian density. Yet even here the influx of Muslim rural migrants (partly due to the location of Khazindar bus terminal in Shubra) since the Second World War expanded Shubra while diluting its Christian density. Indeed as more rural Muslim migrants have moved in to such lower-class neighborhoods as al-Wayli, Zaytoun, Shubra al-Khayma, or al-Azawa al-Hamra, the affluent and middle-class Christians (along with their Muslim counterparts) chose to move out to settle in the more desirable districts of Muhandessin, Heliopolis, and Nozha, where they created ethnically heterogeneous and more cosmopolitan urban localities. The appeal of modern autonomous individuality, mobility, and the independent nuclear family free from traditional bonds and restrictions continues to push new generations of middle-class professional Copts to seek, once they can afford to do so, to reside outside of their historic Coptic quarters. Consequently, Shubra over the years has been left with more variations in terms of housing styles, socioeconomic status, and ethnic composition than other districts (Abu-Lughod, *Cairo*, 210). While relative to other areas in Cairo Shubra still accommodates more concentrated Christian Copts, nonetheless the area has lost its more cohesive ethnic identity or closeness in a bounded spatial location. Ethno-religious dilution in a neighborhood means diminishing the real experience of intimate and durable interaction and sharing with members from one's own ethnic grouping, simultaneously increasing the possibility of greater physical proximity, social interaction, and cultural sharing, in short, coexistence with members of other ethno-religious clusters. So, the old Coptic quarter of Azbakiya and its Shubra extension, where Christians lived together, did business, interacted, and shared in everyday life, has given way to a more heterogeneous mélange of diverse people, interests, and interactions. It is perhaps no surprise that a Coptic intellectual would argue, "Community? What community? There is no such Coptic community in Egypt."[13]

"DISTANCIATED COMMUNITY"

I tend to think, however, that some sense of a "Coptic community" does exist in Egypt. The diminishing of localized, immediate, and territory-based religious "community" has not meant the end of collective identity, communal sentiment, and imagining. A feeling of general threat, discrimination, and distinction or a desire for what Stanley Tambiah calls "leveling" can generate collective affinity among religious members who may not even have met each other. Leveling refers to efforts to equalize entitlements, eliminating the real or perceived advantages enjoyed by the opponents and disadvantages suffered by the self (Tambiah 275). While the modern city, as in Cairo, tends to erode close-knit face-to-face and localized collectives, thus making possible modes of cosmopolitan experience and interaction, it at the same time facilitates broader, even though distanciated and imagined communities. For the modern city is not just a physical space (neighborhood relations, immediate proximities, and the everyday) but also consists of the public sphere—the sphere of virtual communities, political process, media activities, and citizenship. The urban concentration of literacy, electoral campaigns, and mass media (news, novels, daily papers, images, TV, satellite channels, and now the Internet) provides the anonymous religious members the means to associate, develop collective affinity, and form a virtual community. In modern conditions, rumors, the source of so much sectarian tension, spread faster and farther than ever before, thus potentially rendering communal relations even more volatile and precarious. Unlike in premodern times when conflicts would remain mostly enclosed and extinguishable, the modern media has the capacity to broaden a small and insignificant incident into epidemics of generalized violence among overstretched imagined and distanciated communities. Only in late modernity could a few cartoons of the Prophet Muhamad or a statement by Pope Benedict's galvanize Muslim collective outrage in such a global scale and velocity.

In Egypt, the dominance of Islamic discourse in the past three decades has made Christians more self-consciously a "minority." Their internal affinity has been reinforced by both real and imagined acts of discrimination. Copts, in general, speak of how they are underrepresented in the academia and professional unions; deprived of state support for Coptic studies; have no Coptic mayors, governors, college deans, school head teachers; and are absent from high-ranking military positions, judiciary, intelligence, and presidential offices.[14] When the Muslim Brotherhood leader, Mustafa Mashur, stated in the 1990s that Copts as *dhimmi* people were not to be allowed to serve in the Egyptian army it implied a lack of trust in Christians. The mass media, in particular, has been instrumental in alienating Copts as a collective by spreading anti-Christian gossip and rumors, or projecting them as second-class citizens. Popular soap operas or *musalsalaat* often depict Egypt as an Islamic nation thus excluding Christians from its membership (Abu-Lughod, *Dramas of Nationhood;* Abbu-Lughod, "Local Contexts of Islamism"). Many ordinary Christians may not experience or be aware of these facts, but these are usually communicated through publications, Web sites, and more fiercely by Coptic activists in exile. On the other hand, the retreat of the state from social welfare provisions tends to reinforce sectarian divide, in that people are compelled to rely on their own communal support instead of the state, upon which all citizens equally rest. Thus following President Sadat's open-door policy, the Coptic Church took up the task of establishing a network of community development centers in rural and urban areas to provide religious education, literacy classes, women's empowerment, and income generation schemes of various kinds—ones that cater largely to Christian clientele. The 1980s and 1990s saw a more expansive "welfare pluralism," one that was deemed to buttress a new "communal identity" and loyalty (Tadros; Sadra 219–32). Thus, Maged's uncle in Shubra established a welfare association that supports forty poor Coptic families, who are introduced by the local church or related associations, who serve only the Christian families.[15] Thus, while Shubra stands as a distinctive Christian Muslim cosmopolitan locale in the city's imagination, the discourse of exclusivist identities does contribute to lines of tension within Shubra.

What we have then is a coincidence of both a daily experience of interreligious coexistence and a sense of intra-communal belonging among Copts and Muslims. This simultaneity of inclusive inter-communal connectedness and exclusive communal identity gives rise to a different kind of ethno-religious reality, one that is quite distinct from those projected by both primordialist and instrumentalist schools. One might call this "critical communalism" or "postcommunalism" referring to a critical identity that unites the collective sense of the ethno-religious self with the cosmopolitan experience of lifeworld, and in which the sense of the "other" is complicated by the lived experience of interpersonal association, sharing, and trust. In day-to-day life, judgment about "us" and "them" tends to be concrete, selective, and differential, rather than generalized and sweeping. Selective rational judgments moderate generalized praise of self and prejudice against others, diminishing the ground for inward-looking sectarianism and collective conflict in everyday life.

Does this mean that the modern city is free from communal strife? Not quite. The extraordinary tales of sectarian violence in Beirut, Sarajevo, Mumbai, or Delhi attest to the fact that "critical communalism" does not eliminate the possibility of episodic sectarian violence in cosmopolitan conditions. Civil war, destruction of property, killing, and rape are common features of what Horowitz calls the "deadly ethnic riot" in urban places. It is not uncommon to hear astonishing tales of carnage between long-standing neighbors and associates (Mehta).[16] Of course the experience of sectarian divide in Egypt, even in its villages, is in no way comparable to the kind of "routinization," "ritualization," and the seemingly disproportionate scale of collective violence that seems to characterize South Asian or African ethnic relations (Tambiah; Horowitz). Nevertheless, Egypt's urban landscape has not remained immune from occasional communal confrontations. October 2005 saw ten days of sectarian tension and violence between Muslims and Christians in the historically cosmopolitan port city of Alexandria. The incident began by the media giving the news of a DVD recording of a play called "I Was Blind, but Now I Can See." The play tells the story of a young Copt who is persuaded by fundamentalist Muslims to convert to Islam, only to revert to Christianity soon after realizing the moral shortcomings of Muslims. The tabloid press seemed to exploit the DVD to undermine a Christian candidate for the Parliamentary elections in favor of his Muslim rivals. The newspapers pressed the Coptic Church to issue an apology for the DVD. Upon refusal, some five thousand Muslim protesters assembled at the gate of the Church of Mary Gurgess, which had been accused of distributing the DVD. The ensuing fights left 3 people dead, 150 injured, and more than 100 arrested. The incident became a prelude to yet another episode of violence some six months later when on 14 April 2006 a Muslim man stabbed Coptic worshippers in three separate Alexandria churches, causing further sectarian dissension (El-Amrani).

How then can one explain the episodic feuds between individuals and families of different denominations who have been living together through communal divide? This is an extremely challenging task and a satisfactory response is yet to emerge. Suffice it here to suggest that the very coincidence of cosmopolitan interaction on the one hand, and communal belonging on the other, carries within itself the seeds of an exaggerated emphasis on demarcation, which can potentially grow into mass violence of an extraordinary scale. Georg Simmel observed that "the degeneration of difference in convictions into hatred and fight occurs only when there were essential similarities between the parties" (43–45). In other words, when conflict erupts between ethno-religious groups that have had a history of similarity and coexistence, rival parties make an exaggerated attempt to highlight difference and wipe out overlap and fuzziness. Thus, in the words of Tambiah speaking on South Asia, "the greater the blessings of and ambiguities between the socially-constructed categories of difference, the greater the venom of the imposed boundaries, when conflict erupts between the self and the other, 'us' and 'them'" (276). Notwithstanding their significance, these observations reflect only one aspect of the complex whole, in that they relate to indiscriminate intercommunal atrocities in which assailants construct an abstract and generalized picture of the target group, lumping everyone together as the objective of hatred. The fact, however, is that the times of acute tension are also times when individual opponents selectively spare, protect, and rescue neighboring "enemies" from the wrath of indiscriminate assault. They invoke their live experience of sharing and trust with people who happen to belong to a rival sect. In other words, the experience of cosmopolitan exchange renders a Muslim to project a more nuanced and differentiated "Christian people" rather than massing them together as an abstract and totalized other, and vice versa. Thus a Coptic resident referring to the sectarian confrontation in Alexandria in October 2006 said, "This [the clash] is not going to keep me from associating with my Muslim friends." And a Muslim shopkeeper echoed, "In this neighborhood, we Copts and Muslims live together, work together, share the same hardships. It is inconceivable that a problem like this should tear us apart" (Moger and Moger). This process of individual differentiation in judging the "other" resulting from the live experience of interpersonal association, sharing, and trust is likely to contain indiscriminate sectarian divide and dissension.[17] After all, in Egypt's worst urban religious "strife" in Alexandria in October 2006 only three people were killed—and they were killed not by the rival sect members, but by rubber bullets of the police.

NOTES

1. For a fine overview of approaches, see Hutchinson and Smith (3–16).
2. The precise number of Coptic Christians is a matter of contention. According to the government sources, Copts constitute 6% of the population, while Coptic sources claim it be around 18%; see Ibn-Khaldoun Center (6); see also Ibrahim (381).
3. See also most publications of militant Copts in the United States and Canada.
4. The fact is that *interpretations* about Muslim-Christian relations cannot be divorced from its reality. They are part of it. For if "ethnicity" is based largely on a myth of kinship origin based on common ancestry, then the current debate in Egypt about the "reality" of Coptic-Muslim relations is likely to shape that reality. In other words, advancing an argument about how Copts are not a "minority" but "citizens," may indeed galvanize consensus, leading to an actual change in their status.
5. The reports of the conflicts are cited here from the Ibn-Khaldoun Center.
6. Daily papers.
7. The notion of "urban footprints" is discussed in Amin and Thrift.
8. Interview, July 2004, Cairo.
9. Interview with Maged, in Shubra, 10 July 2004.
10. Interview with both in August 2004, in Shubra, Cairo.

11. Interview with Moheb Zaki, Cairo, 31 Jan. 2005.
12. Here, I draw on the definition of ethnic developed by John Hutchinson and Anthony Smith as "a named human population with myths of common ancestry, shared historical memories, one or more elements of common culture, a link with homeland, and a sense of solidarity among at least some of its members." See Hutchinson and Smith (6).
13. Moheb Zaki, interview, 31 Jan. 2005, Cairo.
14. Interview with Moheb Zaki, 31 Jan. 2005, Cairo. See also Zaki.
15. Interview with Maged, Shubra, 10 July 2004.
16. See for instance a tale of riots in Bombay, India, in Mehta.
17. Donald Horowitz's general survey of ethnic riots confirms this conclusion. " . . . when such [indiscriminate and abstract] beliefs change, the deadly riot declines"; see Horowitz (544).

WORKS CITED

Abu-Lughod, Janet. *Cairo: One Thousand Years of a City Victorious*. Princeton: Princeton UP, 1971.
Abu-Lughod, Lila. *Dramas of Nationhood: The Politics of Television in Egypt*. Chicago: Chicago UP, 2005.
———. "Local Contexts of Islamism in Popular Media." ISIM Papers Series, no. 6. Leiden: ISIM, 2006.
African Research Bulletin 37.1 (Jan. 2000).
Amin, Ash, and N. Nigel Thrift. *Cities: Reimagining the Urban*. Cambridge: Polity, 2002.
Appadurai, Arjun. *Modernity at Large*. Minneapolis: U of Minnesota P, 1996.
Atiya, A. S. *A History of Eastern Christianity*. London: Methuen, 1968.
Badawi, Gamal. *Muslimoun wa Aqbat: Min al-Mahd Ilal-Majd*. Cairo: Dar Al-Shoruk, 2000.
———. *Al-Fitna al-Taefiya fi Misr*. Cairo: Arab Press Center, 1977.
Bayat, Asef. "Radical Religion and the Habitus of the Dispossessed: Does Islamic Militancy Have an Urban Ecology?" *International Journal of Urban and Regional Research* 31.3 (September 2007): 579–90.
Burgess, Ernest. "The Growth of the City: An Introduction to a Research Project." *The City Reader*. Ed. Richard LeGates and Frederic Stout. London and New York: Routledge, 1996. 153-61.
Chitham, E. J. (1988). *The Coptic Community in Egypt: Spatial and Social Change*. Occasional Paper Series, no. 32. Durham, Eng.: University of Durham, Center for Middle Eastern and Islamic Studies.
Delanty, Gerard. *Community*. London: Routledge, 2003.
El-Amrani, E. "The Emergence of 'Coptic Question' in Egypt." *Middle East Report on Line* 28 Apr. 2006.
El-Bishri, Tariq. *Al-Muslimoun wa Aqbat*. Cairo: Dar al-Shoruk, 2004.
Geertz, Clifford. "Primordial Ties." *Ethnicity*. Ed. John Hutchinson and Anthony Smith. Oxford: Oxford UP, 1996. 40–5.
Gellner, Ernest. *Nations and Nationalism*. Oxford: Blackwell, 1983.
Giddens, Anthony. *Run Away World*. New York: Routledge, 2003.
Hopkins, Nicholas, and Reem Saad, eds. *Upper Egypt: Identity and Change*. Cairo: American U in Cairo P, 2005.
Horowitz, Donald. *The Deadly Ethnic Riot*. Berkeley: U of California P, 2001.
Hutchinson, John, and Anthony D. Smith, eds. *Ethnicity*. Oxford: Oxford UP, 1996.

Ibn-Khaldoun, Center. *The Copts of Egypt*. London: Minority Rights Group International, 1996.
Ibrahim, Saad Eddin. *Al-Milal wal-Nahal wal-I'raq*. Cairo: Ibn Khaldoun Center, 1994.
Kepel, Giles. *The Revenge of God*. State College: Pennsylvania State UP, 1994.
Labib, Hani. *Al-Muwatinah wal-Awlimah*. Cairo: Dar El-Shorouk, 2004.
Lane, Edward. *Manners and Customs*. London: Knight, 1836.
Marsot, Afaf. *A Short History of Egypt*. Cambridge: Cambridge UP, 1985.
Mehta, Suketu. *Maximum City: Bombay Lost and Found*. New York: Knopf, 2004.
Melucci, A. (1996). "The Post-Modern Revival of Ethnicity." *Ethnicity*. Ed. John Hutchinson and Anthony D. Smith. Oxford: Oxford UP, 1996. 367-70.
Moger, Robin and John Ehab Moger. "All Over a Play." *Cairo Magazine* 27 Oct. 2006.
Park, Robert. *Human Communities*. Glencoe: The Free Press, 1952.
Purcell, Mark. (1998). "A Place for the Copts: Imagined Territory and Spatial Conflict in Egypt." *Ecumene* 5.4 (1998): 432-51.
Redfield, Robert. *The Little Community*. Chicago: U of Chicago P, 1955.
Sadra, Paul. "Class Cleavage and Ethnic Conflict: Coptic Christian Communities in Modern Egyptian Politics." *Islam and Christian-Muslim Relations* 10.2 (1999): 219-35.
Simmel, Georg. *Conflict and the Web of Group Affiliations*. New York: Free Press. 1955. 43-45.
Staffa, Susan Jane. *Conquest and Fusion: The Social Evolution of Cairo, AD 642-1850*. Leiden: Brill, 1977.
Tadros, Mariz. *NGO-State Relations in Egypt: Welfare Assistance in a Poor Urban Community of Cairo*. Diss. U of Oxford, 2004.
Tambiah, Stanley. *Leveling Crowds: Ethnonationalist Conflicts and Collective Violence in South Asia*. Berkeley: U of California P, 1996.
Viand, Gerard. "Short History of Shubra." Unpublished paper. August 2004.
Zaki, Moheb. *Civil Society and Democratization in Egypt*. Cairo: Ibn-Khaldoun Center, 1995.
Zeidan, D. (1999). "The Copts: Equal or Persecuted? The Impact of Islamization on Muslim-Christian Relations in Modern Egypt." *Islam and Christian-Muslim Relations* 10.1 (1999): 53-67.

9 Cosmopolitanism and the City
Interaction and Coexistence in Bukhara

Caroline Humphrey, Magnus Marsden, and Vera Skvirskaja

INTRODUCTION

While the notion of the city implies the presence of certain distinctions—geographical, administrative, social, linguistic, and so forth—the idea of cosmopolitanism suggests mediations or engagements across various boundaries (ethnic, cultural, geographic, and political) (Breckenridge et al. 1–14; Cheah and Robbins). This chapter is an attempt to conceptualize and document ethnographically the mediations that occur within and across the boundaries of present-day Bukhara, Uzbekistan. It describes different aspects of coexistence in Bukhara, a city very much in dialogue with the diversity of its pasts, and inquires what can be learned from them about the cosmopolitan dynamics of its social morphology.

Post-Soviet Bukhara is not in any simple sense a classic example of a global city or cosmopolis, that is, a place claimed by global capital, a center for headquarter operations and international trade (cf. Sassen 92; Hannerz). Although it was an important capital in pre-Soviet times, the city today is a smallish regional center (population c. 300,000) of the Bukhara province. In line with the fate of many other post-Soviet cities, during the last fifteen years it has experienced economic decline and mass emigration of its ethnic diasporas. The only immediately apparent "cosmopolitan" urban scene is tied up with seasonal tourism. During the low tourist season, from October till March, the city is, in local idiom, "dead" (*mertvyi gorod*)—there are no caravans of foreign tourists, backpackers are few and far between, and a large proportion of the city dwellers is away in Russia, Kazakhstan, Dubai, and elsewhere, working as migrant laborers and petty traders. Yet, we also came to recognize that a variety of different if less immediately striking forms of cosmopolitan experience are central to the everyday experiences of city dwellers, and that these continue to exist despite the fact that Bukhara is today a small and even declining regional center in strictly geographical and economic terms.

The city's self-image, as it was recounted to us, is tied to visions of earlier kinds of cosmopolitanism and global interconnections, which often focus on the place as both a trade center and a seat of learning in the wider

Muslim world. Until Soviet times, predominantly Tajik-speaking Bukhara was the capital of its own polity, the Emirate of Bukhara (1740s–1920). This was a city that lay on the medieval Silk Route, whose wealth was based on trade and artisan craftwork, and it maintained distant networks to the Middle East, India, Siberia, and China (Burton); its variegated population was the outcome of this specific economic niche. Interleaved with this mercantile image is another one, now much downplayed in public discourse, of Bukhara as a key and innovative city of Muslim learning and pan-ethnic religious devotion, the intellectual home of influential Muslim scholars and thinkers who associated themselves with a very wide range of disciplines within the Islamic sciences (Sukhareva).

One curious aspect of old Bukhara is that, although it experienced considerable Soviet destruction of mosques, madrasas, public baths, cemeteries, and caravanserais (see details in Gangler, Gaube, and Petroccioli 72), the major monuments of the old city are still intact and there was relatively little new building there. As a result, there can be an illusion of continuity—there they still stand, the old houses and alleyways, the mosques and *mazars* (shrines), even some water tanks and old *chaikhanas* (teahouses). Yet it is obvious that the everyday life of the city, which has extensive modern suburbs, is post-Soviet to the core. Since 1991 the independent Uzbek state has instituted a new national(ist) ideology and authoritarian political regime, it has reorganized the *mahallas* (traditional community organizations) into a new form of monopolistic administration (Massicard and Trevisani 216), and it has its own educational agenda that prioritizes an Uzbek-centered interpretation of the region's history, its specific mode of managing the economy, and its own religious policy. No citizens can escape these institutions and policies unless they leave the country—which many of them do. Those left behind have to graft the actual layered diversity of their own pasts onto the deliberately monolithic present of Uzbekistan.

In the Soviet era, the population, which already included Tajiks, Uzbeks, Jews, Turks, Armenians, Arabs, Tatars, Iranians, and a few Kazakhs, Gypsies, and Kyrgyz (this is an approximation using modern terms) was further diversified. Stalinist policies of resettlement of whole ethnic groups as "enemies of the people," evacuations during World War II, the practice of *ssylka* (exile), and planned labor allocations in the Khrushchev/Brezhnev eras, resulted in influxes of Russians, Crimean and Volga Tatars, Germans, Koreans, Meschetian Turks, Ukrainians, and Poles. The traditional courtyard houses were turned from single extended-family use to "communal apartments"; the original family was confined to one or two rooms, while the others were requisitioned for incomers. As trade and religion all but disappeared as publicly acceptable occupations, upwardly mobile Bukharans (the educated, the factory workers, the state employees) tended to move from the old city to Soviet apartments, leaving the former to teem with a heterogeneous and mysterious mixture of people, living perforce cheek by jowl with strangers, many of whom were forced to accept any means of subsistence. Russian now joined Tajik as a lingua franca of the city. The daily interactions in the communal apartments and courtyards, joint membership in the same *mahalla,* and coexistence in schools and work collectives did not in fact obviate the ethnic, religious, and cultural divides between the various Soviet newcomers and the heterogenous "proper" Bukharans. But it tended to create a situation we might still call "cosmopolitan," that is, fostering positive relationships at the personal level while differences were often kept in the background and remained unspoken.

These Soviet processes have been undone, but in their place—and perhaps stimulated by the precedents—others have appeared in recent years. The diversity of the past, an image in which Bukharans take great pride, has partially ebbed away. The great majority of Jews have upped sticks to Israel or the United States, virtually all of the Germans have disappeared, Armenians, Russians, and Tatars have been flooding away, and many Koreans have left for Russia. The earlier forms of coexistence—the trading and religious cosmopolitanism, as well as "Soviet internationalism" (if it ever really existed)—have gone for ever. At the same time, and principally as a result of Bukharan citizens' participation in networks of labor migration, new types of cosmopolitan dynamics are currently being injected into the city. These too have placed strains on the already delicate dynamic between the city's "newcomers" and "proper" dwellers, and also invested city life with new moral anxieties. The sharpest example we encountered of this, perhaps, is the anxiety that many city dwellers express concerning the immoral image that Bukharans have earned in the wider Muslim world as a result of the supposedly widespread participation of the city's women as sex workers in Dubai, something that undermines both Bukhara's reputation as an old center of Islamic learning and also its more recent aspirations to rekindle this status in post-Soviet Central Asia.

Although the official state ideology claims Bukhara as an integrated part of the new nation-state, the city is not seen by its native inhabitants as "Uzbek." There are no publicly or politically manifest threats to Uzbekistan's sovereignty in Bukhara. Still, discontent with Uzbek domination is often voiced on the ground—from people's discussions of President Karimov's family's business interests in the city to the often undisguised arrogance expressed in relation to rural Uzbek-speaking immigrants, or the "dislike" of the newly introduced Uzbek citizenship.[1]

Yet, what has remained constant, or perhaps has now become emphasized in popular narratives, is an idealized image of tolerance and peaceful coexistence as a particular trait of the city. Emigration is attributed not so much to ethnic tensions as to the overall economic climate and generalized uncertainty. In folk reflections on the ethnic violence that took place in other parts of Uzbekistan prior to and after its independence (but bypassing Bukhara) or on religious "extremism" and "terrorism" elsewhere (e.g., Pakistan), Bukhara features as a "sacred city," another Mecca. The city acquires a truly "global" dimension when its place in Islamic history and learning is recognized, and violence is seen as incompatible with its global religious status. It is as if the accumulated sacredness, manifested and concentrated in numerous shrines, minarets, and domes—the city itself—has the ability to control the violent impulses of man and prevent outbreaks of intolerance.

The way in which people tended to describe and conceptualize Bukhara as a city of tolerance, made it clear for us that, as an ideal, coexistence in the city is largely predicated on the recognition of difference rather than on indifference to or unawareness of differences. In other words, to have coexisted and to *co*exist in the city people should be able to see themselves as different from the very beginning. Clearly, the ideal does not presuppose an interrupted harmony of interactions and all embracing acceptance of the "other," however defined. Rather, coexistence takes different forms in different social spaces and contexts, and in actuality has not always been benign.

What we call "cosmopolitan dynamics" designates a *specific* modality of coexistence. As we have already implied, in more general terms this modality refers to the effective presence of a social order to which all might feel they belong or, as Rapport puts it in his discussion of a cosmopolis, "a social order which might offer a successful accommodation of an ongoing variety of diasporic practice" (181). In particular, it signals the open-endedness of individual subjectivities, experiences, and potentialities for engagement with "otherness" (not only at home, but also in the transnational context of labor migration and visitation). We suggest that to understand how cosmopolitan dynamics work, it is pertinent to analyze how the ideal of coexistence is negotiated in practice, for while the postulated "positive" state of things in Bukhara cannot be discarded as mere ideological mystification or the legacy of Soviet internationalism, neither can it exist independently of people's relationships.

In the sections that follow, we explore ways in which Bukhara people deal with the complexities of coexistence. We attempt to trace the layers of cosmopolitan experience that emerge from the city's Islamico-Persian past, its participation in the Soviet Union, as well as Bukhara people's experiences of labor migration. After first providing some historical information, we discuss three major arenas of coexistence: domestic and neighborhood spaces of interaction; migration and marriage; and religious life.

HISTORICAL BACKGROUND

In the second half of the nineteenth century, the Emirate of Bukhara, governed by rulers from the Persian Manghit dynasty, became a Russian protectorate. Although it lost some territory to the Russian colonial political structure in Central Asia, Turkestan (*Turkestanskiy krai* in Russian), the Emirate retained sovereignty over its internal affairs. In 1920, after prolonged resistance to the Bolsheviks, Emir Mohammed Alim Khan

(1880–1944) was driven into Afghanistan and the Bukhara People's Soviet Republic was established. In 1924 it was proclaimed a socialist republic and was included in the USSR, but soon after it was dismembered and divided up between Uzbekistan, Tajikistan, and Turkmenistan. The city of Bukhara ended up on the Uzbek side.

The intensification of economic and political links between Tsarist Russia and the Emirate led to the establishment of new settlements in close proximity to Bukhara. Kagan—an old settlement some seven kilometers away from the city—expanded and industrialized during the Russian building of the Caspian railway in the last quarter of the nineteenth century. Meanwhile, a small Russian town, New Bukhara (at present, an administrative entity called Kagan), emerged on the other side of the railway as a station settlement and also as the site of the Russian Political Agency, a diplomatic mission of sorts (Nielsen 135). As New Bukhara/Kagan grew, it incorporated surrounding villages and *mahallas,* including the Irani (Shi'i) *mahalla* called Zirabod (*Zirabad* in Russian).

During the pre-Soviet era, the old city of Bukhara was not "open to all" and there were limits to the integration of various ethnic/religious communities into city life. For example, unlike Irani people elsewhere in the city, who had lived in Bukhara for many centuries, the people of Zirabod had come to Bukhara only some two hundred years ago. They were originally from the city of Merv in present-day Turkmenistan, but had been forced to leave. When they arrived in Bukhara, the Emir was said to have told them that they could stay in his city but only so long as they lived outside the city's walls—whence the establishment of their settlement of Zirabod. A similar residential policy was often applied by Bukhara's rulers in relation to the "invaders" who decided to settle in the area after the end of a military campaign, for example, the Arabs.

Bukharan Jews,[2] speakers of a Tajiki-Jewish dialect, by contrast, had always lived within the city's walls, but Jewish residence was largely restricted to a special quarter and they were prohibited from acquiring houses from Muslims. The second half of the eighteenth century saw a particularly active period of building of religious institutions (Sukhareva 115–16), with the Emirate becoming an ardent propagator of Islam in the region. During this period, many Jews were forced (some say, voluntarily decided) to convert to Islam. The converts acquired the local name of "Chala" and were often treated with suspicion by the Muslim population. After Russian colonization of Turkestan, although some Bukharan Jews sought refuge in the Russian-dominated territory, and despite the restrictions imposed on them in Bukhara, they remained active in the economic life of the city: the majority was engaged in the dyeing of textiles and the silk trade, and there were also wealthy merchants who traded with Moscow and other towns in Russia. Thanks in part to the widening contacts with Ashkenazi Jews, schools where the language of instruction was Hebrew were established in Bukhara (*Encyclopaedia Judaica* 1470–74).

And so it was into this widely connected, yet enclosed and differentiated city, that the Soviets introduced new visions and practices of coexistence. We are fortunate in having the work of the indefatigable Russian scholar Sukhareva to hand, which describes in detail the makeup of the city in the late 1920s to 1950s (Sukhareva). The walled old city, with a population of sixty to sixty-five thousand in the mid-1920s, was divided into some 220 *mahallas*,[3] each of which had its own social character. Sometimes this was based on ethnicity or language—there were specifically Jewish, Kyrgyz and Arab *mahallas*, for example. But most communities were mixed—even in the 1920s the inhabitants would call themselves "Tajik" or "Uzbek" without there being anything clearly to distinguish them, and "Uzbeks" would often speak Tajik and vice versa (Sukhareva 122). Most *mahallas* specialized in certain artisan work (making leather goods, weaponry, weaving, working with reeds, etc.), or in a particular occupation (soldiering, religious services). Several of the ethnic populations were rather strictly endogamous (the Arabs and Jews, for example—Sukhareva 130; also Al'meev), while others, such as the Tajik, Uzbek, and Iranian Farsi, tended to marry internally because of their preference for cousin marriages (Sukhareva 140–57). Crossing religious boundaries by changing faith was regarded as more reprehensible than external marriage. Most *mahallas* had their own mosque, and many also contained sacred tombs (*mazars*) that were worshipped by diverse peoples as well as relatives from far away. To simplify a complex reality, we can say that the city consisted of a large number of localities that formed socially inward-looking communities, while at the same time members of these communities also interacted with others in certain specific economic, political, and religious contexts.

This tight-knit and, it seems, locally "readable" cityscape must have been severely shaken by the Soviet transformation. Would the city's tradition of cosmopolitanism, limited as it was to specific kinds of encounters, withstand the influx of radically different incomers, especially when its own political structure (the Emirate) had been destroyed, its high religious culture forced underground, and its cosmopolitan political elites and their followers found refuge in Afghanistan? And how would the previous situation-specific, and not overgenerous, cosmopolitanism react to the injunctions of socialist internationalism—be atheist together! Fight our Soviet enemies together! Go to school together! And please intermarry, because that will make our Party statistics look good.

SPACES OF INTERACTION: HOMES, NEIGHBORHOODS, AND TOMBS

This account will address the place of interaction by working from the most intimate outward. It will start with the places of domestic life, courtyard houses, to show that coexistence in Bukhara frequently begins at home.

Yelia Saizhanova, a middle-aged Tatar[4] teacher, told us that the area she lives in is called Hauz Rashid; that is, it is named after water tank (*hauz*) built by a merchant called Rashid. The tank used to have a beautiful marble pipe, and carriers would take water to the surrounding houses. The *mahalla*, with around 120 houses, also had a small *mechit* for prayers (now closed), notable for its inscription written in 1709 by Obaidullah Khan. In living memory Jews, Tajiks, and Tajik-speaking Uzbeks lived here, and there was also a family of Chala. The occupations were mostly trade and clock and watchmaking, and there was one, rather unsuccessful, money changer. Today the tank itself has been paved over (following an epidemic, the Soviets decided that public tanks were a health hazard), but the open space with shade trees and citrus fruits has survived. Some older men lounge here to chat, but no one could see this as a bustling peopled space. These days the *mahalla* is physically more easily penetrated than it had been. Earlier there was only one main entrance, with a back, almost hidden, exit, whereas today there are several streets debouching into the area. The houses, however, still present a closed exterior: there is one door, kept locked, and windows open onto the interior yard. Yelia's house is entered by means of a low, dark, twisting corridor past some storerooms, before one steps out into a pleasant open courtyard, with flowering bushes and an outside cooking pit, surrounded by one- and two-story living rooms.

The population of Bukharan houses varies according to the history of the people living there and their property status. In Yelia's case, the house with some twelve rooms, is held as private property and was in her husband's mother's name. The sons of the family did not survive the war and the purges, and so this large house ended up in one person's name (her mother-in-law's). Next door, on the other hand, a house of the same size was in public ownership and five families live in it. Yelia recounted the family history of her affines: formerly rich merchants, her mother-in-law's parents had owned expensive carpets, jewelry, fine embroidered clothes, stores of oil and flour, much of which was expropriated in the 1930s. People came at night and took the fine things "to the Museum" (though Yelia never saw them there). The daughter of the family, Yelia's mother-in-law, joined the Party and her brother was a revolutionary. This revolutionary brother was purged under Stalin and sent to Siberia, from where he never returned. The family fell on hard times; Yelia's mother-in-law sold her few remaining pieces of china on the market to survive.

Concerning her own family, Yelia makes a careful differentiation of the various Tatar groups in the city (see note 4), but she sees herself as tolerant and one of a "strong" community that marries with anyone and is at peace with all. (This attitude should be understood in relation to the context: several Tajiks and Uzbeks told us that Tatars do not have high status in Bukhara—they are too Europeanized to fit well with the Central Asian urban culture and, being Muslim, they are counted as foreign to the Slavic groups too.) As a married woman, however, Yelia's preoccupation was with the former merchant's household she married into, which, it gradually was revealed, is far more complex than we had first appreciated. The family is Chala, into which women from other ethnic groups had married, including a Chinese Muslim (Dungan) great-grandmother. Yelia's mother-in-law had married a Chechen. But such is the stigma of the Chala identity that it overrode both the low status of the Dungan grandmother, who arrived in Bukhara as a slave, and current political anxieties about Chechens. Yelia said: "Everywhere people say, 'Ah, but you're Chala.' They look at one another. It is so hurtful. They won't give their children to marry people like us."

This brief summary of a much longer narrative shows that "tolerance" in Bukhara has had to struggle against racist, religious, and political antagonisms. Of these, the religious often appeared to have been the sharpest. The Chala label has been stigmatizing for around two hundred years. The term *chala* is also used in everyday life to denigrate something half-baked or useless, for example, "Your work is *chala*." As a child, Yelia said, her mother-in-law felt perpetually guilty, because her merchant father had been repressed under Stalin. No one wanted to marry her, a Chala, although she was beautiful, and when she reached the age of twenty-four, after returning from the front, she took the initiative and decided to marry a writer she had met only three times. In the registry office, she glanced at the book with the data about her bridegroom and saw that it said 'Chechen." "Well, why not?" she thought. Nor did she know he was a political exile. A year later, he was again repressed, this time sent to exile in Siberia. Yelia's mother-in-law was now caught in a dilemma, for she was a Party member. To safeguard the future of her baby son, as she explained, she wrote to her husband in Siberia sending divorce papers, a decision she later regretted. But the result was that Yelia's husband never met his Chechen father. Working through this tragedy, Yelia's mother-in-law was able to build on her heroic exploits as a field doctor in the army during the war, to construct a strong career in Communist Party politics in the city (this path fits a pattern found elsewhere in the Soviet Union, whereby it was often not local elites but precisely the people outside power networks that "found themselves" in the Party).

After some time talking with Yelia, her aged mother-in-law Mukhtopana came into the room. She had dressed in fine clothes and pinned on her Soviet medals to show us. She described her career as a Soviet "activist" with pride—and along the way described herself as Tajik, an identity she had adopted in the army.[5] "She will not talk about her Chala identity to you," Yelia whispered. Mukhtopana described a city where mixed marriages were forbidden, where interethnic encounters took place largely at neighborhood parties (*mekhman*, "guest"), and where women of her generation had had to confront veiling customs in order to be able to leave the house and go out to attend Russian lessons. She, the daughter of a Chala family, loves Jewish food. But despite her lifetime career in public health, she still has to bow to local perception of ethnic boundaries. Mukhtopana had to hide the fact that she was eating Jewish food in secret, because the Chala keep the Muslim festivals and food rules. Her Tatar daughter-in-law Yelia also observed certain conventions of status discourse. Although she had in fact married into this equivocal family (Tajik, Chala, Chechen), she said she would not in any circumstances marry a Jew,[6] and that even a "black African" would be preferable.[7]

This account reveals that households—even those not forced to incorporate the mixed lodgers of Soviet times—experience the tensions of coexistence in their own relations behind the walls of the courtyard. Somehow, accommodations have to be made, boundaries shifted to include the lived-with relations, secrets kept, and faces maintained, while at the same time other notional boundaries are erected in respect of the social world outside. All households are in dense interactions with neighbors, the families living in the network of lanes that constitute the *guzar,* which approximates to the "traditional" *mahalla.* The neighborhood for people today is both an institution with a head (the *guzarkom*) and a set of practices arising around a location (a linked set of streets). Within this area people know one another, they must stop to talk in the street, they observe common rules of propriety—for example, by fetching water to brush down the dust in the lane outside one's house early in the morning. If one person does this, other neighbors tend to follow, whereas there are localities where no one bothers.

The main encounters of neighbors are at formal parties given for life cycle events. Here a wide range of relatives are invited, but also the neighbors. Carpets are laid out (men and women sit separately); *plov, halissa,* and other special foods are cooked; there is wine and song; presents are given. These events are quite ritualized, with certain named actions that must be performed. Especially important occasions are often seen in terms of *sarvop* (charity, the sharing of wealth). The individual will first tell the family he or she wishes to hold an occasion of this kind; the family will then consult and decide the date, how much to spend, and how widely to invite people. They then inform the *vakkil* (information officer of the *mahalla*), he tells the *mahalla* committee, and then every household is taken a personal invitation to their gate. People of all ethnicities attend such events, including in the past even the exiles and the lodgers, and one Russian woman said she would specially dress in Tajik clothes to fit in better. In fact, neighbors should attend as a matter of course; it is not good enough to say, "You didn't invite me." Sometimes however, strangers and new newcomers are shy to accept even formal written invitations. An Uzbek woman told us about one Ossetian Christian neighbor who never turned up. She felt ashamed (perhaps because she had no husband and her only child had recently died) and she did not know how to behave. But gradually she began to join in and soon became a regular participant, though she continued to wear black mourning clothes. Everyone understood this and approved of it: "People should accept who they are; they should maintain their own customs," people told us.

This is why no one we spoke to in Bukhara ever questioned the partial participation of the Jews at neighborhood events. The Jews used to invite everyone to their celebrations, and all neighbors ate their food. However, the Jews, fearing pollution, would bring their own food to the festivities of other nationalities. If anything, this practice was admired. "Look how admirably the Jews keep their traditions. It is a sign of their high culture. And the Russians too, look how clean they are. We don't want to know about the inside of their lives; just let them live according to their own rules," said one Uzbek woman. She continued that no one wanted Russians to wear Uzbek clothes and pretend to a closeness that doesn't exist. "In the same way," she said, "we don't expect them to interfere with our own traditions." In many statements about these neighborly festivities, we see a trace of what is called in Uzbek *andisha,* which means "appropriate modesty, understanding, and adapting yourself to society."

If the water tanks (*hauz*) that used to provide a focus for neighborly encounters have now mostly disappeared, other sites seem to retain their vitality. One of these is the *mazar,* a shrine at the grave of a respected mullah. One such *mazar* is found in the area called Lezik Hauz, where the pond was bricked up, leaving an open space. We were told this is the gravesite of seven brothers who lived around 1800 and whose descendants lived in all the houses round about. The site consists of a fenced garden with trees surrounding the gravestone, with a *tüh* (a tall pole topped with an open hand, and with a horsehair tuft hanging below) at its head, and nearby a small "fire-oven" where people light candles. Muslims come here from the neighborhood to pray after the Friday mosque. But more intermittently, all kinds of people, including Russians and Koreans (and even Jews), would come to pray for the recovery of children with illnesses. This *mazar* is particularly known for curing speech defects. Here, all day, one way or another, there are people sitting on the bench by the tomb, passing the time of day and discussing politics. The bench tends to be appropriated by descendants of the mullahs, and they will let their strongly Islamic, anti-Russian, and anti-Western views be known to anyone coming to the tomb. They are glad so many people come to pay respects at the *mazar*. Their disapproval, which they do not hide, does not seem to filter out different kinds of encounters. Their presence and their attitudes are an accepted part of the experience of the *mazar.*

We turn now briefly to wider relations in the city, where there are sites for specific kinds of encounters. In such places, the relatively formalized—distanced yet accepted—relations just described are replaced by more diffuse, less predictable, or more fleeting encounters. The *chaikhana* (teahouses), located under trees by tanks, are the preserve of older Uzbek and Tajik men; tables for playing chess are frequented mostly by men (Russians, Tatar); the female public baths, which have been established for at least a century, are places where women of many backgrounds may meet; the tourist cafés are often patronized by local families or groups of young girls

Photo 9.1 Vegetable market, Bukhara. Photo by Caroline Humphrey.

out together for an evening; the children's public library, where the books are mostly in Russian, is a place where any young people who know that language may meet; and some guilds have recently been set up as professional associations.[8] The large covered markets are places for businesslike haggling and they do not seem to be places of much socializing. The early morning open-air vegetable and fruit markets, on the other hand, and the winding lanes leading to them, are prime sites for exchanging gossip and fascinating news of the neighborhood. The Lyabi-Hauz, the paved area around a particularly large water tank close to the main tourist sites, is a particularly interesting place of encounters. Sites in this area change character throughout the day, as they accommodate different functions and people. For example, one space, hung with carpets and other wares for tourists during the day, may be taken over by a local school for a performance by pupils in the evening. Or to take another case, younger women keep well away from a table where old men are sitting smoking, drinking tea, and quietly discussing. They wait until the old men have gone before claiming the table, laughing and talking loudly in Russian, and ordering Western drinks.

Other sites, such as former caravanserais or madrasas now turned to shopping areas for tourists, also promote specific encounters. Physically, they consist of gated courtyards, with a number of small, one-room shops opening off a central yard. The sellers in one such site, the Bukhara Artisan Development Centre, include an Uzbek silk weaver, a Tajik maker of embroidered cloths, an Arab painter of miniatures, some Uzbek girls doing gold-thread embroidery, and many others. Some stalls, for example, selling ceramics, are run by ten- to sixteen-year-old local girls, raucous, playful, and proficient in some English, French, Italian, Russian, or Japanese. Having a shop or a stall allows these youngsters to access certain kinds of excitement, which may not be available elsewhere. This includes the opportunity to talk to foreigners, learn languages, explore emerging sexuality, share close companionship, and earn some money. When the girls are on their own, which is most of the time, while they do try to sell their wares, they prize any kind of contact with tourists—asking questions about other places, inviting them home, and almost always getting promises to correspond with them over e-mail once they have returned home (Venkatesan).

The sellers interact with one another and with the tourists, but the majority also have long-distance economic relations far beyond the city. Gold thread for embroidery, for example, comes from Korea via "Arabistan" (UAE), and many of the rugs are woven in Afghanistan, to which Bukharan traders make journeys to pick them up. Many of the artisans in such centers have inherited their craftsmanship from parents and grandparents. Yet the substantive reality today of Bukhara's earlier identity as a city of trade and artisanship, and cosmopolitan for that reason, is much compromised. High and unpredictable taxes, difficult visa regimes, and governmental interference and takeovers, we were told, make life as a trader extremely difficult, and productive private business almost impossible. The old centripetal pattern, whereby traders would come from all over Asia bearing wares to store at the caravanserais and sell, has not been revived. Now Bukharans have to travel elsewhere to seek out goods for sale, and the market has radically divided: goods designed for domestic consumption are almost entirely different from those aimed at tourists. The "local," "traditional" artisan wares are sold to tourists.

The Bukharans, on the other hand, buy Russian, Turkish, and Chinese goods of "modern" appearance, which are sold at different markets. They even buy factory-made carpets, rather than local rugs. Of course, the high prices of items sold to tourists are a factor here, but there has also been a change in sensibility. The effect is to divorce ordinary Bukharan people (office workers, teachers, even those in the tourist industry) from the traditional professions of the city, thus breaking apart—or rather, failing to reintegrate—the economic links that used to form the arteries of cosmopolitan life. Instead, the new sensibilities tend to be oriented outward, to Russia where so many people go to find work and to the wider Islamic world.

OF MIGRATION, MARRIAGE, AND THE RUSSIAN LEGACY

The general pattern of post-Soviet migration in the territory of the former USSR has tended toward ethnic consolidation (Pilkington). This is very much the case for contemporary Bukhara: while the majority of ethnic Russians and Russian nationals move back to Russia, there is a steady inflow of rural Uzbek migrants (*kishlachnye*, i.e., from a *kishlak*, a village) from Bukhara's hinterlands and other Uzbek provinces. In this context, it is interesting that Bukharans not only assert the uniqueness and superiority of their "sacred Bukhara," but also emphasize that Bukhara is a "European" city. Ignoring the peasant inflow, they point to the wide boulevards, new fancy cafés that serve European food, the diversity of women's clothing in the city (their bold modern outfits), and their freedom of movement. Such native representations of Bukhara as part of "Europe" (*evropa*) of course also gloss over the complexity of recent transformations in the city and experiences of its dwellers.

Russians are not the only ethnic community to leave Bukhara in large numbers. The Bukharan Jews have now all but disappeared from the city, leaving from five hundred to a thousand people behind. In the old Jewish quarter, which is popular with tourists, some of the recently vacated property has been turned into guesthouses and small hotels by new Tajik/Uzbek owners. The old Jewish cemetery has been recently restored and a new Jewish school opened, but these developments are due to the efforts of foreign Jewish organizations that are also engaged in promoting or facilitating emigration.

It is the relative absence of Russians combined with an ongoing Russian cultural influence that was most obvious in the city's landscape and local practices. Here we refer to different forms of engagement with Russians and the Russian or Soviet legacy, both in the city and beyond. The city dwellers' ties with Russia nearly appear to be as strongly felt and thought about as they were during the Soviet era. Our middle-aged and elderly interlocutors spoke fluent Russian and many had firsthand experience of Soviet Russia and other Soviet republics. As elsewhere in the former USSR, the main routes from Bukhara were organized school trips, exchange programs, tourism, and holidays, and, for male Bukharans, obligatory military service. Today, Russia is the main destination for Uzbekistan's illegal migrants, seasonal laborers, and traders.

During the tourist low season, the city is partially deserted due to this mass migration of temporary labor, but the emigration of Russians has left a more permanent void. We were told that prior to independence, the streets of Bukhara were visually dominated by the "Europeans."[9] The "Europeans" were enthusiastic *flâneurs* and introduced idle strolling as a form of cultural pastime. Nowadays, street conversations in Russian are few and far between, and during the low season, the evening streets are largely empty. "Native" non-Slav Bukharans, it is said, do not have a tradition of idle walking, preferring to spend their free time at home or in a *chaikhana*. Nor is strolling after sunset now looked upon positively by the authorities—ever present police patrols encourage youths and idlers to stay indoors. People with some means may opt for a night club where Russian and Western tunes are played interchangeably with Arab, Turkish, Iranian, and Central Asian *estrada* (folk and pop music). Those who now stroll the streets of Bukhara by night are prostitutes and occasional drunks—those "who have no shame."[10]

The fate of Russian/Soviet cultural institutions in the city is, perhaps, nowhere as stark as in Bukhara's theater, situated across the street from the magnificent walls of the Ark, the former residence of Bukhara's Emirs. Constructed by the Soviets in the early 1930s, the theater's shabby building is now squeezed between two busy restaurants and looks permanently shut. In fact, there was some life in this apparently deserted building. According to the theater's head producer, a Tajik-speaking man in his early fifties, the days of Anton Chekhov's plays had gone forever—theater was a Soviet cultural imposition that had not succeeded in evoking much interest among Uzbeks. Instead, the theater scrapes a living by organizing events for children, such as New Year celebrations, and by occasionally staging "propaganda" plays that address contemporary problems—unemployment, alcoholism, drug addiction, and so on. The tickets are distributed mainly in schools and other state institutions. In other words, a visit to the theater is often a state-organized event and considered obligatory.

We were invited to attend one such performance and were shown around by an old-time actress. Some seventy young people from the Bukhara's medical school came to watch the pay (performed in Uzbek). In forty minutes we were shown a story of a young alcoholic and drug addict who killed his mother while on drugs and who was later killed by a drug dealer. After a short break this bloody drama was followed by a concert—one by one the same actors appeared on stage in ethnic costumes or in sparkling modern garb and performed folk dances and Uzbek/Tajik songs. Within a few minutes, the whole audience was dancing and clapping energetically by the stage and in the aisles between the chairs. "If the theater is to survive," our actress-guide explained, "it has to have some appeal."

Insofar as they can be deduced from transformations enacted upon the city landscape, official attitudes toward the legacy of a Russian presence have been far from unequivocal. For instance, the Soviet monument to the Unknown Soldier commemorating the victory in World War II was disassembled, leaving only plaques with the names of Bukharans who vanished during the war. A new sculpture to "Mother and a Child" has been erected on the same square, and newly married couples often visit the monument to lay flowers or take a picture for their bridal photo album, thus reproducing a Soviet ritual whereby the newly wed paid homage to the Unknown Soldier.

However, while some central symbols of the Soviet past have been removed from the city's surface, the presence of a Russian/Slav population has been acknowledged in the form of a new Russian Orthodox church. The spacious old railway station near the modern city center was converted into an Orthodox church in 1993. Local Russians petitioned for the construction of the church in 1992 by collecting signatures, and asked the Moscow Patriarchy to grant permission. This was duly given and the new church approved by the Bukhara's city council. The opening of the new Orthodox church is not so much indicative of the growing numbers of believers and converts to Orthodoxy, as of the desire of the remaining "traditionally" Orthodox population to manifest its presence and a sense of community. Many Russian oldtimers in Bukhara still prefer to attend the old Russian church in the town of Kagan for major celebrations.

In the late 1980s to early 1990s, the prevailing spirit was of ethnic and cultural revival of Bukhara's many minorities, rather than emigration, and it resulted not only in attempts to resurrect religious traits of ethnic communities, but also in the establishment of various national cultural centers (e.g., a Russian center, a Turkish center, an Armenian center, and so on). Thus the project of post-Soviet coexistence has taken on a new institutionalized form whereby each ethnic community has to be represented. The leaders of these centers have been engaged in organizing regular joint public events, very similar to Soviet festivals of national cultures. Yet, in the course of the 1990s, many of these cultural centers were gradually transformed into legal fictions: the majority of the ethnic diaspora and/or the leaders of these communities simply left the city. The Russian cultural center, for instance, which has distanced itself from the new Orthodox church, was reinvigorated in the early 2000s by a former military man, a Russian born in Uzbekistan, and it now mainly deals with the rights of local Russians and assists them in applying for Russian citizenship and passports.

At the time of our fieldwork, the Orthodox church was one of twelve non-Muslim confessions represented in the city. In contrast to post-Soviet Russia, where foreign Protestant and Catholic missions are often seen as a threat to Russian security and culture (Skvirskaja), the Karimov government appears to view "religious pluralism" and non-Muslim foreign sects as a buffer against the thread of Islamization.[11] In people's narratives, the spread or visibility of new and old religions in the city is also used to emphasize the discourse on tolerance and peaceful coexistence as well as to dwell on ambiguities and negotiations related to religious matters. The case of different Islamic doctrines in the city we explore in the next section; here we would like to focus on the overall religious landscape.

Religious affiliation in the city does not always follow from one's ethnic identification (e.g., Tatars are Muslims, but there are also some who are Christians), and one's religious identification is not necessarily firmly fixed. Let us give an example. During one wedding, we befriended three female friends of the bride's well-to-do family of Bukhara's Imams. The women introduced themselves as Tajik-speaking Uzbeks and later explained that they were recorded as Uzbeks in their passports (see Footnote 3), used Russian to talk to each other, and represented three different confessions: one was Muslim, another Russian Orthodox, and the third, a recent convert to Protestant Christianity. The latter, Gulya, a widow in her early forties and a follower of the Korean Protestant Church *Sym Bochym* ("The Annunciation"), converted to Christianity because she was attracted by the singing and various social activities organized by the church. For a single woman who cares about her reputation, Gulya said, there are not many opportunities left to socialize widely and enjoy a collective life in the city. "Muslim women do not go to mosque here." After her husband's death and some of her friends' departure to Russia, the Korean church has become Gulya's main focus of social life.

Gulya's younger friend, Dylia, was married to a man of mixed Russian-Azeri descent whose family arrived in Bukhara from Armenia after World War II. In the mid-1990s, Dylia's husband became a Muslim, while Dylia herself had followed the suit of her Russian friends and opted for Orthodox Christianity. For Dylia, an important factor in her decision to adopt Orthodox Christianity was her perceived affiliation with Russian culture: while she traced her ancestry to local Tajik-speaking Bukharans, she had graduated from a Russian school and Russian was the language she used at home with her husband and children.

Coexistence of different confessions in various configurations within one family is thus widespread in Bukhara, and it is mixed, interethnic marriages that often give rise to such coexistence. Marriage between Uzbek/Tajik-speaking people and Slavs was fairly common in the Soviet past and appears to be still practiced today, albeit on a different scale. Although the variations in "love marriages" (e.g., those that do not involve matchmaking by the families of the future spouses) cannot be reduced to one stable scenario, marriages between Muslim men and Slav women seem to have been more common than between Russian/Ukrainian men and local Uzbek women.[12] During the Soviet period, it was not unusual for young Uzbek men who served in the army or studied in Russia or Ukraine to bring home a "Russian" bride.

In some cases, a non-Muslim bride could be required formally to convert to Islam. We came to know several Slav women, now in their early sixties, who married young to Muslim men and in the course of their life in Bukhara not only became practicing Muslims, but also largely renounced European dress and used exclusively Tajik language. It is notable, however, that these women were not urbanites, but came to Bukhara from the Russian, Ukrainian, or Moldovan countryside. Whether or not a Slav woman married to a local Muslim goes "native" (or even more "native" than many natives themselves, for many Bukhara's Muslim women have adopted full European dress) is largely up to the woman herself. Many of our interlocutors insisted that it was rare, especially during the last few decades, to meet a Russian woman wearing Uzbek dress or reading *namaz* (a Muslim prayer).

A common solution regarding the religious affiliation of children from such mixed marriages consists either in letting children choose their religion themselves when they reach maturity (a popular approach during the late Soviet period[13]) or in sharing out siblings between the different confessions. In the case of Dylia's family, whom we mentioned earlier, her six-year-old daughter has been baptised into Russian Orthodoxy, while her son is a Muslim. "The daughter is mine. My husband talked to the daughter about Islam, but she told him that she was 'Mummy's girl' and eventually he gave up." The decision about the religious affiliation of the couple's children was preceded by some heated debates between Dylia and her husband, but as Dylia stated, by now, their decision illustrates an approach that has almost become a new custom. The priest in the new Russian church also told us that he has encountered many such instances: it is all right to baptise daughters, but there is an expectation that sons follow their fathers' religion and become Muslims.

In the face of the complexity posed by these mixed marriages, many of our interlocutors were eager to point out that the city dwellers, are generally relaxed about religion (see also next section): religious affiliation and certain choices that it might entail should be seen as a matter of personal inclination, rather than only of one's ethnic identification. Olga, a woman in her early twenties, with a Russian mother and Uzbek father, told us about her younger sister who had decided to become a Muslim because she wanted to marry a local Muslim, stay at home, and become a good housewife. Olga saw herself as the antipode of her sister—she was making money as a hairdresser, was not particularly interested in any religion, enjoyed dating boys, and frequented night clubs with a high turnover of "Europeans." Olga has adopted a Russian "cultural style" (Ferguson) that allowed her to lead a life she wanted, while her sister has adopted Islam to have a very different life. Neither of the choices was seen as more respectable or desirable than the other in Olga's family.

Many people see Bukhara as a special place, precisely because it appears to accommodate this diversity without any overt conflicts. There is a sense then in which many Bukharans see Russian or Soviet influence (e.g., secularization of public life) as something that has a distinctly positive dimension (i.e., "Europe"). Furthermore, some elements of Russian/Soviet ritual have become integral to "indigenous" Bukharan customs. Our acquaintances were eager to invite us along to wedding celebrations or show us video recordings of their own weddings, because these festivities were seen as events where "real" and the most colorful Bukharan traditions were on full display.

The wedding ritual stretches over several days and is a very complex and elaborate occasion. The day of official marriage—when the bride and groom sign their marriage certificate in the presence of a representative of the state—is marked by a banquet usually organized in a restaurant. In the case of the well-to-do families, the banquet alone hosts more than three hundred people—relatives, neighbors, colleagues, friends, friends of the friends, and so on. What was especially striking about the event and the aspect seen by locals as "fun" (*ba mazah*) was its European or Russian complexion. Whether a couple was rich or poor, the bride and groom were invariably dressed in European wedding outfits, vodka was consumed by both men and women, and the dance floor was open to all after the bride and groom had performed the first dance—a waltz. After the waltz men and women danced together to the sound of Uzbek, Tajik, Iranian, and Azeri music; hired dancing girls in Oriental outfits made sure that the guests performed to best of their abilities and were generous with money. An occasional elder might murmur disapprovingly that nowadays Uzbeks were like Russians, but other guests were quick to point out that the elder in question was just a simple villager (*kishlachnyi*). A proper traditional Bukharan wedding should feature a bride with bare shoulders in a white dress and a waltz, even if after the waltz the newly wed couple might remain virtually motionless—the main activity is seemingly endless bowing to show respect to the guests.

A very different, although perhaps now central, aspect of Tajik-speaking Bukharans' engagement with Russians relates to their experiences and aspirations as labor migrants and traders. These experiences play a significant role in people's conceptions of themselves and their city. For many, and not only those who have firsthand experience of illegal work in Russia, the image of Uzbek migrants in Russia sets limits to the vision of Bukhara as "Europe" and to perceptions of themselves as "cosmopolitan" subjects accustomed to life and easy interaction with different ethnic or religious groups.

In present-day Russia, people of Central Asian origin are called "blacks" (*chernie*), and for some of our older interlocutors this attribute was considered not merely offensive, but above all incomprehensible: "Why do Russians call us blacks? In Soviet times, we were all the same." Young men still bring wives back home from their trips in Russia, but the wives are now rarely Russian, but instead other Uzbek migrant laborers. We did not come across, however, any evidence that the negative perception of Uzbeks in Russia, and the discontent it provokes, had any profound impact on Bukharans' attitude toward Bukhara's Russians or to Russians more generally. Many local Russians are now also engaged in seasonal labor migration and, similarly to non-Slav seasonal laborers or Russian return migrants (i.e., those who emigrated back to Russia), when in Russia, they are often considered to be somehow the "other" (*chuzhie*), that is, culturally different (cf. Pilkington 172–83). In other words, there is a plane of experience of migrant life shared by Slav and non-Slav Bukharans alike and people are well aware that outside Uzbek borders they might be more firmly linked by their migrant status.

Yet, despite awareness or experience of racism, many young Bukharans aspire to work and live (at least for some time) in Russia. Some young men we befriended, from a madrasa student to an antiquaries seller, said that they would happily master different professions in an effort to find a job in Russia, and many were concerned with their inability to speak Russian properly. There are very few Russian schools left in the city and the new generation is schooled to grow up largely monolingual in Uzbek. A good knowledge of Russian is one of the main prerequisites to become a successful labor migrant or trader. For the younger generation of Bukharans who do not speak Russian at home, the desire to master the language has become a stimulus for what we might call "strategic friendships." For instance, Olim, a Tajik-speaking man in his early twenties, told us that he and his acquaintances sought out metis and Russian-speaking friends with whom to practice their Russian. He also hoped that his future wife (there was still none in sight) would be a graduate from a Russian school.

Very outspoken and proud about his long-standing, although not moneyed, Bukharan ancestry, Olim boldly endorsed the Russian representation of Uzbeks as "blacks." He had spent two seasons in Russia working for a Bukharan trader, for "without a rich father, Russia is the only way to make a living here." We were having dinner with his friends in a Russian restaurant when Olim suddenly burst out: "After all, it is not surprising that Russians called Uzbeks 'blacks.' The Uzbeks they [Russians] meet are often *kishlachnye* [the villagers] or real Uzbeks. They live like cattle in Russia, they economize on everything, ten people sleep in one room, they do not wash or dress properly. Russians don't like it, we don't like it here either . . ." To illustrate his emotional speech, Olim pointed to a group of people at the other end of the restaurant. "Look at them," he said, "just look how they are dressed—a jacket, a tie, and trainers! They are indoors, but they are wearing hats. Look how they move! They are real Uzbeks—*kishlachnye*—and they are taking over the city".

To summarize, the legacy of a Russian presence, as well as the current rules of engagement with Russians, form a complex matrix of sociality in the city. The latter-day political economy is such that few in the city can imagine their present or future not as somehow linked to Russia or the

Russian-speaking environment. While Soviets (Russians) may have been perceived by some as civilized "colonizers" (a common theme of post-independence Uzbek nationalism), popular concerns are not about whether it is good or bad that Russians have largely left the city, but rather about those who are moving in. Older residents and those who consider themselves native Bukharans are anxious lest the influx of rural Uzbek migrants may simply transform Bukhara into yet another poor, provincial "Uzbek" city. It is feared that if this were to happen, then the city's European outlook as well as its "cosmopolitanism" might well become mere ghosts from the past.

ISLAM AND MUSLIM LIFE IN BUKHARA

There is a growing body of scholarly literature on the forms of the Islamic tradition in contemporary Central Asia, the role played by religious ideas and organizations in the region's politics, and the changing position that "being Muslim" plays in the identities of Central Asians (see Roy, *The Failure of Political Islam;* Kandiyoti and Azimova; Heyat). Much of this work challenges arguments made in more popular accounts of the region, which often seek to emphasize the dangers the newly independent Muslim-majority countries face in the form of "Islamization" and the growth of "political Islam" (Rashid). Rasanayagam, most notably, has documented the ways in which Muslims in village and urban settings in Uzbekistan today seek to live up to the range of ideas the country's *ulama* have regarding correct Muslim practice, at the same as combining in creative ways different types of Muslim thought and identity during the course of their daily lives.

In many Muslim settings, notably Pakistan and India, there is a long and important tradition of conflict between Sunni and Shi'i Muslims (see Bayly). Many historians and anthropologists have argued that such conflict has increased over the past century, as Muslims participating in expanding mass education and literacy have become more aware of the doctrinal differences that exist in the *umma* (worldwide Muslim community), and these differences have been further hardened by the "proxy wars" that Shi'i Iran and Sunni Saudi Arabia have fought in countries like Pakistan (Nasr). Here we seek to deal with these issues in the case of Bukhara, which is a home to a substantial population of Sunni and Shi'i or Irani Muslims. Some people we spoke to claimed that the "Irani" population living in the city numbered as many as 120,000, although this estimate seems exaggerated.[14] There are also significant differences, divisions, and even tensions among Bukhara's Iranis. In order to explore these complex issues, we focus on the ways in which Bukhara people talk and think about the type of differences that exist between Shi'i and Sunni Muslims and the place occupied by Irani people in city life.

Dilshoda, a student at Bukhara University, showed us around Bukhara's mosques and markets and told us that Irani people lived throughout the city, but in *mahalla* Zirabod, in Kagan, "all" (*hamash*) people were Irani. Irani women, she told us, wore different clothes and big black veils (*kalon panjir-e siyoh*). Irani people in the city more generally had separate feasts marking the end of a day's fasting in Ramadan, and played mostly Persian songs and music at their wedding as opposed to the Uzbek-Tajik mixture of songs played at the wedding receptions of non-Irani Bukharans.

We were struck by the degree to which Bukhara people tended to identify a group of city dwellers as "Irani" and thus distinct from other "nationalities" (*millet*) living in the city.[15] At the same time, there was relatively little sensitivity about openly introducing somebody as "an Irani." One way in which Bukhara people represent and talk about the cosmopolitan makeup of city life is by openly recognizing the importance of different types of "communities" there. These communities may be defined in terms of either religion or ethnicity, or, as in the case of "Iranis," a complex folding together of the two. Yet when we asked our interlocutors how the city's Shi'i Muslims differed from its Sunnis, they told us that everyone in Bukhara belonged to the same religion. At most, they claimed, Bukhara's Shi'i Muslims were different from the city's Sunnis only because they practiced one ritual a year that the Sunnis did not: Muharram.

When many Bukhara people presented Bukhara as a city of special peace (*aman*), they were aware that this image of the city could be easily contrasted to that in other Muslim settings. "Bukhara is not Fergana; Bukhara is not Pakistan," we were often told. What is important is that people do not see their city as being a once great Islamic city that now exists on the periphery of the modern Muslim world. For many Bukhara people, despite the years of Soviet rule, their city's status as one of Islam's most important centers remains unchallenged. We want to extend our discussion of the diversity of forms of Muslim life found in Bukhara by treating such diversity as more than a product of either doctrinal or ethnic forms of distinction, and exploring, rather, the ways in which Bukhara people openly reflect about the state of life in their city and the role they see Islam as playing in their lives.

The complexity of the ways in which Bukhara people think about their and the city's relationship to other Muslim countries and localities was especially pronounced in what they said and thought about the nature of women's roles in Bukhara life. People told us that women in Bukhara were "free" (*azod*) in comparison to some other Muslim regions. Yet, we also encountered deep-seated and persistent anxieties about sexuality and the dangers of premarital cross-sexual relationships, not only from Bukhara's parents but also from the city youth as well. So here too, not only in Bukhara people's representation of their city, it is possible to see a clear distinction between idealized images on the one hand, and a very different types of ethnographic reality on the other.

Where there was little concern among Bukhara people about women working and traveling in public, attitudes toward the women's participation in spaces more clearly identifiable with pleasure were more complex and ambivalent. For instance, one day as we were walking with Dilshoda in the old part of the city, she saw a girl from her neighborhood who was aged about seventeen. The girl waved to her, said *salaam*, and then walked away. Dilshoda immediately told us that she thought the girl had been "meeting boys" in one of the city's cafés or restaurants because she had not asked Dilshoda if she would like to walk back home with her. Dilshoda went on to tell us that many Bukhara girls told their parents that they were going to school but actually spent the day visiting friends and chatting with boys in restaurants.

Another space in Bukhara that was the source of much ambivalent judgment, especially regarding the presence of women, was the nightclub. There are about six nightclubs in the city, some based in expensive hotels, others in purposefully built discos. While many people do drink, it is also possible and acceptable to go to a nightclub and refuse to do so. On our visits to the nightclubs, we were told that the people gathered were from an array of "national" backgrounds, including, especially, Korean, Russian, Uzbek, and Tajik. Thus, the nightclub is in no sense seen as an alien space in which only "Europeans" are able to feel active and comfortable. The playing of Oriental pop music later into the night often appeared to be what enticed dancers to the floor. Yet, many nightclubs embody a different and non-Bukharan type of pleasure associated with wasteful attitude toward money, and, especially, the unconstrained mixing of men and women in spaces free from the gaze of kin and neighbors. The threat posed by the city's nightclubs to Bukhara's youth, however, seemed to be relatively specific in the minds of many people. One young man, who intended to embark on a university degree course in Tashkent, told us that most of the women who attended these clubs were "from Dubai" (*ad dubai*). This, he explained, meant Bukhara girls who had worked, largely in the sex trade, in Dubai.

Various transnational connections were manifest in Bukhara, but here we would like to turn to those that were a focus of a number of revealing conversations about the nature of Muslim life as lived by the city's Muslims. Many of our interlocutors, for instance, were critical of the state-run madrasa in the center of Bukhara. We were told that the students who went there were taught Arabic not so that they could become good Muslims but so they could spy not only on other people in the city, but also on Bukhara people who went to live and work in Dubai and the Gulf states. Thus, in the same way that mullahs are seen as compromised religiously and morally because of their associations with state officialdom, so is this city's central madrasa considered a place of surveillance and control. Skepticism toward the city's religious authorities is partly related to the degree to which most if not all Bukhara people see them as instruments of state control. There is, of course, a very high level of state intrusion into the activities of Islamic movements in Uzbekistan—many groups, such as Hizb-e Tahir, a worldwide Islamist party calling for the forging of a transnational Islamic caliphate—are banned by the Uzbek government. While there were fleeting instances when we did glimpse the underlying presence of anxieties surrounding new forms of "political Islam" in the city, this was not a dimension of religious life in the city that we were invited to explore by our interlocutors.

This is not to say, of course, that debates between Sunni Muslims about what it meant to live a Muslim life were not a visible feature of Muslim life in the city. Nor does it mean we were not able to sense a steady public influence of emergent forms of Islamic piety in the city. There was a great desire to know about Islam and the traditions of the city, and many people did say these were "taken from them" during the Soviet period. Some did not see the need for urgent change: they called themselves "atheists" and while proud of their city's heritage and happy that their children were learning about Islam, did not themselves intend to embrace publicly pious forms of Islamic lifestyle. Others were more pained about their inability to understand even the most basic of Islamic concepts. One man in his mid-forties who worked for an insurance company told us he knew nothing about Islam, but had read books by Persian poets, Hafiz Shirazi, Jallaludin Rumi, Khusrow, and Omar Khayyam during his school years in Russian. Others, like Leila, a young woman in her early twenties who studies English at Bukhara University, told us how she had started learning Arabic so that she would be able to read the Qur'an.

Despite the fact that Bukhara's connections both with other regions of the onetime Soviet Union (other than the metropolitan cities of Russia), and with the wider Islamic world have lessened over the past century, one still sees glimpses of a conception of Bukhara as part of a world less shaped by narrow forms of ethnic identity or even religious affiliation, than by a shared orientation toward a wider and more cosmopolitan world of Persianate linguistic and cultural forms. Bukhara people, both Irani and non-Irani, are aware of the presence of the Islamic Republic of Iran and its importance in their lives. They do not conceptualize Iran in a one-dimensional way as being a country of strict Islamic values or even "fundamentalism," but rather reflect in nuanced and sophisticated ways about the form of the Muslim world of which they are a part.

There are two mosques in Bukhara that are known by many of the city's people to be "Irani." If most Bukharan people are aware that their city is home to a significant Irani population, then knowledge about the location of their mosques is less widely possessed. In one way, this is indicative of a general degree of indifference toward detailed knowledge about the region's different "communities." These mosques are sometimes also referred to as Shi'i or Jaffariya. As with Shi'i mosques in other settings, these two mosques have the name of Ali in Persian script written on the wall, along with black cloth that symbolizes the martyrdom of Hussein and Hassan at the battle of Karbala. From the outside these mosques are not easily distinguishable from other Sunni mosques in the city, but from the inside they are different and follow the model of Shi'i mosques in other parts of the Muslim world.

The Imams of both mosques told us that they had received no formal education either in Islam or in the Shi'i teachings and scriptures. They had, rather, been taught the practices of Shi'i Islam by their fathers—men knowledgeable about religion, although they did specify whether these men had also been Irani Imams. Both of the Imams told us that during the Soviet era the important Shi'i festival of Muharram was illegal, and, thus, it had not been possible for Shi'i Muslims in Bukhara to commemorate the martyrdom of Hassan and Hussein at the battle of Karabala. However, during the Soviet years the city's Iranis did mark the festival of Muharram in the confines of their homes, where they recited prayers commemorating the two martyrs, and flagellated themselves in a way similar to that widely practiced by Shi'i Muslims in other Muslim settings. Both of these Irani mosques remained closed throughout the Soviet era, and, it had been impossible for Shi'i Muslims to attend prayers, learn about their religion, or travel to the pilgrimage sites in Iran.

Anxieties concerning the continuing vitality of forms of ritual and Shi'i Islamic forms of knowledge did not, however, cease with the end of the Soviet era in 1991. The ongoing need to transmit Shi'i religious knowledge was an important concern for both the Irani Imams. This was a topic of conversation, however, that they obviously did not feel they could talk freely about with us. Initially, we asked one of the Imams how many Irani boys from the city traveled to Iran in search for religious knowledge. He replied that when there were good madrasas and mosques in Uzbekistan, why should Bukhara boys need to travel to Iran? He sought to deny the suggestion that the city's Irani and non-Irani people held different ideas about Islamic religious doctrine. Another Shi'i Imam commented that while there had once been Irani and non-Irani people, now all people living in the city were mixed (*qati qati*) and different groups intermarried.

We recognized that the search for a specific type of Shi'i knowledge among the Irani community was more complex when we visited the central madrasa in Bukhara, Mir-e Arab. This government madrasa teaches the principles of Hanafi Sunni Islam. It is famous across Uzbekistan as Bukhara's only official registered madrasa for boys, and its religious scholars teach young men from across Uzbekistan,[16] both the Islamic sciences and the worldly subjects. The general public are not allowed to enter the madrasa. There is, however, the shrine of the man who founded the school inside its outer wall, and people from Bukhara and beyond do visit this shrine, where prayers are recited by one of the madrasa's teachers. On this occasion, it was the Arabic teacher who recited the prayers and then gave a short talk about the shrine's history in Tajik. When we asked about Iranis, he told us that while some did enroll for tuition many did not, because they preferred to travel to Azerbaijan, as they were able to learn their "religion" there. Strikingly, this man said that the Irani "religion" (*mazhab*) was different from the Sunni Islam taught in the Sunni Mir-e Arab. So for some of the city's population, religious differences between the Bukhara's Shi'i and Sunni are great enough both to claim that they belong to different religious traditions and also to generate long-distance travel for Shi'i religious knowledge that is not easily available in the region.

The city's Sunni religious authorities did openly reflect, then, upon the differences between the Sunni and Shi'i doctrinal traditions, yet they did not do so in a way that simply posited the gradual emergence of ethnic-like sectarian identities in the city. One day we met with the main Sunni authority in Bukhara: he is the Imam of the city's central mosque, the Masjid-e Kalon. He has written several books on the Naqshbandiyya Sufi brotherhood, or *tariqa*, and so we asked him whether the city's Irani people went to the city's shrine of the founder of the Naqshbandiyya. He replied that "Sufism transcends external differences between religious systems," thereby suggesting that Bukhara's rich Sufi tradition plays a significant role in contributing to the harmonious nature of interpersonal relationships between Sunni and Shi'i Muslims in the city. There were several occasions when we witnessed this interaction. One of our Irani friends, for instance, asked us to join his family on the occasion of Eid-ul Fitr on their annual visit to the great shrine of the Sufi master and founder of the Naqshbandiyya brotherhood, Bakhaudin Naqshband, despite the fact that the shrine's mosque Imam is Sunni. We were also taken by Sunni Bukhara friends to visit what are said to be the shrines of two of Shi'i Islam's most holy men: Hussein and Hassan. These are located on the periphery of a town, Nuratta, a two-hour drive away from Bukhara. The custodians of both of these shrines call themselves Sunni, suggesting a complex interaction between Sufism and Shi'i Islam within and beyond Bukhara.

It should not be assumed, however, that Bukhara's Sufi tradition is an inevitable source of tolerance for the city's Sunni and Shi'i Muslims. For one thing, in Uzbekistan as elsewhere in Central and South Asia, Sufi shrines and the networks of social relationships that surround them, are invoked in significant ways in order to enhance the legitimacy of the state, and the ideas its officials hold about the need to modernize its people. We noted at the shrine of Bakhauidin Naqshband, for example, that there were signs telling worshippers that it was impermissible for Muslims to pray to the saint and that they could only use his name as a vehicle to pray to God. The shrine, then, is being used as a vehicle by the government authorities who run and control it to reform the "backward, superstitious, and irrational" practices of Muslims in the region who attend it. At the same time, the shrine had also undergone a significant facelift financed by the Uzbek government: whereas there had once been a village located just outside the major shrine, this had been demolished and replaced with a concrete walkway and carefully tended garden.

The importance of travel to both Iran and Azerbaijan is a particular feature of Irani identity in Bukhara. It points to two separate issues. On the one hand, it suggests that Shi'i thought and religious practice is central to Bukhara Irani identity: the choice to send children for education to

Azerbaijan, a Turkic-speaking yet largely Shi'i country, is one indicator that religious and not only national or ethnic identity configurations are important for them. On the other hand, it is also a reflection on both the imagined and lived experience of Bukhara's connectedness with a wider world both of Shi'i Islam and also of a Persian cultural heritage. It suggests that a Persianate culture that values traditions of refinement and sophistication remains a powerful source of faith and values for both Irani and non-Iran Bukhara people.

It was also not unusual for Sunni Bukhara Tajik-speaking people to visit the shrine of Imam Reza in Mashhad, Iran, at the invitation of their Bukhara Irani friends. One relatively wealthy hotelier, Ahmed, had visited Mashhad with his wife and some of his Irani friends. He had enjoyed his visit and found the shrine a place of great beauty and exceptional religiosity. Ahmed was keen to tell us that while he was in the shrine local Iranians had asked him whether he was a Shi'i or a Sunni. And he had replied saying that he was from the great Islamic city of Bukhara where people did not think about who was Sunni and who was Shi'i; they were, rather, happy to be Muslims and believe in one God.

All this is striking because it implies a level of coexistence and plurality between Bukhara's Sunni and Shi'i Muslims. In some other Muslim-majority settings, Sunnis (let alone agreeing to eat meat killed by Shi'i Muslims) refuse even to sit with a Shi'i who is eating. What we discovered in Bukhara however was that while complex tensions do exist between Irani and non-Irani people, there continues also to be great potential for experiencing moments of intensely shared religious faith and experience. This is especially interesting because it often involves traveling to a context not only outside of the city but also Uzbekistan: the shrine of Imam Reza in majority-Shi'i Iran.

CONCLUSION

The city, as Anna Tsing has recently reflected, can be used as a metaphor to talk about cosmopolitanism in different contexts (see also Derrida; Rapport). In Tsing's vision, shifting urban histories are like "lineages," "that is, shards of genealogies through which present forms have emerged" (127). The city makes cosmopolitanism its own through these contingent lineages. In this paper, however, we have adopted a reverse perspective and talked about the city by looking not so much at histories and genealogies, but at a particular modality of coexistence that exhibits multiply layered and imperfectly interleaved cosmopolitan dynamics at work. As our study shows, certain tensions lie at the center of people's experiences of their city: tensions between the Bukharans' projection of their city as a site of harmonious or peaceful coexistence—those public images of a historically shared city with expansive cosmopolitan connections both within and beyond—and an emphasis on people's boundaries and reserved intimate spaces on the other.

Thus, coexistence in Bukhara should not be seen in the simple image of separate social "blocks" grating against one another. Rather, it takes place in the chameleon colors of the most intimate of relations, as well as in diverse spaces of the town, and appears as an interweaving of partial connections and a holding apart of certain other relations. Coexistence seems hard won here. Only in a few situations in everyday life, such as the neighborhood life cycle parties and the *mazars*, are older patterns of formalized courteous engagement maintained. These occasions can be inclusive and cordial because no one speaks about, and therefore everyone accepts, the accompanying limitations: "I will offer you food, but I would not marry your daughter"; "I come to this *mazar*, but I do not attend your mosque," and so forth. But in the rest of city life, by far the greater part, including the places we have not been able to describe here such as schools and the new administrative *mahallas*, no interaction can easily be taken for granted. Not only has the pre-Soviet image of a city of functional diversity disappeared forever, but even the fairly recent Soviet notion of socialist internationalism has gone. The final nail in the coffin of internationalism is the experiences of overt racism by labor migrants in Russia.

Yet, despite the emergences of new enmities (such as hostility to rural newcomers, the "real Uzbeks"), Bukharans are feeling their way into new kinds of cosmopolitan dynamics. Interestingly, labor migration and religion in general are major spheres where this can happen. We have shown that when interest in religion is on the rise and people are newly able to convert, they are able to find ways of negotiating the coexistence of different confessions and approaches toward religious life even within one family. As regards Islam, in particular, its heterogeneity clearly contributes to the practices of coexistence in the city today, as, indeed, it did in the past. While anthropologists have documented the ways in which Islam, and Muslim ritual practices generally, were nurtured in a range of spaces ranging from secret to semipublic during Soviet rule, there are fewer discussions of the ways in which diverse Islamic doctrinal traditions were also able to remain a vital part of Muslim life in the region during these years. In other words, Bukhara people not only maintained the position of Islam in a dynamic and important way in their city, but the city itself continues to be a social and urban space that nurtures and sustains different types of Islamic doctrinal teachings and the various Muslim identities formed around them. Some forms of coexistence within the city are thus closely tied to branching links and imaginaries far beyond, to Persianate culture and a variety of holy sites in Asia.

In a similar vein, the "shards of genealogies" that the city still encompasses are not simply contained within Bukahra's boundaries. While references to the past are often used by the native Bukharans to object to linguistic and cultural "Uzbekization" of their city, the new political economy with its impetus to labor migration creates novel conditions for dealing with "otherness." Although these experiences are not always benign, the overall effect is a production of new cosmopolitan subjectivities beyond, as it were, the simple "generosity with respect to cultural difference" (Humphrey 151) that people were accustomed to during the Soviet period. Cosmopolitanism of present-day Bukhara, now in great part evolving around labor migration and new connections with the Farsi-speaking religious and political realms, folds distant links into intimate settings.

NOTES

1. In the Soviet period, ethnicity was recorded in passports and understood as one's "nationality" (*natsional'nost'*). In the post-Soviet period, the practice of recording ethnicity in passports has been abandoned. Thus, many native Bukharans told us first that they were Uzbek, but then commented that their *millet* (nationality/ethnicity) was Tajik but that on their passport it said that they were only Uzbek. When they reflected upon these matters they also often told us that Uzbek was what the "government" (*hokumat*) called them, thereby suggesting that they see Uzbekness as an artificial and imposed form of ethnic or nation identity in contrast to their understandings of themselves as Tajik-speaking Bukharan people.
2. The term "Bukharan Jews" refers to Central Asian Jews who had supposedly come from Khiva and Persia. This term was applied to these communities by Ashkenazi Jews and the Russian government. The first evidence of a Jewish community in Bukhara dates back to the thirteenth century (*Encyclopaedia Judaica* 1470).
3. Mahallas varied in size. Around 1900, the 220 mahallas contained from 10 to 350 houses (Sukhareva 144; Gangler, Gaube, and Petruccioli 73–80).
4. The Tatars in Bukhara consist of three groups, the Volga, Kazan, and Crimean Tatars. Yelia's family are Volga Tatars, closest in culture to the Russians. They came to Bukhara mostly in the 1920s and 1930s, fleeing from famine and collectivization in Russia, and they chose Bukhara because of the common Islamic religion. Volga and Kazan Tatars distinguish themselves from Crimean Tatars, whom they see as less well-educated, "darker," and more clannish. The Crimean Tatars in Bukhara did not arrive voluntarily but were sent by force under Stalin during World War II.
5. The Red Army was an institution where ethnic mixing was common. Mukhtopana, who had medical training, became an officer and, unusually, she implied, she had Russian, Ukrainians, and Uzbeks serving under her.
6. This boundary is very strongly upheld by both Jews and non-Jews in Bukhara. The Bukharan Jews are considered one of the most Jewish-conscious groups among Soviet Jewry (see *Encyclopaedia Judaica* 1474). We were told of three love affairs between young Jews and Uzbeks, in each case ending in tragedy and social exclusion.
7. Yelia described an encounter in her youth. She had gone to Moscow and in some crowd at a theater she suddenly saw a black hand on her arm (an African was standing behind her). This shocked her so much that she fainted. She is now very ashamed of this moment, her naivety and lack of appreciation of common humanity. But she told the story as a way of explaining the involuntary strong feelings people have about intermarriage.

8. Bukhara used to have many artisan and professional guilds before the Soviet era. These were often associated with specific *mahallas*. Now, there is an active guild of guesthouse keepers, another for women entrepreneurs, and a few others for particular trades.
9. *Evropeitsi*, the term often used to designate the Slav population.
10. While drinking alcohol is fully acceptable in many Uzbek/Tajik households and often accompanies a brief prayer before a meal, any public appearance in a drunken state is highly stigmatized.
11. On the Uzbek state's "fear of Islamism," see Everett-Heath (193–96).
12. The picture becomes more complex if we take into account extramarital relations. It is not unusual for Muslim men in Bukhara, both married and single, to have long-term relationships and children with Slav or Christian women. For discussion of similar practices in Tajikistan, see Colette Harris (114–33).
13. This strategy appears to be closely related to the way in which children from mixed marriages were free to choose their "ethnicity" to be recorded in their internal Soviet passports at the age of sixteen.
14. There are other communities of Shi'i Muslims in Uzbekistan, and Shi'i Muslims in Bukhara are aware of these, and the ways in which they differ from Shi'is in Bukhara. Samarqand, for instance, is home to a significant population of Shi'i Muslims, yet these are said not to be "Irani," but Turkish, or *turkha*. Roy suggests these Shi'i are probably descended from an urban elite of Iranian origin but ethnically Turcophone traders (*The Failure of Political Islam* 143). Neither Rasanayagam's work on Samarqand nor Louw's account of everyday experiences of Islam in Bukhara note the vitality of Shi'i forms of Islamic identity in these cities today.
15. The use of the term "Irani" by Bukhara people to describe the city's "Shi'i" peoples suggests the complexity of the relationship between "regional" and "confessional" identities in the city today. Nineteenth-century accounts of Bukhara talk about the city's "Shiites" and not "Iranis." The category "Irani" may, then, reflect the attempts made during the Soviet era to categorize Central Asian identities more in terms of "nationality" than "religion."
16. Notably there were no foreign students.

WORKS CITED

Al'meev, Robert. *Burkharskiye Yevrei (istoriko-kul'turnyi ocherk)*. Bukhara: Ministerstvo po delam kul'tury, 1998.

Bayly, Christopher Alan. A. The Pre-History of Communalism: Religious Conflict in India, 1700–1860. *Modern Asian Studies* 19.2 (1985): 177–203.

Breckenridge, Carol A, Sheldon Pollock, Homi Bhabha and Dipesh Chakrabarty. *Cosmopolitanism*. Durham, N.C.: Duke University Press, 2002.

Burton, Audrey. *Bukharan Trade, 1558–1718*. Bloomington: Indiana University Research Institute of Inner Asian Studies, 1993.

Cheah, Pheng and Bruce Robbins. *Cosmopolitics: Thinking and Feeling Beyond the Nation*. University of Minnesota Press, 1998.

Derrida, Jacques. *On Cosmopolitanism and Forgiveness*. London: Routledge, 2001.

Encyclopaedia Judaica. Jerusalem: Keter, 1971.

Everett-Heath, Tom. "Instability and Religious Identity in a Post-Soviet World: Kazakhstan and Uzbekistan." *Central Asia: Aspects of a Transition*. Ed. Tom Everett-Heath. London: RoutledgeCurzon, 204–36.

Gangler, Anette, Heinz Gaube, and Attilio Petruccioli. *Bukhara—The Eastern Dome of Islam. Urban Development, Urban Space, Architecture and Population*. Stuttgart: Aexel Menges, 2004.
Ferguson, James. *Expectations of Modernity*. Berkeley: U of California P, 1999.
Hannerz, Ulf. "The World in Creolization." *Africa* 57.4 (1987): 546–59.
Harris, Colette. *Control and Subversion, Gender Relations in Tajikistan*. London: Pluto, 2004.
Heyat, Farideh. Women and the Culture of Entrepreneurship in Soviet and post-Soviet Azerbaijan. *Markets and Moralities: Ethnographies of Post-Socialism*. Ed. Ruth Mandel and Caroline Humphrey. New York: Berg, 2002. 19–32.
Humphrey, Caroline 2004: 'Cosmopolitanism and kosmopolitizm in the political life of Soviet Citizens.' *Focaal: European Journal of Anthropology* 44 (2004) 138–34.
Kandiyoti, Denis and Nadira Azizmova. "The Communal and the Sacred: Women's Worlds of Ritual in Uzbekistan." *Journal of Royal Anthropological Institute* 10.2 (2004): 327–49.
Louw, Maria E. "The Heart with God, the Hand at Work: Being Muslim in Post-Soviet Bukhara." Diss. University of Copenhagen, 2004.
Massicard, Elise, and Tommaso Trevisani. "The Uzbek Mahalla: Between State and Society." *Central Asia: Aspects of Transition*. Ed. Tom Everett-Heath. London: RoutledgeCurzon, 205–6. .
Nasr, Seyyed Vali Reza "The Rise of Sunni Militancy in Pakistan: The Changing Role of Islamism and the Ulama in Society and Politics." *Modern Asian Studies* 34.1 (2000): 139–80.
Nielsen, V. *Uistokov sovremennogo gradostroitel'stva Uzbekistana*. Tashkent: Izdatel'stvo literatury i iskusstva, 1988.
Pilkington, Hilary. *Migration, Displacement and Identity in Post-Soviet Russia*. London: Routledge, 1998.
Rapport, Nigel. "Diaspora, Cosmopolis, Global Refuge: Three Voices of the Supra-national City." *Locating the Field, Space, Place and Context in Anthropology*. Ed. by Simon Coleman and Peter Collins. Oxford: Berg, 2006. 179–97.
Rasanayagam, Johan. "Healing with Spirits and the Formation of Muslim Selfhood in Post-Soviet Uzbekistan." *Journal of the Royal Anthropological Institute* 12.2 (2006): 377–93.
Rashid, Ahmed. *Jihad: The Rise of Militant Islam in Central Asia*. New Haven: Yale UP, 2002.
Roy, Oliver. 1994. *The Failure of Political Islam*. London: I.B.Tauris, 1994.
———. *The New Central Asia: The Creation of Nations*. London: I.B.Tauris, 2000.
Sassen, Sasika. *The Global City: New York, London, Tokyo*. Princeton: Princeton UP, 2001.
Skvirskaja, Vera. "New Economic Forms and Subjectivity in Post-Socialist Russia: The Case of a Rural Periphery, Yamal-Nenets Autonomous Region." Diss. Cambridge University, 2005.
Sukhareva, O. E. *Bukhara XIX—nachalo XXv (pozdnefeodal'nyi gorod I ego naselenie)*. Moscow: Nauka, 1966.
Tsing, Anna L. *Friction. An Ethnography of Global Connection*. Princeton: Princeton UP, 2005.
Venkatesan, Soumhya 2005 "She Is My Sister; but Buy from Me": Competition and Co-Existence in the Tourist Markets of Bukhara City, Uzbekistan. Preliminary report, 2005.
Ziya, Muhammad-Sharif-e sadr-e. *The Personal Biography of a Bukharan Intellectual. The Diary of Muhammad-Sharif-e sadr-e Ziya*. Ed. Edward A. Allworth, Intro. Muhammad-jon-i Shakuri, Trans. Rustam M. Shukurov. Leiden: Brill, 2004.

Contributors

Yasmeen Arif is Visiting Assistant Professor at the Interdisciplinary Center for the Study of Global Change at the University of Minnesota, Twin Cities Campus. In 2009 she will be a Quadrant fellows at the Institute for Advanced Study, University of Minnesota. She is finishing a manuscript titled, "Afterlife: Reclaiming Life after Catastrophe," for a multidisciplinary research project that explores lifeworlds that emerge in and from conditions of damage and devastation. Apart from her fieldwork and writing on violence in Lebanon and India, she has written on the theory and history of anthropological knowledge production.

Asef Bayat is Professor of Sociology and Middle Eastern Studies at the University of Leiden and Director, Institute for the Study of Islam in the Modern World. He is the author of *Making Islam Democratic: Social Movements and the Post-Islamist turn* (Stanford University Press, 2007), *Workers and Revolution* (London: Zed Books, 1987), *Work, Power and Politics* (London and New York: Monthly Review Press, 1991), and *Street Politics* (New York: Columbia University Press, 1998). His areas of scholarly interest include development, urban space, and subaltern and radical politics in the Middle East, Iran, and Egypt.

Caroline Humphrey is Professor of Asian Anthropology at the Department of Social Anthropology, King's College, University of Cambridge, a fellow of the British Academy and a fellow of King's College. She is coeditor of the journal *Inner Asia* and an editor of the Inner Asia Monograph series. She has written and edited several books and numerous articles including *Karl Marx Collective: Economy, Society and Religion in a Siberian Collective Farm* (Cambridge: Cambridge University Press, 1983), *Shamans and Elders: Experience, Knowledge and Power among the Daur* (Oxford: Clarendon Press, 1996), and *The Unmaking of Soviet Life: Everyday Economies after Socialism* (Ithaca: Cornell University Press, 2002). Thematically her work covers postsocialism, nomads, shamanism (including shamans in the city), Jainism and Central Asia, theories of ritual, and Soviet and post-Soviet society. Her recent projects include a study of the political language of democratic Mongolia, long-term field research on Buddhism and local politics in contemporary Inner Mongolia, China, and work on architecture and ideology in Russia and the post-Socialist cities of Asia.

Engin F. Isin holds a Chair in Citizenship and Professor in Politics and International Studies (POLIS) at the Faculty of Social Sciences, the Open University, UK. He served as Canada Research Chair and Professor in the Division of Social Science at York University, Toronto, Canada, between 2001 and 2006. His research has focused on the origins and transformations of "occidental citizenship" as a political and legal institution that enables various ways of being political. He is the author of *Cities Without Citizens: Modernity of the City as a Corporation* (Montreal: Black Rose Books, 1992), *Citizenship and Identity* (coauthored with Patricia K. Wood; London: Sage, 1999), and *Being Political: Genealogies of Citizenship* (Minneapolis: University of Minnesota Press, 2002), and has edited *Democracy, Citizenship and the Global City* (London: Routledge, 2000). He has coedited with Bryan S. Turner, *Handbook of Citizenship Studies* (London: Sage, 2002), and with Gerard Delanty, *Handbook of Historical Sociology* (London: Sage, 2003); and most recently with Greg Nielsen, *Acts of Citizenship* (London: Zed Books, 2008).

John Lie is Dean of International and Area Studies and Class of 1959 Professor at the University of California, Berkeley. He is the author of *Modern Peoplehood* (Cambridge: Harvard University Press, 2004), *Multiethnic Japan* (Cambridge: Harvard University Press, 2001), *Han Unbound: The Political Economy of South Korea* (Stanford: Stanford University Press, 1998), *Sociology of Contemporary Japan*. A special issue of *Current Sociology*, Vol. 44 (1996), and *Blue Dreams: Korean Americans and the 1992 Los Angeles Riots* (coauthored with Nancy Abelmann; Cambridge: Harvard University Press, 1995).

Magnus Marsden is Lecturer in Social Anthropology of South and Central Asia at the School of Oriental and African Studies, University of London. He has conducted extensive fieldwork in Chitral, northern Pakistan, and published widely on everyday forms of Chitrali Islam. His more recent project is on Persianate expressions of Islam in the connected regions of Tajikistan and Afghanistan. In addition to journal articles in *American Ethnologist, Journal of the Royal Anthropological Institute, Journal of Asian Studies,* and *Modern Asian Studies and Contributions to Indian Sociology,* he is the author of *Living Islam: Muslim Religious Experience in Pakistan's North-West Frontier* (Cambridge: Cambridge University Press, 2005).

Shail Mayaram is Professor at the Centre for the Study of Developing Societies, Delhi. Publications include *Against History, Against State: Counterperspectives from the Margins* (New York: Columbia University

Press, 2003; Delhi: Permanent Black, 2004); *Resisting Regimes: Myth, Memory and the Shaping of a Muslim Identity* (Delhi: Oxford University Press, 1997); and *Creating a Nationality: The Ramjanmabhumi Movement and the Fear of Self* (coauthored with Ashis Nandy, Shikha Trivedi, Achyut Yagnik; Delhi: Oxford University Press, 1995). She is a member of the Subaltern Studies collective and has coedited *Subaltern Studies: Muslims, Dalits and the Fabrications of History*, Vol. 12 (Delhi: Permanent Black, 2005). Her interests include marginality, subalternity, state formation, Hindus and Muslims and cities.

Aihwa Ong is Professor of Anthropology at the University of California, Berkeley. An anthropologist of globalization, her interests include neoliberalism, modernity, citizenship, and sovereignty in Southeast Asia, China, and the United States. She is the author of the award-winning *Flexible Citizenship* (Durham: Duke University Press, 1999), *Buddha Is Hiding: Refugees, Citizenship and the New America* (Berkeley and Los Angeles: University of California Press, 2003), and *Neoliberalism as Exception: Mutations in Citizenship and Sovereignty* (Durham: Duke University Press, 2006). Her co-edited volumes include *Global Assemblages: Technology, Politics and Ethics as Anthropological Problems* (coedited with Stephen J. Collier; Blackwell, 2005) and *Privatizing China, Socialism from Afar* (Ithaca: Cornell University Press, 2008). Ong's writings have been translated into German, Italian, and Chinese.

Yeoh Seng Guan teaches at the School of Arts and Sciences, Monash University. He studies urban anthropology with particular emphasis on subaltern practices, civil society, and transnational spatial politics/flows with a regional focus on Southeast Asia. His research interests include anthropologies of the city, religion, media, and gender. He has been concerned with issues of memory, peace building, democratic multiculturalism, the postcolonial city, religion, ritual performance, and social change. Seng Guan's recent publications include "House, Kampung and Taman: Spatial Hegemony and the Politics (and Poetics) of Space," *Crossroads: Interdisciplinary Journal for Southeast Asian Studies* 17.2: forthcoming; "The Unbearable Likeness of Democratic Multiculturalism," in *Another Malaysia Is Possible*, ed. M. Nadarajah (Kuala Lumpur: National Office for Human Development, 2004); "Creolised Utopias: Squatter Colonies and the Postcolonial City in Malaysia," *Sojourn* 16 (2001): 102–24; "Producing Locality: Space, Houses and Public Culture in a Hindu Festival in Malaysia," *Contributions to Indian Sociology* 35.1 (2001): 33–64.

Vera Skvirskaja is a Research Associate at the Department of Social Anthropology, University of Cambridge. She has worked on kinship, new economic forms, and religious change in rural communities in arctic Siberia. Her current research interests include urban anthropology with a special focus on practices of coexistence, cosmopolitan subjectivity, migration, and diaspora in the context of the post-Soviet city.

Emily T. Yeh is an Assistant Professor of Geography at the University of Colorado, with interests in the governance of society and nature in Tibetan areas of China. She has examined the role of state policies, markets, and ideologies of nature and nation in structuring highly unequal environmental and economic outcomes, and how these in turn are inscribed on the material landscape. Specific research projects have included examinations of violent conflicts over access to natural resources, the clash of religious and state authority in the resolution of disputes, the political economy and cultural politics of agricultural and urban development, and the ways in which Tibetans and Han migrants have been differently positioned with respect to their ability to benefit from economic reform. She is also working on the emergence of environmental subjectivities, and the interplay of transnational environmentalism and religious nationalism in contemporary Tibet.

Index

A
Abrahamson, Mark, 6
Agamben, Giorgio, 22, 24
Ainu, 164, 173
Aitmatov, Chingiz, 21
Ajmer, xv, 12
Akbar, 15–16
AkgŸndŸz, Ahmet, 40, 51
Alexandria, 198, 199
Algeria, colonial, 47–48, 52
Ankara, 51–53
Amdo, 76–77
Appiah, Anthony, 54
Armenian, 41–42
Asia, idea of, 1, 2–5. *See also* frontier
Asian values, 148
Aum Shinrikyo, 161, 174
awqaf: administration of, 36, 41, 46; centralization of, 43–45, 48, 50; Church, 35, 39–40; communal, 43, 45, 48; non-Muslim, 35–39, 41–47; Istanbul, 35–38, 41, 50; Jewish, 40–42, 49; monastic, 39–40; Muslim, 35, 38–39, 41–44, 46–48; religious status of, 48; family structure, 43, 48
Azbakiya (Cairo), 194, 195

B
Baghdad, 1, 4, 7
Balkans, 40
baths, public, 36–37, 49
Bangsa Malaysia, 137
Bandung, 3, 26n8
Barkor, 57, 60–1, 64, 68, 71–72, 82n2
Barisan Nasional, 138, 148, 156n7
Basra, 1

bazaar, 12, 13, 15, 37, 124, 142, 148, 150; Grand, 12; Mughal mina, 13; souk, 13, 18, 106; hat, 13; Malay, 142
benefactors, 36
beneficence, non-Muslim, 35, 37, 39, 41, 43, 45, 47; Ottoman, 35, 37, 39, 43, 45, 47, 49, 51–53
Beirut, vii, xiii, xvi, 1, 4, 18, 20, 21, 23, 26n3, 26n6, 28n27, 38, ch 5, 198; downtown, 106–112, 114; southern suburbs, 105–114
Braude, Benjamin, 35–36, 51
Brickfields, 134, 150, 151
Burakumin, 162–168, 169, 172–173; Liberation League, 166–169
Bhabha, Homi, 137
Bharucha, Rustam, 3, 5, 8, 20
Bombay, 4, 8, 17, 21, 200n16. *See* Mumbai
Bön, 82n1
Buddhism, 3, 11, 14, 21, 56–7, 62–4, 67, 69–70, 76–77, 80, 81, 82n1, 83n7, 147
Bukhara, viii, xi, xiii, xv, xvi, 4, 7, 13, ch 9
Byzantium, 7

C
Cairo, viii, xi, xiii, 2, 8, 12, 13, 15, 18, 22, 28n18, 38, ch 8
capital, 2, 8, 15, 17, 19, 20, 27n13, 55, 56, 86, 87, 88, 89, 92, 93, 94, 108, 114, 148, 154, 185, 202; capitalism, 4, 8, 20, 54, 77, 104, 135, 156n8
Caribbean, 3, 4
cartography, 1, 2, 95

Castells, Manuel, 8–9
Chala, 206, 208, 209, 210
Chander, Naveen and Naresh Goswami, 23
Cheah, Pheng, 55
Chicago School of Urban Sociologists, 180
China, xi, xiii, 3, 9, 12, 14, 19, 20, 21, 23, ch 3, 86, 87, 88, 90, 91, 92, 94, 203, 208
Chinese: Muslims, 56, 61, 64, 67, 70, 81, 83n14; new, 75–9; conflict with Tibetans, 76–78; Han 56, 64–71, 77, 79, 81; vegetable farmers, 71–72; in Japan, 162, 170
Churches: Byzantine, 35; Greek, 17; Korean, 217; Roman Catholic, 13; Russian, 218; Syrian Orthodox, 19. See also Christians
Christians, 7, 14, 15, 16, 17, 18, 19, 36, 41–2, 51, 113, 114 , 217; Copt, 18, 19, ch 8, 101–130, 182; Maronite, 18, 19, 106, 126n8
citizen, 36, 39, 41, 44–45, 48, 52
citizenship, 3, 10, 14, 16, 23, 24, 29n29, 38, 43, 44, 45, 48, 49, 94, 164, 183, 184, 196, 204, 216; acts of, 38; genealogies of, 52; Oriental, 38, 48–49, 52; Ottoman, 38, 43–45, 48–49, 52
civism, 38
Çizakça, Murat, 37, 51
cities: Buddhist, 11; other global cities, 5–8; Islamic, 7; post Soviet city, 16; sacred city, 3, 12, 204; world class city, 6, 135, 137, 174n4. See also Baghdad, Beirut, Bukhara, Cairo, Damascus, Kuala Lumpur
Clifford, James, 54
Cochin, 11, 17
coercive amity, 56, 66–67, 71, 79, 82. See also minzu tuanjie.
conflict. See violence
conviviality, xiii, 10, 54, 56, 81, 95, 148
Constantinople, 7, 14, 35, 36; Ecumenical patriarch of, 36
compassion. See nyingjé
Constantinople. See Istanbul 7,14, 35,36

Coptic Christians. See also Christians
Cordoba 28n17
cosmopolitanism, xiii, xiv, xv, ch 1; alternative, 11–19; discrepant, 54; everyday, 180; mundane, 101–102, 114, 123, 124; Ottoman, 14, 42, 49, 50; rooted, 54; prenationalist, 62, 80; subaltern, vii, xiv, 10, 19–26, 54, 55–6, 69, 73, 79–81, 132–133; vernacular, 55; cosmopolitan being, 1, 4, 8, 10, 11, 19, 21, 23; cosmopolitan democracy, 9; cosmopolitan living, regimes of 94–96;
decosmopolitanization, 79; and Buddhism, 62–4, 82, 83n7
civilization, xiii, xv, xvi, 1, 2, 5, 9, 10, 11, 19, 28n24, 54, 55, 67, 69, 78, 184; clash of, 54, 69, 78

D
Damascus, xv, 4
Dara Shikoh, 15, 16
Davis, Mike, 22, 23
Dalai Lama 60; Fifth, 57, 61–63, 77, 82nn5 6; Fourteenth, 55, 69–70, 72–73, 81–82
development, Tibet, 56–57, 73, 83n11
de Certeau, Michel, 132, 133, 154, 155
Delhi, vii, xi, xiii, xvi, 6, 13, 15, 16, 17, 20, 21, 23, 24, 25, 38, 86, ch 5, 198
democracy, xiv, 1, 9, 10, 19, 23, 24
dhimmi (non-Muslim minority), 43, 182
difference, negotiation of, 35, 38, 40, 49–50

E
Edirne, 35
Egypt, 18, 19. See also Cairo
endowment, 39, 47–48; family, 47–48, 52; public, 39, 48, 52
engagement, civic 37
ethnic evolutionism, 87, 91–94
ethnic governmentality, 89–91
Essential (Clearance of Squatters) Act 1969, 136
Euergetism, Greek, 52
EyŸp Sultan, 37
Europe , xiv, 2, 3, 4, 14, 18, 19, 21, 26n5, 58, 131, 214, 219; Europeanization, 26n8

F

Fatehpur Sikri, 15
Fatih KŸlliyesi, 37, 51
Fener, 35
Fethiye, Mosque of, 35
Fetwa, 39–40
finance. *See* capital
Fletcher, Joseph, 26n4
foreign workers in Japan, 162, 168–169
Frank, Andre Gunder, 2
frontier, 26n2, 26n9, 106, 126
Frug, Gerald, 48, 51
fundamentalism, 22,104, 224
Furnivall, John, 136

G

Geertz, Clifford, 179
Gellner, Ernest, 180
Gierke, Otto, 51
gift-giving, acts of, 37–38, 49–50, 52
globality, 4, 5, 6, 7, 8, 88, 138
globalization, 2, 6, 9, 22, 26n4, 26n13, 55, 96n2, 148, 155, 181, 235
governmentality, vii, 20, 28n20, 86, 87, 90, 92, 136, 154
guilds, 36, 39, 48
Gujarat, 23

H

habitus, 139, 153
Hannerz, Ulf, 54
harmony ideology (in Japan), 170–1
Harvey, David, 26n7, 88, 96n4
hawkers, 24, 29n32, 142, 143, 151, 152, 153, 158n33
healing, ritual, 13
Held, David and Daniele Archibuigi, 9
Hezbollah, 105–113
Hindus, xi, xiv, 1, 3,6, 9, 12, 13, 14, 15, 16, 21, 22, 23, 24, 25, 26, 26n2, 28n28, 48, 58, 89, 116, 131, 132, 138, 139, 145, 147, 149, 150, 151, 153, 156n11, 156n12, 157n27, 157n32, 158n34
Hong Kong, 5, 6, 27n11, 28n18, 86, 88
Hui. *See also* Chinese Muslim.
hybridity, 55, 79

I

identity, 38, 42, 49, 50, 53
Ikeda, Daisaku, 21
Imber, Colin, 38, 51
imperial ideology (in Japan), 163, 170

Inalcik, Halil, 35, 51
Indian Ocean, 2, 3
India, viii, xi, xv, xvi, 1, 3, 5, 7, 8, 12, 13, 15, 17, 20, 21, 23, 47, 48, 59, 68, 74, 91, 91–94, 114, 119, 120, 127n5, 163, 200n16, 203, 221; High Courts of India, 47–48, 52; Little India, ch 6
Indonesia, 3, 27n11, 90, 146, 163
Internationalism, Soviet, 204, 205
institutions, civic, 39, 49–50; *waqf*, 38–41, 45–46, 49–50
Irani, 206, 221, 222, 224, 225, 226, 227, 230n14, 230n15; Iranians in Japan, 168
Islam, 3, 6, 7, 12, 15, 17, 19, 21, 27n16, 28n17, 28n20, 30, 37, 39, 40, 42, 47, 48, 49, 62, 87, 112, 113, 128n22, 131, 132, 135, 136, 138, 142, 144, 146, 147, 148, 184, 185, 189, 193, 197, 203, 204, 205, 211, 214, 217, 221, 222, 223, 224, 225, 227, 228, 229n4, 230n14; Islamic governmentality, 28n20, 136; Islamist movements, 18
Istanbul, xiii, 2, 7, 13, 14, 16, 18, 19, 22, ch 2, 78

J

Japan, 3, 9, 16. *See also* Tokyo
Jerusalem, 52
Jews, 7, 13, 14, 18, 22, 36, 41, 42, 43, 46, 194, 195, 203, 204, 206, 207, 208, 211, 214, 229n2, 229n6; Ottoman, 36, 41–43, 46, 51; Bukharan, 206, 214, 229n2, 229n6; in Cairo, 194
jizya, 18, 182
Jokhang Temple, 57, 76, 82n2

K

Kabul, 1, 21
Kagan, 206, 216, 222
Kant, Immanuel, 21, 54, 81, 95, 97n15
Karbala, 1, 224
Kermeli, Eugenia, 38, 40, 52
Keyman, Fuat, 50, 52
Khache. *See* Muslim
Koreans in Japan, 162–3, 165–7, 171–3
Kuala Lumpur, viii, xi, xiii,14, 20, 27n11, 86, 87, ch 6
Kurds, 17

L

Lausanne Treaty, 46
Law, Islamic, 40, 42, 47–48, 51–52; of gift, 50, 52; Ottoman, 40, 42, 45–48, 50–52; *waqf*, 40, 45–46, 48, 50–52
Lebanon, xvi, 1, 2, 18, 19, 188. *See also* Beirut
Lefebvre, Alexandre, 37–38, 42, 52
Lefebvre, Henri, 2, 37, 38, 42, 127n3
Leh, xi, 12, 13, 60
Lhasa, vii, xi, xiii, 10, 14, ch 3
Lie, John, viii, 9, 16, 27n10, 104, 161, 162, 164
Living together, vii, viii, xiii, xv, 1, 9, 10, 11, 13, 29n32, 50, 54, 55, 56, 57,59, 61, 63, 64, 65, 67, 69, 71, 73, 75, 77, 78, 79, 80, 81, 83, 85, 95, 132, 179, 182, 198
London, 52

M

Ma Bufang, 76–7
madrasa, 16, 37, 143, 203, 213, 220, 223, 225
Mandal, Sumit, 132
Ma Rong, 68, 71
mahalla, 16, 203, 204, 206, 207, 208, 210, 222, 228, 229n3, 230n8
Mahathir Mohamad, 136, 137, 138, 143, 156n7
Mahmood, Saba, 21
Malacca Sultanate, 135
Malaysia, 9, 19, 20, 27n11, 28n20, 87, 89. *See also* Kuala Lumpur
mamak, 143, 145, 155n3, 157n25
mazar, 13, 203, 207, 211, 228
McGee, Terry, 136
Middle East, 1, 2, 19, 35, 49, 74, 146, 154, 157n19, 203
migrant labour. *See also* migration
migration, 4, 18, 55, 65, 71, 73, 94, 105, 122, 188, 204, 205, 214, 215, 220, 228, 229, 236
migrants, 4, 24, 27n11, 28n26, 54, 65, 67–8, 71–3, 75–9, 83n12, 96, 136, 141, 143, 144, 145, 152, 153, 154, 156n3, 156n8, 156n18, 157n29, 202, 219, 220
minzu tuanjie, 56, 64–7, 71–3, 76–80; *Zhonghua minzu*, 73; *minzu fenlie*. *See* splittism
millets, 14, 15, 35, 36, 37, 38, 39, 43, 49, 50, 222, 229n1

minorities, 40, 42, 44
modernity, 3, 11, 16, 19, 20, 23, 26n4, 48, 49, 70, 137, 179, 180, 181, 197; early modernity, 26n4
modernization, Turkish, 42, 44, 46–50, 52
Ambikaipaker, Mohan, 137
Mongols, 4, 59, 67; Pax Mongolica, 14
monoethnic ideology in Japan, 16, 162–164, 167, 172-3
Mubarak, Hosni, 186
Mumbai, 5, 6, 22, 23, 28n18, 198
Muslims, 7, 12, 13, 16, 17, 18, 28n28, 39, 41, 43, 44, 45, 46, 48, 56, 59, 60, 63, 73, 75, 76, 77, 79, 83 n 13, 87, 111, 113, 116, 138, 143, 146, 148, 151, 154, 155n3, 157n19, 182, 183, 184, 186, 189, 190, 191, 192, 193, 194, 195, 197, 198, 199, 206, 211, 217, 218, 221, 222, 223, 224 225, 226, 227, 230n14; Barkor, 61–62, 74, 78; Hebalin, 61–63, 74–75, 78–79; Ladakhi, 61; Kashmiri, 59, 61–63, 74–75, 78, 83n13; Shi'i, 19, 112,127n16; Sunni, 1, 7, 18, 106, 127n12, 221, 224, 225, 226, 227; Druze, 18, 106, 110, 127n12. *See also* Chinese Muslims
Muslim Brothers, 185, 197

N

Najaf, 1
Nandy, Ashis, xv, 11, 17, 23
nation, 42, 44, 50
nationalism, 3, 5, 16, 17, 20, 38, 42–43, 52, 54, 55, 69, 71, 78, 79, 80, 81, 96n10, 104, 116, 173, 174n5, 185, 189, 221; Chinese, 56, 67, 71, 78–9; Han, 67, 71, 78, 81; official (state), 80–1; postcolonial, 55, 69, 81; Tibetan, 56, 71
nationality, 56. *See also minzu tuanjie*
nation-state, 3, 9, 19, 20, 44, 46, 55, 56, 78, 89, 116, 135, 148, 204
Nazareth, 40
Negri, Antonio, 24, 29n33
neighbourhood, 17–19; Hebalin, 61, 75, 79
Neuwirth, Robert, 23
Nishkam, 119–121

NGOs in Beirut, 112–113; in Delhi, 119–121. *See also* Nishkam
Non-Muslims, Ottoman, 39, 41, 43–46
nyingjé, 63–4, 69, 81

O

obedience, 36
obligation, 43
Okinawans, 162, 164, 173
Old Testament, 39
Ong, Aihwa, vii, 9, 10, 20, 28n20, 28n24, 82, 83n11, 86, 88, 90, 92, 94, 96, 96n5, 96n8, 96n10, 97n16, 97n18, 136
Orientalists, French, 47–48
Ottoman, vii, 7, 14, 15, 35, 36, 37, 38, 39, 40, 42, 43, 44, 45, 46, 47, 48, 49, 50, 78, 188; tolerance, 42, 49, 51–52

P

Palestine, 40, 52
Palestinians, 18, 23
Pamuk, Orhan, 15
pastoral, 4, 8
peasant, 4, 5, 8, 214
persona, juristic, 39, 45–46
planetarization, 104
pluralism, 42, 49, 51
Pope Benedict, 197
poverty, 24, 71, 118, 123, 158n34, 164, 172
Powers, David, 36, 47–48, 52
practices: civic gift-giving, 7, 50
primordialists, 179
properties, civic, 37, 49–50; rural, 37; status of awqaf, 40, 44, 46, 48
Putrajaya, 137

R

Raju, CK, 28n19
Ramadan, 138, 142, 148, 153, 157n30, 189, 191, 222,
Rambo, 152, 153
reconstruction, 107–112
rehabilitation, strategies of, 102 -103, 105–106, 117. *See also* reconstruction
reforms, Tanzimat, 42–43
Regulations, Vestiary, 41
religion, xv, 3, 7, 17, 11, 12, 15, 16, 27n11, 28n28, 42, 43, 50, 63, 69, 73, 74, 75, 76, 77, 78,80, 82n1, 95, 111, 119, 120, 129n28, 155n1, 179, 180, 183, 189, 190, 193, 203, 217, 218, 222, 225, 228, 229n4, 230n15
rgya Khache. *See also* Chinese Muslim
Rhys, Jean, 27n10
rights, group 36, 42, 46, 49–50; human, 51; negotiation of group, 38, 49–50
Park, Robert, 180
Russia, 44
Russians, 13, 16, 203, 204, 211, 214, 215, 216, 219, 220, 221, 229n4

S

Sadat, Anwar, 185, 197
Samarqand, 4, 12, 230n14
Sarajevo, 198
Sassen, Saskia, 3, 5, 6, 21, 27n14, 88, 96n3, 135, 202
Science, xv, 7, 82, 91, 92, 94, 203, 225; Arab, 7, 8, 28n18, 182, 184, 194, 203, 206, 207, 213, 215, 225
Shanghai, xv, 5, 6, 20, 86
Shari'a, 138, 185
Shi'i, 105, 113, 105, 106, 111, 112, 126n8, 126n13, 127n16
Shubra (Cairo), 187–192
Shuyun, Sun, 14
Sikhs, 114–122
Silk Route, ix, 3, 12, 12, 203
Simmel, Georg, 198
Singapore, xvii, 3, 6, 8, 13, 14, 19, 20, 27n11, ch 4, 135, 157n21
slums, 22, 23, 28n28, 136, 137, 140
sociality, xv, 17, 19, 21, 23, 95, 96, 143, 144, 220
sociability, 21, 49
Solidere, 108 -110
sovereignty, 8, 20, 28n24, 48, 50, 66–7, 70, 73, 81, 83n11, 116, 136, 204, 205
Spivak, Gayatri C, xvi, 4, 26, 27n12, 28n22, 28n23
splittism, 66–7; splittist, 70, 73
Srongtsen Gampo, 57, 67
State: Ottoman, 43–50, 52; Turkish, 46–47, 50, 52
Subrahmanyam, Sanjay, 26n4
sufi, 1, 4, 7, 16, 27n16, 126n4, 226; sufi orders: Chishtiyya, 12, 15; Naqshbandiyya, 226 ; Qadiriyya, 7
Sunni, 1, 7, 18, 106, 126n8, 221, 222, 224, 225, 226, 227
Swettenham, Frank, 134

synagogues, 39, 41, 46

T

Tagore, Rabindranath, 3, 5
Taylor, Charles, iv
Tehran, 38
Tenshin, Okakura, 5
Thessalonica, 35
Thornton, William; and Songok Han Thornton, 22, 32
Tibetan protests: failed uprising of 1959, 55, 68, 74; 1987–89, 68, 71–73; 2008, 81–82
Tokyo, viii, xiii, 6, 16, 86, ch 7
tolerance, 7, 10, 15, 42, 49, 101, 124, 148, 193, 204, 205, 209, 217, 226
trade, xv, 3, 11, 12, 13, 14, 16, 27n13, 29n30, 56, 57, 62, 63, 75, 77, 78, 80, 83n14, 88, 96n7,102, 133, 142, 143, 151, 182, 202, 203, 206, 208, 213, 223
Tunku Abdul Rahman , 135
Turkey, 3, 7, 17, 19. *See also* Istanbul

U

Uberoi, Jit Pal Singh, xvi, 1, 26n2, 26n9, 129n28
unity of the nationalities. *See minzu tuanjie.*
urban ecosystem, 88–89
urban imaginaries, 2, 21

V

Varshney, Ashutosh, 11
vendors. *See* hawkers

violence, xiii, xvi, 2, 11, 15, 17, 18, 19, 20, 23, 27n11, 29n32, 41, 56, 62, 69, 73, 76, 79, 81–2, 101, 102, 103,104, 107, 111, 114, 116, 122, 123, 124, 125, 126, 129n24, 129n27, 129n28, 130n39, 132, 170, 184, 185, 186, 196, 198, 204, 205
Visvanathan, Shiv, 8

W

Wang kopi, 151, 152
waqf, family, 40, 48, 52; Hayri, 39–40; HŸrri, 39–40; logic of, 50; Muslim family, 40, 48, 52; Ottoman, 36–40, 45–46, 48–52
welfare pluralism, 197
Wencheng, Princess, 57, 67
Widows Relocation Colony, 115–122
Wink, Andre, 3
workers, xi, 4, 23, 24, 25, 26, 27n11, 28n24, 29n30, 64, 86, 92, 93, 94, 96, 110, 136, 141, 143, 144, 145, 152, 153, 156n3, 156n18, 157n29, 162, 163, 168n2, 168n3, 169n3, 170, 171, 174, 203, 204, 214. *See also* migration, slums, subaltern cosmopolitanism

Y

Yediyildiz, Bahaeddin, 52

Z

Zubaida, 10, 35, 49